WHAT'S ON THE DISC

Here is an overview of the contents of the Classroom in a Book disc

The *Adobe Flash Professional CS6 Classroom in a Book* disc includes the lesson files that you'll need to complete the exercises in this book, as well as other content to help you learn more about Adobe Flash Professional CS6 and use it with greater efficiency and ease. The diagram below represents the contents of the disc, which should help you locate the files you need.

These same disc files are available to eBook users via electronic download. Please click here to go to the last page in your eBook for instructions.

Lesson files

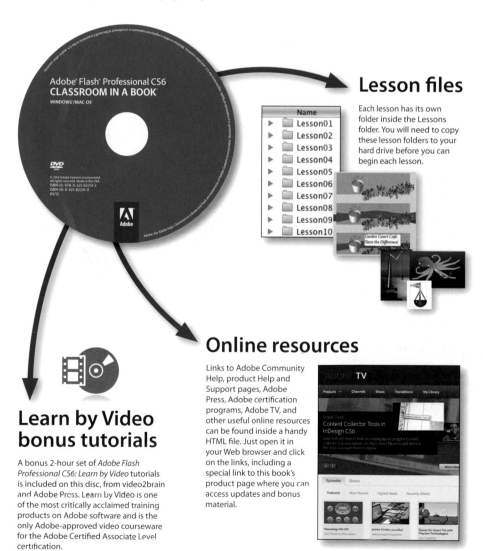

Each lesson has its own folder inside the Lessons folder. You will need to copy these lesson folders to your hard drive before you can begin each lesson.

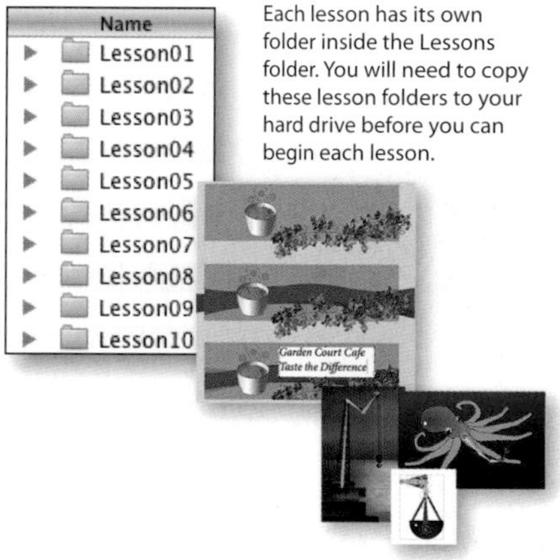

Online resources

Links to Adobe Community Help, product Help and Support pages, Adobe Press, Adobe certification programs, Adobe TV, and other useful online resources can be found inside a handy HTML file. Just open it in your Web browser and click on the links, including a special link to this book's product page where you can access updates and bonus material.

Learn by Video bonus tutorials

A bonus 2-hour set of *Adobe Flash Professional CS6: Learn by Video* tutorials is included on this disc, from video2brain and Adobe Press. Learn by Video is one of the most critically acclaimed training products on Adobe software and is the only Adobe-approved video courseware for the Adobe Certified Associate Level certification.

CONTENTS

Adobe Flash Professional CS6

CLASSROOM IN A BOOK®

The official training workbook from Adobe Systems

Adobe

Adobe® Flash® Professional CS6 Classroom in a Book®

Adobe Press books are published by Peachpit, a division of Pearson Education located in Berkeley, California. For the latest on Adobe Press books, go to www.adobepress.com. To report errors, please send a note to errata@peachpit.com. For information on getting permission for reprints and excerpts, contact permissions@peachpit.com.

Acquisitions Editor: Rebecca Gulick
Writer: Russell Chun
Development and Copy Editor: Stephen Nathans-Kelly
Production Coordinator and Compositor: Danielle Foster
Technical Reviewer: Keith Gladstien
Keystroker: H. Paul Robertson
Proofreader: Liz Welch
Indexer: Valerie Haynes Perry
Cover Designer: Eddie Yuen
Interior Designer: Mimi Heft

Printed and bound in the United States of America

ISBN-13: 978-0-321-82251-2
ISBN-10: 0-321-82251-X

9 8 7 6 5 4 3 2

GETTING STARTED

Adobe Flash Professional CS6 provides a comprehensive authoring environment for creating interactive and media-rich applications. Flash is widely used to create engaging projects integrating video, sound, graphics, and animation. You can create original content in Flash or import assets from other Adobe applications such as Photoshop or Illustrator, quickly design animation and multimedia, and use Adobe ActionScript 3.0 to integrate sophisticated interactivity.

Use Flash to build innovative and immersive Web sites, to create stand-alone applications for the desktop, or to create apps to distribute to mobile devices running on the Android or the iOS system.

With extensive controls for animation, intuitive and flexible drawing tools, and a powerful object-oriented coding language, Flash delivers one of the only robust environments that let your imagination become reality.

About Classroom in a Book

Adobe Flash Professional CS6 Classroom in a Book is part of the official training series for Adobe graphics and publishing software developed with the support of Adobe product experts. The lessons are designed so you can learn at your own pace. If you're new to Flash, you'll learn the fundamental concepts and features you'll need to use the program. Classroom in a Book also teaches many advanced features, including tips and techniques for using the latest version of this application.

What's New

The lessons in this book provide opportunities to use some of the new features and improvements in Flash Professional CS6, including:

- An updated Document panel for quick access to document settings
- Powerful controls for managing layers

- Stage resizing that scales all your content proportionally
- Auto-Save and Auto-Recovery, new options that can ease your mind over potential lost work due to crashes.
- Additional options for symbols, Convert to Bitmap and Export as Bitmap, which provide greater control over graphics handling.
- Outputting animations as a Sprite sheet or PNG sequences to support alternative approaches to animation.
- A new feature for inverse kinematics called Pinning, which allows finer control for armatures.
- A tab ruler for TLF text for positioning of text with layout precision.
- An improved Code Snippets panel featuring a fast, visual way of applying code to objects on the Stage.
- Additional code snippets available in the Code Snippets panel, many geared particularly toward mobile device interactions.
- A streamlined Publish Settings dialog box.
- Better workflow for sharing resources across multiple FLA files
- Revamped interface for Adobe Media Encoder for more efficient processing of your media files.
- A simulator for mobile device interactions to allow testing gestures such as pinches and swipes within Flash.
- Many more incremental feature improvements and overall better performance.

Prerequisites

Before you begin using *Adobe Flash Professional CS6 Classroom in a Book*, make sure your system is set up correctly and that you've installed the required software. You should have a working knowledge of your computer and operating system. You should know how to use the mouse and standard menus and commands, and also how to open, save, and close files. If you need to review these techniques, see the printed or online documentation included with your Microsoft Windows or Apple Mac OS software.

Installing Flash

You must purchase the Adobe Flash Professional CS6 software either as a standalone application or as part of the Adobe Creative Suite. The following specifications are the minimum required system configurations.

Windows:

- Intel® Pentium 4, Intel Centrino®, Intel Xeon®, or Intel Core™ Duo (or compatible) processor
- Microsoft® Windows XP with Service Pack 3 or Windows 7
- 2 GB of RAM required (3 GB recommended)
- 1024 x 768 display
- 2.5 GB of available hard-disk space (additional free space required during installation)
- Internet connection required for product activation
- QuickTime 7.x software required for multimedia features and PNG import.
- DirectX version 9.0c or higher

Mac OS

- Multicore Intel processor
- Mac OS X 10.6.x or 10.7.x
- 2 GB of RAM required (3 GB recommended)
- 1024 x 768 display
- 2.5 GB of available hard-disk space (additional free space required during installation)
- Internet connection required for product activation
- QuickTime 7.x software required for multimedia features and PNG import

For updates on system requirements and complete instructions on installing the software, visit www.adobe.com/go/flash_systemreqs.

Install Flash from the Adobe Flash Professional CS6 application DVD, or from the disk image you downloaded from Adobe, onto your hard drive. You cannot run the program from the installation disc. Follow the onscreen instructions.

Make sure that your serial number is accessible before installing the application. You can find the serial number on the back of the DVD case, or if you downloaded the software from Adobe, the serial number will be in your emailed receipt.

Copying the Lesson Files

The lessons in *Adobe Flash Professional CS6 Classroom in a Book* use specific source files, such as image files created in Adobe Illustrator, video files created in Adobe After Effects, audio files, and prepared Flash documents. To complete the lessons in this book, you must copy these files from the *Adobe Flash Professional CS6 Classroom in a Book* CD (inside the back cover of this book) to your hard drive. Follow these steps to copy the lesson files:

1 On your hard drive, create a new folder in a convenient location and name it **FlashProCS6_CIB**, following the standard procedure for your operating system:

- **Windows:** In Windows 7 or Vista, right-click and choose New > Folder. Then enter the new name for your folder.
- **Mac OS:** In the Finder, choose File > New Folder. Type the new name and drag the folder to the location you want to use.

Now, you can copy the source files onto your hard drive.

2 Drag the Lessons folder (which contains folders named Lesson01, Lesson02, and so on) from the *Adobe Flash Professional CS6 Classroom in a Book* CD onto your hard drive to your new FlashProCS6_CIB folder.

When you begin each lesson, navigate to the folder with that lesson number to access all the assets, sample movies, and other project files you need to complete the lesson.

If you have limited storage space on your computer, you can copy each lesson folder as you need it, and then delete it after you've completed the lesson if desired. Some lessons build on preceding lessons; in those cases, a starting project file is provided for you for the second lesson or project. You do not have to save any finished project if you don't want to or if you have limited hard drive space.

Copying the sample movies and projects

You will create and publish SWF animation files in some lessons in this book. The files in the End folders (01End, 02End, and so on) within the Lesson folders are samples of completed projects for each lesson. Use these files for reference if you want to compare your work-in-progress with the project files used to generate the sample movies. The end project files vary in size from relatively small to a couple of megabytes, so you can either copy them all now if you have ample storage space or copy just the end project file for each lesson as needed. Then you can delete it when you finish that lesson.

How to Use the Lessons

Each lesson in this book provides step-by-step instructions for creating one or more specific elements of a real-world project. Some lessons build on projects created in preceding lessons; most stand alone. All the lessons build on each other in terms of concepts and skills, so the best way to learn from this book is to proceed through the lessons in sequential order. In this book, some techniques and processes are explained and described in detail only the first few times you perform them.

The organization of the lessons is also project-oriented rather than feature-oriented. That means, for example, that you'll work with symbols on real-world design projects over several lessons rather than in just one chapter.

Additional Resources

Adobe Flash Professional CS6 Classroom in a Book is not meant to replace documentation that comes with the program or to be a comprehensive reference for every feature. Only the commands and options used in the lessons are explained in this book. For comprehensive information about program features and tutorials, please refer to these resources:

Adobe Community Help: Community Help brings together active Adobe product users, Adobe product team members, authors, and experts to give you the most useful, relevant, and up-to-date information about Adobe products.

To access Community Help: To invoke Help, press F1 or choose Help > Flash Help.

Adobe content is updated based on community feedback and contributions. You can add comments to both content or forums—including links to web content, publish your own content using Community Publishing, or contribute Cookbook Recipes. Find out how to contribute at www.adobe.com/community/publishing/download.html

See community.adobe.com/help/profile/faq.html for answers to frequently asked questions about Community Help.

Adobe Flash Professional CS6 Help and Support: www.adobe.com/support/flash/ is where you can find and browse Help and Support content on Adobe's site.

Adobe Forums: forums.adobe.com lets you tap into peer-to-peer discussions, questions and answers on Adobe products.

Adobe TV: tv.adobe.com is an online video resource for expert instruction and inspiration about Adobe products, including a How To channel to get you started with your product.

Adobe Design Center: www.adobe.com/designcenter offers thoughtful articles on design and design issues, a gallery showcasing the work of top-notch designers, tutorials, and more.

Adobe Developer Connection: www.adobe.com/devnet is your source for technical articles, code samples, and how-to videos that cover Adobe developer products and technologies.

Resources for educators: www.adobe.com/education offers a treasure trove of information for instructors who teach classes on Adobe software. Find solutions for education at all levels, including free curricula that use an integrated approach to teaching Adobe software and can be used to prepare for the Adobe Certified Associate exams.

Also check out these useful links:

Adobe Marketplace & Exchange: www.adobe.com/cfusion/exchange/ is a central resource for finding tools, services, extensions, code samples and more to supplement and extend your Adobe products.

Adobe Flash Professional CS6 product home page: www.adobe.com/products/flash

Adobe Labs: labs.adobe.com gives you access to early builds of cutting-edge technology, as well as forums where you can interact with both the Adobe development teams building that technology and other like-minded members of the community.

Adobe Certification

The Adobe training and certification programs are designed to help Adobe customers improve and promote their product-proficiency skills. There are four levels of certification:

- Adobe Certified Associate (ACA)
- Adobe Certified Expert (ACE)
- Adobe Certified Instructor (ACI)
- Adobe Authorized Training Center (AATC)

The Adobe Certified Associate (ACA) credential certifies that individuals have the entry-level skills to plan, design, build, and maintain effective communications using different forms of digital media.

The Adobe Certified Expert program is a way for expert users to upgrade their credentials. You can use Adobe certification as a catalyst for getting a raise, finding a job, or promoting your expertise.

If you are an ACE-level instructor, the Adobe Certified Instructor program takes your skills to the next level and gives you access to a wide range of Adobe resources.

Adobe Authorized Training Centers offer instructor-led courses and training on Adobe products, employing only Adobe Certified Instructors. A directory of AATCs is available at partners.adobe.com.

For information on the Adobe Certified programs, visit www.adobe.com/support/certification/main.html.

1 GETTING ACQUAINTED

Lesson Overview

In this lesson, you'll learn how to do the following:

- Create a new file in Flash
- Adjust Stage settings and document properties
- Add layers to the Timeline
- Manage keyframes in the Timeline
- Work with imported images in the Library panel
- Move and reposition objects on the Stage
- Open and work with panels
- Select and use tools in the Tools panel
- Preview your Flash animation
- Save your Flash file
- Access online resources for Flash

This lesson will take less than 1 hour to complete. Copy the Lesson01 folder from the *Adobe Flash Professional CS6 Classroom in a Book* CD onto your hard drive if it's not already there.

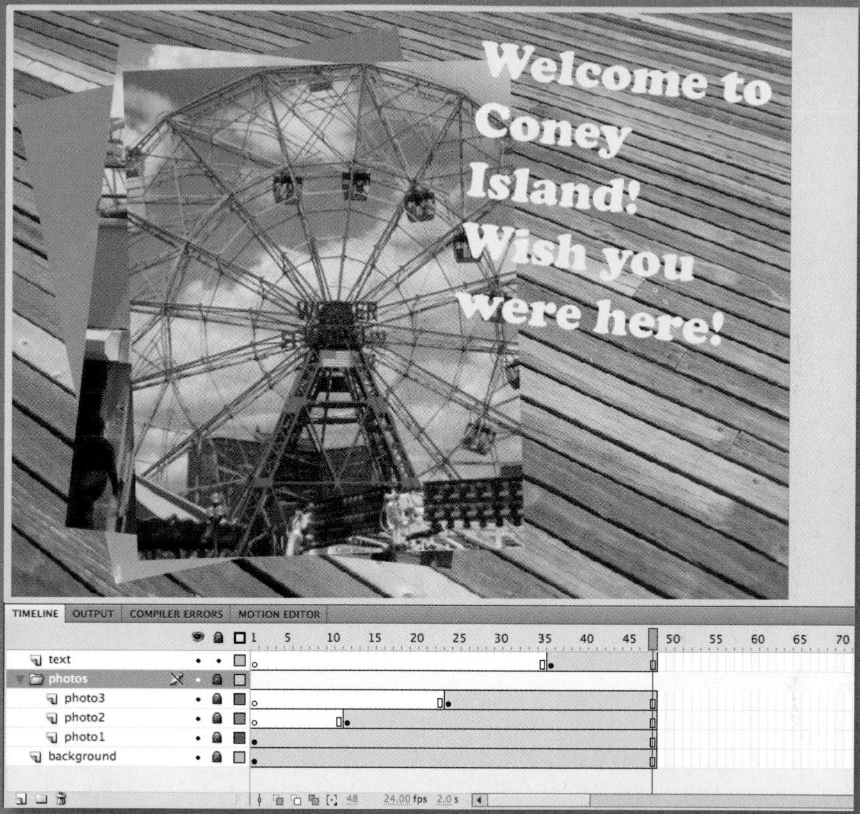

In Flash, the Stage is where the action takes place, the Timeline organizes frames and layers, and other panels let you edit and control your creation.

Starting Flash and Opening a File

The first time you start Flash you'll see a Welcome screen with links to standard file templates, tutorials, and other resources. In this lesson, you'll create a simple animation to showcase a few vacation snapshots. You'll add the photos and a title, and in the process you'll learn about positioning elements on the Stage and placing them along the Timeline. It's important to understand that the Stage is used to organize your visual elements spatially, and the Timeline is used to organize your elements temporally.

Note: You can also start Flash by double-clicking a Flash file (*.fla or *.xfl), such as the 01End.fla file that is provided to show you the completed project.

Note: If your computer is missing a font that the final project contains, Flash displays a warning dialog box. You can manually choose a substitute if you wish, or simply click Use Default and Flash will do so automatically.

1 Start Adobe Flash Professional CS6. In Windows, choose Start > All Programs > Adobe Flash Professional CS6. In Mac OS, click Adobe Flash Professional CS6 in the Applications folder or the Dock.

2 Choose File > Open. In the Open dialog box, select the 01End.fla file in the Lesson01/01End folder and click Open to see the final project.

3 Choose File > Publish Preview > HTML.

   Flash creates the necessary files (an HTML file and a SWF file) to display the final animation in your default browser. An animation plays. During the animation, several overlapping photos appear one by one, ending with a title.

4 Close the browser.

Creating a New Document

You'll create the simple animation that you just previewed by starting a new document.

1 In Flash, choose File > New.

The New Document dialog box opens.

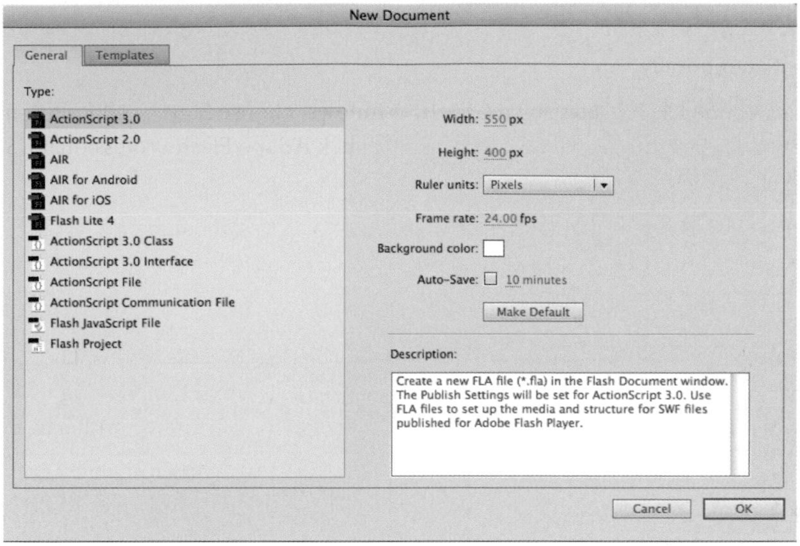

2 Under the General tab, choose ActionScript 3.0.

ActionScript 3.0 is the latest version of Flash's scripting language, which you use to add interactivity. In this lesson, you will not be working with ActionScript, but you still must choose with which version your file is compatible. Choosing ActionScript 3.0 creates a new document configured for playback in a desktop browser (such as Chrome, Safari, or Firefox) with Flash Player.

The other options target alternative playback environments. For example, AIR for Android and AIR for iOS create new documents configured for playback with AIR on an Android or an Apple mobile device.

Note: For simple projects, such as the example animation you'll create in this lesson, creating a single FLA document is sufficient. However, for more complex projects that require coordination with multiple developers or for projects intended for playback in several different environments (desktop and mobile), it's best to use the Project panel (Window > Project) to create a new project. A project helps organize multiple assets. You'll learn about the Project panel in Lesson 10, "Publishing Flash Documents."

3 On the right-hand side of the dialog box, you can choose the dimensions of the Stage by entering new pixel values for the Width and Height. Enter **800** for Width and **600** for Height. Keep the Ruler units as Pixels.

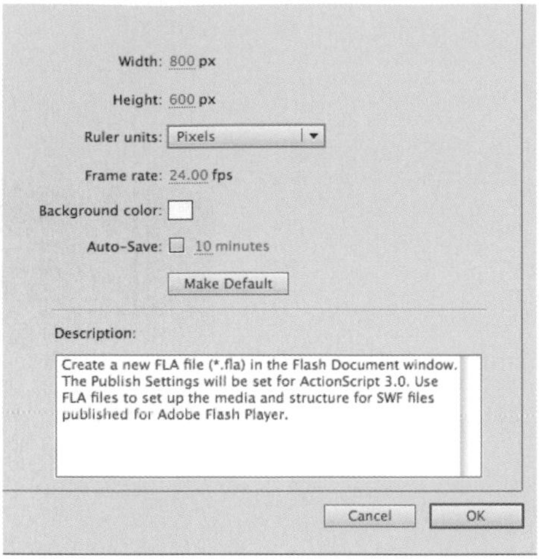

Leave the Frame rate and Background color for the Stage at their default settings. You can always edit these document properties, as explained later in this lesson.

4 Click OK.

Flash creates a new ActionScript 3.0 file with all the specified settings.

5 Choose File > Save. Name the file **01_workingcopy.fla**, and from the Format/Save as Type pull-down menu choose Flash CS6 document (*.fla). Save it in the 01Start folder. Saving your file right away is a good working habit that ensures your work won't be lost if the application or your computer crashes. You should always save your Flash file with the extension .fla to identify it as the Flash source file.

Getting to Know the Workspace

The Adobe Flash Professional work area includes the command menus at the top of the screen and a variety of tools and panels for editing and adding elements to your movie. You can create all the objects for your animation in Flash, or you can import elements you've created in Adobe Illustrator, Adobe Photoshop, Adobe After Effects, and other compatible applications.

By default, Flash displays the menu bar, Timeline, Stage, Tools panel, Properties inspector, and a few other panels. As you work in Flash, you can open, close, dock, undock, and move panels around the screen to fit your work style or your screen resolution.

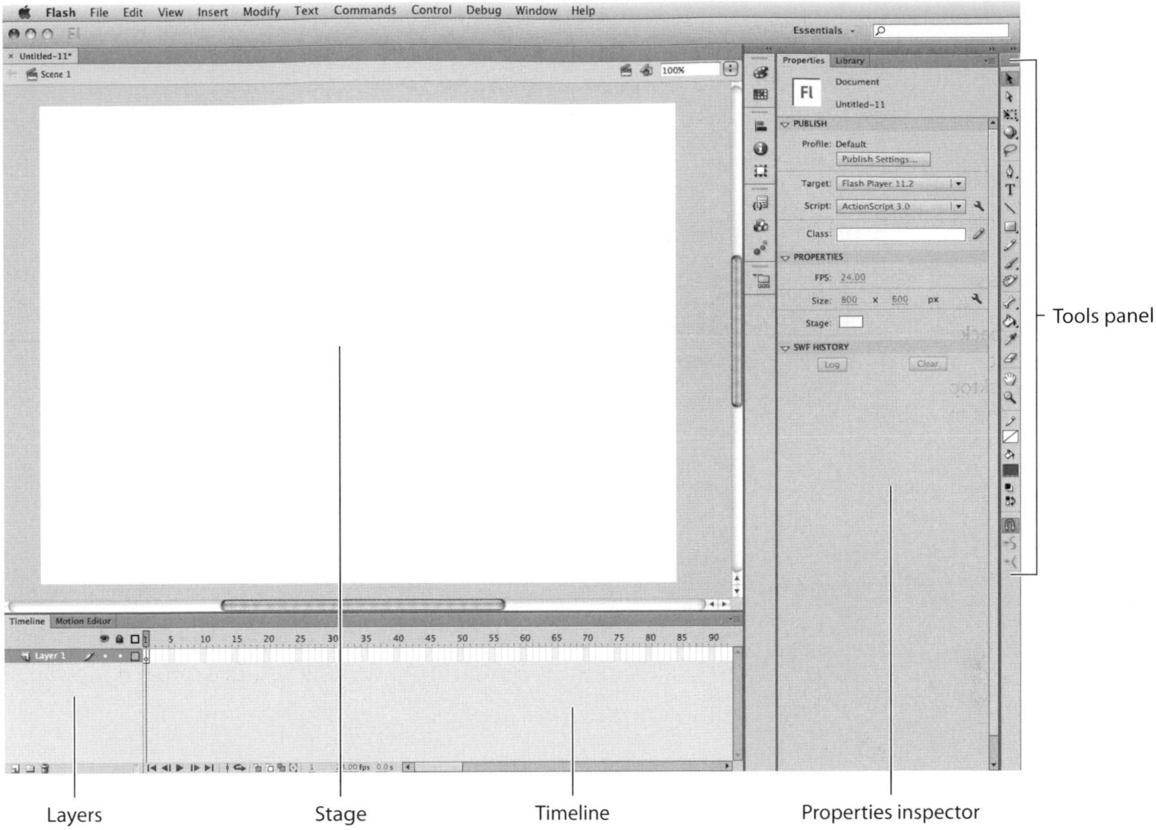

Choosing a new workspace

Flash also provides a few preset panel arrangements that may better suit the needs of particular users. The various workspace arrangements are listed in a pull-down menu at the top right of the Flash workspace or in the top menu under Window > Workspace.

1 Click the Essentials button at the top right of the Flash workspace and choose one of the other predefined workspaces.

   The various panels are rearranged and resized according to their importance to the particular user. For example, the Animator and Designer workspaces put the Timeline at the top for easy and frequent access.

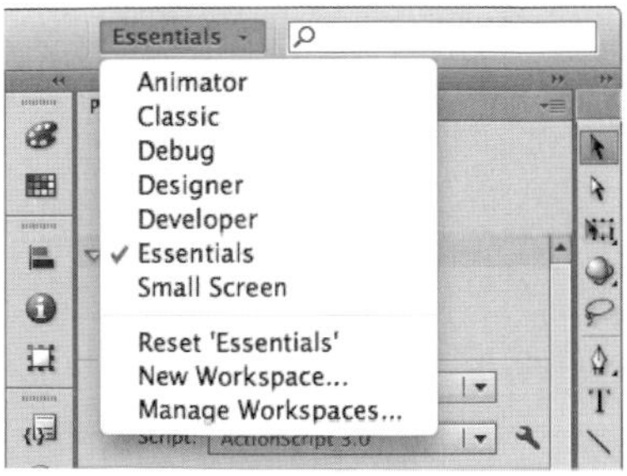

2 If you've moved some of the panels around and want to return to one of the prearranged workspaces, choose Window > Workspace > Reset and the name of the preset workspace.

3 To return to the default workspace, choose Window > Workspace > Essentials. In this Classroom in a Book, we'll be using the Essentials workspace.

Saving your workspace

If you find an arrangement of panels comfortable for your style of work, you can save the custom workspace to return to it at a later date.

1 Click the Workspace button at the top-right corner of the Flash workspace and choose New Workspace.

The New Workspace dialog box appears.

2 Enter a name for your new workspace. Click OK.

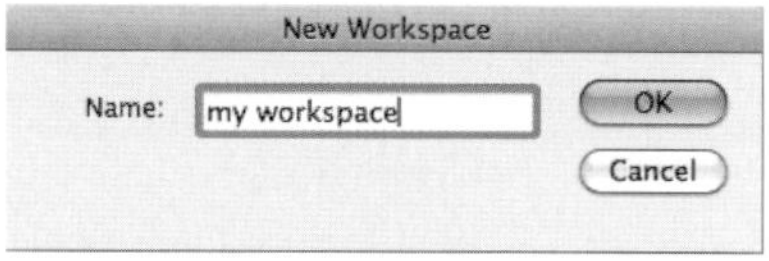

Flash saves the current arrangement of panels. Your workspace is added to the options in the Workspace pull-down menu, which you can access at any time.

About the Stage

The big white rectangle in the middle of your screen is called the Stage. As with a theater stage, the Stage in Flash is the area that viewers see when a movie is playing. It contains the text, images, and video that appear on the screen. Move elements on and off the Stage to move them in and out of view. You can use the rulers (View > Rulers) or grids (View > Grid > Show Grid) to help you position items on the Stage. Additionally, you can use the Align panel and other tools you'll learn about in the lessons in this book.

By default, you'll see the gray area off the Stage where you can place elements that won't be visible to your audience. The gray area is called the Pasteboard. To just see the Stage, choose View > Pasteboard to deselect the option. For now, leave the option selected.

To scale the Stage so that it fits completely in the application window, choose View > Magnification > Fit in Window. You can also choose different magnification view options from the pop-up menu just above the Stage.

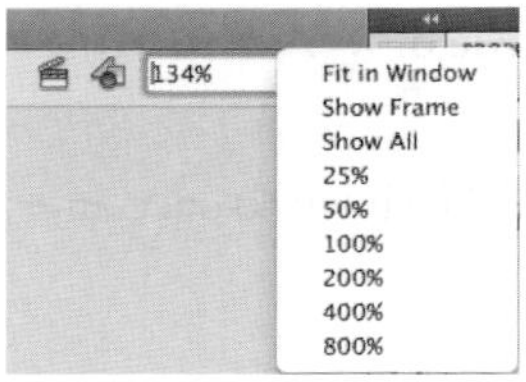

Changing the Stage properties

Now you'll change the color of the Stage. The Stage color, and other document properties such as the Stage dimensions and frame rate, are available in the Properties inspector, which is the vertical panel just to the right of the Stage.

1 At the bottom of the Properties inspector, note that the dimensions of the current Stage are set at 800 x 600 pixels, which you chose when you created the new document.

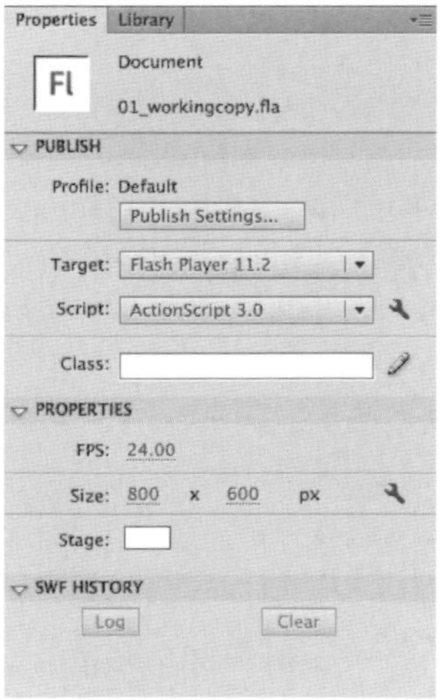

2 Click the Background color button next to Stage and choose a new color from the color palette. Choose dark gray (#333333).

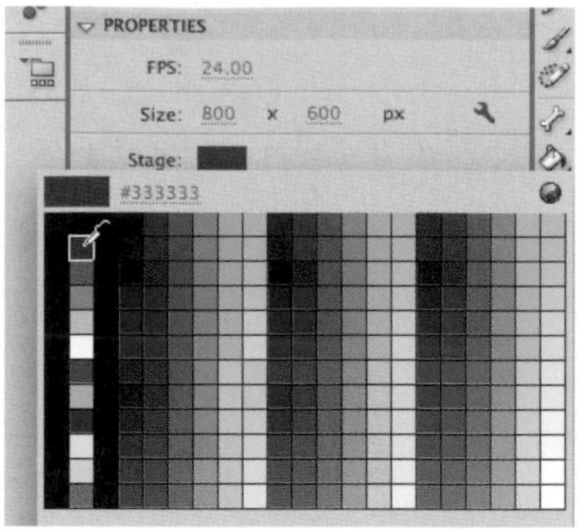

Your Stage is now a different color. You can change the Stage properties at any time.

Working with the Library Panel

Note: You'll learn much more about symbols in Lesson 3, "Creating and Editing Symbols."

The Library panel is accessible from a tab just to the right of the Properties inspector. The Library panel is where you store and organize symbols created in Flash, as well as imported files, including bitmaps, graphics, sound files, and video clips. Symbols are often-used graphics used for animation and for interactivity.

About the Library panel

The Library panel lets you organize library items in folders, see how often an item is used in a document, and sort items by type. When you import items into Flash, you can import them directly onto the Stage or into the library. However, any item you import onto the Stage is also added to the library, as are any symbols you create. You can then easily access the items to add them to the Stage again, edit them, or see their properties.

To display the Library panel, choose Window > Library, or press Ctrl+L (Windows) or Command+L (Mac).

Importing an item to the Library panel

Often, you'll be creating graphics directly with Flash's drawing tools and saving them as symbols, which are stored in the library. Other times you'll be importing media such as JPEG images or MP3 sound files, which are also stored in the library. In this lesson, you'll import several JPEG images into the library to be used in the animation.

1 Choose File > Import > Import to Library. In the Import to Library dialog box, select the background.jpg file in the Lesson01/01Start folder, and click Open.

2 Flash imports the selected JPEG image and places it in the Library panel.

3 Continue importing photo1.jpg, photo2.jpg, and photo3.jpg from the 01Start folder. Don't import the last image, photo4.jpg. You'll use that image later in this lesson.

You can also hold down the Shift key to select multiple files and import all of them at once.

4 The Library panel displays all the imported JPEG images with their filenames and a thumbnail preview. These images are now available to be used in your Flash document.

Adding an item from the Library panel to the Stage

To use an imported image, simply drag it from the Library panel onto the Stage.

● **Note:** You can also choose File > Import > Import to Stage, or Ctrl+R (Windows) or Command+R (Mac) to import an image file to the Library and put it on the Stage all in one step.

1 Choose Window > Library to open the Library panel if it isn't already open.

2 Select the background.jpg item in the Library panel.

3 Drag the background.jpg item onto the Stage and place it approximately in the center of the Stage.

Understanding the Timeline

The Timeline is located below the Stage. Like films, Flash documents measure time in frames. As the movie plays, the playhead, shown as a red vertical line, advances through the frames in the Timeline. You can change the content on the Stage for different frames. To display a frame's content on the Stage, move the playhead to that frame in the Timeline.

At the bottom of the Timeline, Flash indicates the selected frame number, the current frame rate (how many frames play per second), and the time that has elapsed so far in the movie.

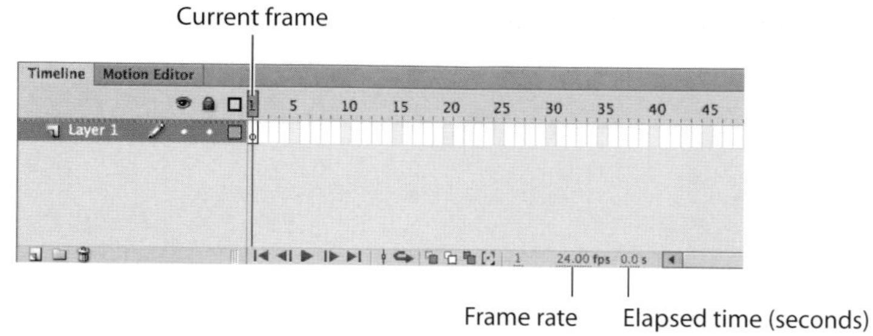

The Timeline also contains layers, which help you organize the artwork in your document. At the moment, your project only has one layer, which is called Layer 1. Think of layers as multiple film strips stacked on top of each other. Each layer can contain a different image that appears on the Stage, and you can draw and edit objects on one layer without affecting objects on another layer. The layers are stacked in the order in which they overlap each other, so that objects on the bottom layer in the Timeline are on the bottom of the stack on the Stage. You can hide, lock, or show the contents of layers as outlines by clicking the dots in the layer under the layer option icons.

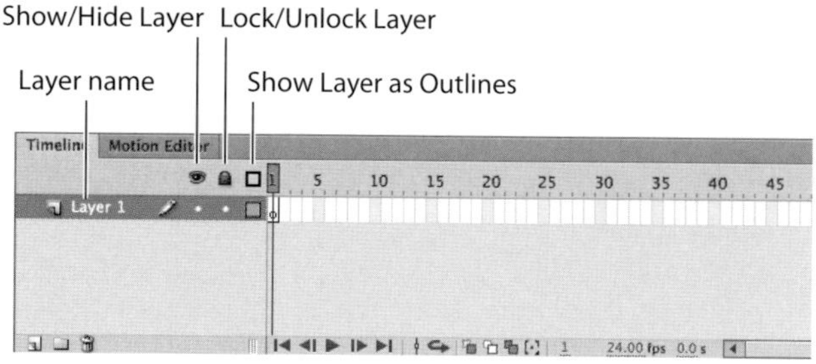

Renaming a layer

It's a good idea to separate your content on different layers and name each layer to indicate its contents so that you can easily find the layer you need later.

1 Select the existing layer in the Timeline, called Layer 1.

2 Double-click the name of the layer to rename it and type **background**.

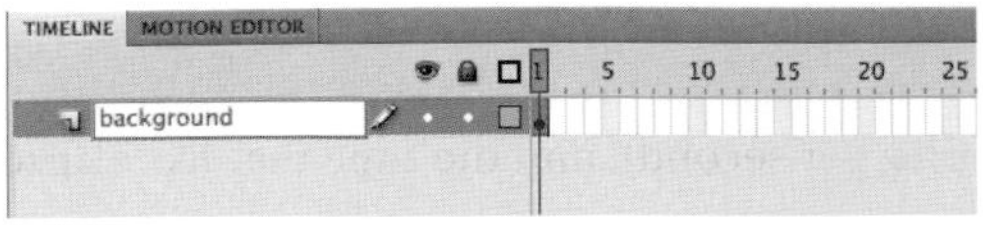

3 Click outside the name box to apply the new name.

4 Click the dot below the lock icon to lock the layer. Locking a layer prevents you from accidentally making changes to it.

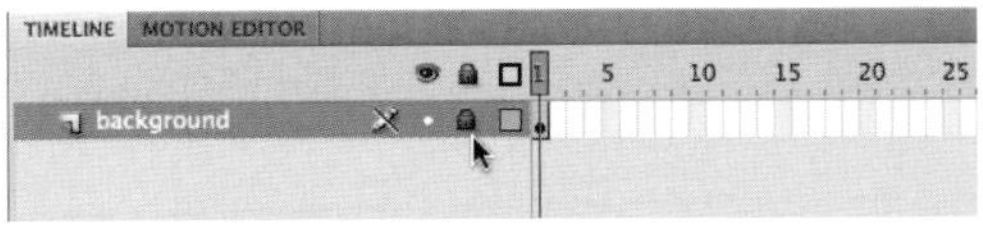

The pencil icon with a diagonal slash that appears after the layer name indicates that you can't make edits to the layer because it is locked.

Adding a layer

A new Flash document contains only one layer, but you can add as many layers as you need. Objects in the top layers will overlap objects in the bottom layers.

1 Select the background layer in the Timeline.

2 Choose Insert > Timeline > Layer. You can also click the New Layer button ( ) below the Timeline. A new layer appears above the background layer.

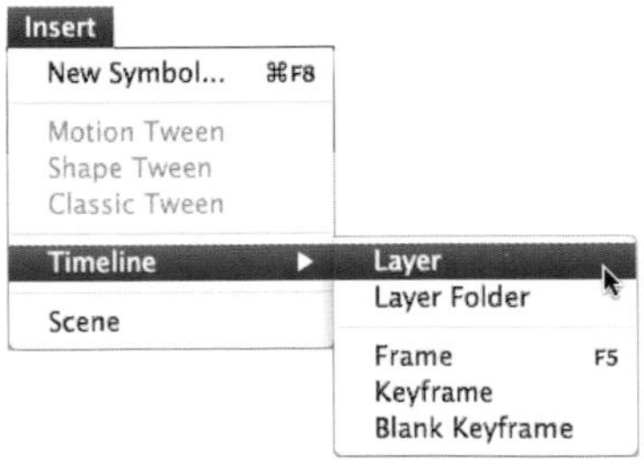

3 Double-click the new layer to rename it and type **photo1**. Click outside the name box to apply the new name.

Your Timeline now has two layers. The background layer contains the background photo, and the newly created photo1 layer above it is empty.

4 Select the top layer called photo1.

5 Choose Window > Library to open the Library panel if it isn't already open.

6 Drag the library item called photo1.jpg from the library on to the Stage.

The photo1 JPEG appears on the Stage and overlaps the background JPEG.

7 Choose Insert > Timeline > Layer or click the New Layer button below the Timeline to add a third layer.

8 Rename the third layer **photo2**.

Working with Layers

If you don't want a layer, you can easily delete it by selecting it and then clicking the Delete button below the Timeline.

If you want to rearrange your layers, simply click and drag any layer to move it to a new position in the layer stack.

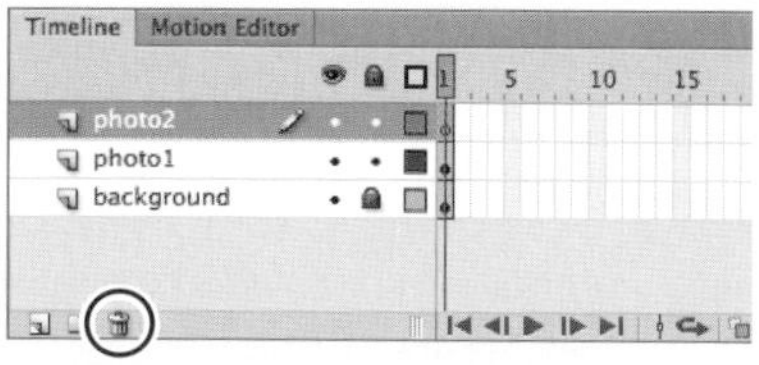

Inserting frames

So far, you have a background photo and another overlapping photo on the Stage, but your entire animation exists for only a single frame. To create more time on the Timeline, you must add additional frames.

1 Select frame 48 in the background layer.

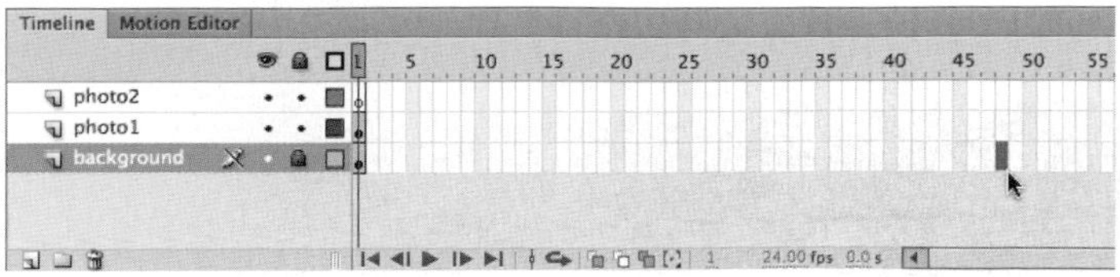

2 Choose Insert > Timeline > Frame (F5). You can also right-click (Windows) or Ctrl-click (Mac) and choose Insert Frame from the context menu that pops up.

Flash adds frames in the background layer up to the selected point, frame 48.

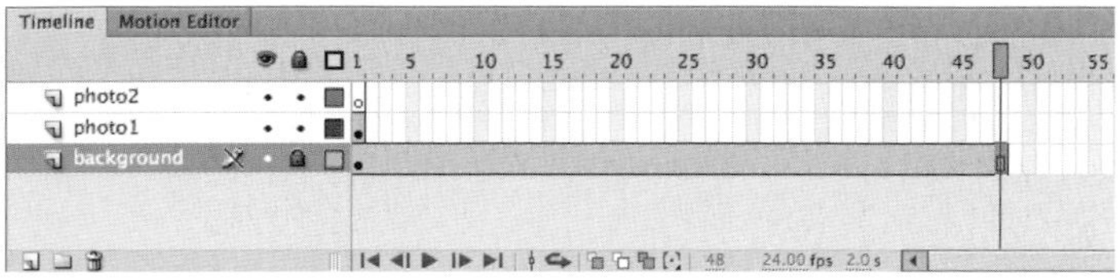

3 Select frame 48 in the photo1 layer.

4 Choose Insert > Timeline > Frame (F5). You can also right-click/Ctrl-click and choose Insert Frame from the context menu.

Flash adds frames in the photo1 layer up to the selected point, frame 48.

5 Select frame 48 in the photo2 layer and insert frames on this layer.

You now have three layers, all with 48 frames on the Timeline. Since the frame rate of your Flash document is 24 frames per second, your current animation lasts two seconds.

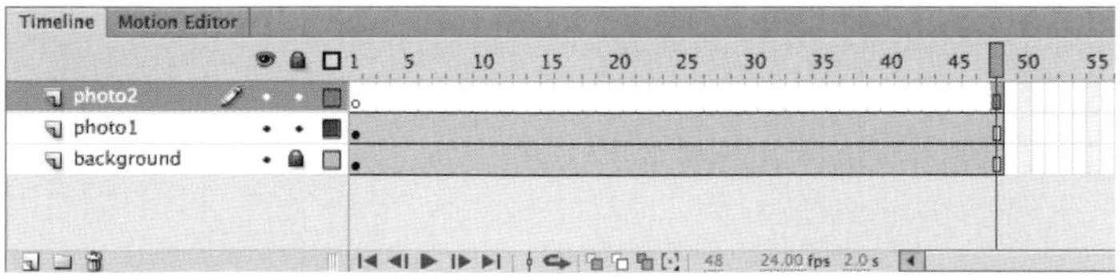

Selecting Multiple Frames

Just as you can hold down the Shift key to select multiple files on your desktop, you can hold down the Shift key to select multiple frames on the Flash Timeline. If you have several layers and want to insert frames into all of them, hold down the Shift key and click on the point at which you want to add frames in all of your layers. Then choose Insert > Timeline > Frame.

Creating a keyframe

A keyframe indicates a change in content on the Stage. Keyframes are indicated on the Timeline as a circle. An empty circle means there is nothing in that particular layer at that particular time. A filled-in black circle means there is something in that particular layer at that particular time. The background layer, for example, contains a filled keyframe (black circle) in the first frame. The photo1 layer also contains a filled keyframe in its first frame. Both layers contain photos. The photo2 layer, however, contains an empty keyframe in the first frame, indicating that it is currently empty.

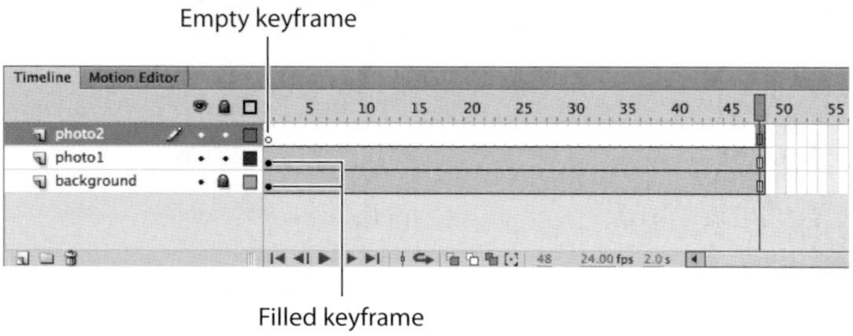

You'll insert a keyframe in the photo2 layer at the point in time when you want the next photo to appear.

1 Select frame 24 on the photo2 layer. As you select a frame, Flash displays the frame number beneath the Timeline.

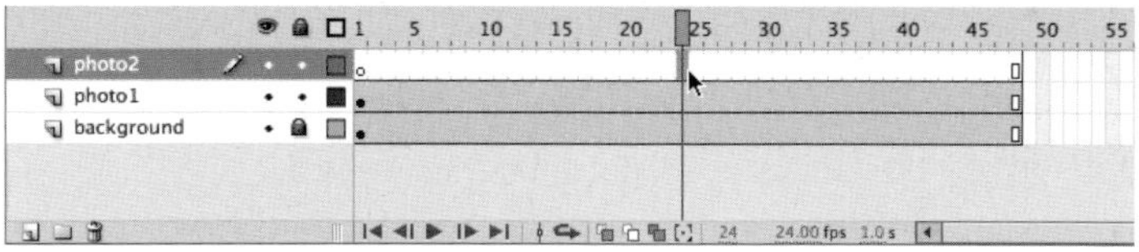

2 Choose Insert > Timeline > Keyframe (F6).

A new keyframe, indicated by an empty circle, appears in the photo2 layer in frame 24.

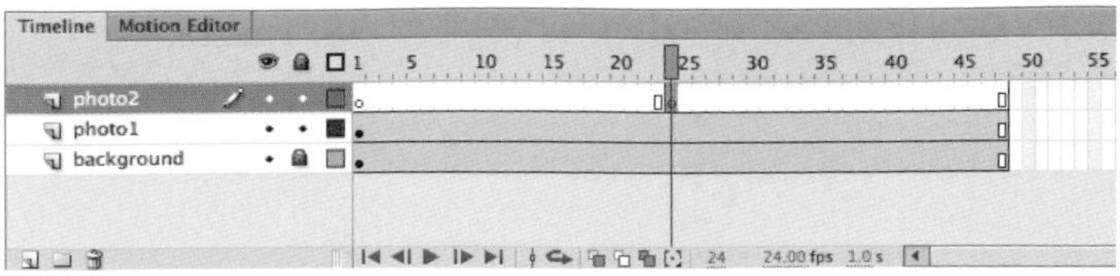

3 Select the new keyframe at frame 24 in the photo2 layer.

4 Drag the photo2.jpg item from your library onto the Stage.

The empty circle at frame 24 becomes filled, indicating there is now a change in the photo2 layer. At frame 24, your photo appears on the Stage. You can click and drag the red playhead from the top of the Timeline to "scrub," or show what's happening on the Stage at any point along the Timeline. You'll see that the background photo and photo1 remain on the Stage throughout the Timeline but photo2 appears only at frame 24.

Understanding frames and keyframes is essential for mastering Flash. Be sure you understand how the photo2 layer contains 48 frames with 2 keyframes—an empty keyframe at frame 1 and a filled keyframe at frame 24.

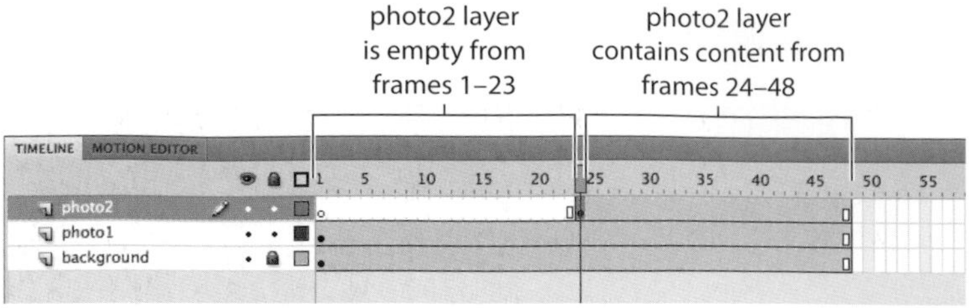

Moving a keyframe

If you want your photo2.jpg to appear later or earlier, you need to move the keyframe in which it appears later or earlier along the Timeline. You can easily move any keyframe along the Timeline by simply selecting it and then dragging it to a new position.

1 Select the keyframe in frame 24 on the photo2 layer.

2 Move your mouse cursor slightly, and you'll see a box icon appear near your cursor indicating that you can reposition the keyframe.

3 Click and drag the keyframe to frame 12 in the photo2 layer.

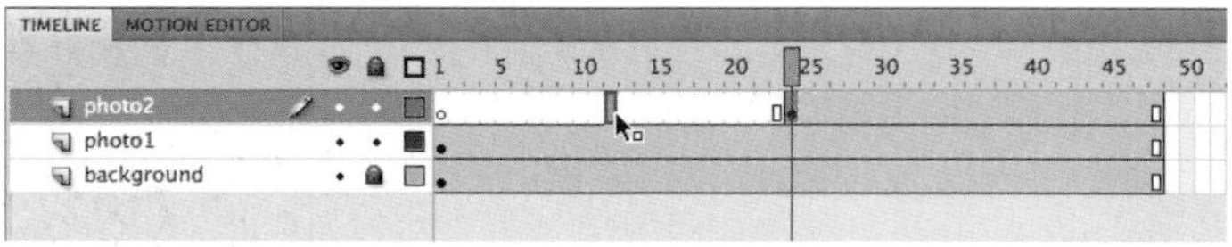

The photo2.jpg now appears on the Stage much earlier in the animation.

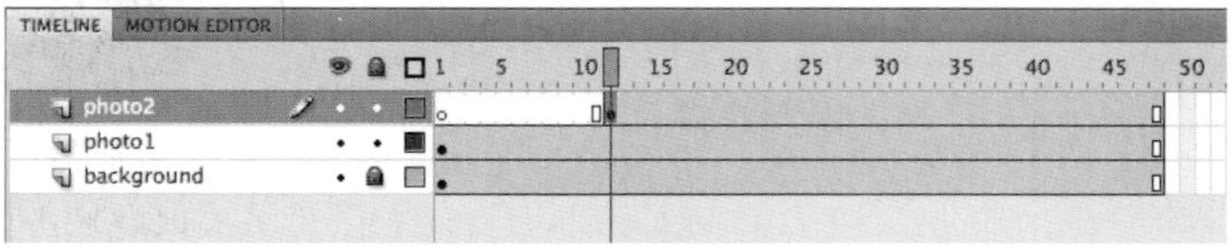

Removing Keyframes

If you want to remove a keyframe, do not press the Delete key! Doing so will delete the contents of that keyframe on the Stage. Instead, select the keyframe and choose Modify > Timeline > Clear Keyframe (Shift+F6). Your keyframe will be removed from the Timeline.

Organizing Layers in a Timeline

At this point, your working Flash file has only three layers: a background layer, a photo1 layer, and a photo2 layer. You'll be adding additional layers for this project, and like with most other projects, you'll end up having to manage multiple layers. Layer folders help you group related layers to keep your Timeline organized and manageable, just like you make folders for related documents on your desktop. Although it may take some time to create the folders, you'll save time later because you'll know exactly where to look for a specific layer.

Creating layer folders

For this project, you'll continue to add layers for additional photos, and you'll place those layers in a layer folder.

1 Select the photo2 layer and click the New Layer button at the bottom of the Timeline ( ).

2 Name the layer **photo3**.

3 Insert a keyframe at frame 24.

4 Drag the photo3.jpg from the library onto the Stage.

You now have four layers. The top three contain photos of scenes from Coney Island that appear at different keyframes.

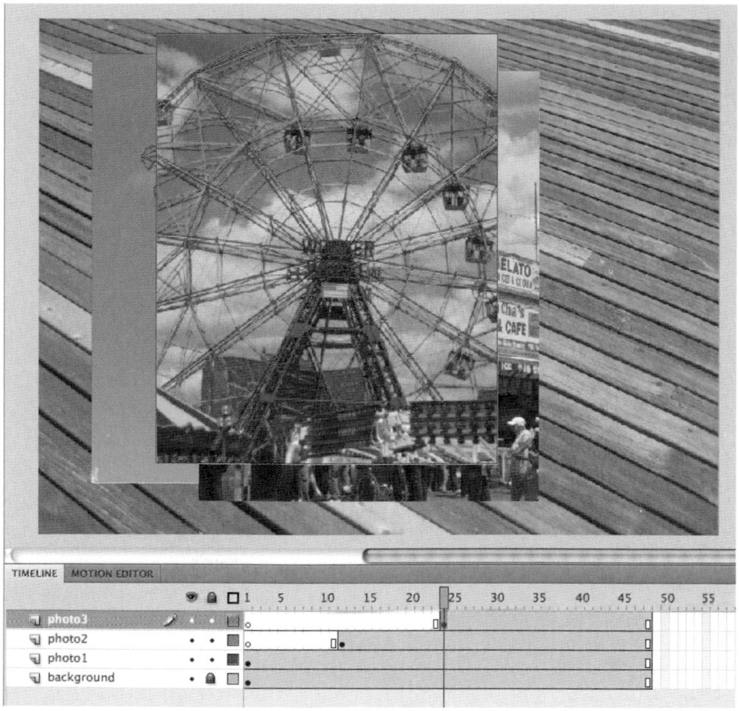

5 Select the photo3 layer and click the New Folder icon at the bottom of the Timeline ( ).

A new layer folder appears above the photo3 layer.

6 Name the folder **photos**.

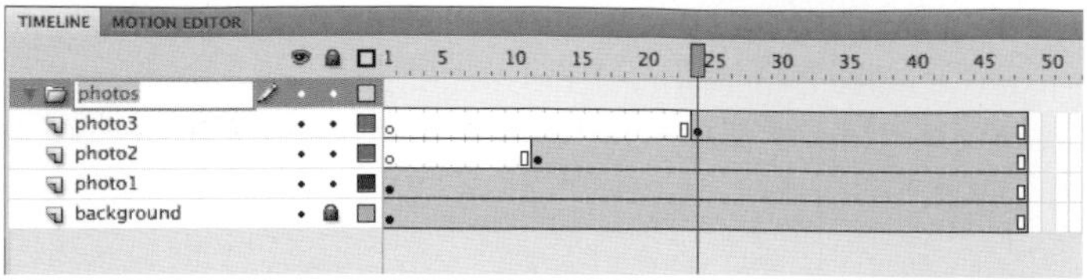

Adding layers to layer folders

Now you'll add the photo layers to the photo folder. As you arrange layers, remember that Flash displays content in the layers in the order in which they appear in the Timeline, with the top layer's content at the front and the bottom layer's content at the back.

1 Drag the photo1 layer into the photos folder.

Notice how the bold line indicates the destination of your layer. When a layer is placed inside a folder, the layer name is indented.

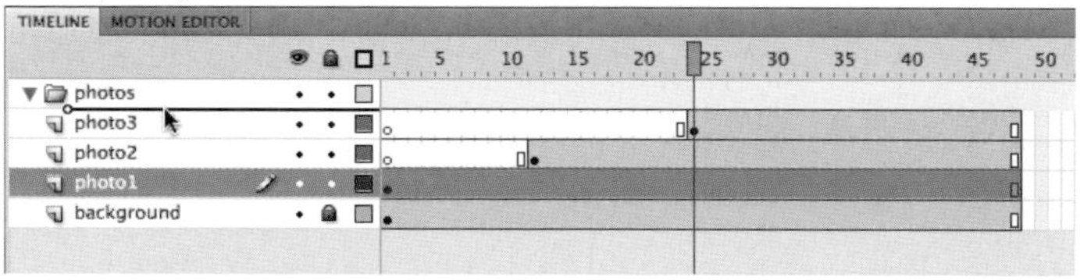

2 Drag the photo2 layer into the photos folder.

3 Drag the photo3 layer into the photos folder.

All three photo layers should be in the photos folder.

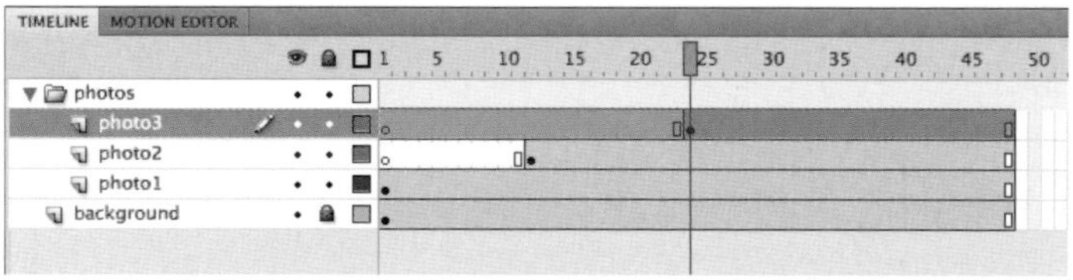

You can collapse the folder by clicking the arrow. Expand the folder by clicking the arrow again. Be aware that if you delete a layer folder, you delete all the layers inside that folder as well.

Changing the appearance of the Timeline

You can adjust the Timeline's appearance to accommodate your workflow. When you want to see more layers, select Short from the Frame View pop-up menu in the upper-right corner of the Timeline. The Short option decreases the height of frame cell rows. The Preview and Preview in Context options display thumbnail versions of the contents of your keyframes in the Timeline.

You can also change the width of the frame cells by selecting Tiny, Small, Normal, Medium, or Large.

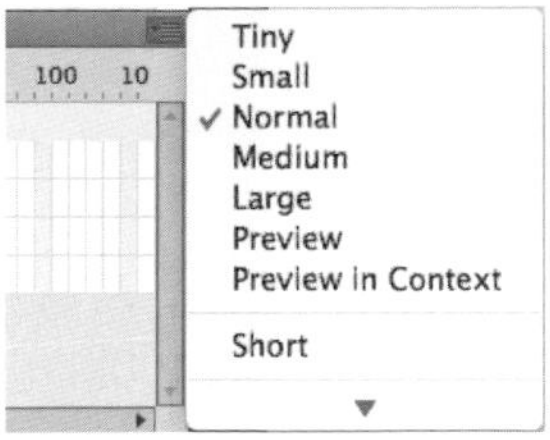

Cut, Copy, Paste, and Duplicate Layers

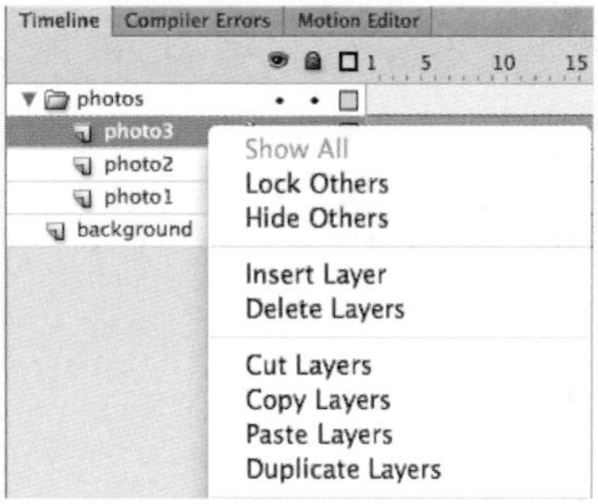

When managing multiple layers and layer folders, you can rely on cut, copy, paste, and duplicate layer commands to make your workflow easier and more efficient. All the properties of the selected layer are copied and pasted, including its frames, keyframes, any animation, and even the layer name and type. Layer folders and their contents can also be copied and pasted.

To cut or copy any layer or layer folder, simply select the layer and right-click/Ctrl-click the layer. In the contextual menu that appears, choose Cut Layers or Copy Layers.

Right-click/Ctrl-click on the Timeline again, and choose Paste Layers. The layer or layers that you cut or copied are pasted into the Timeline. Use Duplicate Layers to copy and paste in one operation.

You can also Cut, Copy, Paste, or Duplicate layers from the top Flash menu. Choose Edit > Timeline > and choose Cut Layers, Copy Layers, Paste Layers, or Duplicate Layers.

Using the Properties Inspector

The Properties inspector gives you quick access to the attributes you're most likely to need. What appears in the Properties inspector depends on what you've selected. For example, if nothing is selected, the Properties inspector includes options for the general Flash document including changing the Stage color or dimensions; if an object on the Stage is selected, the Properties inspector shows its *x* and *y* coordinates and its width and height, among other information. You'll use the Properties inspector to move your photos on the Stage.

Positioning an object on the Stage

Note: If the Properties inspector is not open, choose Window > Properties, or press Ctrl/Command+F3.

You'll begin by moving the photos with the Properties inspector. You'll also use the Transform panel to rotate the photos.

1 At frame 1 of the Timeline, select the photo1.jpg image that you dragged onto the Stage in the photo1 layer. A blue outline indicates that the object is selected.

2 In the Properties inspector, type **50** for the X value and **50** for the Y value. Press Enter/Return to apply the values. You can also click and drag your mouse cursor over the X and Y values to change their positions. The photo moves to the left side of the Stage.

The X and Y values are measured on the Stage from the top-left corner. X begins at 0 and increases to the right, and Y begins at 0 and increases downward. The registration point for imported photos is at the top-left corner.

3 Choose Window > Transform to open the Transform panel.

4 In the Transform panel, select Rotate, and type **-12** in the Rotate box, or click and drag over the value to change the rotation. Press Enter/Return to apply the value.

The selected photo on the Stage rotates 12 degrees counterclockwise.

5 Select frame 12 of the photo2 layer. Now click on the photo2.jpg on the Stage.

6 Use the Properties inspector and Transform panel to position and rotate the second photo in an interesting way. Use X=**80**, Y=**50**, and a Rotate of **6** to give it some contrast with the first photo.

Working with Panels

Just about everything you do in Flash involves a panel. In this lesson, you use the Library panel, Tools panel, Properties inspector, Transform panel, History panel, and the Timeline. In later lessons, you'll use the Actions panel, the Color panel, the Motion panel, and other panels that let you control various aspects of your project. Because panels are such an integral part of the Flash workspace, it pays to know how to manage them.

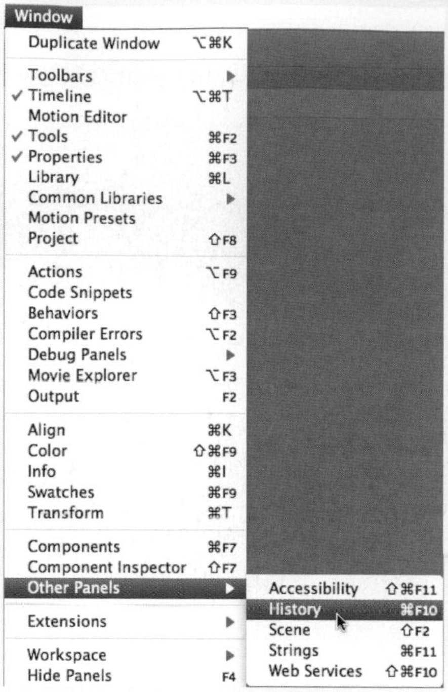

To open any panel in Flash, choose its name from the Window menu. In a few cases, you may need to choose the panel from a submenu, such as Window > Other Panels > History.

By default, the Properties inspector, Library panel, and Tools panel appear together at the right of the screen; the Timeline and Motion Editor are at the bottom; and the Stage is on the top. However, you can move a panel to any position that is convenient for you.

- To undock a panel from the right side of the screen, drag it by its tab to a new location.
- To dock a panel, drag it by its tab into the dock at a new position on the screen. You can drag it to the top, bottom, or in between other panels. A blue highlight indicates where you can dock a panel.
- To group a panel with another, drag its tab onto the other panel's tab.
- To move a panel group, drag the group by its dark gray top bar.

You also have the option of displaying most of the panels as icons to save space but still maintain quick access. Click the upper-right arrows to collapse the panels to icons. Click the arrows again to expand the panels.

7 Select frame 24 in the photo3 layer. Now click on photo3.jpg on the Stage.

8 Use the Properties inspector and Transform panel to position and rotate the third photo in an interesting way. Use X=**120**, Y=**55**, and a Rotate of **–2** so all your photos have visual variety.

● **Note:** When images are scaled or rotated in Flash, they may appear jagged. You can smooth them out by double-clicking the bitmap icon in the Library panel. In the Bitmap Properties dialog box that appears, select the Allow Smoothing option.

Using the Tools Panel

The Tools panel—the long, narrow panel on the far right side of the work area—contains selection tools, drawing and type tools, painting and editing tools, navigation tools, and tool options. You'll use the Tools panel frequently to switch to tools designed for the task at hand. You'll most often be using the Selection tool, which is the black arrow tool at the top of the Tools panel, for selecting and clicking on items on the Stage or the Timeline. When you select a tool, check the options area at the bottom of the panel for more options and other settings appropriate for your task.

Selecting and using a tool

When you select a tool, the options available at the bottom of the Tools panel and the Properties inspector change. For example, when you select the Rectangle tool, the Object Drawing mode and Snap To Objects options appear. When you select the Zoom tool, the Enlarge and Reduce options appear.

The Tools panel contains too many tools to display all at once. Some tools are arranged in hidden groups in the Tools panel; only the tool you last selected from a group is displayed. A small triangle in the lower-right corner of the tool's button indicates there are other tools in the group. Click and hold the icon for the visible tool to see the other tools available, and then select one from the pop-up menu.

You'll use the Text tool to add a title to your animation.

1 Select the top layer in the Timeline, and then click the New Layer button.

2 Name the new layer **text**.

3 Lock the other layers below it so you don't accidentally move anything into them.

4 In the Timeline, move the playhead to frame 36 and select frame 36 in the text layer.

5 Choose Insert > Timeline > Keyframe (F6) to insert a new keyframe at frame 36 in the text layer.

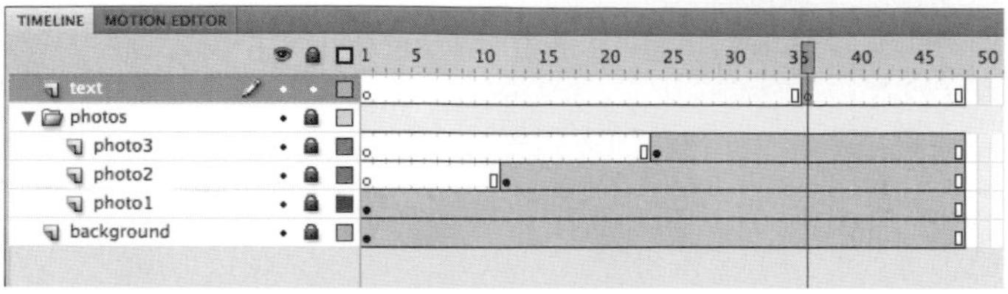

You will create text to appear at frame 36 in this layer.

6 In the Tools panel, select the Text tool, which is indicated by the large capital letter T.

7 In the Properties inspector, choose Classic Text from the pull-down menu. Choose Static Text from the pull-down menu that appears below.

Classic Text is a mode for adding simple text that doesn't require sophisticated options such as multiple columns or wrapping around other objects. Static Text is the option for any text that is used for display purposes. Dynamic and Input Text are special text options for more interactive purposes and can be controlled with ActionScript. You'll learn about more advanced text options in Lesson 7, "Using Text."

8 Select a font and size in the Properties inspector. Your computer may not have the same fonts as those shown in this lesson, but choose one that is close in appearance.

9 Click the colored square in the Properties inspector to choose a text color. You can click on the color wheel at the upper right to access the OS Color Picker, or you can change the Alpha percentage at the upper right, which determines the level of transparency.

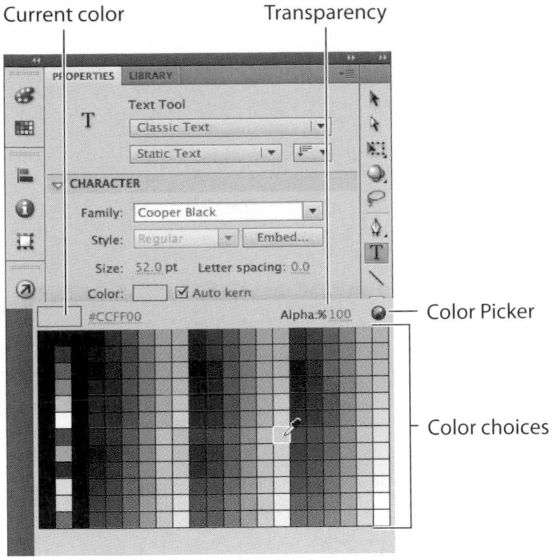

10 Make sure the empty keyframe in frame 36 of the title layer is selected, and then click on the Stage where you want to begin adding text. You can either click once and begin typing, or you can click and drag to define the width of your text field.

11 Type in a title that describes the photos that are being displayed on the Stage.

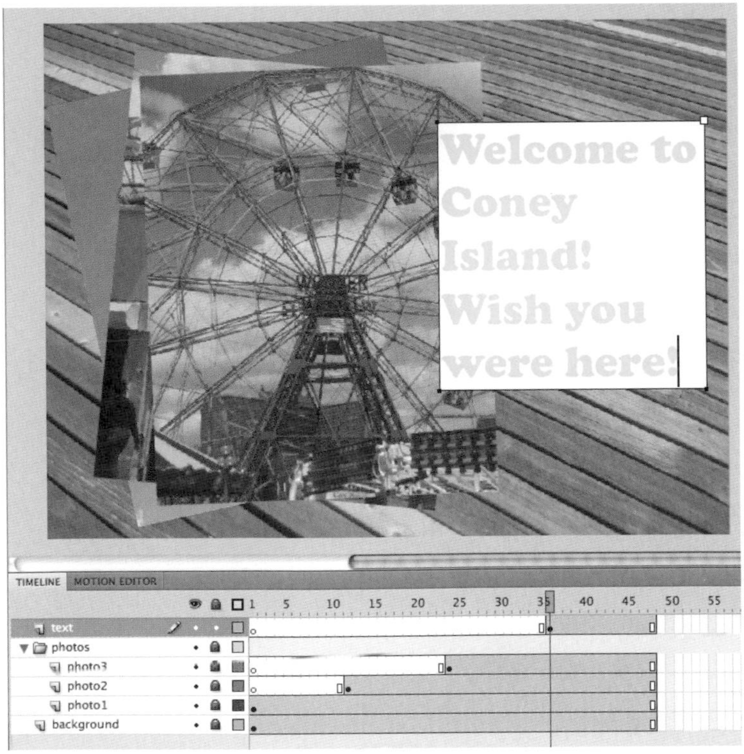

Tools Panel Overview

The Tools panel contains selection tools, drawing and painting tools, and navigation tools. The options area in the Tools panel lets you modify the selected tool. The expanded menu on the right shows the hidden tools. The black squares on the expanded menu to the right indicate the default tool that appears on the Tool panel. The single capital letters in parentheses indicate the keyboard shortcuts to select those tools. Notice how the tools are grouped together by similar function.

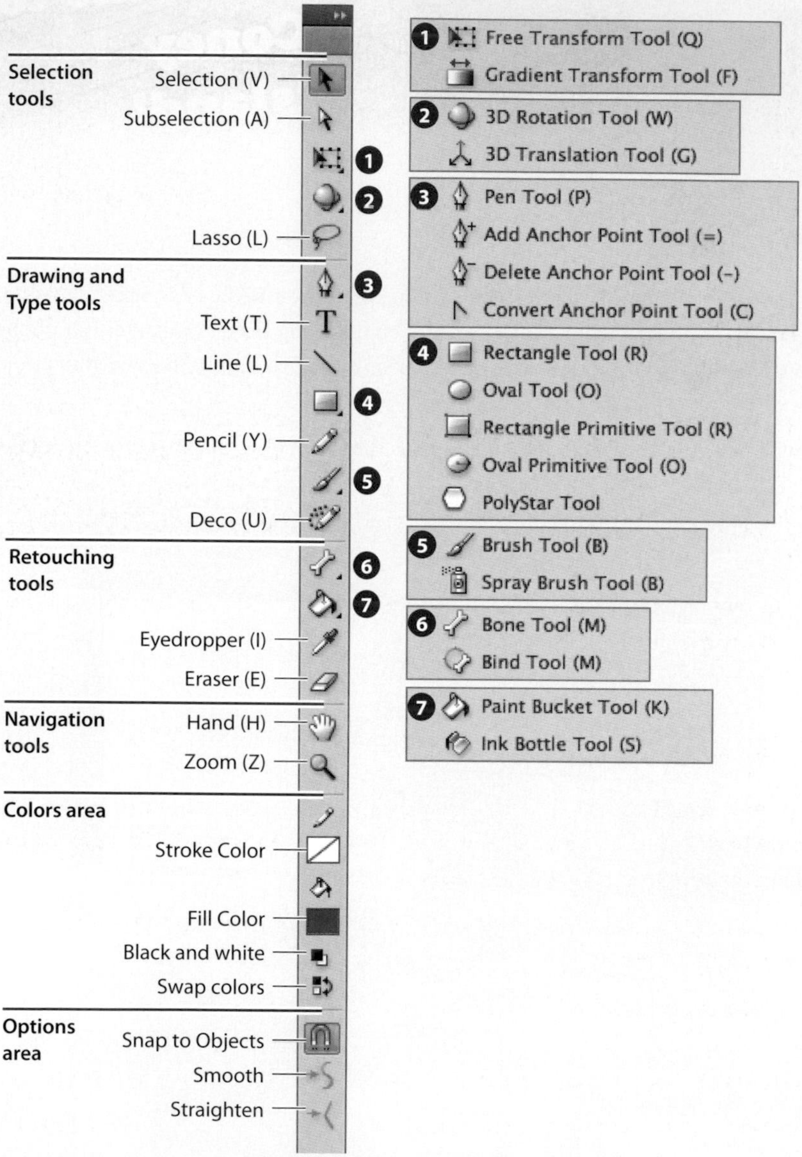

12 Exit the Text tool by selecting the Selection tool ( ).

13 Use the Properties inspector or the Transform panel to reposition or rotate your text on the Stage, if desired. Or, choose the Selection tool and simply drag your text to a new position on the Stage. The X and Y values in the Properties inspector update as you drag the text around the Stage.

14 Your animation for this lesson is finished! Compare the Timeline in your file with the Timeline in the final file, 01End.fla.

Undoing Steps in Flash

In a perfect world, everything would go according to plan. But sometimes you need to move back a step or two and start over. You can undo steps in Flash using the Undo command or the History panel.

To undo a single step in Flash, choose Edit > Undo or press Ctrl/Command+Z. To redo a step you've undone, choose Edit > Redo.

To undo multiple steps in Flash, it's easiest to use the History panel, which displays a list of all the last 100 steps you've performed. Closing a document clears its history. To access the History panel, choose Window > Other Panels > History.

For example, if you aren't satisfied with the newly added text, you can undo your work and return your Flash document to a previous state.

1 Choose Edit > Undo to undo the last action you made. You can choose the Undo command multiple times to move backward as many steps as are listed in the History panel. You can change the maximum number of Undo commands by selecting Flash > Preferences.

2 Choose Window > Other Panels > History to open the History panel.

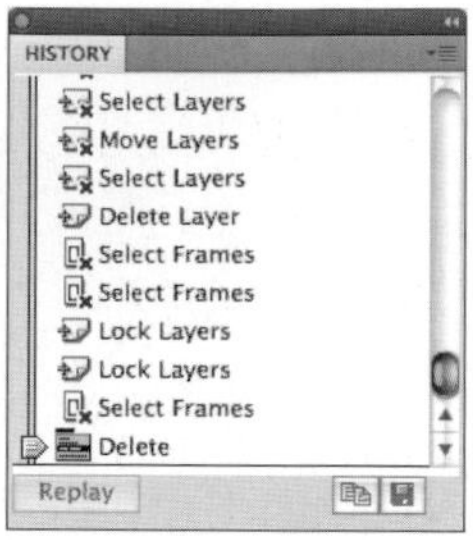

● **Note:** If you remove steps in the History panel and then perform additional steps, the removed steps will no longer be available.

3 Drag the History panel slider up to the step just before your mistake. Steps below that point are dimmed in the History panel and are removed from the project. To add a step back, move the slider back down.

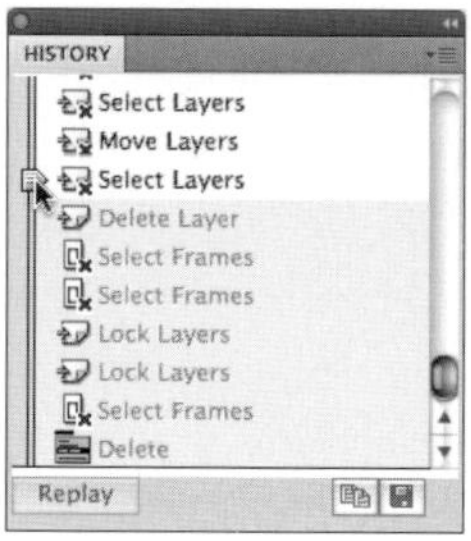

Previewing Your Movie

As you work on a project, it's a good idea to preview it frequently to ensure that you're achieving the desired effect. To quickly see how an animation or movie will appear to a viewer, choose Control > Test Movie > in Flash Professional. You can also press Ctrl+Enter or Command+Return to preview your movie.

1 Choose Control > Test Movie > in Flash Professional.

Flash creates a SWF file in the same location as your FLA file and opens and plays the file in a separate window. A SWF file is the compressed, published file that you would upload to the Web to play in a browser on the desktop.

Flash automatically loops your movie in this preview mode. If you don't want the movie to loop, choose Control > Loop to deselect the option.

2 Close the preview window.

3 Click on the Stage with the Selection tool. Note at the bottom of the Properties inspector that the SWF History displays and keeps a log of the file size, date, and time of the most recent SWF file published. This will help you keep track of your work progress and revisions.

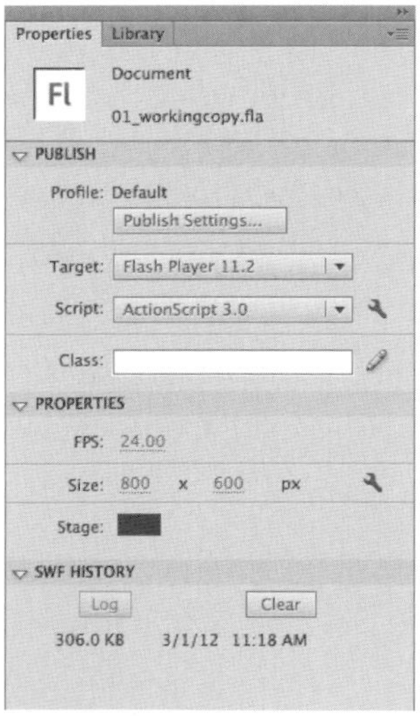

Modifying the Content and Stage

When you first started this lesson, you created a new file with the Stage set at 800 pixels by 600 pixels. However, your client may later tell you that they want the animation in several different sizes to accommodate different layouts. For example, they'd like to create a smaller version with a different aspect ratio for a banner ad. Or, they may want to create a version that will run on AIR for Android devices, which have specific dimensions.

Fortunately, you can modify the Stage even after all your content is put in place. When you change the Stage dimensions, Flash provides the option of scaling the content with the Stage, automatically shrinking or enlarging all your content proportionally.

Stage Resizing and Content Scaling

You'll create another version of this animated project with different Stage dimensions.

1 At the bottom of the Properties inspector, note that the dimensions of the current Stage are set at 800 x 600 pixels. Click the Edit button next to the Stage size (the wrench icon).

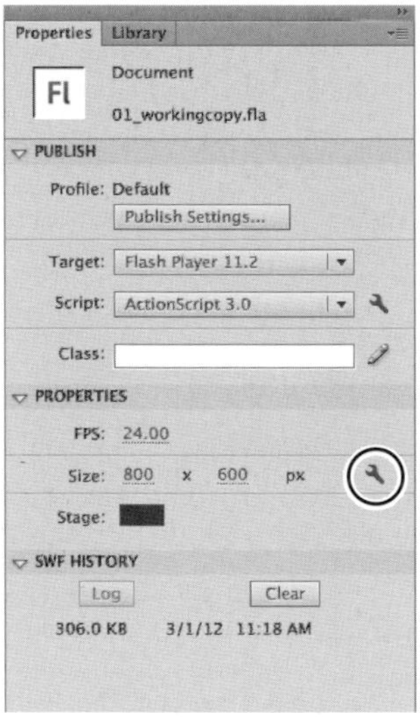

The Document Settings dialog box appears.

2 In the Width and Height boxes, enter new pixel dimensions. Enter **400** for the Width and **300** for the Height.

Notice that as you enter new values for the Width and the Height, the option to Scale content with stage becomes enabled.

3 Check the option to Scale content with stage.

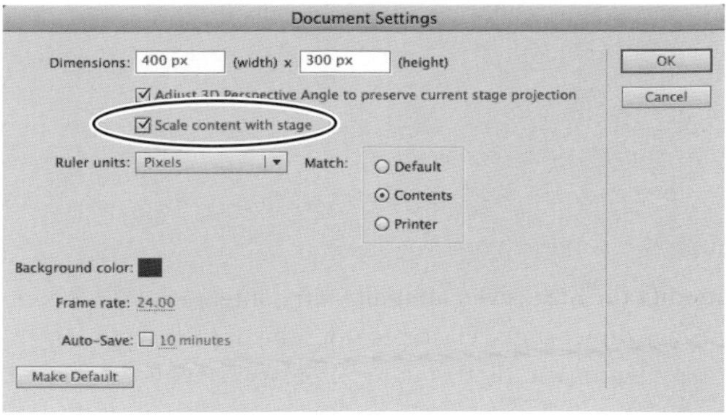

4 Click OK.

Flash modifies the dimensions of the Stage and automatically resizes all the content. If your new dimensions are not proportional to the original size, Flash will resize everything to maximize the content to fit. This means that if your new Stage size is wider than the original, there'll be extra Stage space to the right. If your new Stage size is taller than the original, there'll be extra Stage space on the bottom.

5 Choose File > Save As, and choose Flash CS6 Document for the Format. Name the file **01_workingcopy_resized.fla**.

You now have two Flash files, identical in content but with different Stage dimensions. Close this file and re-open **01_workingcopy.fla** to continue this lesson.

Saving Your Movie

A mantra in multimedia production is "Save early, save often." Applications, operating systems, and hardware crash more often than anyone wants, and at unexpected and inconvenient times. You should always be saving your movie at regular intervals to ensure that, if a crash does happen, you won't have lost too much of your time.

Flash can help alleviate much of the worry over lost work. The Auto-Save feature automatically saves your file at specified intervals, and the Auto-Recovery feature creates a backup file in case of a crash.

Using Auto-Save

The Auto-Save feature, when enabled, saves your Flash file automatically at regular intervals that you set. You can set your Flash file to Auto-Save anywhere between 1 minute and 1440 minutes (24 hours).

1 At the bottom of the Properties inspector, click the Edit button next to the Stage size (the wrench icon).

   The Document Settings dialog box appears.

2 Check the Auto-Save option and enter a desired interval for each save.

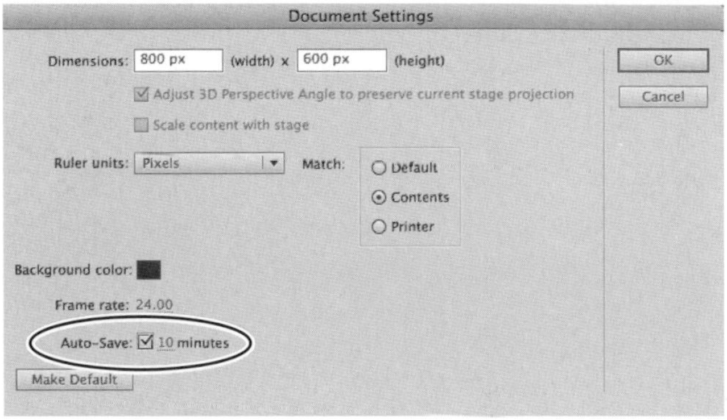

3 Click OK.

   Rest easy. Your old Flash file will be replaced by the open document at the predetermined intervals. An open document that has unsaved changes is indicated by an asterisk at the end of its filename at the top of the document window.

Using Auto-Recovery for a backup

The Auto-Recovery feature works a little differently from the Auto-Save feature. The Auto-Recovery feature is a preference set for the Flash application for all documents, while the Auto-Save feature is specific for each document.

The Auto-Recovery feature saves a backup file, so that in case of a crash, you have an alternate file to return to.

1 Choose Flash > Preferences (Mac) or Edit > Preferences (Windows).

   The Preferences dialog box appears.

2 Choose the General category from the left column.

3 Select the Auto-Recovery option and enter a time (in minutes) for the interval that Flash creates a backup file.

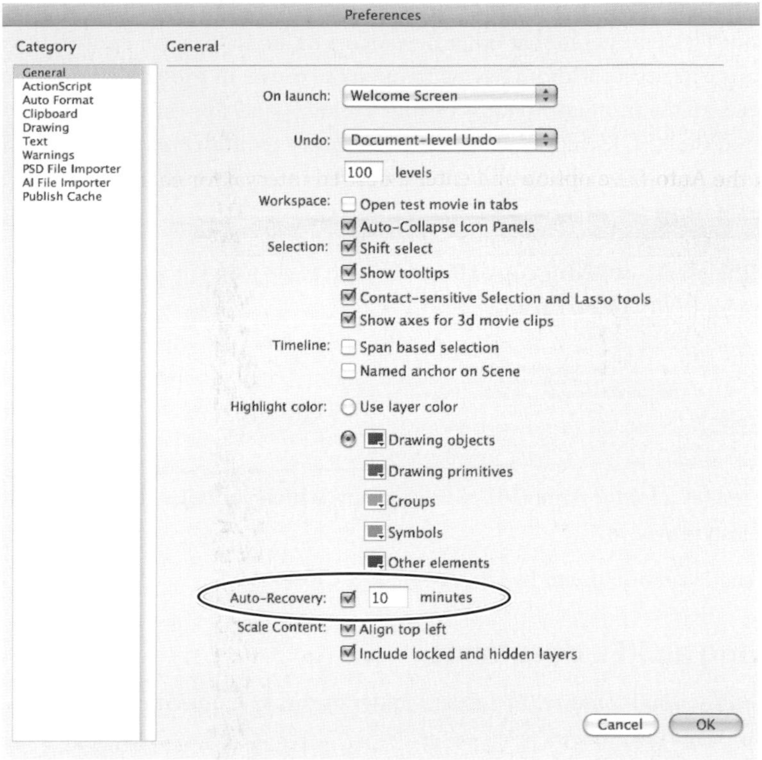

4 Click OK.

Flash creates a new file in the same location as your FLA with **RECOVER_** added to the beginning of the filename.

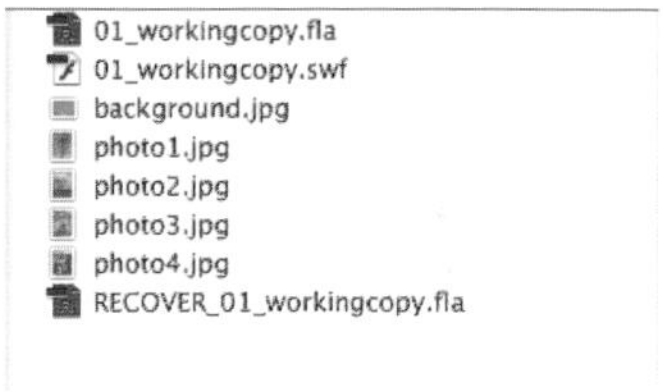

The file remains as long as the document is open. When you close the document or when you quit Flash safely, the file is deleted.

Saving an XFL document

You've already saved your Flash movie as an FLA file, but another option is to save your movie in an uncompressed format known as XFL. The XFL format is actually a folder of files rather than a single document. The XFL file format exposes the contents of your Flash movie so that other developers or animators can easily edit your file or manage its assets without having to open the movie in the Flash application. For example, all the imported photos in your Library panel appear in a Library folder within the XFL format. You can edit the library photos or swap them with new photos. Flash will make the substitutions in the movie automatically.

1 Choose File > Save As.

2 Name the file **01_workingcopy.xfl** and choose Flash CS6 Uncompressed Document (*.xfl). Click Save.

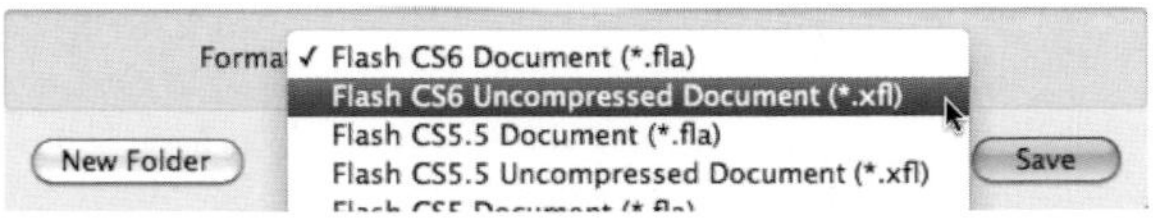

Flash creates a folder named 01_workingcopy, which contains all the files for your Flash movie.

3 Close the Flash document by choosing File > Close.

Modifying an XFL document

In this exercise, you'll modify the Library folder of the XFL document to make changes to your Flash movie.

1 Open the LIBRARY folder inside the 01_workingcopy folder.

The folder contains all the photos you imported into your Flash movie.

2 Select the photo3.jpg file and delete it.

3 Drag the photo4.jpg file from the 01Start folder and move it to the LIBRARY folder inside the 01_workingcopy folder. Rename photo4.jpg as **photo3.jpg**.

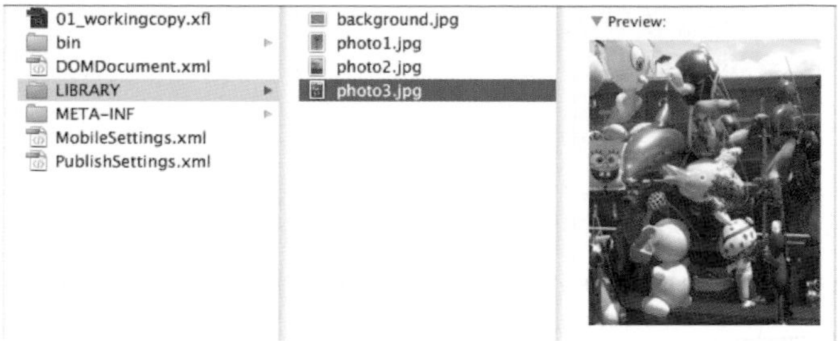

Swapping out photo3.jpg with a new image in the LIBRARY folder automatically makes the change in the Flash movie.

4 To open an XFL document, double-click the .xfl file.

The last image in keyframe 24 of your Timeline has been swapped with the photo4.jpg image with which you made the substitution.

Publishing Your Movie

When you're ready to share your movie with others, publish it from Flash. For some projects, that means posting an HTML file and a SWF file to the Web so your audience can view it in a desktop browser. For other projects, it may involve publishing an application file for your audience to download and view on a mobile device. Flash provides options to publish for a variety of platforms. You'll learn more about publishing options in Lesson 10 "Publishing Flash Documents."

For this lesson, you'll create an HTML file and a SWF file. The SWF file is your final Flash movie, and the HTML file tells the Web browser how to display the SWF file. You'll need to upload both files to the same folder on your Web server. Always test your movie after uploading it to be certain that it's working properly.

1 Choose File > Publish Settings, or click the Publish Settings button in the Profile section of the Properties Inspector.

   The Publish Settings dialog box appears. The output formats appear on the left, and their corresponding settings appear on the right.

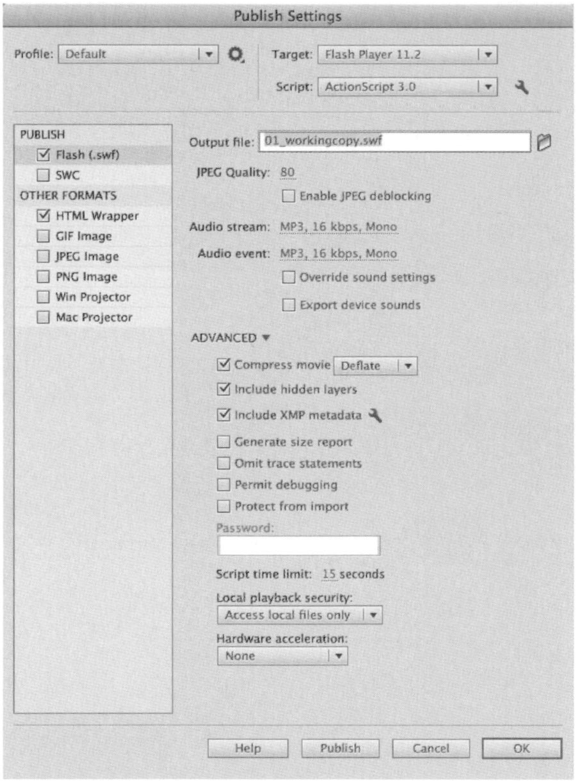

2 Check the Flash and HTML Wrapper options if they are not already checked.

3 Select HTML Wrapper.

The options for the HTML file determine how the SWF file appears in the browser. For this lesson, keep all the default settings. If the Loop check box is selected, deselect it.

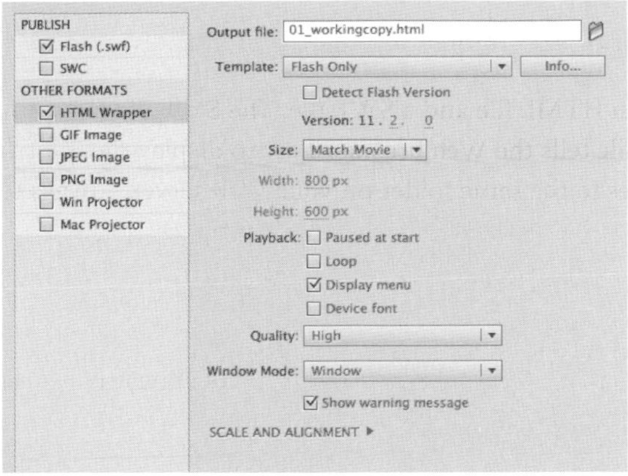

4 Click Publish at the bottom of the Publish Settings dialog box.

5 Click OK to close the dialog box.

6 Navigate to the Lesson01/01Start folder to see the files Flash created.

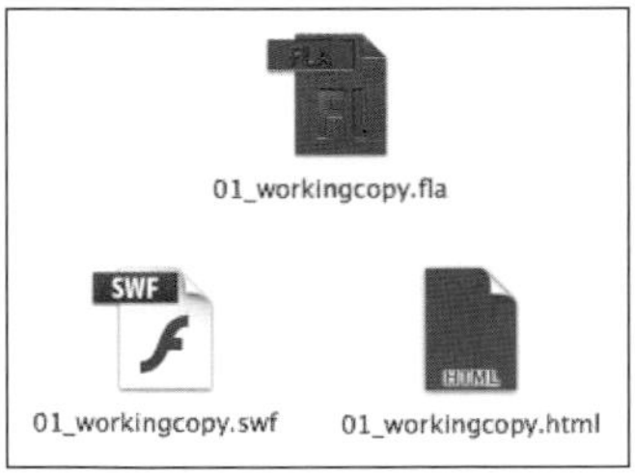

Finding Resources for Using Flash

For complete and up-to-date information about using Flash panels, tools, and other application features, visit the Adobe Web site. Choose Help > Flash Support Center.

You'll be connected to the Adobe Flash Professional Help site where you can search for answers in the support documents. There are links to helpful tutorials, forums, product guides, product updates, and more.

Don't be shy about going beyond the Adobe Web site and searching elsewhere on the Web for additional resources. There are numerous worldwide sites, blogs, and forums dedicated to Flash users, from beginner to advanced.

Note: If Flash detects that you're not connected to the Internet when you start the application, choosing Help > Flash Support Center opens the Help HTML pages installed with Flash. For more up-to-date information, view the Help files online or download the current PDF for reference.

Checking for Updates

Note: To set your preferences for future updates, choose Help > Updates, and then click Preferences in the Adobe Application Manager. Select the applications for which you want Adobe Application Manager to check for updates. Click OK to accept the new settings.

Adobe periodically provides updates to its Creative Suite applications. You can easily obtain these updates through Adobe Application Manager, as long as you have an active Internet connection.

1 In Flash, choose Help > Updates.

   The Adobe Application Manager automatically checks for updates available for your Adobe software.

2 In the Adobe Application Manager dialog box, select the updates you want to install, and then click Download And Install Updates to install them.

Review Questions

1 What is the Stage?

2 What's the difference between a frame and a keyframe?

3 What's a hidden tool, and how can you access it?

4 Name two methods to undo steps in Flash and describe them.

5 How can you find answers to questions you have about Flash?

Review Answers

1 The Stage is the rectangular area viewers see when a movie is playing. It contains the text, images, and video that appear on the screen. Objects that you store on the Pasteboard outside of the Stage do not appear in the movie.

2 A frame is a measure of time on the Timeline. A keyframe is represented on the Timeline with a circle and indicates a change in content on the Stage.

3 Because there are too many tools to display at once in the Tools panel, some tools are grouped, and only one tool in the group is displayed. (The tool you most recently used is the one shown.) Small triangles appear on tool icons to indicate that hidden tools are available. To select a hidden tool, click and hold the tool icon for the tool that is shown, and then select the hidden tool from the menu.

4 You can undo steps in Flash using the Undo command or the History panel. To undo a single step at a time, choose Edit > Undo. To undo multiple steps at once, drag the slider up in the History panel.

5 Choose Help > Flash Support Center to browse or search for information about using Flash CS6 and ActionScript 3.0. Use the site as the launching off point for free tutorials, tips, and other resources for Flash users.

2 WORKING WITH GRAPHICS

Lesson Overview

In this lesson, you'll learn how to do the following:

- Draw rectangles, ovals, and other shapes
- Understand the differences between drawing modes
- Modify the shape, color, and size of drawn objects
- Understand fill and stroke settings
- Make symmetrical and decorative patterns
- Create and edit curves
- Apply gradients and transparencies
- Group elements and convert art to bitmaps
- Create and edit text

This lesson will take approximately 90 minutes to complete. If needed, remove the previous lesson folder from your hard drive and copy the Lesson02 folder onto it.

You can use rectangles, ovals, and lines to create interesting, complex graphics and illustrations in Flash. Edit their shapes and combine them with gradients, transparencies, text, and filters for even greater possibilities.

Getting Started

Start by viewing the finished movie to see the animation you'll be creating in this lesson.

1 Double-click the 02End.html file in the Lesson02/02End folder to view the final project in a browser.

The project is a simple static illustration for a banner ad. This illustration is for Garden Court Cafe, a fictional company that's promoting its store and coffee. In this lesson, you'll draw the shapes, modify them, and learn to combine simple elements to create more complex visuals. You won't create any animation just yet. After all, you must learn to walk before you can run! And learning to create and modify graphics is an important step before doing any Flash animation.

2 In Flash, choose File > New. In the New Document dialog box, choose ActionScript 3.0.

3 On the right-hand side of the dialog box, make the Stage size **700** pixels by **200** pixels and make the color of the Stage a light brown by clicking the icon next to Background color. Click OK.

4 Choose File > Save. Name the file **02_workingcopy.fla** and save it in the 02Start folder. Saving your file right away is a good working habit (even if you've enabled the Auto-Recovery feature) and ensures that your work won't be lost if the application or your computer crashes.

Understanding Strokes and Fills

Every graphic in Flash starts with a shape. A shape is made of two components: the *fill*, or the insides of the shape; and the *stroke*, or the outlines of the shape. If you always keep these two components in mind, you'll be well on your way to creating beautiful and complicated visuals.

The fill and the stroke are independent of each other, so you can modify or delete either without affecting the other. For example, you can create a rectangle with a blue fill and a red stroke, and then later change the fill to purple and delete the red stroke entirely. All you'll be left with is a purple rectangle without an outline. You can also move the fill or stroke independently, so if you want to move the entire shape, make sure that you select both its fill and stroke.

Creating Shapes

Flash includes several drawing tools, which work in different drawing modes. Many of your creations will begin with simple shapes such as rectangles and ovals, so it's important that you're comfortable drawing them, modifying their appearance, and applying fills and strokes.

You'll begin by drawing the cup of coffee.

Using the Rectangle tool

The coffee cup is essentially a cylinder, which is a rectangle with an oval at the top and an oval at the bottom. You'll start by drawing the rectangular body. It's useful to break down complicated objects into their component parts to make drawing them easier.

Note: Each color has a hexadecimal value in Flash, HTML, and many other applications. Light gray is #999999, white is #FFFFFF, and black is #000000. You may find it handy to memorize the values for the colors you use most often.

1 In the Tools panel, select the Rectangle tool ( ). Make sure the Object Drawing mode icon ( ) is *not* selected.

2 Choose a stroke color ( ) and a fill color ( ) from the bottom of the Tools panel. Choose #663300 (dark brown) for the stroke and #CC6600 (light brown) for the fill.

3 On the Stage, draw a rectangle that is a little taller than it is wide. You'll specify the exact size and position of the rectangle in step 6.

4 Select the Selection tool ( ).

5 Drag the Selection tool around the entire rectangle to select its stroke and its fill. When a shape is selected, Flash displays it with white dots. You can also double-click a shape, and Flash will select both the stroke and fill of the shape.

6 In the Properties inspector, type **130** for the width and **150** for the height. Press Enter/Return to apply the values.

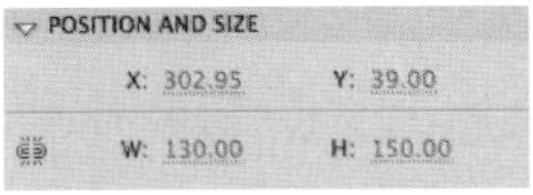

Using the Oval tool

Now you'll create the opening at the top and the rounded bottom.

1 In the Tools panel, press and hold your mouse cursor over the Rectangle tool to access the hidden tools. Choose the Oval tool.

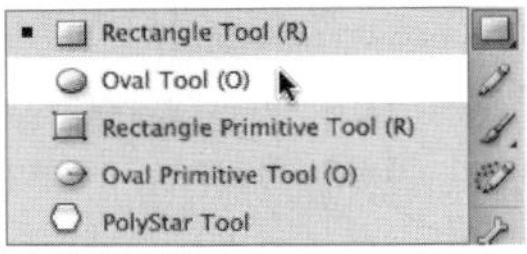

Note: Flash applies the default fill and stroke to the rectangle and oval, which are determined by the last fill and stroke you applied.

2 Make sure the Snap to Objects option ( ) is enabled. This option forces shapes that you draw on the Stage to snap to each other to ensure that lines and corners connect to one another.

3 Click inside the rectangle and drag across it to make an oval inside the rectangle. The Snap to Objects option makes the sides of the oval connect to the sides of the rectangle.

4 Draw another oval near the bottom of the rectangle.

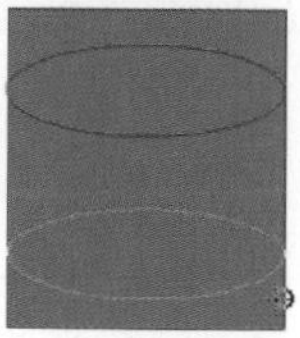

Making Selections

To modify an object, you must first be able to select different parts of it. In Flash, you can make selections using the Selection, Subselection, or Lasso tool. Typically, you use the Selection tool to select an entire object or a section of an object. The Subselection tool lets you select a specific point or line in an object. With the Lasso tool, you can make a freeform selection.

Selecting strokes and fills

Now you'll make the rectangle and ovals look more like a coffee cup. You'll use the Selection tool to delete unwanted strokes and fills.

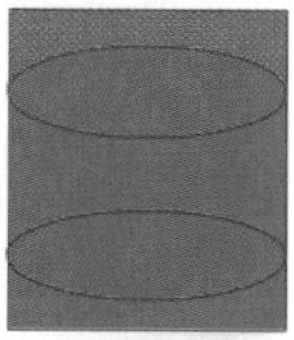

1 In the Tools panel, select the Selection tool ( ).

2 Click the fill above the top oval to select it.

The shape above the top oval becomes highlighted.

3 Press the Delete key.

The shape is deleted.

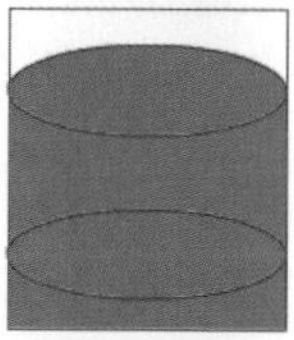

4 Select each of the three line segments above the top oval and press the Delete key.

The individual strokes are deleted, leaving the top oval connected to the rectangle.

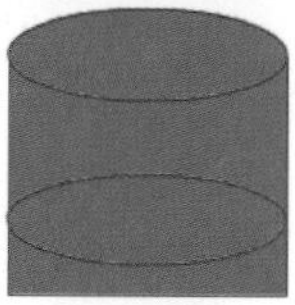

Note: Hold down the Shift key when making selections to select multiple fills or strokes together.

5 Now select the fill and strokes below the bottom oval, as well as the inside arc at the bottom of the cup, and press the Delete key.

The remaining shape appears as a cylinder.

Editing Shapes

When drawing in Flash, you'll often start with the Rectangle and Oval tools. But to create more complex graphics, you'll use other tools to modify those base shapes. The Free Transform tool, the Copy and Paste commands, and the Selection tool can help transform the plain cylinder into a coffee cup.

Using the Free Transform tool

The coffee cup will look more realistic if you taper the bottom rim. You'll use the Free Transform tool to change its overall shape. With the Free Transform tool, you can change an object's scale, rotation, or skew (the way it is slanted), or distort an object by dragging control points around a bounding box.

Note: If you press Alt or Option while moving one of the control points, the selected object is scaled relative to its transformation point, represented by the circle icon. You can move the transformation point anywhere, even outside the object. Press Shift to constrain the object proportions. Press Ctrl/Command to deform the object from a single control point.

1 In the Tools panel, select the Free Transform tool ().

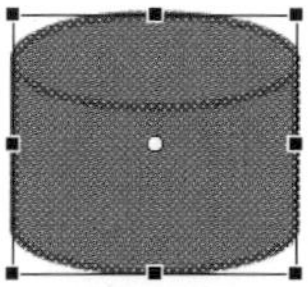

2 Drag the Free Transform tool around the cylinder on the Stage to select it.

   Transformation handles appear on the cylinder.

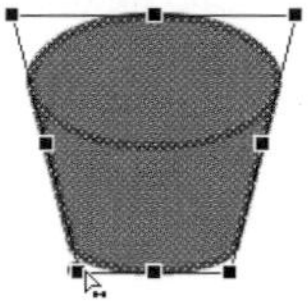

3 Press Ctrl/Command+Shift as you drag one of the lower corners inward. Holding these keys while dragging lets you move both corners the same distance simultaneously.

4 Click outside the shape to deselect it.

   The bottom of the cylinder is narrow, and the top is wide. It now looks more like a coffee cup.

Using Copy and Paste

Use Copy and Paste commands to easily duplicate shapes on the Stage. You'll set the surface level of the coffee by copying and pasting the top rim of the coffee cup.

1 Choose the Selection tool. Hold down the Shift key and select the top arc and bottom arc of the coffee cup opening.

2 Choose Edit > Copy (Ctrl/Command+C). The top strokes of the oval are copied.

3 Choose Edit > Paste in Center (Ctrl/Command+V).

   A duplicate oval appears on the Stage.

4 In the Tools panel, if it's not already selected, select the Free Transform tool.

   Transformation handles appear on the oval.

5 Press the Shift key and the Alt/Option key as you drag on the corners inward. Make the oval about 10 percent smaller. Pressing the Shift key lets you change the shape uniformly so the oval maintains its aspect ratio. Pressing the Alt/Option key changes the shape from its transformation point.

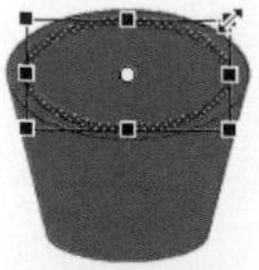

6 Select the Selection tool.

7 Drag the oval over the rim of the coffee cup so it overlaps the front lip.

8 Click outside the selection to deselect the oval.

9 Select the lower part of the smaller oval and delete it.

Your coffee cup now is filled with coffee!

Changing shape contours

With the Selection tool, you can push and pull lines and corners to change the overall contours of any shape. It's a fast and intuitive way of working with shapes.

1 In the Tools panel, select the Selection tool.

2 Move your mouse cursor close to one of the sides of the coffee cup.

A curved line appears near your cursor, indicating that you can change the curvature of the stroke.

3 Click and drag the stroke outward.

Note: Hold down the Alt/Option key while dragging the sides of a shape to add a new corner.

The sides of the coffee cup bend, giving the coffee cup a slight bulge.

4 Click and drag the other side of the coffee cup outward slightly.

The coffee cup now has a more rounded body.

Changing strokes and fills

If you want to change the properties of any stroke or fill, you can use the Ink Bottle tool or the Paint Bucket tool. The Ink Bottle tool is used to change fill colors, and the Paint Bucket tool is used to change stroke colors.

1 In the Tools panel, select the Paint Bucket tool ( ).

2 In the Properties inspector, choose a darker brown color (#663333).

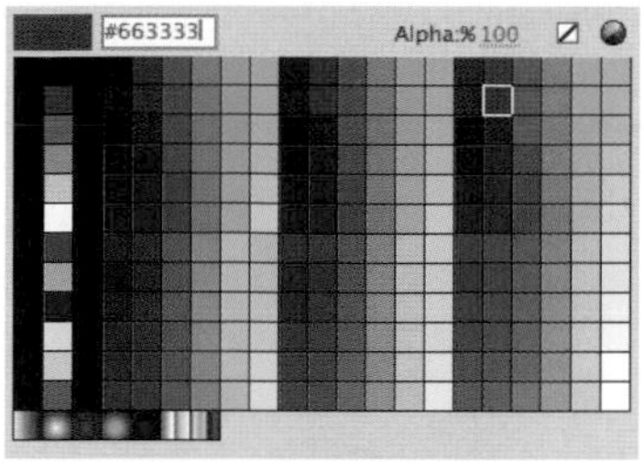

Note: If your Paint Bucket tool changes the fill in surrounding areas, there may be a small gap that allows the fill to spill over. Close the gap, or at the bottom of the Tools panel, choose to close different gap sizes for your Paint Bucket tool.

3 Click the top surface of the coffee that is inside the cup.

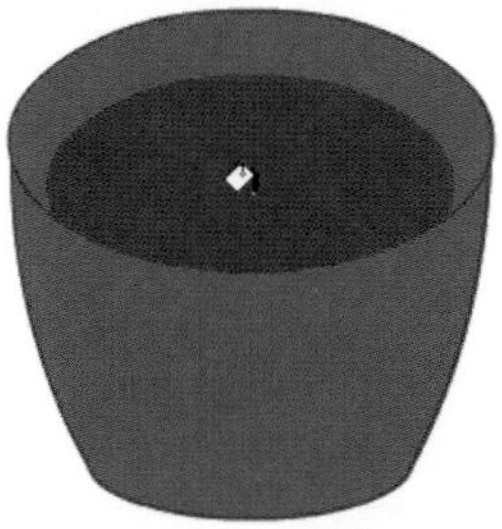

The fill of the top oval changes to the darker brown color.

4 In the Tools panel, select the Ink Bottle tool ( ) that is hidden under the Paint Bucket tool.

5 In the Properties inspector, choose a darker brown color (#330000).

6 Click the top stroke above the surface of the coffee.

The stroke around the surface of the coffee changes to a darker brown color.

Note: You can also select a stroke or a fill and change its color in the Properties inspector without using the Paint Bucket or Ink Bottle tool.

Flash Drawing Modes

Flash provides three drawing modes that determine how objects interact with one another on the Stage and how you can edit them. By default, Flash uses Merge Drawing mode, but you can enable Object Drawing mode or use the Rectangle Primitive or Oval Primitive tool to use Primitive Drawing mode.

Merge Drawing mode

In this mode, Flash merges drawn shapes, such as rectangles and ovals, where they overlap, so that multiple shapes appear to be a single shape. If you move or delete a shape that has been merged with another, the overlapping portion is permanently removed.

Object Drawing mode

In this mode, Flash does not merge drawn objects; they remain distinct and separate, even when they overlap. To enable Object Drawing mode, select the tool you want to use, and then click the Object Drawing icon in the options area of the Tools panel.

To convert an object to shapes (Merge Drawing mode), select it and press Ctrl/Command+B. To convert a shape to an object (Object Drawing mode), select it and choose Modify > Combine Objects > Union.

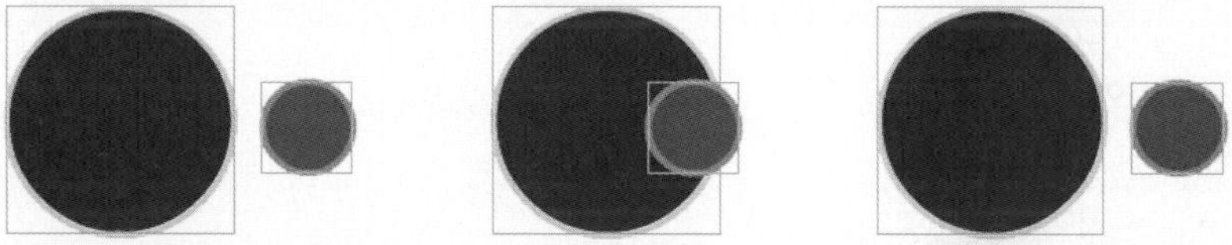

Primitive Drawing mode

When you use the Rectangle Primitive tool or the Oval Primitive tool, Flash draws the shapes as separate objects. Unlike with regular objects, however, you can modify the corner radius and start and end angle of rectangle primitives, and adjust the inner radius of oval primitives using the Properties inspector.

Using Gradient and Bitmap Fills

The *fill* is the interior of the drawn object. Currently, you have a solid tan color, but you can also have a gradient or a bitmap image (such as a JPEG file) as a fill, or you can specify that the object has no fill at all.

In a *gradient*, one color gradually changes into another. Flash can create *linear* gradients, which change color horizontally, vertically, or diagonally; or *radial* gradients, which change color moving outward from a central focal point.

For this lesson, you'll use a linear gradient fill to add three-dimensionality to the coffee cup. To give the appearance of a top layer of foaming cream, you'll import a bitmap image to use as the fill. You can import a bitmap file in the Color panel.

Creating gradient transitions

You'll define the colors you want to use in your gradient in the Color panel. By default, a linear gradient moves from one color to a second color, but you can use up to 15 color transitions in a gradient in Flash. A *color pointer* determines where the gradient changes from one color to the next. Add color pointers beneath the gradient definition bar in the Color panel to add color transitions.

You'll create a gradient that moves from tan to white to dark tan on the surface of the coffee cup to give it a rounded appearance.

1 Choose the Selection tool. Select the fill that represents the front surface of the coffee cup.

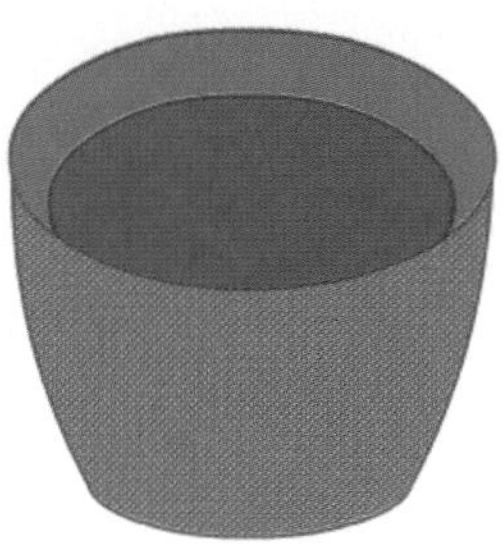

2 Open the Color panel (Window > Color). In the Color panel, choose the Fill color icon and select Linear gradient.

The front surface of the coffee cup is filled with a color gradient from left to right.

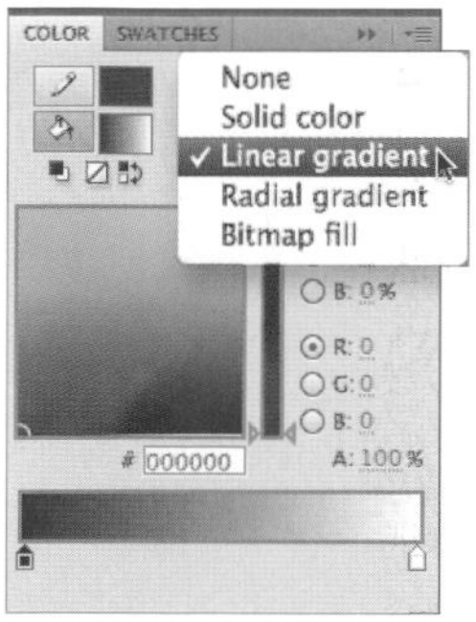

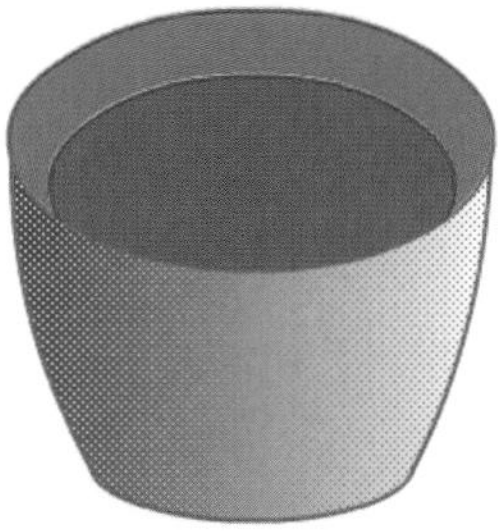

3 Select the color pointer on the left of the color gradient in the Color panel (the triangle above it turns black when selected), and then type **FFCCCC** in the Hex value field to specify a light tan color. Press Enter/Return to apply the color. You can also choose a color from the color picker or double-click the color pointer to choose a color from the color swatches.

4 Select the far-right color pointer, and then enter **B86241** for a dark tan color. Press Enter/Return to apply the color.

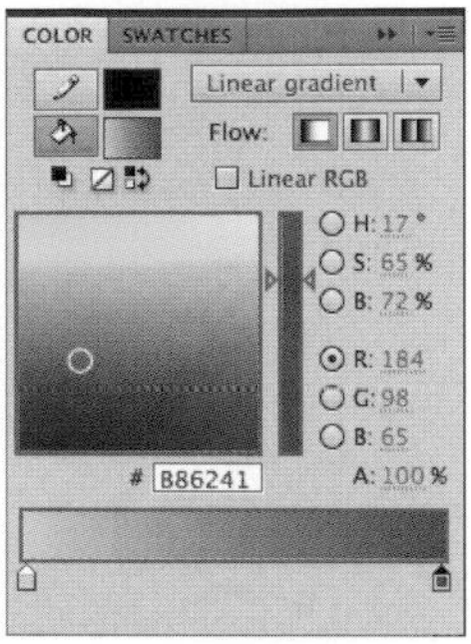

The gradient fill for the coffee cup gradually changes from light tan to dark tan across its surface.

5 Click beneath the gradient definition bar to create a new color pointer.

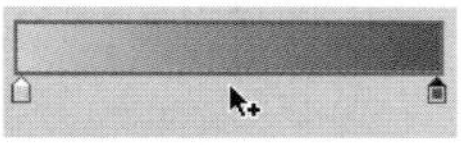

6 Drag the new color pointer to the middle of the gradient.

7 Select the new color pointer, and then type **FFFFFF** in the Hex value field to specify white for the new color. Press Enter/Return to apply the color.

The gradient fill for the coffee cup gradually changes from light tan to white to dark tan.

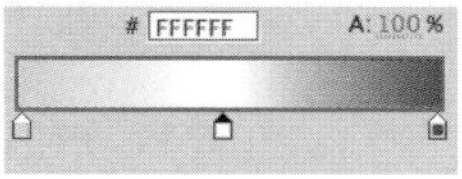

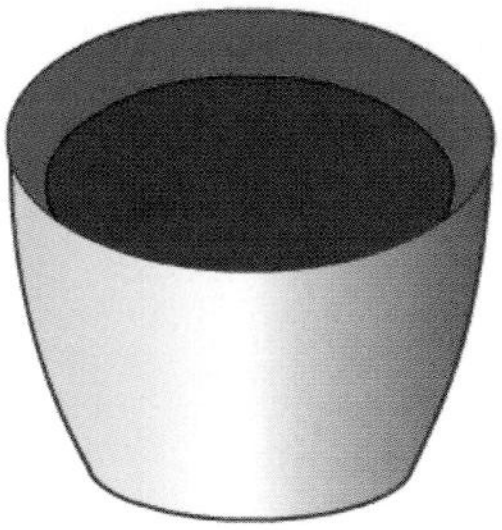

8 Deselect the fill on the Stage by clicking elsewhere on the Stage. Choose the Paint Bucket tool and make sure the Lock Fill option ( ) at the bottom of the Tools panel is deselected.

The Lock Fill option locks the current gradient to the first shape to which it was applied so that subsequent shapes extend the gradient. You'll want a new gradient for the back surface of the coffee cup, so the Lock Fill option should be deselected.

9 With the Paint Bucket tool, select the back surface of the coffee cup.

The gradient is applied to the back surface.

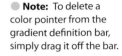

Note: To delete a color pointer from the gradient definition bar, simply drag it off the bar.

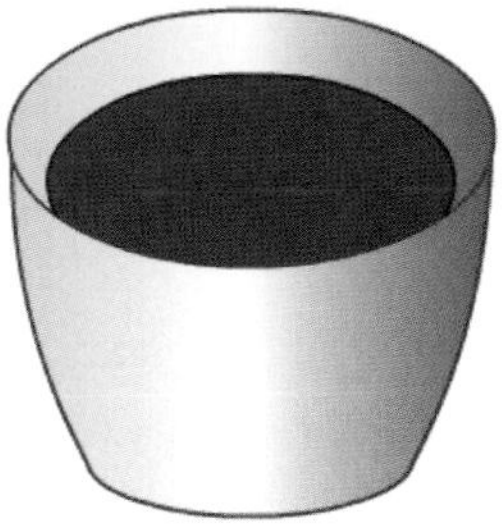

Using the Gradient Transform tool

In addition to choosing colors and positioning the color pointers for a gradient, you can adjust the size, direction, or center of a gradient fill. To squeeze the gradient in the front surface and reverse the gradient in the back surface, you'll use the Gradient Transform tool.

1 Select the Gradient Transform tool. (The Gradient Transform tool is grouped with the Free Transform tool.)

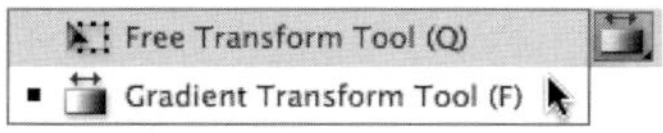

2 Click the front surface of the coffee cup. Transformation handles appear.

3 Drag the square handle on the side of the bounding box inward to squeeze the gradient tighter. Drag the center circle to move the gradient to the left so the white highlight is positioned slightly left of center.

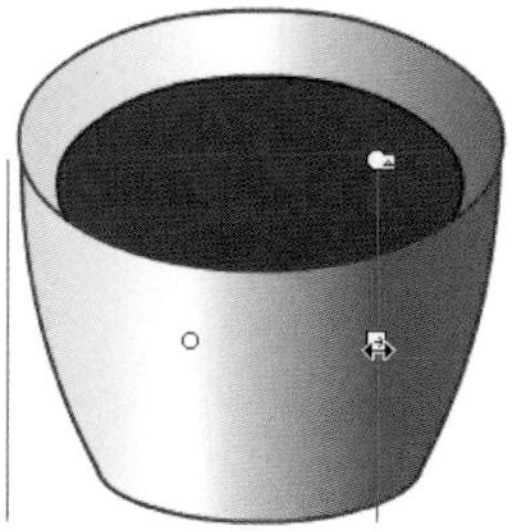

4 Now click the back surface of the coffee cup. Transformation handles appear.

Note: Move the center circle to change the center of the gradient; drag the arrow circle to rotate the gradient; or drag the arrow in the square to stretch the gradient.

5 Drag the round handle on the corner of the bounding box to rotate the gradient 180 degrees so the gradient fades from dark tan to the left to white to light tan on the right. Drag the square handle on the side of the bounding box inward to make the gradient tighter.

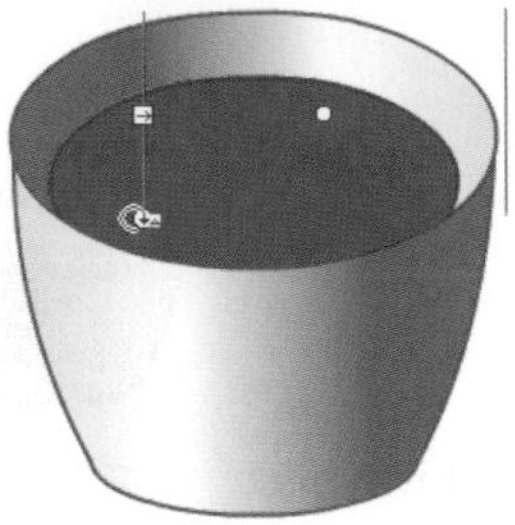

The coffee cup now has more realism because the shadows and highlights make it appear that the front surface is convex and the back surface is concave.

Adding a bitmap fill

You'll make this cup of coffee a little fancier by adding a frothy layer of cream. A JPEG image of foam will be used as a bitmap fill.

1 Select the top surface of the coffee with the Selection tool.

2 Open the Color panel (Window > Color).

3 Select Bitmap fill.

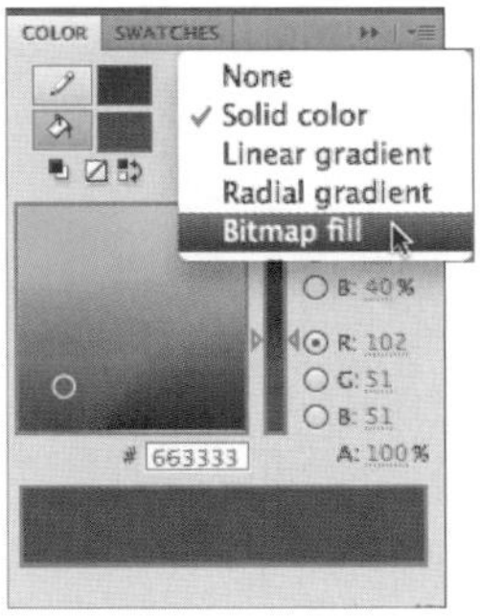

4 In the Import to Library dialog box, navigate to the coffeecream.jpg file in the Lesson02/02Start folder.

Note: You can also use the Gradient Transform tool to change the way a bitmap fill is applied.

5 Select the coffeecream.jpg file and click Open.

The top surface of the coffee fills with the foam image.

The cup of coffee is complete! Rename the layer containing your completed drawing **coffee cup**. All that's left to do is to add some bubbles and hot steam.

Grouping objects

Now that you're finished creating your cup of coffee, you can make it into a single group. A group holds together a collection of shapes and other graphics to preserve their integrity. When grouped, you can move the elements that comprise the coffee cup as a unit without worrying that the cup might merge with underlying shapes. Use groups to organize your drawing.

1 Select the Selection tool.
2 Select all the shapes that make up the cup of coffee.
3 Choose Modify > Group.

   The cup of coffee is now a single group. When you select it, a blue outline indicates its bounding box.

4 If you want to change any part of the cup of coffee, double-click the group to edit it.

   Notice that all the other elements on the Stage dim, and the top horizontal bar above the Stage displays Scene 1 Group. This indicates that you are now in a particular group and can edit its contents.

5 Click the Scene 1 icon in the horizontal bar at the top of the Stage, or double-click an empty part of the Stage, and return to the main scene.

Note: To change a group back into its component shapes, choose Modify > Ungroup (Shift+Ctrl+G [Windows] or Shift+Command+G [Mac]).

Making Patterns and Decorations

You can make intricate patterns with the Deco tool ( ), which has different brushes and configurations. Many options allow you to quickly and easily build symmetrical designs, grids, or branching-type flourishes. In this lesson, you'll use the Deco tool to create symmetrical fizzy shapes and dashed lines to give the banner ad more punch, and floral decorations to adorn the edges.

Creating a symbol for a pattern

Before you can use the Deco tool's symmetry brush, you must create a symbol to be used as the base shape that will repeat. You'll learn more about symbols in the next lesson.

1 From the top menu, choose Insert > New Symbol.

2 In the Create New Symbol dialog box that appears, enter **line** for the name and choose the Graphic Type symbol. Click OK.

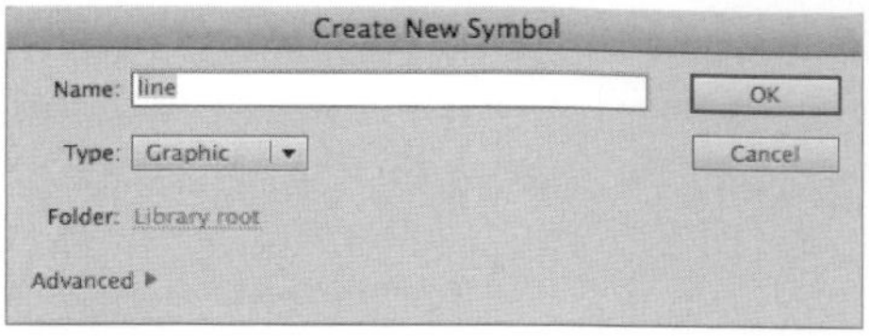

Flash immediately takes you to symbol editing mode. Notice the top horizontal bar above the Stage, which indicates you are currently editing the symbol called **line**. You will now draw a line for this symbol.

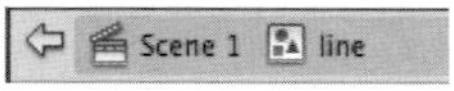

3 Select the Line tool ().

Note: A hairline stroke maintains a uniform thin thickness regardless of how large or small you scale it.

4 Select a brown color for the stroke and Hairline for the Stroke Style.

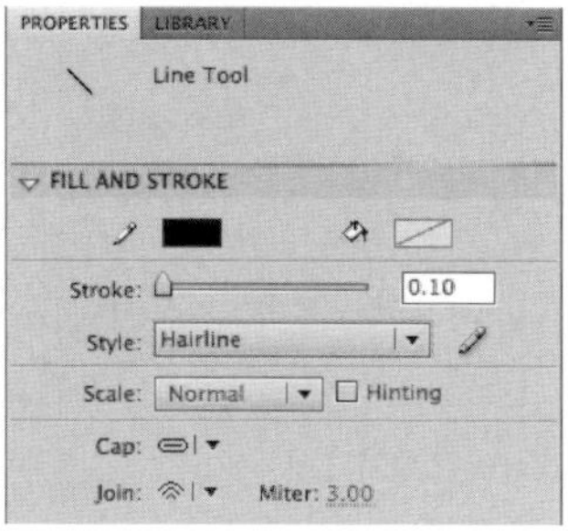

5 Hold down the Shift key while you draw a line across the center of the Stage where you see a crosshair representing the center point of your symbol. Make the line about 25 pixels high.

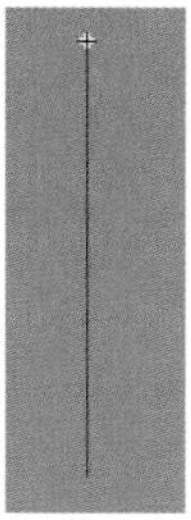

6 Click on Scene 1 on the horizontal bar above the Stage to return to the main Timeline. Your new symbol called line has been created and is stored in your Library panel for later use.

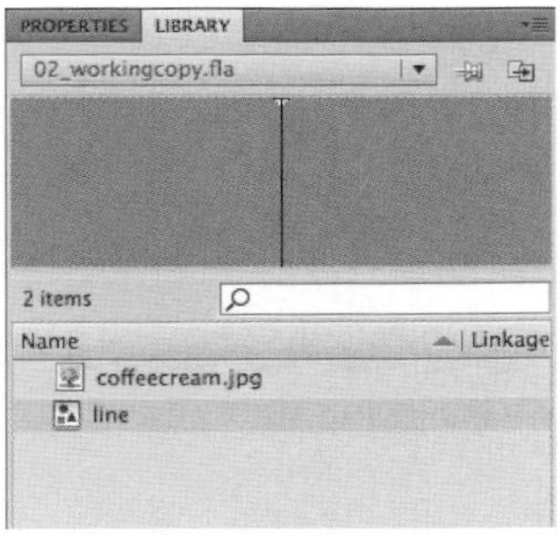

Using the Deco tool Symmetry Brush

You'll create a star shape with the Deco tool.

1 On the Timeline, insert a new layer and name it **coffee aroma**. You'll draw your symmetrical shapes in this layer.

2 In the toolbar, select the Deco tool ( ).

3 In the Properties inspector, under Drawing Effect, choose Symmetry Brush.

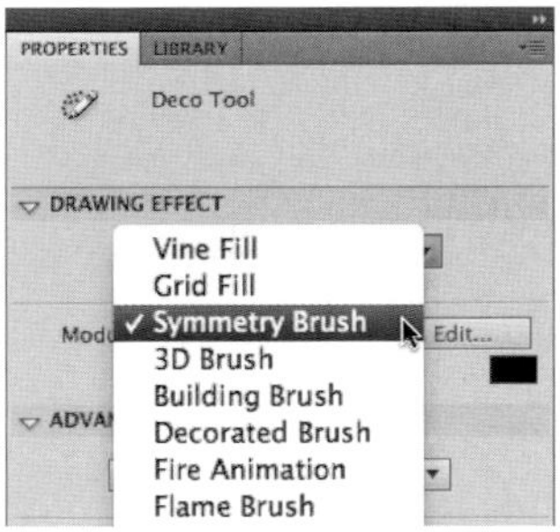

4 Click the Edit button next to Module to change the shape that will repeat.

5 In the Select Symbol dialog box, choose the line symbol. Click OK.

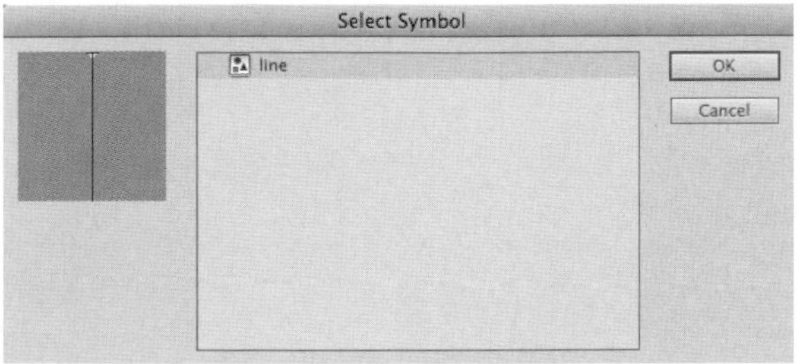

6 Under Advanced Options, choose Rotate Around.

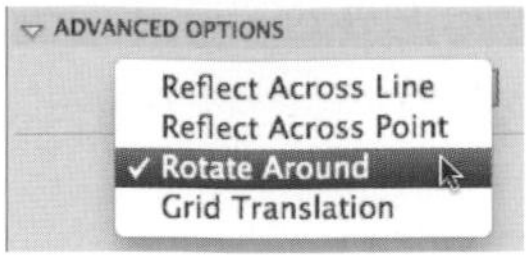

With these Deco tool options, you can create a repeating pattern of the line symbol that is symmetrical around a point. A green guide appears on the Stage that shows the center point, the main axis, and a secondary axis that determines how frequently the symbol is repeated.

7 Click on the Stage to place your symbol and, while keeping your mouse button depressed, drag it around the green guides until you get the radial pattern you desire. The initial line should be vertical.

8 Drag the secondary green axis closer to the main axis to increase the repetitions.

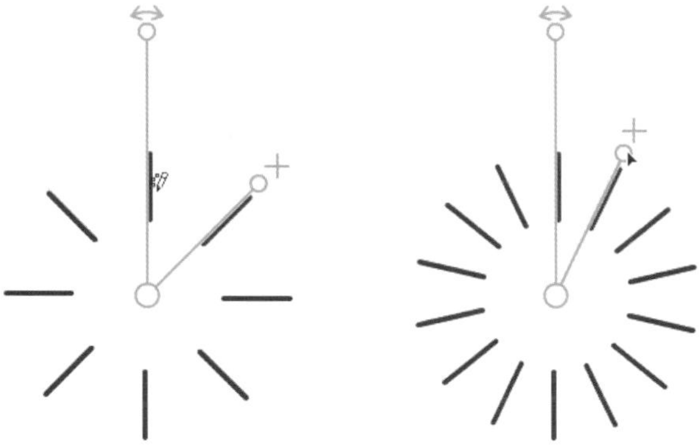

9 When you're done, select the Selection tool to exit the Deco tool.

The resulting pattern is a group consisting of a number of line symbols.

Aligning objects

Now you'll create a center bubble for the radiating lines. The bubble should be located exactly in the center of the radiating lines, and for that, you can turn to the Align panel. The Align panel, as you might guess, aligns any number of selected objects horizontally or vertically. It can also distribute objects evenly.

1 Select the Oval tool.

2 Select a brown color for the stroke and no fill. To select no fill, choose the color box that has a diagonal red line through it. Select Hairline for Stroke Style.

3 Select the coffee aroma layer. Hold down the Shift key while you draw a small circle on the Stage.

4 Now select the Selection tool.

5 Drag the Selection tool over both the star-shaped group and the newly drawn oval. You might have to lock the lower layer so you don't accidentally select the shapes in the lower layers.

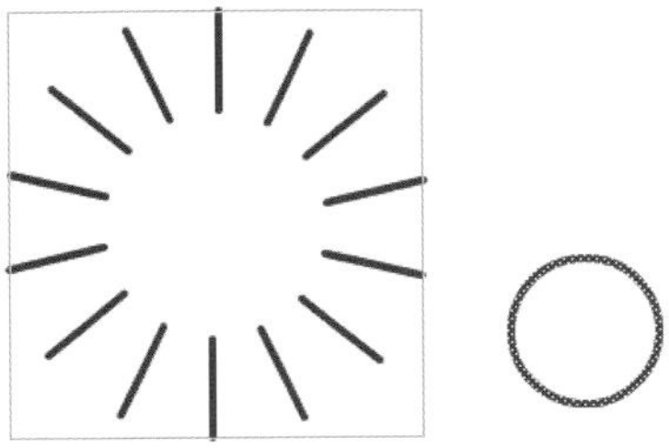

6 Open the Align panel (Window > Align).

7 Click the Align horizontal center button.

The star-shaped group and the oval become aligned horizontally.

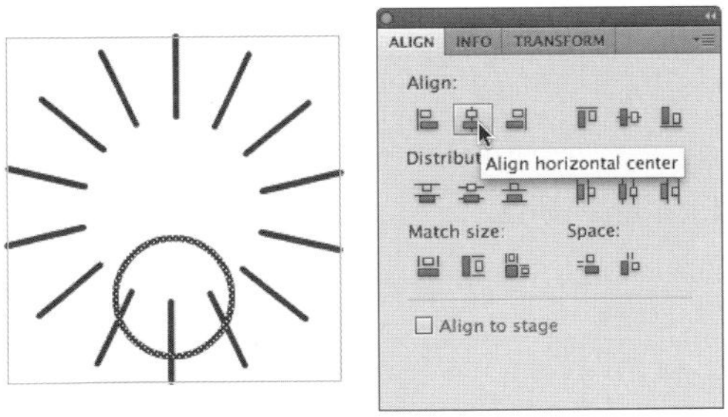

8 Click the Align vertical center button.

The star-shaped group and the oval become aligned vertically.

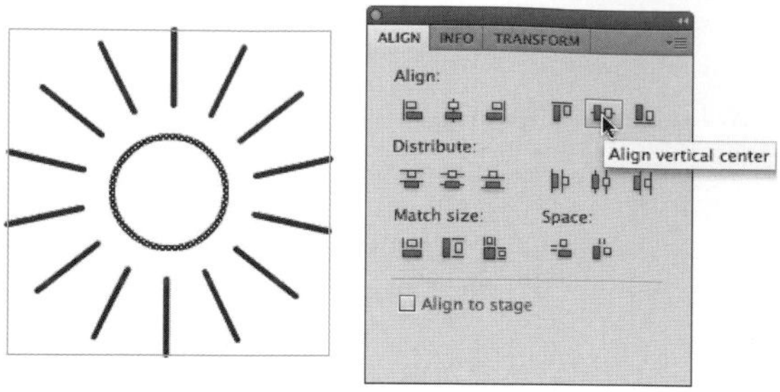

Breaking apart and grouping objects

You used the Deco tool to create the group of radiating lines and the Align panel to center the bubble with the lines. Now you'll group the fizzy shape into a single entity. To do so, you'll break apart the group of radiating lines and regroup them with the oval.

1 With the Selection tool, drag a selection around the entire star so that all the lines and the circle are selected.

2 Choose Modify > Break Apart.

The group of lines breaks into its component parts and becomes a collection of line symbols.

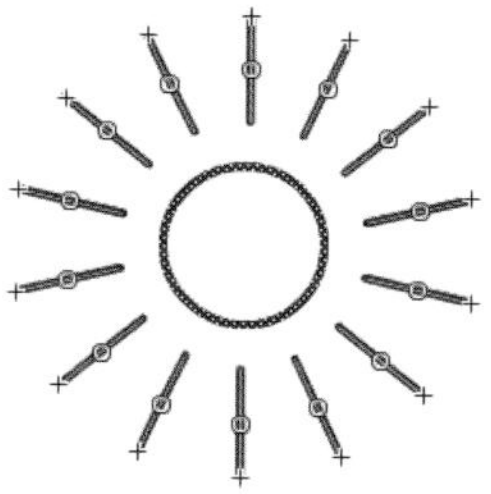

3 Choose Modify > Break Apart one more time.

The collection of line symbols breaks into its component parts and becomes a collection of strokes.

4 Choose Modify > Group.

The lines and center circle become a single group.

5 Copy and paste the group to create multiple bubbles just over the coffee cup. Use the Transform tool to scale the bubbles to different sizes.

Using the Deco tool Decorated Brush

Now you'll explore the Deco tool's Decorated Brush, which creates decorated borders and complex line patterns.

1 In the toolbar, select the Deco tool ( ).

2 In the Properties inspector, choose the Decorated Brush option.

3 In Advanced Options, select Dashed Line. Choose a dark brown color for the Pattern color and leave Pattern size and Pattern width at their default values.

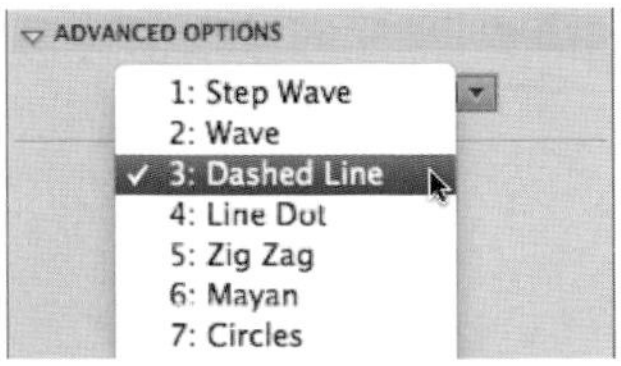

> **Note:** The Line and Pencil tools can also create dashed lines and different line patterns, but they can't make repeated complex patterns like the Deco tool can. In the Properties inspector, click the Edit Stroke Style button to customize the stroke for dashed lines.

4 On the Stage, draw several curvy lines above the coffee cup.

The Decorated Brush creates dashed lines giving your coffee cup a little more life!

Using the Deco tool Flower Brush

Now you'll create flower patterns to decorate the borders of the banner ad.

1 In the toolbar, select the Deco tool ( ).

2 In the Properties inspector under Drawing Effect, choose the Flower Brush option.

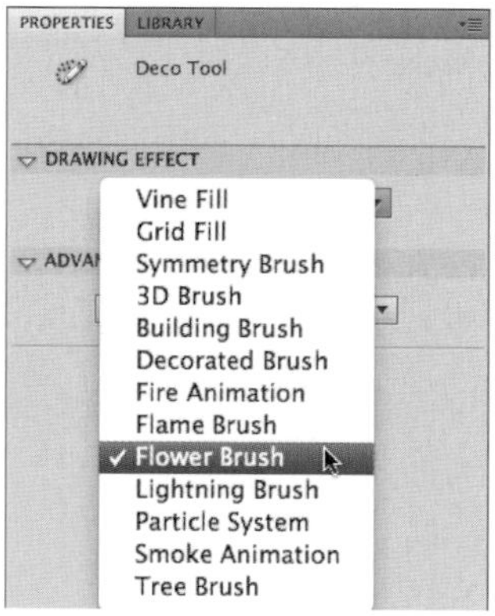

3 In Advanced Options, select Garden flower. Select the Branch option and leave the colors and sizes at their default values.

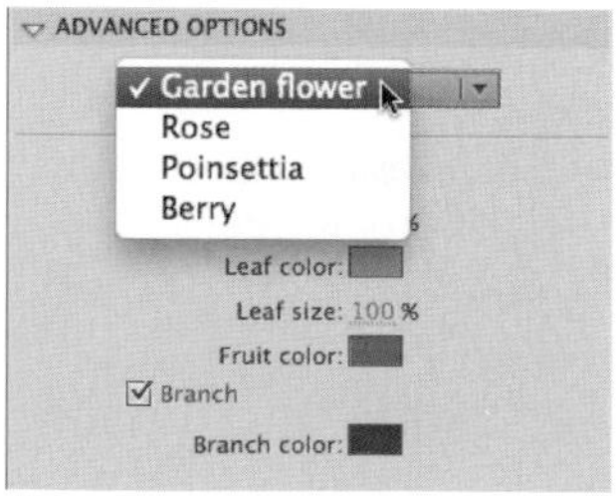

4 Draw a swooping branch of flowers across the lower portion of the Stage.

The flowers, leaves, fruits, and branches are generated repeatedly as you move your brush over the Stage.

5 If it's not already chosen, choose the Selection tool. Select all the flowers, leaves, fruits, and branches. Choose Modify > Group.

The flower decorations are combined into a single group so you can move or modify them as a unit.

Converting Vector Art to Bitmap Art

Vector art, especially art with complex curves and many shapes like the flowers you just created, can be processor-intensive, and can take its toll on mobile devices where performance suffers. An option called Convert to Bitmap provides a way to turn selected artwork on the Stage into a single bitmap, which can be less taxing on the processor.

Once an object is converted to a bitmap, you can move the object without worrying about it merging with underlying shapes. However, the graphics are no longer editable with Flash's editing tools.

1 Choose the Selection tool.

2 Click on the group of flowers.

3 Choose Modify > Convert to Bitmap.

The flowers become a bitmap and the bitmap is stored in the Library panel.

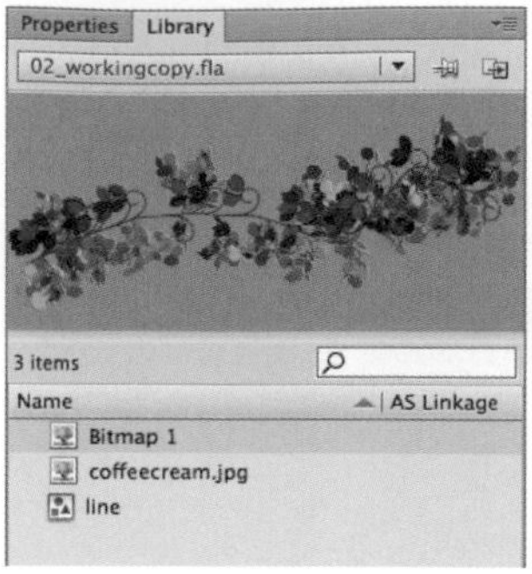

Creating Curves

You've used the Selection tool to pull and push on the edges of shapes to intuitively make curves. For more precise control, you can use the Pen tool ( ).

Using the Pen tool

Now you'll create a soothing, wave-like background graphic.

1 Choose Insert > Timeline > Layer, and name the new layer **dark brown wave**.

2 Drag the layer to the bottom of the layer stack.

3 Lock all the other layers.

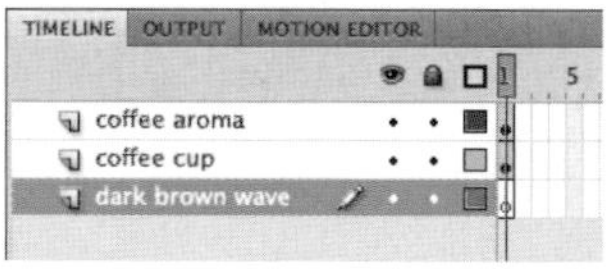

4 In the Tools panel, select the Pen tool ( ).

5 Set the Stroke color to dark brown.

6 Begin your shape by clicking on the Stage to establish the first anchor point.

7 Click on another part of the Stage to indicate the next anchor point in your shape. When you want to create a smooth curve, click and drag with the Pen tool.

A handle appears from the anchor point, indicating the curvature of the line.

8 Continue clicking and dragging to build the outline of the wave. Make the wave wider than the Stage.

9 Close your shape by clicking on the first anchor point. Don't worry about making all the curves perfect. It takes practice to get used to the Pen tool. You'll also have a chance to refine your curves in the next part of the lesson.

10 Select the Paint Bucket tool.

11 Set the Fill color to a dark brown.

12 Click inside the outline you just created to fill it with color and delete the stroke.

Editing curves with the Selection and Subselection tools

Your first try at creating smooth waves probably won't be very good. Use the Selection tool or the Subselection tool to refine your curves.

1 Choose the Selection tool.

2 Hover over a line segment and look at the curve that appears near your cursor. This indicates that you can edit the curve. If a corner appears near your cursor, this indicates that you can edit the vertex.

3 Drag the curve to edit its shape.

4 In the Tools panel, select the Subselection tool ( ).

5 Click on the outline of the shape.

6 Drag the anchor points to new locations or move the handles to refine the overall shape.

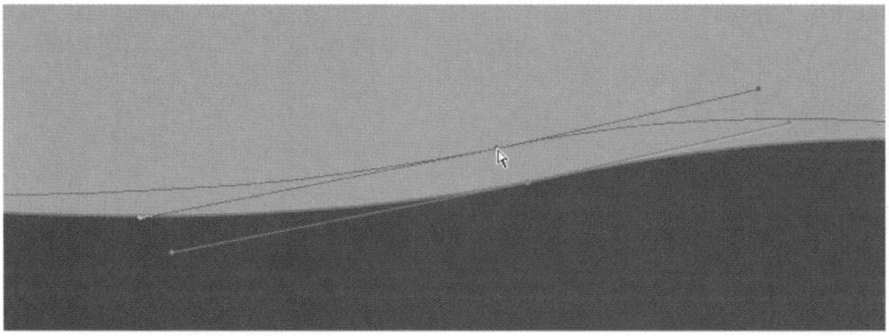

Deleting or adding anchor points

Use the hidden tools under the Pen tool to delete or add anchor points as needed.

1 Press and hold on the Pen tool to access the hidden tools under it.

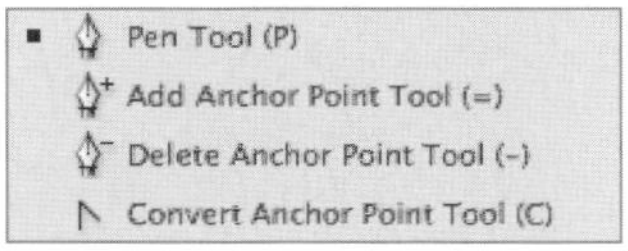

2 Select the Delete Anchor Point tool ( ).

3 Click on an anchor point on the outline of the shape to delete it.

4 Select the Add Anchor Point tool ( ).

5 Click on the curve to add an anchor point.

Creating Transparencies

Next, you'll create a second wave to overlap the first wave. You'll make the second wave slightly transparent to create more overall depth. Transparency can be applied to either the stroke or the fill. Transparency is measured as a percentage and is referred to as alpha. An alpha of 100% indicates that a color is totally opaque, whereas an alpha of 0% indicates that a color is totally transparent.

Modifying the alpha value of a fill

1 Select the shape in the dark brown wave layer.

2 Choose Edit > Copy.

3 Choose Insert > Timeline > Layer and name the new layer **light brown wave**.

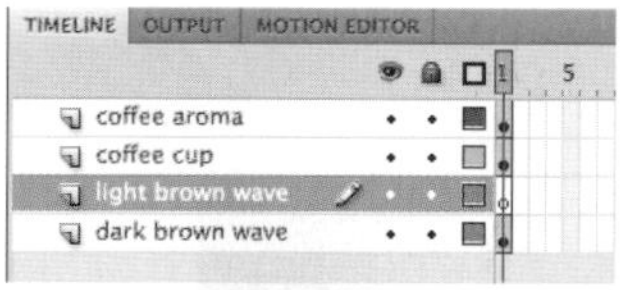

4 Choose Edit > Paste in Place (Ctrl/Command+Shift+V).

The Paste in Place command puts the copied item in the exact same position from where it was copied.

5 Choose the Selection tool and move the pasted shape slightly to the left or to the right so the crests of the waves are somewhat offset.

6 Select the fill of the shape in the light brown wave layer.

7 In the Color panel (Window > Color), set the fill color to a slightly different brown hue (CC6666), and then change the Alpha value to **50%**.

● **Note:** You can also change the transparency of a shape from the Properties inspector by clicking the Fill Color icon and changing the Alpha value in the pop-up color menu.

The color swatch at the bottom of the Color panel previews your newly selected color. Transparencies are indicated by the gray grid that can be seen through the transparent color swatch.

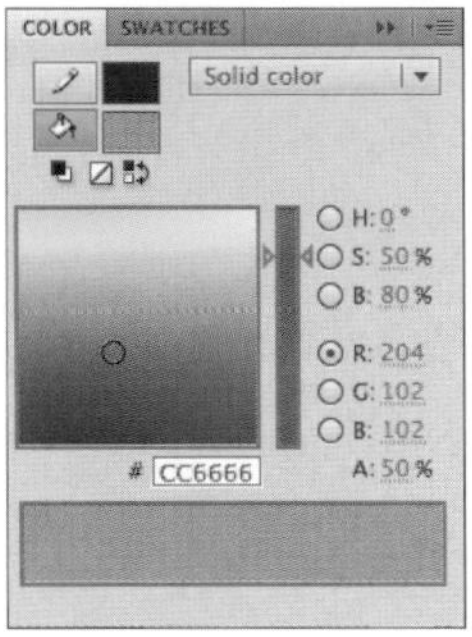

Matching the color of an existing object

If you want to match a color exactly, you can use the Eyedropper tool ( ) to sample a fill or a stroke. After you click on a shape with the Eyedropper tool, Flash automatically provides you with the Paint Bucket tool or the Ink Bottle tool with the selected color and associated properties that you can apply to another object.

1 In the Tools panel, choose the Eyedropper tool.

2 Click on the fill of the shape in the dark brown wave layer.

Your tool automatically changes to the Paint Bucket with the sampled fill color.

3 Click on the shape in the light brown wave layer.

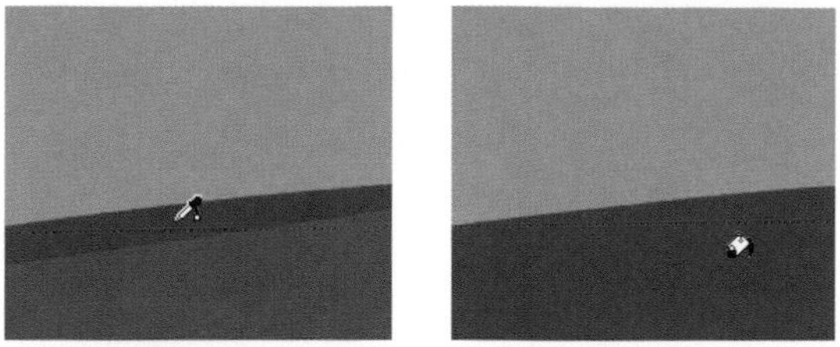

The fill in the light brown wave layer changes to match that of the one in the dark brown wave layer. Undo this step to return to the two different colored wave shapes.

Creating and Editing Text

Finally, let's add text to complete this illustration. Flash has two text options, Classic Text and a more advanced text engine called Text Layout Framework (TLF) Text. You'll learn more about TLF Text in Lesson 7. For this project, you'll use the simpler Classic Text option.

When you create static text on the Stage and publish your project, Flash automatically includes all the necessary fonts to display the text correctly. That means you don't have to worry about your audience having the required fonts to see the text as you intended it.

Using the Text tool

1 Select the top layer.

2 Choose Insert > Timeline > Layer and name the new layer **text**.

3 Choose the Text tool (T).

4 In the Properties inspector, select Classic Text and choose Static Text.

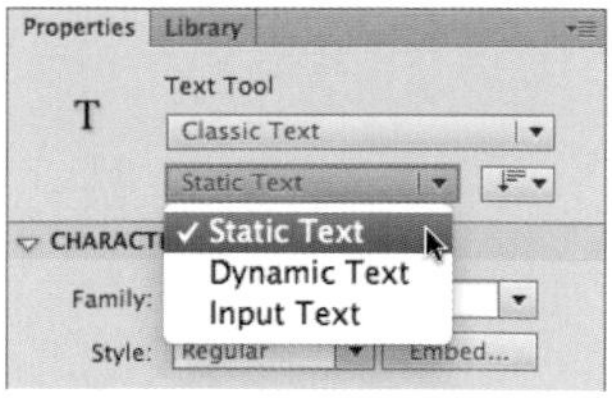

5 Under the Character options, choose a font, style, size, and color.

6 Under the Paragraph options, you have additional choices for formatting the text such as justification or spacing. Choose values there or accept the defaults.

7 Click on the Stage and begin typing. Enter **Garden Court Cafe Taste the Difference**. Alternately, you can click and drag out a text box to define the maximum width of your text.

8 Exit the Text tool by choosing the Selection tool.

Review Questions

1 What are the three drawing modes in Flash, and how do they differ?

2 How can you draw a perfect circle using the Oval tool?

3 When would you use each of the selection tools in Flash?

4 What does the Align panel do?

Review Answers

1 The three drawing modes are Merge Drawing mode, Object Drawing mode, and Primitive Drawing mode.

- In Merge Drawing mode, shapes drawn on the Stage merge to become a single shape.
- In Object Drawing mode, each object is distinct and remains separate, even when it overlaps another object.
- In Primitive Drawing mode, you can modify the angles, radius, or corner radius of an object.

2 To draw a perfect circle, hold down the Shift key as you drag the Oval tool on the Stage.

3 Flash includes three selection tools: the Selection tool, the Subselection tool, and the Lasso tool.

- Use the Selection tool to select an entire shape or object.
- Use the Subselection tool to select a specific point or line in an object.
- Use the Lasso tool to draw a freeform selection area.

4 The Align panel aligns any number of selected elements horizontally or vertically and can distribute elements evenly.

3 CREATING AND EDITING SYMBOLS

Lesson Overview

In this lesson, you'll learn how to do the following:

- Import Illustrator and Photoshop artwork
- Create new symbols
- Edit symbols
- Understand the difference between symbol types
- Understand the difference between symbols and instances
- Use rulers and guides to position objects on the Stage
- Adjust transparency and color, and turn visibility on or off
- Apply blending effects
- Apply special effects with filters
- Position objects in 3D space

This lesson will take about an hour and a half to complete. If needed, delete the previous lesson folder from your hard drive and copy the Lesson03 folder onto it.

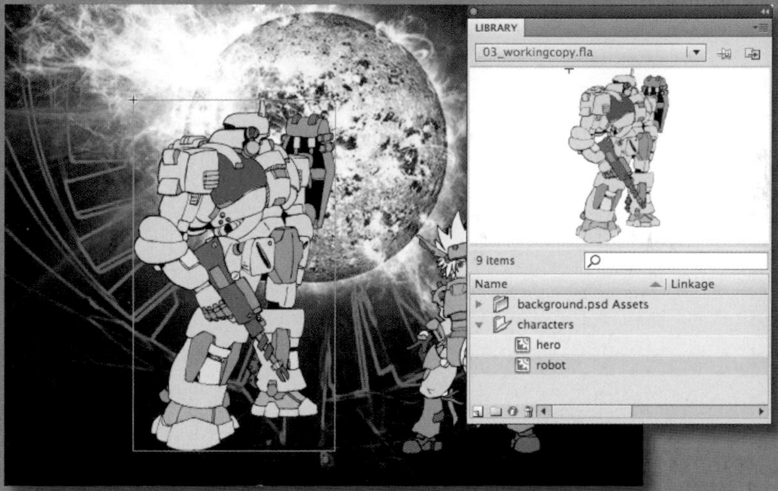

Symbols are reusable assets that are stored in your Library panel. The movie clip, graphic, and button symbols are three types of symbols that you will be creating and using often for special effects, animation, and interactivity.

Getting Started

Start by viewing the final project to see what you'll be creating as you learn to work with symbols.

1 Double-click the 03End.html file in the Lesson03/03End folder to view the final project in your browser.

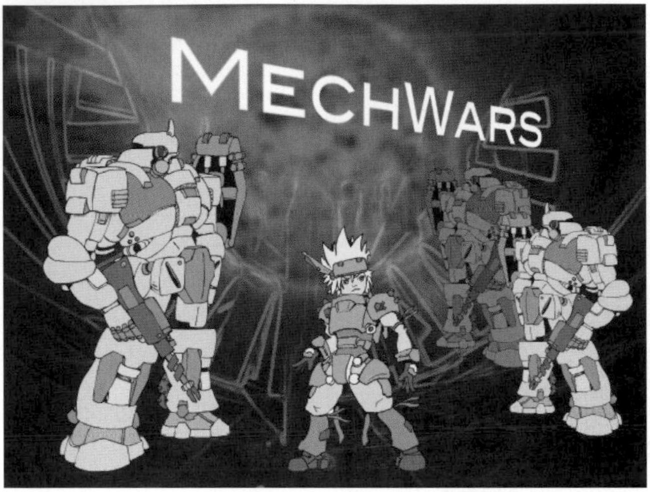

The project is a static illustration of a cartoon frame. In this lesson, you'll use Illustrator graphic files, imported Photoshop files, and symbols to create an attractive static image with interesting effects. Learning how to work with symbols is an essential step to creating any animation or interactivity.

2 Close the 03End.html file.

3 In Flash, choose File > New. In the New Document dialog box, choose ActionScript 3.0.

4 On the right-hand side of the dialog box, change the Stage to **600** pixels wide by **450** pixels high. Click OK.

5 Choose File > Save. Name the file **03_workingcopy.fla** and save it in the 03Start folder.

Importing Illustrator Files

As you learned in Lesson 2, you can draw objects in Flash using the Rectangle, Oval, and other tools. However, for complex drawings, you may prefer to create the artwork in another application. Adobe Flash Professional CS6 supports a variety of graphic formats, including Adobe Illustrator files, so you can create original artwork in that application and then import it into Flash.

When you import an Illustrator file, you can choose which layers in the file to import and how Flash should treat those layers. You'll import an Illustrator file that contains all the characters for the cartoon frame.

1 Choose File > Import > Import to Stage.

2 Select the characters.ai file in the Lesson03/03Start folder.

3 Click Open.

4 In the Import to Stage dialog box, make sure the top level "hero" and "robot" layers are selected. You can expand the groups below them to see their individual drawing paths.

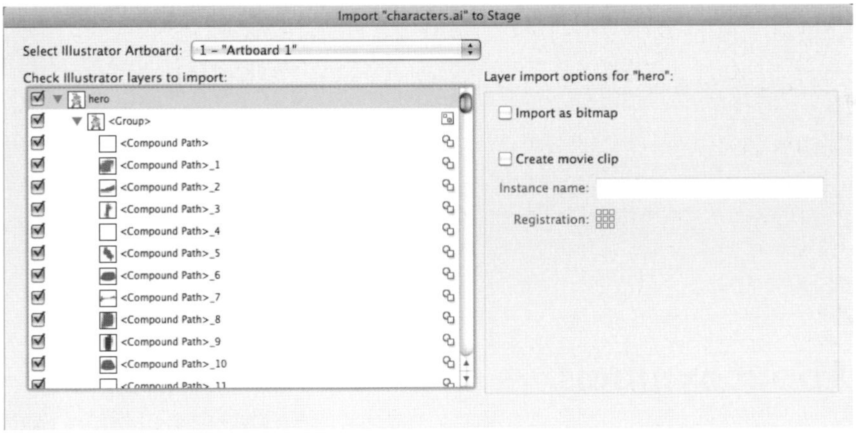

If you want to import only certain layers, you can deselect the layers you want to omit.

5 Choose Flash Layers from the Convert layers to menu, and then select Place objects at original position. Click OK.

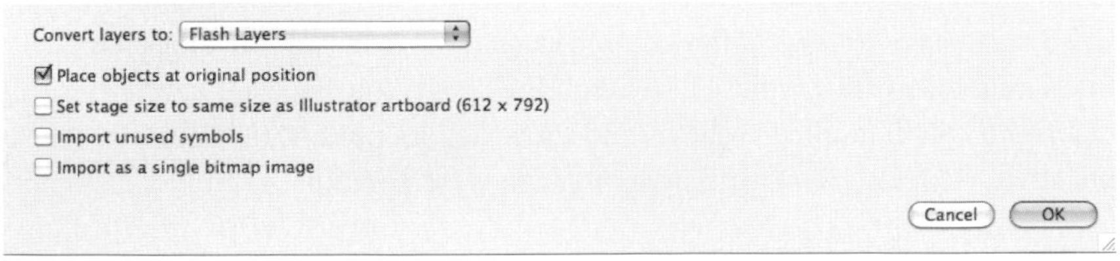

Flash imports the Illustrator graphics, and all the layers from the Illustrator file also appear in the Timeline.

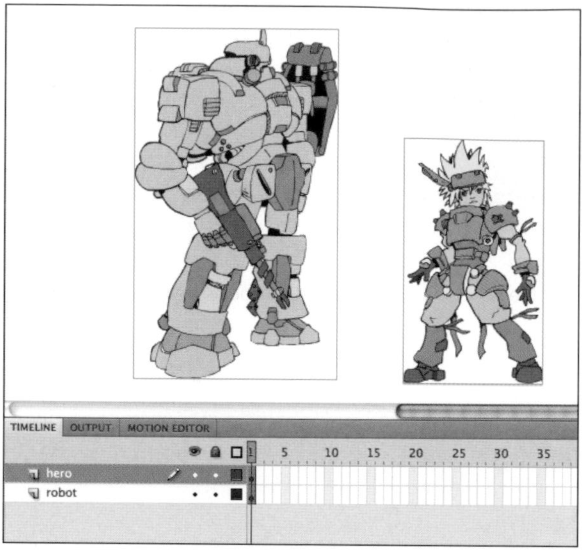

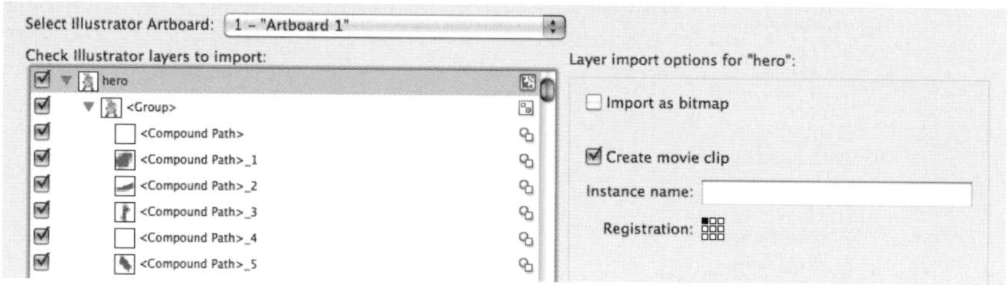

Note: You can select any object displayed in your Illustrator file and choose to import it as a symbol or a bitmap image. In this lesson, you'll just import the Illustrator graphic and take the extra step of converting it to a symbol so you can see the entire process.

About Symbols

A *symbol* is a reusable asset that you can use for special effects, animation, or interactivity. There are three kinds of symbols that you can create: the graphic, button, and movie clip. Symbols can reduce the file size and download time for many animations because they can be reused. You can use a symbol countless times in a project, but Flash includes its data only once.

Symbols are stored in the Library panel. When you drag a symbol to the Stage, Flash creates an *instance* of the symbol, leaving the original in the Library. An instance is a copy of a symbol located on the Stage. You can think of the symbol as an original photographic negative, and the instances on the Stage as prints of the negative. With just a single negative, you can create multiple prints.

Using Adobe Illustrator with Flash

Flash Professional CS6 can import Illustrator files and automatically recognize layers, frames, and symbols. If you're more familiar with Illustrator, you may find it easier to design layouts in Illustrator, and then import them into Flash to add animation and interactivity.

Save your Illustrator artwork in Illustrator AI format, and then choose File > Import > Import To Stage or File > Import > Import To Library to import the artwork into Flash. Alternatively, you can even copy artwork from Illustrator and paste it into a Flash document.

Importing Layers

When an imported Illustrator file contains layers, you can import them in any of the following ways:

- Convert Illustrator layers to Flash layers
- Convert Illustrator layers to Flash keyframes
- Convert each Illustrator layer to a Flash graphic symbol
- Convert all Illustrator layers to a single Flash layer

Importing Symbols

Working with symbols in Illustrator is similar to working with them in Flash. In fact, you can use many of the same symbol keyboard shortcuts in both Illustrator and Flash: Press F8 in either application to create a symbol. When you create a symbol in Illustrator, the Symbol Options dialog box lets you name the symbol and set options specific to Flash, including the symbol type (such as movie clip) and registration point location.

If you want to edit a symbol in Illustrator without disturbing anything else, double-click the symbol to edit it in isolation mode. Illustrator dims all other objects on the artboard. When you exit isolation mode, the symbol in the Symbols panel—and all instances of the symbol—are updated accordingly.

Use the Symbols panel or the Control panel in Illustrator to assign names to symbol instances, break links between symbols and instances, swap a symbol instance with another symbol, or create a copy of the symbol.

Copying and Pasting Artwork

When you copy and paste (or drag and drop) artwork between Illustrator and Flash, the Paste dialog box appears. The Paste dialog box provides import settings for the Illustrator file you're copying. You can paste the file as a single bitmap object, or you can paste it using the current preferences for AI files. (To change the settings, choose Edit > Preferences [Windows] or Flash > Preferences [Mac].) Just as when you import the file to the Stage or the Library panel, when you paste Illustrator artwork, you can convert Illustrator layers to Flash layers.

FXG File Format

The FXG file format is a cross-platform graphics file format that you can also use to easily move your artwork between Flash and other Adobe graphics programs such as Illustrator. If you want to export your Flash artwork as an FXG file, choose File > Export > Export Image and select Adobe FXG. Import FXG artwork as you would any other external file by choosing File > Import > Import To Stage or File > Import > Import To Library.

It's also helpful to think of symbols as containers. Symbols are simply containers for your content. A symbol can contain a JPEG image, an imported Illustrator drawing, or a drawing that you created in Flash. At any time, you can go inside your symbol and edit it, which means editing or replacing its contents.

Each of the three kinds of symbols in Flash is used for a specific purpose. You can tell whether a symbol is a graphic ( ), button ( ), or movie clip ( ) by looking at the icon next to it in the Library panel.

Movie clip symbols

Movie clip symbols are one of the most common, powerful, and flexible of symbols. When you create animation, you will typically use movie clip symbols. You can apply filters, color settings, and blending modes to a movie clip instance to enhance its appearance with special effects.

Also notable is the fact that each movie clip symbol contains its own independent Timeline. You can have an animation inside a movie clip symbol just as easily as you can have an animation on the main Timeline. This makes very complex animations possible; for example, a butterfly flying across the Stage can move from left to right as well as have its wings flapping independently of its movement.

Most important, you can control movie clips with ActionScript to make them respond to the user. For instance, a movie clip can have drag-and-drop behavior.

Button symbols

Button symbols are used for interactivity. They contain four unique keyframes that describe how they appear when the mouse is interacting with them. However, buttons need ActionScript functionality to make them do something.

You can also apply filters, blending modes, and color settings to buttons. You'll learn more about buttons in Lesson 6 when you create a nonlinear navigation scheme to allow the user to choose what to see.

Graphic symbols

Graphic symbols are the most basic kind of symbol. Although you can use them for animation, you'll rely more heavily on movie clip symbols.

Graphic symbols are the least flexible symbols, because they don't support ActionScript and you can't apply filters or blending modes to a graphic symbol. However, in some cases when you want an animation inside a graphic symbol to be synchronized to the main Timeline, graphic symbols are useful.

Creating Symbols

In the previous lesson, you learned how to create a symbol to be used for the Deco tool. In Flash, there are two main ways to create a symbol. The first is to have nothing on the Stage selected, and then choose Insert > New Symbol. Flash will bring you to symbol-editing mode where you can begin drawing or importing graphics for your symbol.

The second way is to select existing graphics on the Stage, and then choose Modify > Convert to Symbol (F8). Whatever is selected will automatically be placed inside your new symbol.

Both methods are valid; which you use depends on your particular workflow preferences. Most designers prefer to use Convert to Symbol (F8) because they can create all their graphics on the Stage and see them together before making the individual components into symbols.

Note: When you use the command Convert to Symbol, you aren't actually "converting" anything; rather, you're placing whatever you've selected inside of a symbol.

For this lesson, you will select the different parts of the imported Illustrator graphic, and then convert the various pieces to symbols.

1 On the Stage, select the cartoon character in the hero layer.

2 Choose Modify > Convert to Symbol (F8).

3 Name the symbol **hero** and select Movie Clip for the Type.

4 Leave all other settings as they are. The Registration indicates the registration point of your symbol. Leave the registration at the top-left corner.

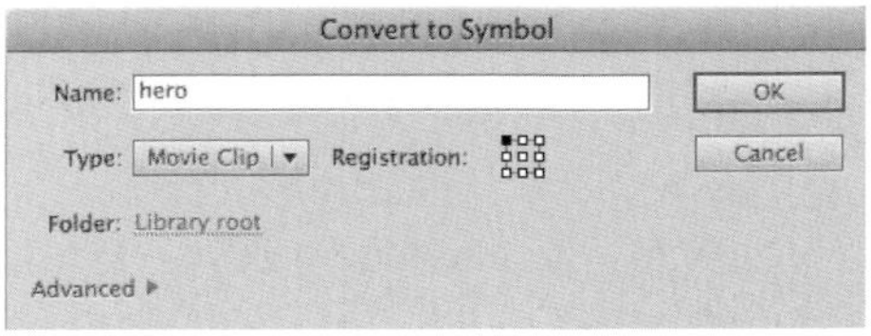

5 Click OK. The hero symbol appears in the Library.

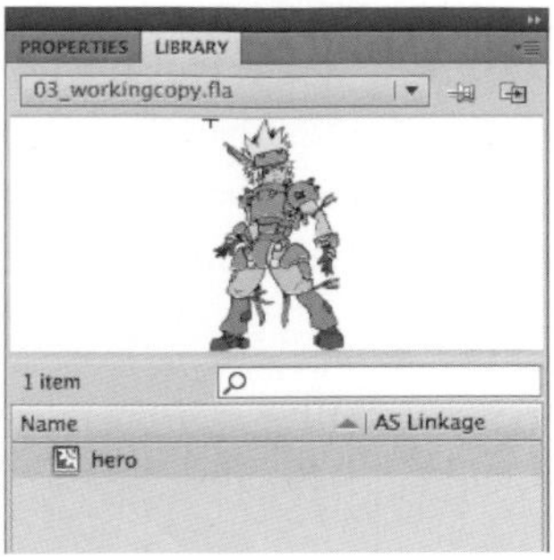

6 Select the other cartoon character in the robot layer and convert it to a movie clip symbol as well. Name it **robot**.

   You now have two movie clip symbols in your Library and an instance of each on the Stage as well.

Importing Photoshop Files

You'll import a Photoshop file for the background. The Photoshop file contains two layers with a blending effect. A blending effect can create special color mixes between different layers. You'll see that Flash can import a Photoshop file with all the layers intact and retain all the blending information as well.

1 Select the top layer in your Timeline.

2 From the top menu, choose File > Import > Import to Stage.

3 Select the background.psd file in the Lesson03/03Start folder.

4 Click Open.

5 In the Import to Stage dialog box, make sure all layers are selected. A check mark should appear in the check box next to each layer.

6 Choose the flare layer in the left window.

7 In the import options on the right, choose Bitmap image with editable layer styles.

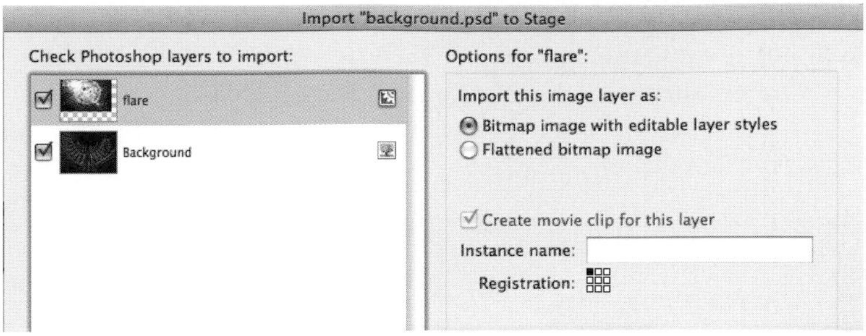

The movie clip symbol icon appears to the right of the Photoshop layer, indicating that the imported layer will be made into a movie clip symbol. The other option, Flattened bitmap image, will not preserve any layer effects such as transparencies or blending.

8 In the left window, choose the Background layer.

9 In the import options on the right, choose Bitmap image with editable layer styles.

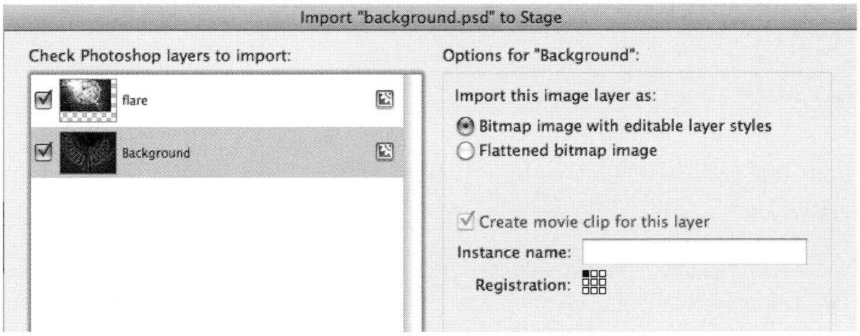

10 At the bottom of the dialog box, set the Convert layers to Flash Layers option, and select Place layers at original position.

You also have the option of changing the Flash Stage size to match the Photoshop canvas. However, the current Stage is already set to the correct dimensions (600 pixels x 450 pixels).

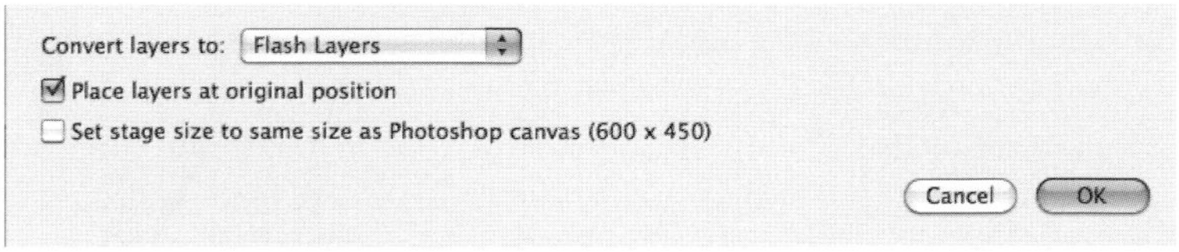

11 Click OK. The two Photoshop layers are imported into Flash and placed on separate layers on the Timeline.

The Photoshop images are automatically converted into movie clip symbols and saved in your Library. All the blending and transparency information is preserved. If you select the image in the flare layer, you'll see that the Blending option is set to Lighten in the Properties inspector under the Display section.

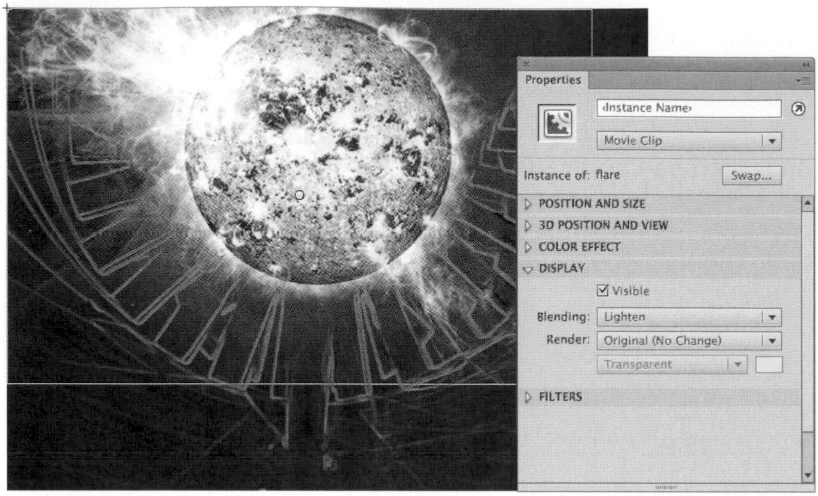

12 Drag the robot and the hero layers to the top of the Timeline so they overlap the background layers.

Note: If you want to edit your Photoshop files, you don't have to go through the entire import process again. You can edit any image on the Stage or in the Library panel in Adobe Photoshop or any other image-editing application. Right-click/Ctrl-click an image on the Stage or an image in the Library and choose Edit with Adobe Photoshop to edit in Photoshop, or select another Edit with the option to choose your preferred application. Flash launches the application, and once you have saved your changes, your image is immediately updated in Flash.

Editing and Managing Symbols

You now have multiple movie clip symbols in your Library and several instances on the Stage. You can better manage the symbols in your Library by organizing them in folders. You can also edit any symbol at any time. If you decide you want to change the color of one of the robot's arms, for example, you can easily go into symbol-editing mode and make that change.

About Image Formats

Flash supports multiple image formats for import. Flash can handle JPEG, GIF, PNG, and PSD (Photoshop) files. Use JPEG files for images that include gradients and subtle variations, such as those that occur in photographs. GIF files are used for images with large solid blocks of color or black and white line drawings. Use PNG files for images that include transparency. Use PSD files if you want to retain all the layer, transparency, and blending information from a Photoshop file.

Converting a Bitmap Image to a Vector Graphic

Sometimes you'll want to convert a bitmap image to a vector graphic. Flash handles bitmap images as a series of colored dots (or pixels); vector graphics are handled as a series of lines and curves. This vector information is rendered on the fly, so that the resolution of vector graphics is not fixed like a bitmap image. That means you can zoom in on a vector graphic and your computer will always display it sharply and smoothly. Converting a bitmap image to a vector often has the effect of making it look "posterized" because subtle gradations are converted to editable, discrete blocks of color, which can be an interesting effect.

To convert a bitmap to a vector, import the bitmap image into Flash. Select the bitmap and choose Modify > Bitmap > Trace Bitmap. The options determine how faithful of a trace the vector image will be to the original bitmap.

In the following figure, the left image is an original bitmap and the right image is a vector graphic.

Exercise caution when using the Trace Bitmap command, because a complicated vector graphic is often more memory- and processor-intensive than the original bitmap image.

Adding folders and organizing the Library

1 In the Library panel, right-click/Ctrl-click in an empty space and select New Folder. Alternatively, you can click the New Folder button ( ) at the bottom of the Library panel or from the options menu at the upper-right corner of the Library panel.

A new folder is created in your Library.

2 Name the folder **characters**.

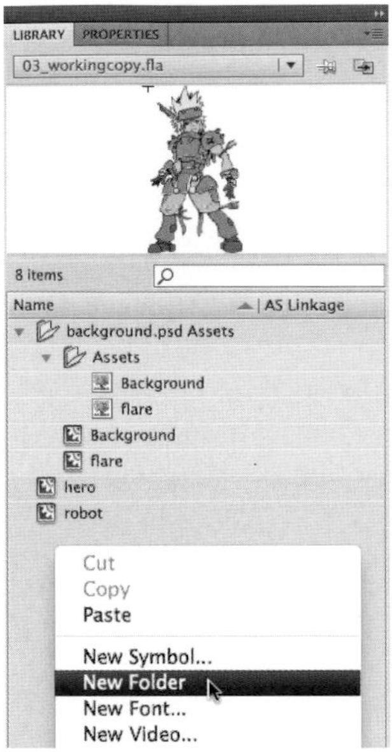

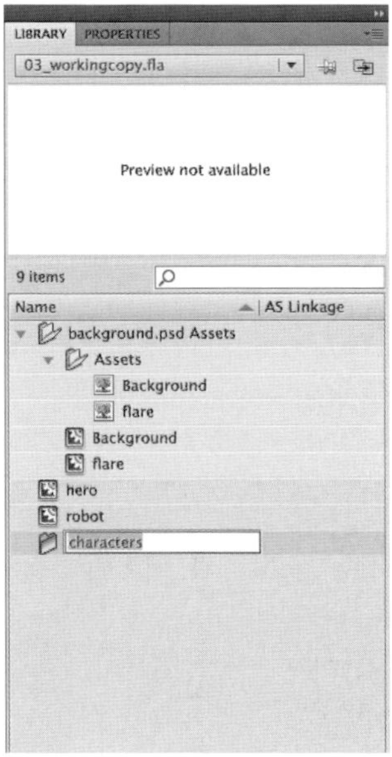

3 Drag the hero and the robot movie clip symbols into the characters folder.

4 You can collapse or expand folders to hide or view their contents and keep your Library organized.

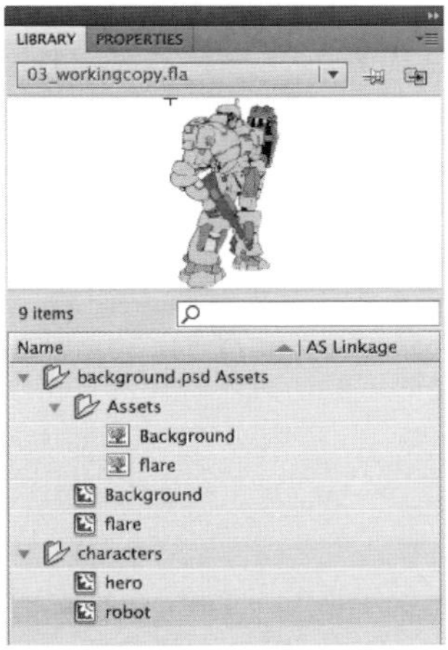

Editing a symbol from the Library

1 Double-click the robot movie clip symbol in the Library.

Flash takes you to symbol-editing mode. In this mode, you can see the contents of your symbol—in this case, the robot on the Stage. Notice on the top horizontal bar that you are no longer in Scene 1 but are inside the symbol called robot.

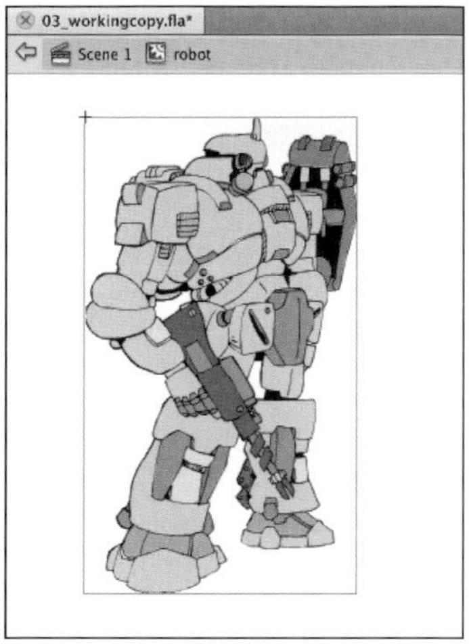

2 Double-click the drawing to edit it. You will need to double-click the drawing groups several times to drill down to the individual shape that you want to edit.

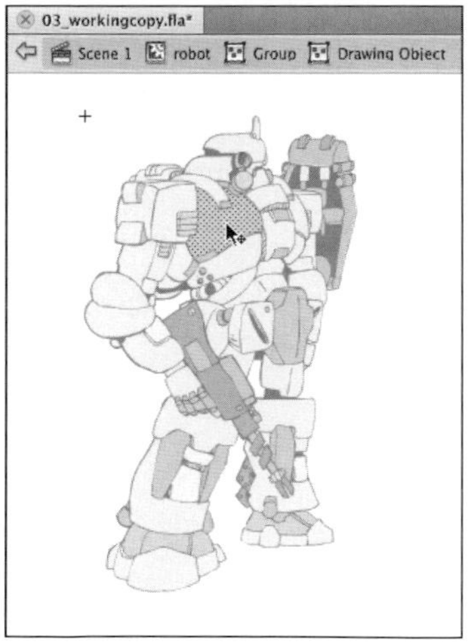

3 Choose the Paint Bucket tool. Select a new fill color and apply it to the shape on the robot drawing.

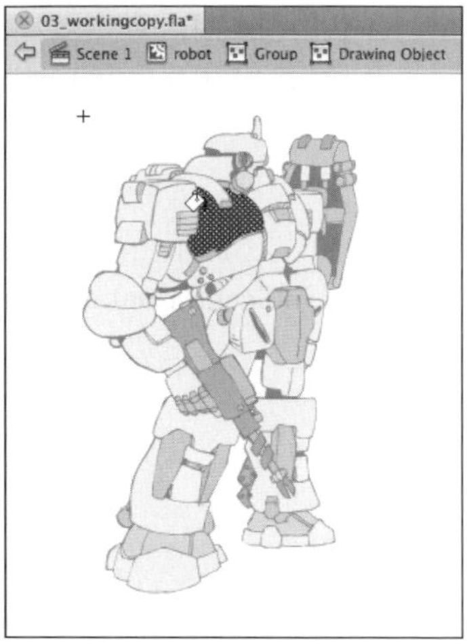

Note: You can quickly and easily duplicate symbols in the Library. Select the Library symbol, right-click/Ctrl-click, and choose Duplicate. Or, from the top-right Options menu in the Library, choose Duplicate. An exact copy of the selected symbol will be created in your Library.

4 Click on Scene 1 on the top horizontal bar above the Stage to return to the main Timeline.

The movie clip symbol in the Library reflects the changes you made. The instance on the Stage also reflects the changes you made to the symbol. All instances of the symbol on the Stage will change if you edit the symbol.

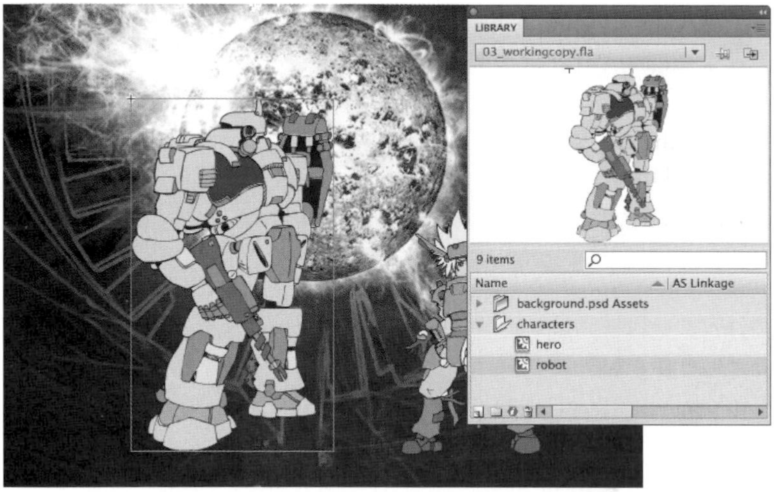

Editing a symbol in place

You may want to edit a symbol in context with the other objects on the Stage. You can do so by double-clicking an instance on the Stage. You'll enter symbol-editing mode, but you'll also be able to see the symbol's surroundings. This editing mode is called editing in place.

1 Using the Selection tool, double-click the robot movie clip instance on the Stage.

   Flash dims all other objects on the Stage and takes you to symbol-editing mode. Notice on the top horizontal bar that you are no longer in Scene 1 but are inside the symbol called robot.

2 Double-click the drawing to edit it. You will need to double-click the drawing groups several times to drill down to the individual shape that you want to edit.

3 Choose the Paint Bucket tool. Select a new fill color and apply it to the shape on the robot drawing.

4 Click on Scene 1 on the top horizontal bar above the Stage to return to the main Timeline. You can also just double-click any part of the Stage outside the graphic with the Selection tool to return to the next higher group level.

The movie clip symbol in the Library panel reflects the changes you made. The instance on the Stage also reflects the changes you made to the symbol. All instances of the symbol will change according to the edits you make to the symbol.

Breaking apart a symbol instance

If you no longer want an object on the Stage to be a symbol instance, you can use the Break Apart command to return it to its original form.

1 Select the robot instance on the Stage.

2 Choose Modify > Break Apart.

Flash breaks apart the robot movie clip instance. What's left on the Stage is a group, which you can break apart further to edit as you please. Undo the Break Apart command to return the robot object back to a symbol instance.

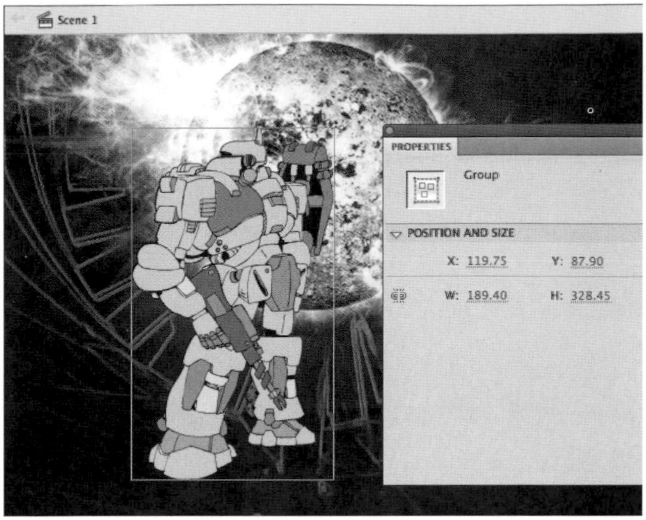

Changing the Size and Position of Instances

You can have multiple instances of the same symbol on the Stage. Now you'll add a few more robots to create a small robot army. You'll learn how to change the size and position (and even rotation) of each instance individually.

1 Select the robot layer in the Timeline.

2 Drag another robot symbol from the Library onto the Stage.

A new instance appears.

3 Choose the Free Transform tool.

Control handles appear around the selected instance.

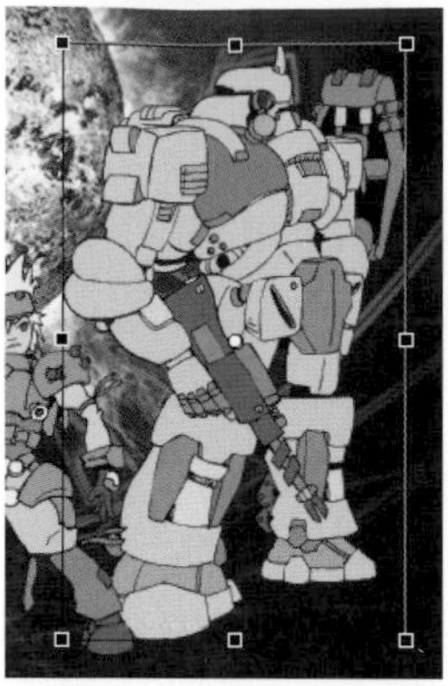

4 Drag the control handles on the sides of the selection to flip the robot so it is facing in the other direction.

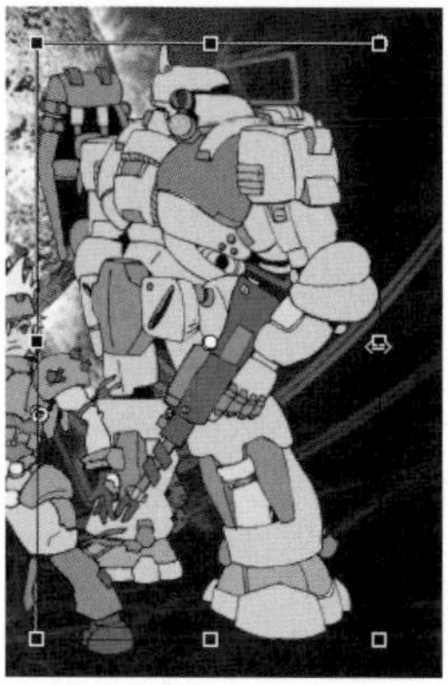

5 Drag the control handles on the corner of the selection while holding down the Shift key to reduce the size of the robot.

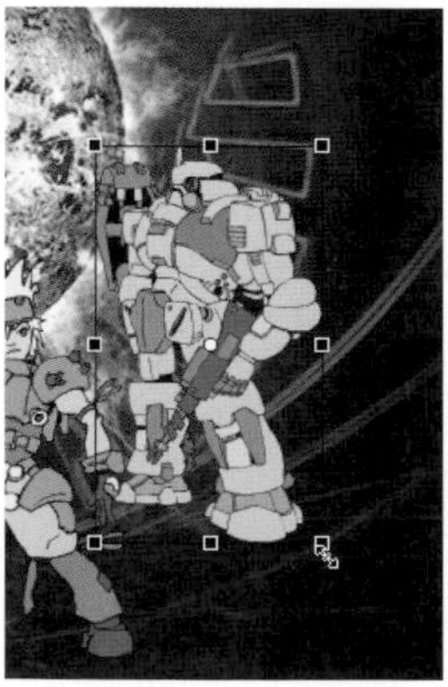

6 Drag a third robot from the Library onto the Stage. With the Free Transform tool, flip the robot, resize it, and make it overlap the second robot.

   The robot army is growing!

Using rulers and guides

You may want to be more precise in your placement of your symbol instances. In Lesson 1, you learned how to use the X and Y coordinates in the Properties inspector to position individual objects. In Lesson 2 you learned to use the Align panel to align several objects to each other. Another way to position objects on the Stage is to use rulers and guides. Rulers appear on the top and left edge of the Pasteboard to provide measurement along the horizontal and vertical axes. Guides are vertical or horizontal lines that appear on the Stage but do not appear in the final published movie.

1 Choose View > Rulers (Ctrl+Alt+Shift+R/Option+Shift+Command+ R).

   Horizontal and vertical rulers measuring in pixels appear along the top and left edges of the Pasteboard. As you move objects on the Stage, tick marks indicate the bounding box positions on the rulers.

2 Click the top horizontal ruler and drag a guide onto the Stage.

A colored line appears on the Stage that you can use as a guide for alignment.

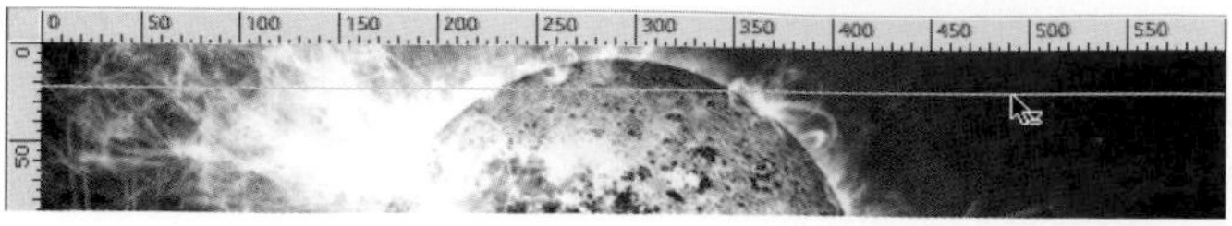

3 Double-click the guide with the Selection tool.

The Move Guide dialog box appears.

4 Enter **435** as the new pixel value of the guide. Click OK.

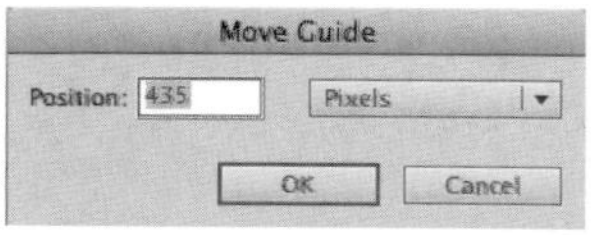

The guide is repositioned 435 pixels from the top edge of the Stage.

5 Choose View > Snapping > Snap to Guides and make sure Snap to Guides is selected.

Objects will now snap to any guides on the Stage.

Note: Choose View > Guides > Lock Guides to lock your guides. This prevents you from accidentally moving them. Clear all guides by choosing View > Guides > Clear Guides. Change the color of the guides and the snapping accuracy by choosing View > Guides > Edit Guides.

6 Drag the robot instance and the hero instance so their bottom edges align with the guide.

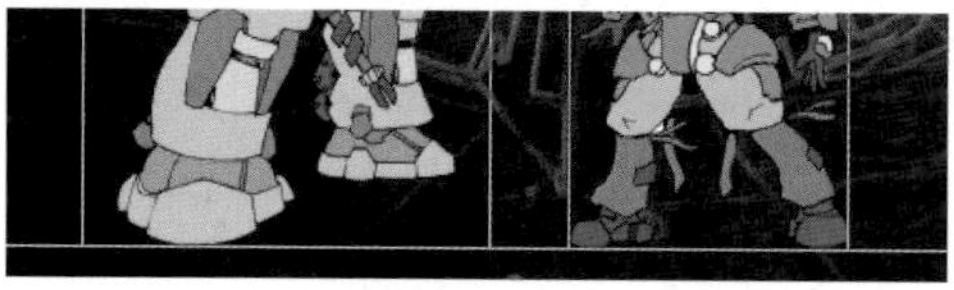

Changing the Color Effect of Instances

The Color Effect option in the Properties inspector allows you to change several properties of any instance. These properties include brightness, tint, or alpha.

Brightness controls how dark or light the instance appears, tint controls the overall coloring, and alpha controls the level of opacity. Decreasing the alpha value decreases the opacity and increases the amount of transparency.

Changing the brightness

1 Using the Selection tool, click the smallest robot on the Stage.

2 In the Properties inspector, choose Brightness from the Color Effect Style menu.

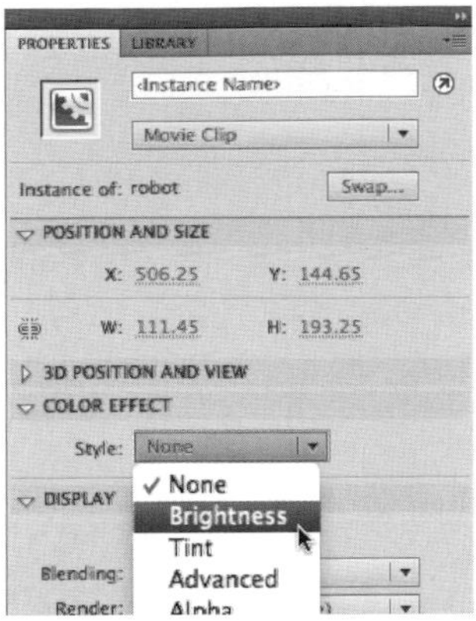

3 Drag the Bright slider to **-40%**.

The robot instance on the Stage becomes darker and appears to recede into the distance.

Changing the transparency

1 Select the glowing orb in the flare layer.

2 In the Properties inspector, choose Alpha from the Color Effect Style menu.

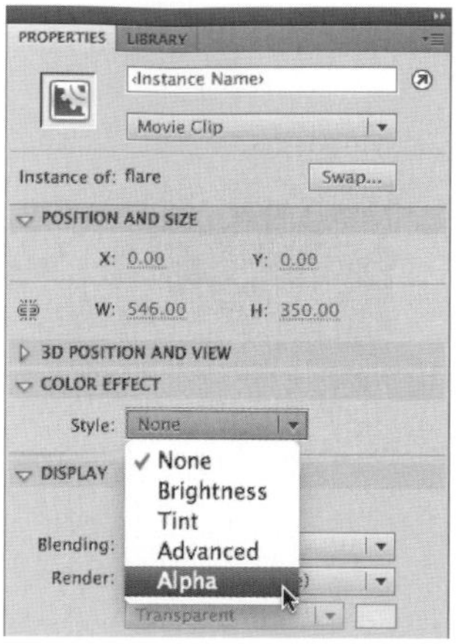

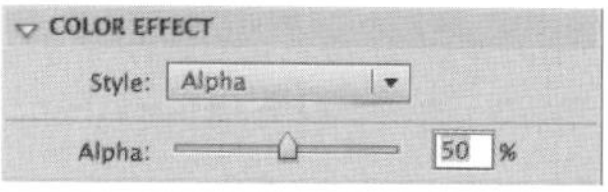

Note: To reset the Color Effect of any instance, choose None from the Style menu.

3 Drag the Alpha slider to a value of **50%**.

The orb in the flare layer on the Stage becomes more transparent.

Understanding Display Options

The Display section in the Properties inspector for movie clips offers options for controlling the instance's visibility, blending, and rendering.

Visible option for movie clips

The Visible property makes objects either visible or invisible to the audience. You can directly control the Visible property of movie clip instances on the Stage by selecting or deselecting the option in the Properties inspector.

1 Select the Selection tool.

2 Select one of the robot movie clip instances on the Stage.

3 In the Properties inspector, under the Display section, notice that the Visible option is checked by default, meaning that the instance is visible.

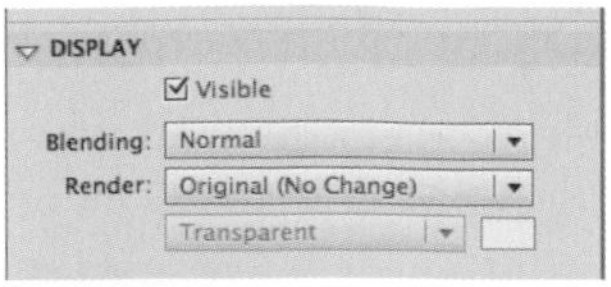

4 Deselect the Visible check box.

The selected instance becomes invisible.

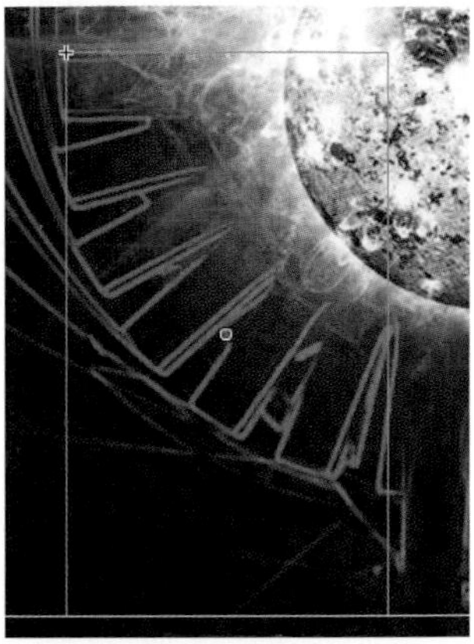

The instance is present on the Stage, and you can still move it to a new position, but the audience won't be able to see it. Use the Visible option to turn instances on or off during the course of your movie, rather than deleting them entirely. You can also use the Visible option to position invisible instances on the Stage in order to make them visible later on with ActionScript, the coding language of Flash.

Check the Visible option to make the robot visible on the Stage again.

Blending effects

Blending refers to how the colors of an instance interact with the colors below it. You saw how the instance in the flare layer had the Lighten option applied to it (carried over from Photoshop), which integrated it more with the instance in the Background layer.

There are many kinds of Blending options. Some have surprising results, depending on the colors in the instance and the colors in the layers below it. Experiment with all the options to understand how they work. The following figure shows some of the Blending options and their effects on the robot instance over a blue-black gradient.

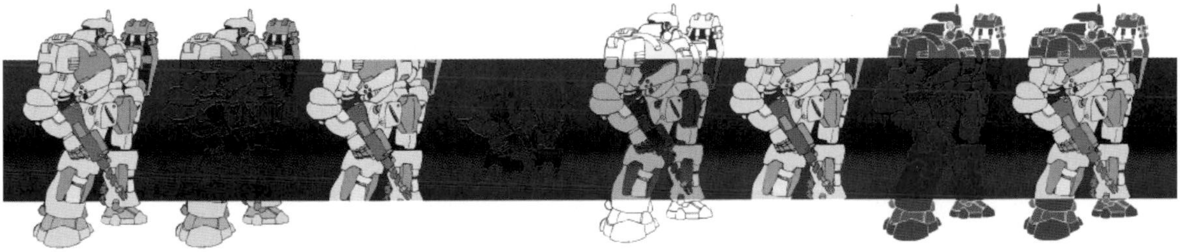

Export as Bitmap

The robots and the hero character in this lesson are movie clip symbols containing complex vector graphics imported from Illustrator. Vector art, however, can be processor-intensive, and can take its toll on performance and playback. A rendering option called Export as Bitmap can help. The Export as Bitmap option renders the vector art as a bitmap, reducing the performance load. The movie clip remains as editable vector graphics in the FLA file, however, so you can still modify the artwork.

1 Select the Selection tool.

2 Select the hero movie clip instance on the Stage.

3 In the Properties inspector, choose Export as Bitmap for the Render option.

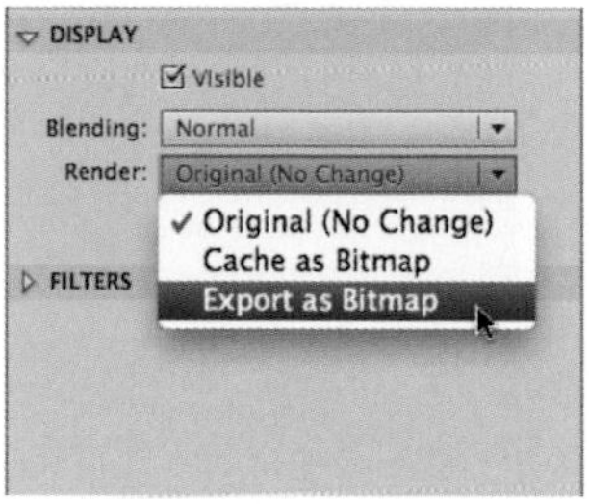

The hero movie clip instance appears as it will be rendered when published. You may see a slight "softening" of the illustration because of the rasterization of the art.

4 In the pulldown menu under the Render options, leave the selection as Transparent.

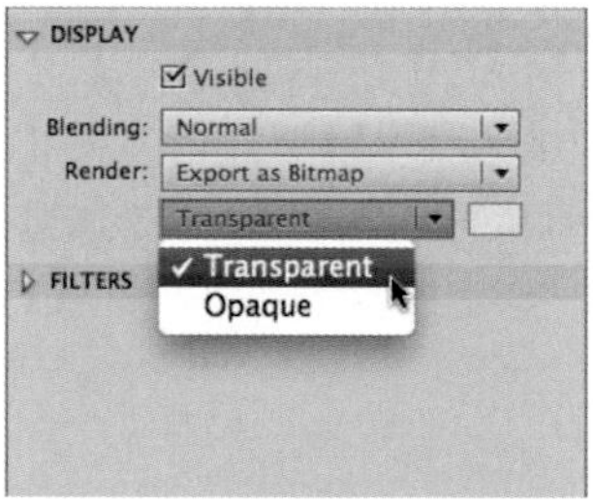

The Transparent option renders the background in your movie clip symbol as transparent. Alternately, you can choose Opaque and pick a color for the background of your movie clip symbol.

Applying Filters for Special Effects

Filters are special effects that you can apply to movie clip instances. Several filters are available in the Filters section of the Properties inspector. Each filter has different options that can refine the effect.

Applying a blur filter

You'll apply a blur filter to some of the instances to help give the scene a greater sense of depth.

1 Select the glowing orb in the flare layer.

2 In the Properties inspector, expand the Filters section.

3 Click the Add filter button at the bottom of the Filters section and select Blur.

The Blur filter appears in the Filters window with options for Blur X and Blur Y.

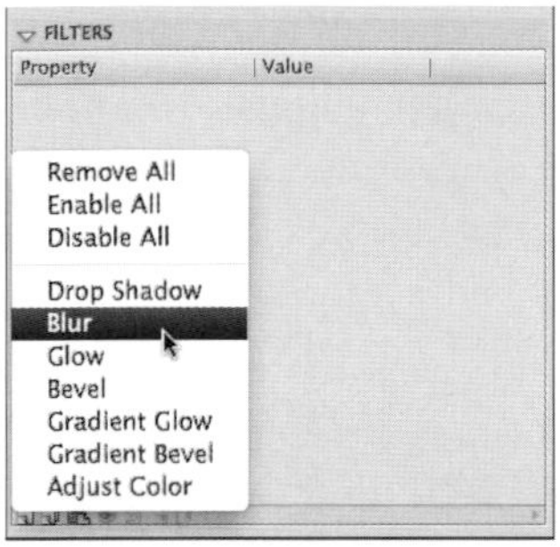

4 If they aren't linked already, click the link icons next to the Blur X and Blur Y options to link the blur effect in both directions.

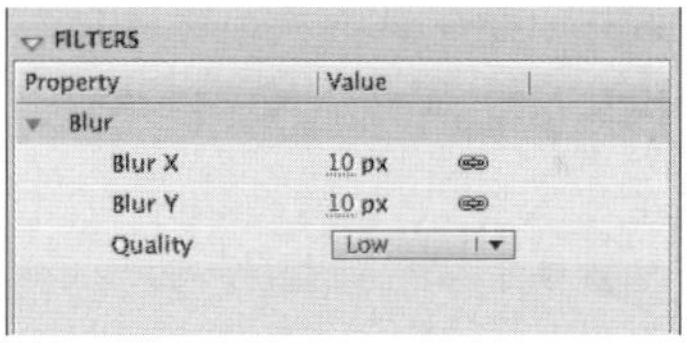

5 Set the Blur X and Blur Y value to **10** pixels.

The instance on the Stage becomes blurry, helping to give an atmospheric perspective to this scene.

● **Note:** It's best to keep the Quality setting for filters on Low. Higher settings are processor-intensive and can bog down performance, especially if you've applied multiple filters.

More Filter Options

At the bottom of the Filters window is a row of options to help you manage and apply multiple filters.

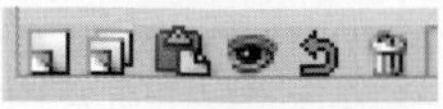

The Presets button lets you save a particular filter and its settings so you can apply it to another instance. The Clipboard button lets you copy and paste any selected filter. The Enable or Disable Filter button lets you see your instance with or without the filter applied. The Reset Filter button resets the filter parameters to their default values.

Positioning in 3D Space

You also have the ability to position and animate objects in real three-dimensional space. However, objects need to be either movie clip symbols or TLF Text to move them in 3D. Two tools allow you to position objects in 3D: the 3D Rotation tool and the 3D Translation tool. The Transform panel also provides information for position and rotation.

Understanding the 3D coordinate space is essential for successful 3D placement of objects. Flash divides space using three axes: the *x*, *y*, and *z* axes. The *x* axis runs horizontally across the Stage with *x*=0 at the left edge. The *y* axis runs vertically with *y*=0 at the top edge. The *z* axis runs into and out of the plane of the Stage (toward and away from the viewer) with *z*=0 at the plane of the Stage.

Changing the 3D rotation of an object

You'll add some text to your image, but to add a little more interest, you'll tilt it to put it in perspective. Think about the beginning text introduction to the *Star Wars* movies, and see if you can achieve a similar effect.

1 Insert a new layer at the top of the layers stack and rename it **text**.

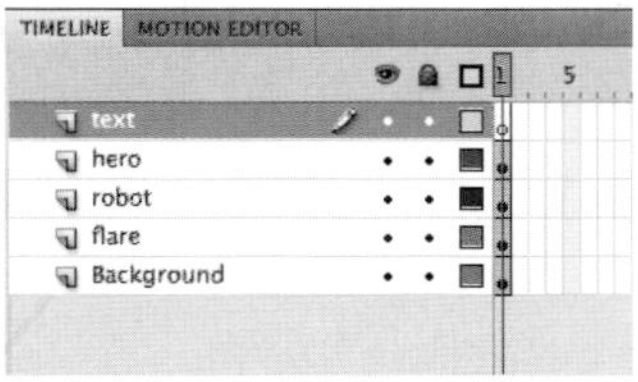

2 Choose the Text tool from the Tools panel.

3 In the Properties inspector, choose TLF Text, Read Only, and select a large-size font with an interesting color that will add some pizzazz. Your font could appear a little differently than what's shown in this lesson, depending on the fonts available on your computer.

4 Click on the Stage in your text layer and begin typing your title.

5 To exit the Text tool, select the Selection tool.

6 Choose the 3D Rotation tool ().

A circular, multicolored target appears on the instance. This is a guide for the 3D rotation. It's useful to think of the guides as lines on a globe. The red longitudinal line rotates your instance around the *x* axis. The green line along the equator rotates your instance around the *y* axis. The circular blue guide rotates your instance around the *z* axis.

7 Click on one of the guides—red for *x*, green for *y*, or blue for *z*—and drag your mouse in either direction to rotate your instance in 3D space.

You can also click and drag the outer orange circular guide to freely rotate the instance in all three directions.

Global vs. Local Transformations

When you choose the 3D Rotation or 3D Translation tool, be aware of the Global Transform option (it appears as a three-dimensional cube) at the bottom of the Tools panel. When the Global Transform option is depressed, rotation and positioning are relative to the global, or Stage, coordinate system. The 3D display over the object that you're moving shows the three axes in constant position, no matter how the object is rotated or moved. Notice in the following image how the 3D display is always perpendicular to the Stage.

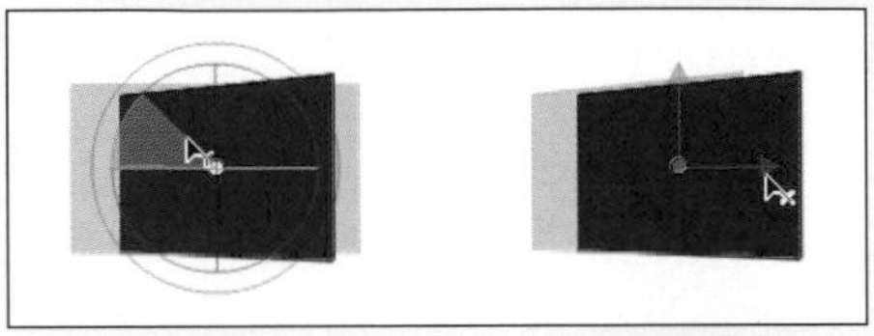

However, when the Global option is turned off (the button is raised), rotation and positioning is relative to the object. The 3D display shows the three axes oriented relative to the object, not the Stage. For example, in the following image, notice that the 3D Translation tool shows the *z* axis pointing out from the rectangle, not from the Stage.

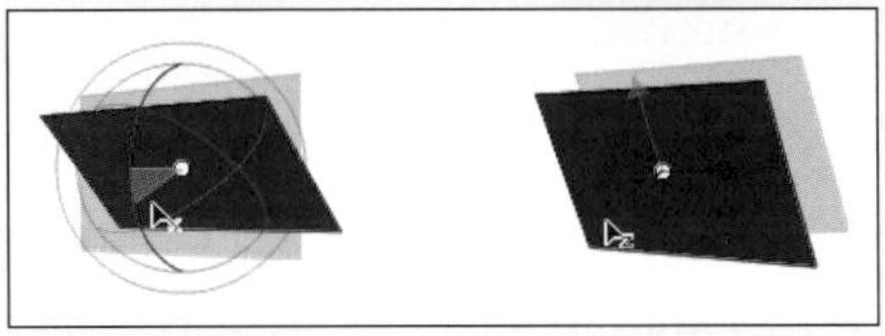

Changing the 3D position of an object

In addition to changing an object's rotation in 3D space, you can move it to a specific point in 3D space. Use the 3D Translation tool, which is hidden under the 3D Rotation tool.

1 Choose the 3D Translation tool ().

2 Click on your text.

   A guide appears on the instance. This is a guide for the 3D translation. The red guide represents the *x* axis, the green is the *y* axis, and the blue is the *z* axis.

3 Click on one of the guide axes and drag your mouse in either direction to move your instance in 3D space. Notice that your text stays in perspective as you move it around the Stage.

Resetting the rotation and position

If you've made a mistake in your 3D transformations and want to reset the position and rotation of your instance, you can use the Transform panel.

1 Choose the Selection tool and select the instance that you want to reset.

2 Open the Transform panel by choosing Window > Transform.

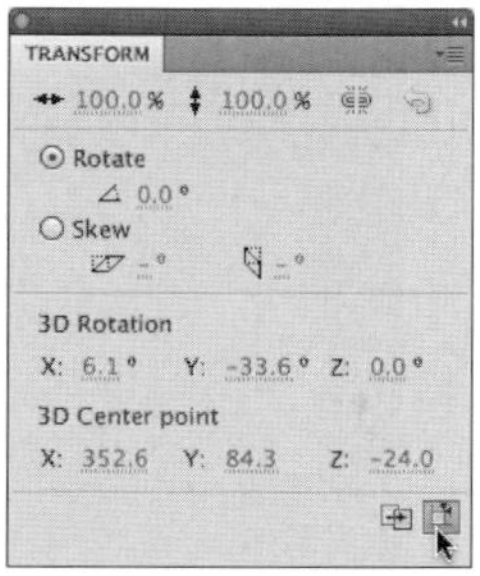

The Transform panel shows all the values for the *x*, *y*, and *z* angles and positions.

3 Click the Remove Transform button in the lower-right corner of the Transform panel.

The selected instance returns to its original settings.

Understanding the vanishing point and the perspective angle

Objects in 3D space represented on a 2D surface (such as the computer screen) are rendered with perspective to make them appear as they do in real life. Correct perspective depends on many factors, including the vanishing point and the perspective angle, both of which can be changed in Flash.

The vanishing point determines where on the horizon parallel lines of a perspective drawing converge. Think of railroad tracks and how the parallel tracks converge to a single point as they recede into the distance. The vanishing point is usually at eye level in the center of your field of view, so the default settings are exactly in the middle of the Stage. You can, however, change the vanishing point setting so it appears above or below eye level, or to the right or left.

The perspective angle determines how quickly parallel lines converge to the vanishing point. The greater the angle the quicker the convergence, and therefore, the more severe and distorted the illustration appears.

1 Select an object on the Stage that has been moved or rotated in 3D space.

2 In the Properties inspector, expand the 3D Position and View section.

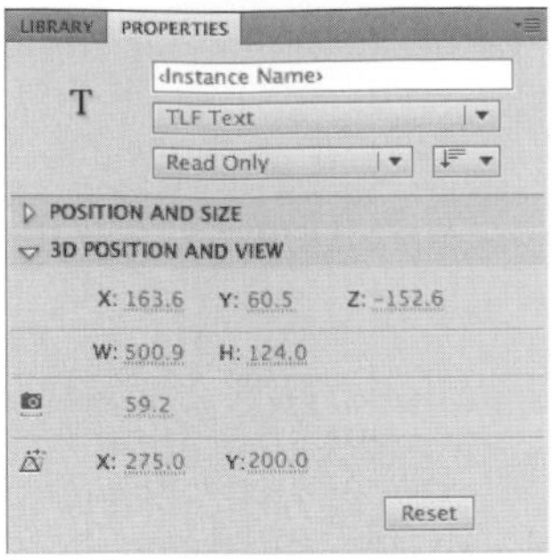

3 Click and drag on the X and Y values of the Vanishing Point to change the vanishing point, which is indicated on the Stage by intersecting gray lines.

4 To reset the Vanishing Point to the default values (to the center of the Stage), click the Reset button.

5 Click and drag on the Perspective Angle value to change the amount of distortion. The greater the angle, the more the distortion.

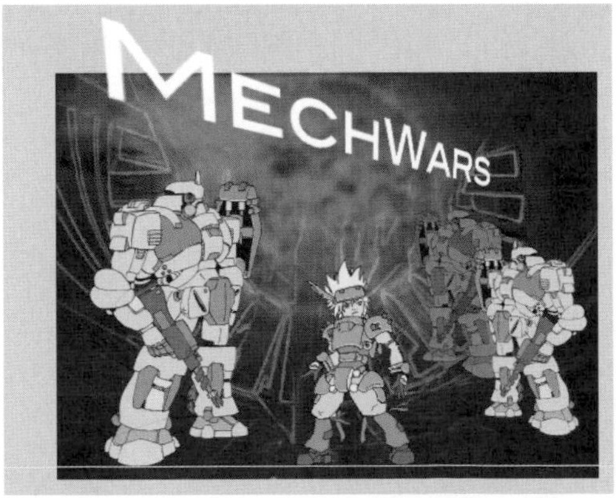

Review Questions

1 What is a symbol, and how does it differ from an instance?

2 Name two ways you can create a symbol.

3 When you import an Illustrator file, what happens if you choose to import layers as layers? As keyframes?

4 How can you change the transparency of an instance in Flash?

5 What are the two ways to edit symbols?

Review Answers

1 A *symbol* is a graphic, button, or movie clip that you create once in Flash and can then reuse throughout your document or in other documents. All symbols are stored in your Library panel. An *instance* is a copy of a symbol located on the Stage.

2 You can create a symbol by choosing Insert > New Symbol, or you can select existing objects on the Stage and choose Modify > Convert to Symbol.

3 When you import layers of an Illustrator file into Flash as layers, Flash recognizes the layers in the Illustrator document and adds them as separate layers in the Timeline. When you import layers as keyframes, Flash adds each Illustrator layer to a separate frame in the Timeline and creates keyframes for them.

4 The transparency of an instance is determined by its alpha value. To change the transparency, select Alpha from the Color Effect menu in the Properties inspector, and then change the alpha percentage.

5 To edit a symbol, either double-click the symbol in the Library to enter symbol-editing mode, or double-click the instance on the Stage to edit it in place. Editing a symbol in place lets you see the other objects around the instance.

4 ADDING ANIMATION

Lesson Overview

In this lesson, you'll learn how to do the following:

- Animate the position, scale, and rotation of objects
- Adjust the pacing and timing of your animation
- Animate transparency and special effects
- Change the path of an object's motion
- Create animation inside symbols
- Change the easing of the motion
- Animate in 3D space

This lesson will take approximately two hours to complete. If needed, remove the previous lesson folder from your hard drive and copy the Lesson04 folder onto it.

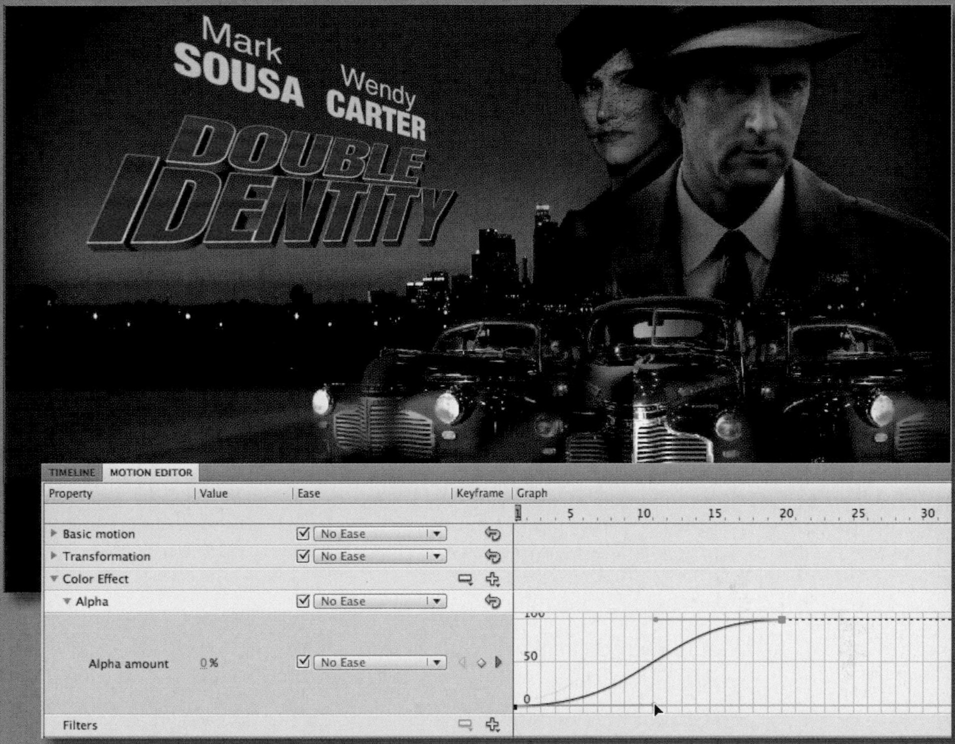

Use Flash Professional CS6 to change almost any aspect of an object—position, color, transparency, size, rotation, and more—over time. Motion tweening is the basic technique of creating animation with symbol instances.

Getting Started

Start by viewing the finished movie file to see the animated title page that you'll create in this lesson.

1 Double-click the 04End.html file in the Lesson04/04End folder to play the animation in a browser.

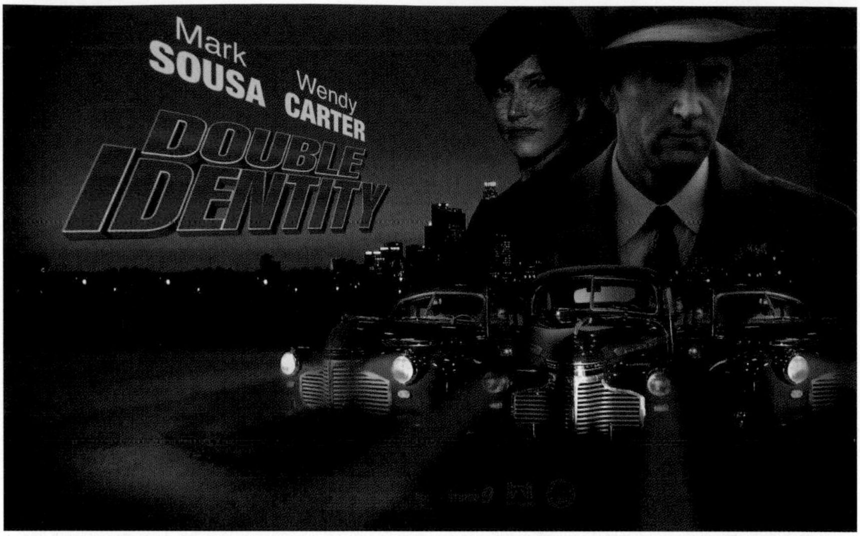

The project is an animated splash page for an imaginary soon-to-be-released motion picture. In this lesson, you'll use motion tweens to animate several components on the page: the cityscape, the main actors, several old-fashioned cars, and the main title.

2 Close the 04End.html file.

3 Double-click the 04Start.fla file in the Lesson04/04Start folder to open the initial project file in Flash. This file is partially completed and already contains many of the graphic elements imported into the Library for you to use.

4 From the view options above the Stage, choose View > Magnification > Fit in Window so that you can see the entire Stage on your computer screen.

5 Choose File > Save As. Name the file **04_workingcopy.fla**, and save it in the 04Start folder.

Saving a working copy ensures that the original start file will be available if you want to start over.

About Animation

Animation is the movement, or change, of objects through time. Animation can be as simple as moving a box across the Stage from one frame to the next. It can also be much more complex. As you'll see in this lesson, you can animate many different aspects of a single object. You can change an object's position on the Stage, change its color or transparency, change its size or its rotation, and even animate the special filters that you saw in the previous lesson. You also have control over an object's path of motion, and even its easing, which is the way an object accelerates or decelerates.

In Flash, the basic workflow for animation goes like this: Select an object on the Stage, right-click/Ctrl-click, and choose Create Motion Tween. Move the red playhead to a different point in time and move the object to a new position. Flash takes care of the rest.

Motion tweens create animation for changes in position on the Stage and for changes in size, color, or other attributes. Motion tweens require you to use a symbol instance. If the object you've selected is not a symbol instance, Flash will automatically ask to convert the selection to a symbol. Flash also automatically separates motion tweens on their own layers, which are called Tween layers. There can be only one motion tween per layer without any other element in the layer. Tween layers allow you to change various attributes of your instance at different key points over time. For example, a spaceship could be on the left side of the Stage at the beginning keyframe and at the far-right side of the Stage at an ending keyframe, and the resulting tween would make the spaceship fly across the Stage.

The term "tween" comes from the world of classic animation. Senior animators would be responsible for drawing the beginning and ending poses for their characters. The beginning and ending poses were the keyframes of the animation. Junior animators would then come in and draw the "in-between" frames, or do the "in-betweening." Hence, "tweening" refers to the smooth transitions between keyframes.

Understanding the Project File

The 04Start.fla file contains a few of the animated elements already or partially completed. Each of the six layers—man, woman, Middle_car, Right_car, footer, and ground—contains an animation. The man and woman layers are in a folder called actors, and the Middle_car and Right_car layers are in a folder called cars.

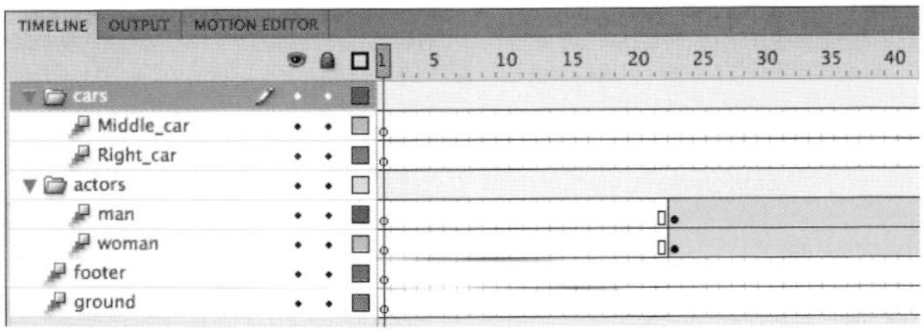

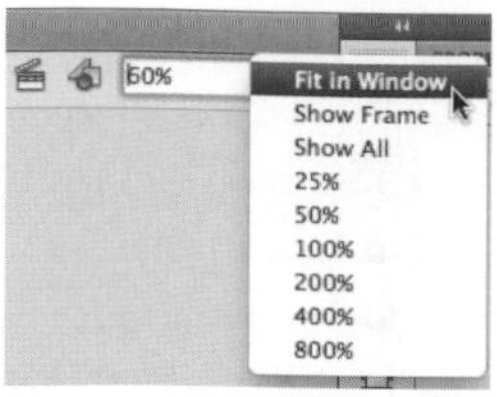

You'll be adding more layers to add an animated cityscape, refining the animation of one of the actors, as well as adding a third car and a 3D title. All the necessary graphic elements have been imported into the Library panel. The Stage is set at a generous 1280 pixels by 787 pixels to fill up a high-resolution monitor, and the Stage color is black. You might need to choose a different view option to see the entire Stage. Choose View > Magnification > Fit in Window from the view options at the top-right corner of the Stage to view the Stage at a magnification percentage that fits your screen.

Animating Position

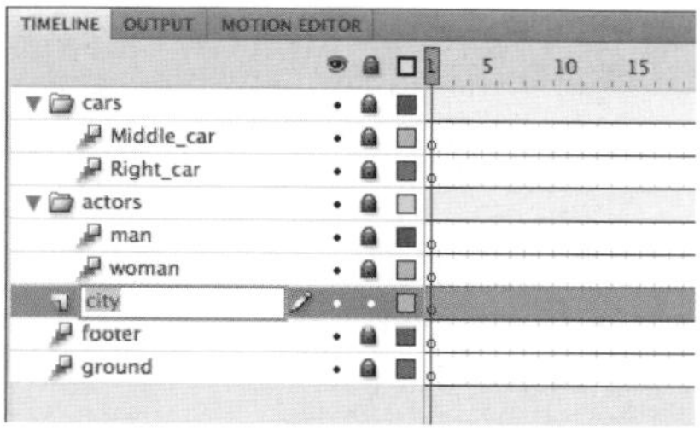

You'll start this project by animating the cityscape. It will begin slightly lower than the top edge of the Stage, and then rise slowly until its top is aligned with the top of the Stage.

1 Lock all the existing layers so you don't accidentally modify them. Create a new layer above the footer layer and rename it **city**.

2 Drag the bitmap image called cityBG.jpg from the bitmaps folder in the Library panel to the Stage.

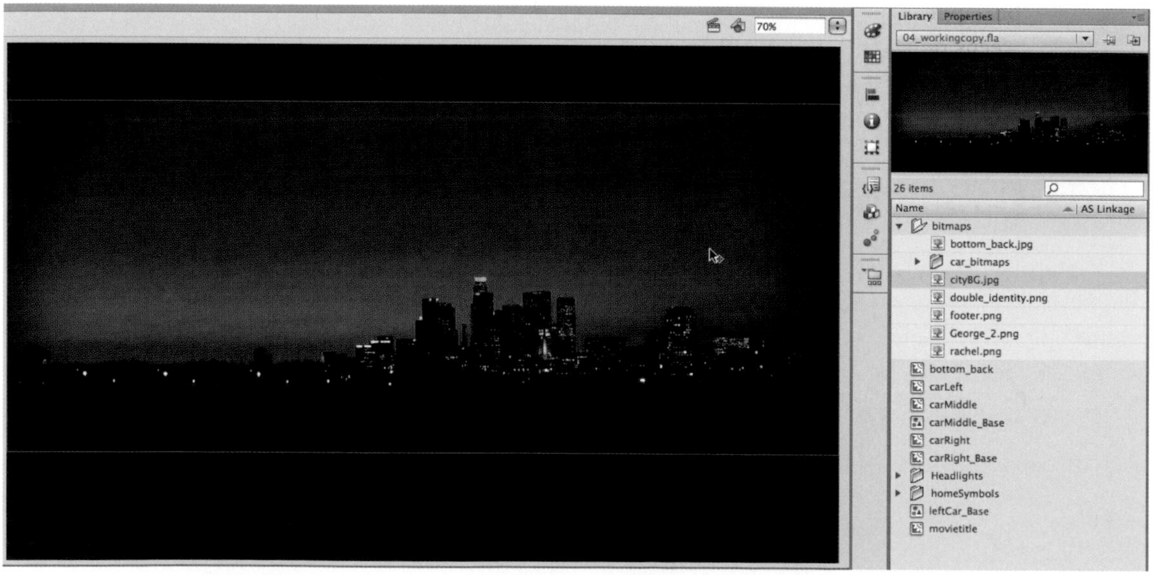

3 In the Properties inspector, set the value of X to **0** and the value of Y to **90**.

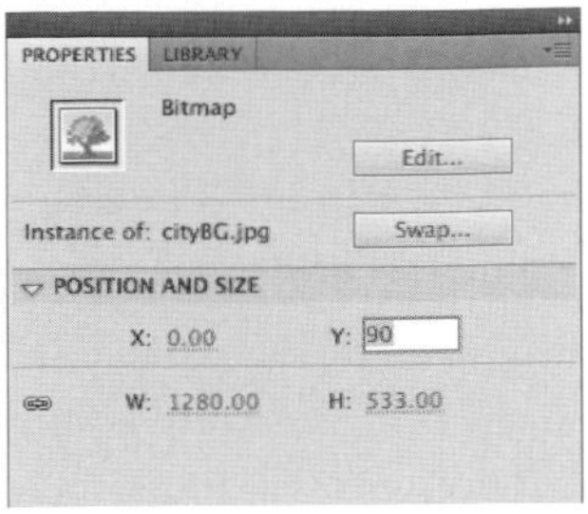

This positions the cityscape image just slightly below the top edge of the Stage.

4 Right-click/Ctrl-click on the cityscape image and choose Create Motion Tween. From the top menu, you can also select Insert > Motion Tween.

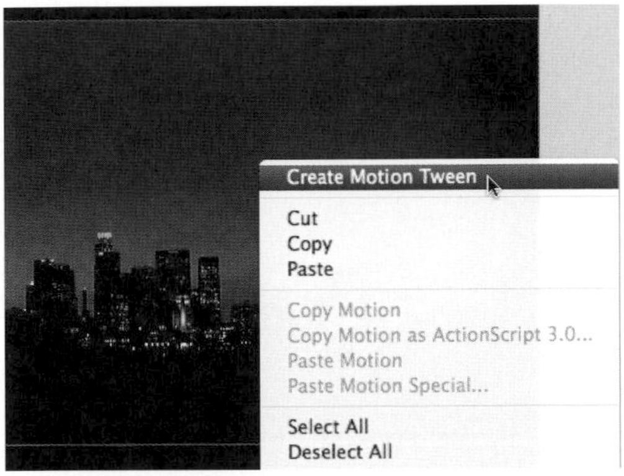

5 A dialog box appears warning you that your selected object is not a symbol. Motion tweens require symbols. Flash asks if you want to convert the selection to a symbol so it can proceed with the motion tween. Click OK.

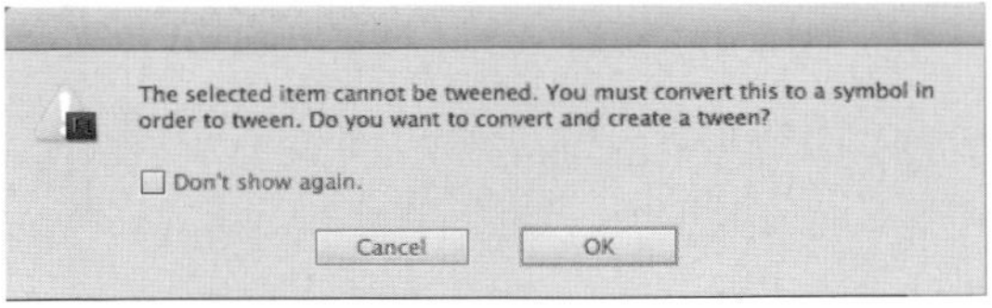

Flash automatically converts your selection to a symbol, which is stored in your Library panel. Flash also converts the current layer to a Tween layer so you can begin to animate the instance. Tween layers are distinguished by a special icon in front of the layer name, and the frames are tinted blue. Tween layers are reserved for motion tweens, and hence, no drawing is allowed on a Tween layer.

6 Move the red playhead to the end of the tween span at frame 190.

7 Select the instance of the cityscape on the Stage, and while holding down the Shift key, move the instance up the Stage.

Holding down the Shift key constrains the movement to right angles.

8 For more precision, set the value of Y to **0** in the Properties inspector.

A small black diamond appears in frame 190 at the end of the tween span. This indicates a keyframe at the end of the tween. Flash smoothly interpolates the change in position from frame 1 to frame 190 and represents that motion with a motion path. Hide all the other layers to see the results of the motion tween on the cityscape.

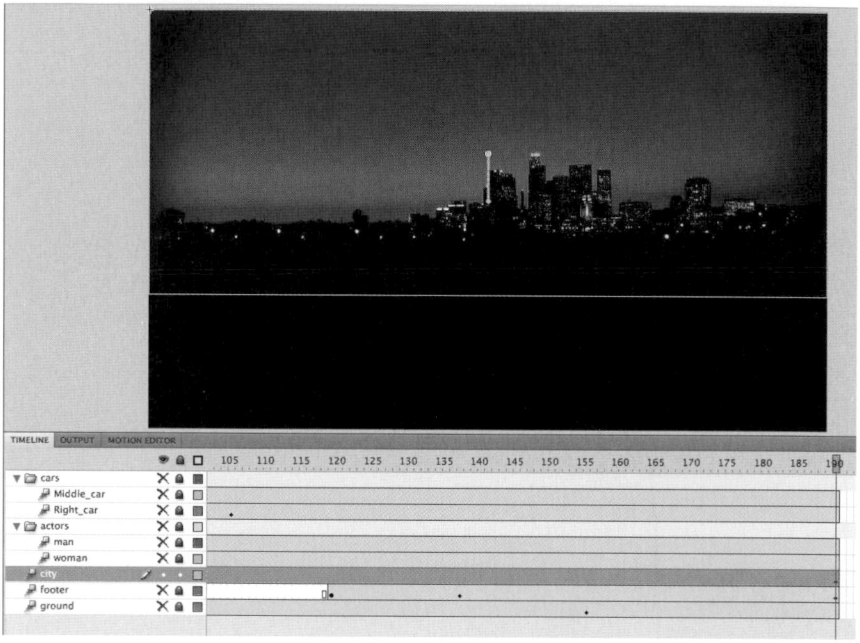

> **Note:** Remove a motion tween by right-clicking/Ctrl-clicking the motion tween on the Timeline or the Stage and choosing Remove Tween.

9 Drag the red playhead back and forth at the top of the Timeline to see the smooth motion. You can also choose Control > Play (Enter) to make Flash play the animation.

Animating changes in position is simple, because Flash automatically creates keyframes at the points where you move your instance to new positions. If you want to have an object move to many different points, simply move the red playhead to the desired frame, and then move the object to its new position. Flash takes care of the rest.

Using the Controller to Preview the Animation

The Controller panel allows you to play, rewind, or go step-by-step backward or forward through your Timeline to review your animation in a controlled manner.

Choose Window > Toolbars > Controller to display a separate controller panel, or use the playback controls that are integrated at the bottom of the Timeline.

1 Click any of the playback buttons on the controller below the Timeline to go to the first frame, go to the last frame, play, stop, or move forward or backward one frame.

2 Choose the loop option and click the play button.

The playhead loops, allowing you to see the animation over and over for careful analysis.

3 Move the front or rear brackets on the Timeline to define the range of frames that you want to see looped.

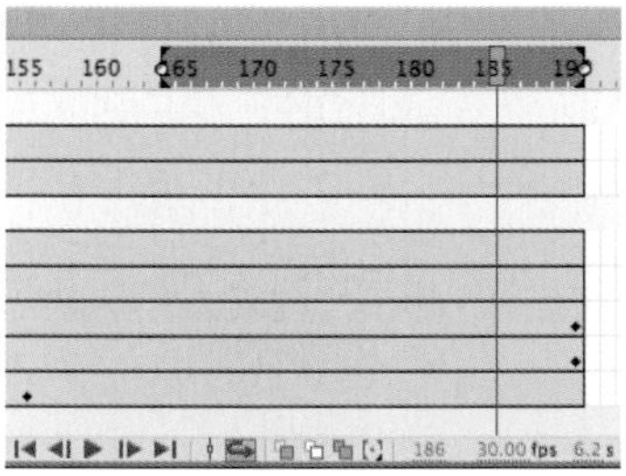

The playhead loops within the bracketed frames. Click on the loop option again to turn it off.

Changing the Pacing and Timing

You can change the duration of the entire tween span or change the timing of the animation by clicking and dragging keyframes on the Timeline.

Changing the animation duration

If you want the animation to proceed at a slower pace, taking up a much longer period of time, you need to lengthen the entire tween span between the beginning and end keyframes. If you want to shorten the animation, you need to decrease the tween span. Lengthen or shorten a motion tween by dragging the ends on the Timeline.

1 Move your mouse cursor close to the end of the tween span in the city layer.

Your cursor changes to a double-headed arrow, indicating that you can lengthen or shorten the tween span.

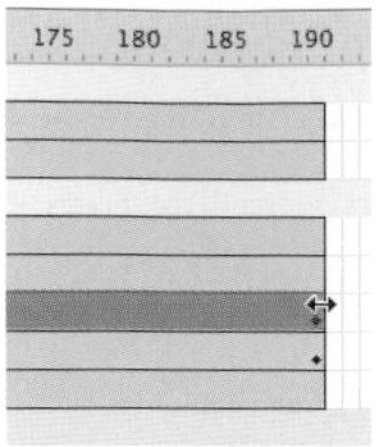

2 Click and drag the end of the tween span back toward frame 60.

Your motion tween shortens to 60 frames, so now the cityscape takes a much shorter time to move.

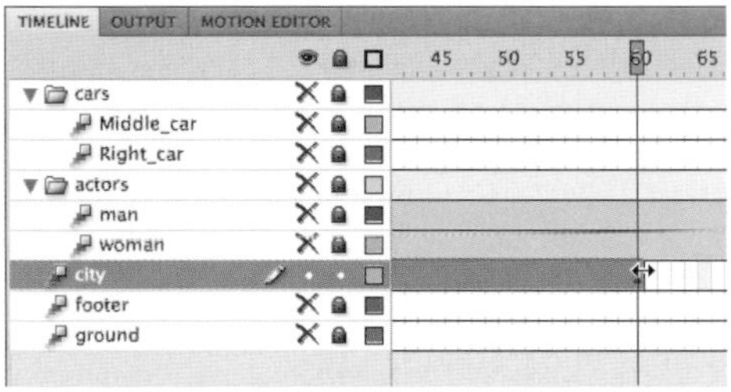

3 Move your mouse cursor close to the beginning of the tween span (at frame 1).

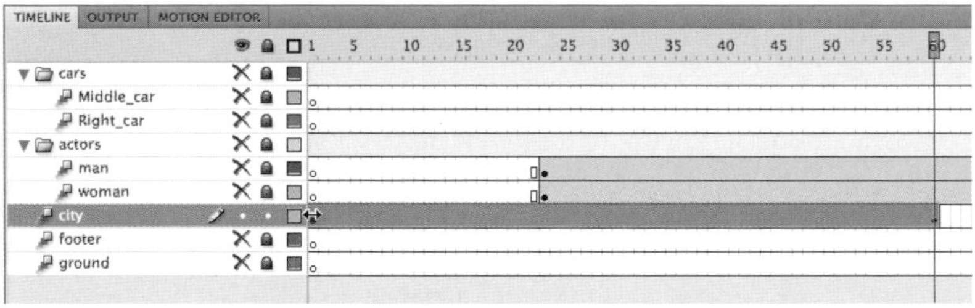

● **Note:** If you have multiple keyframes in a tween, dragging out your tween spans will distribute all your keyframes uniformly. The timing of your entire animation remains the same; only the length changes.

4 Click and drag the beginning of the frame span forward to frame 10.

Your motion tween begins at a later time, so it now plays only from frame 10 to frame 60.

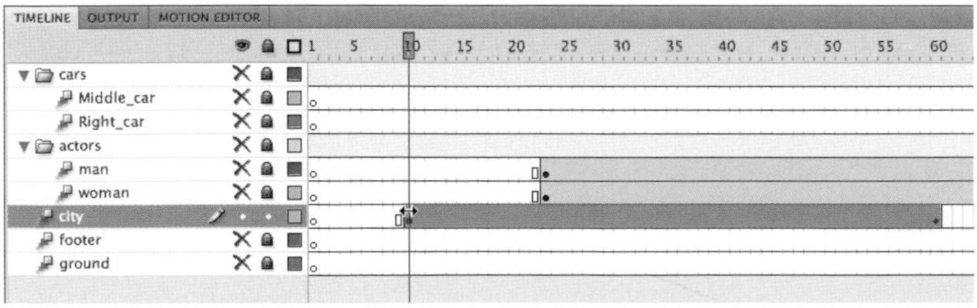

Adding frames

You'll want the last keyframe of your motion tween to hold for the remainder of the animation. Add frames by Shift-dragging the end of a tween span.

1 Move your mouse cursor close to the end of the tween span.

2 Hold down the Shift key and click and drag the end of the tween span forward to frame 190.

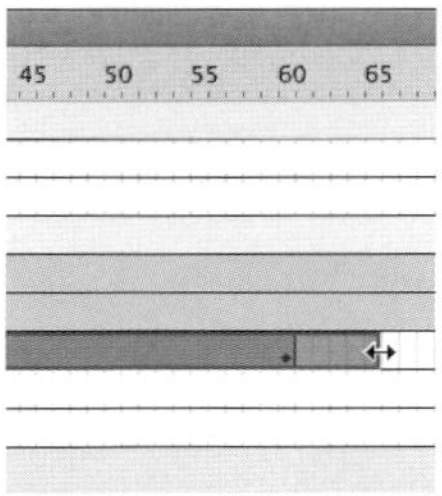

The last keyframe in the motion tween remains at frame 60, but additional frames are added to frame 190.

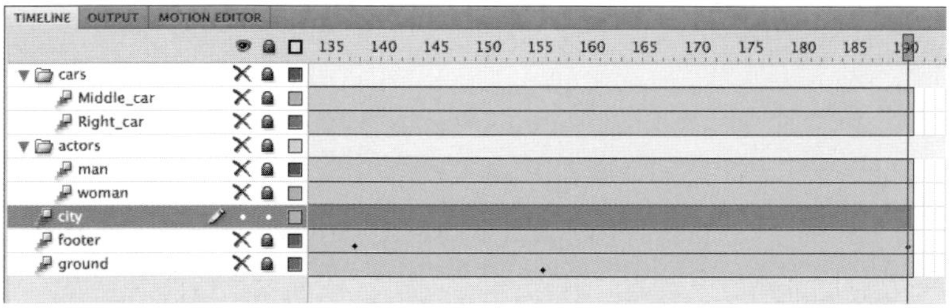

Note: You can also add individual frames by choosing Insert > Timeline > Frame (F5) or remove individual frames by choosing Edit > Timeline > Remove Frames (Shift+F5).

Moving keyframes

When you click on a motion tween on the Timeline, the entire span is selected. This allows you to move the entire motion tween forward or backward in time as a single unit. However, if you want to move particular keyframes within a motion tween to change the pacing of the animation, you have to select individual frames. Holding down the Ctrl (Windows)/Command (Mac) key will let you select single frames or a span of frames within a motion tween.

1 Ctrl-click/Command-click on the keyframe at frame 60.

Just the keyframe at frame 60 is selected. A tiny box appears next to your mouse cursor indicating that you can move the keyframe.

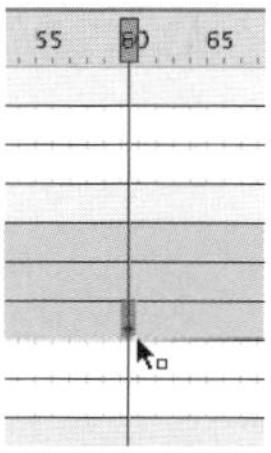

2 Click and drag the keyframe to frame 40.

The last keyframe in the motion tween moves to frame 40, so the motion of the cityscape proceeds quicker.

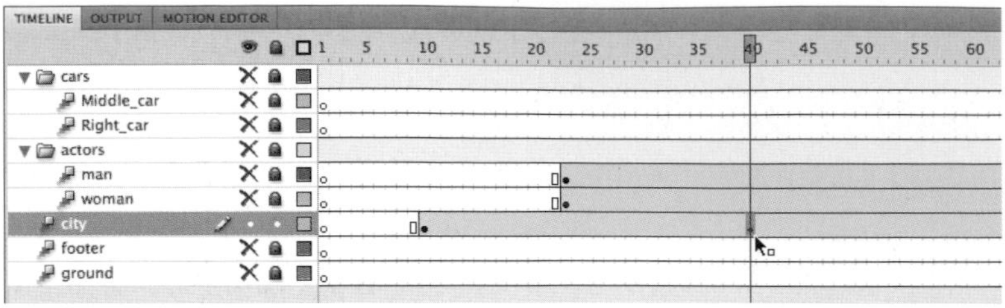

Animating Transparency

In the previous lesson, you learned how to change the color effect of any symbol instance to change the transparency, tint, or brightness. You can change the color effect of an instance in one keyframe and change the value of the color effect in another keyframe, and Flash will automatically display a smooth change, just as it does with changes in position.

You'll change the cityscape in the beginning keyframe to be totally transparent but keep the cityscape in the ending keyframe opaque. Flash will create a smooth fade-in effect.

1 Move the red playhead to the first keyframe of the motion tween (frame 10).

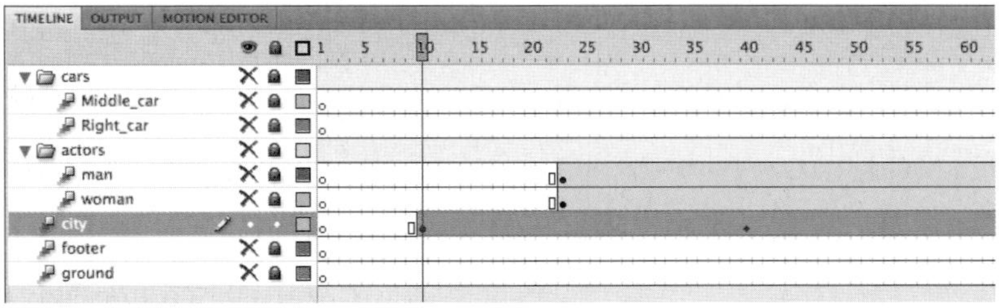

2 Select the cityscape instance on the Stage.

3 In the Properties inspector, choose the Alpha option for Color Effect.

4 Set the Alpha value to **0**%.

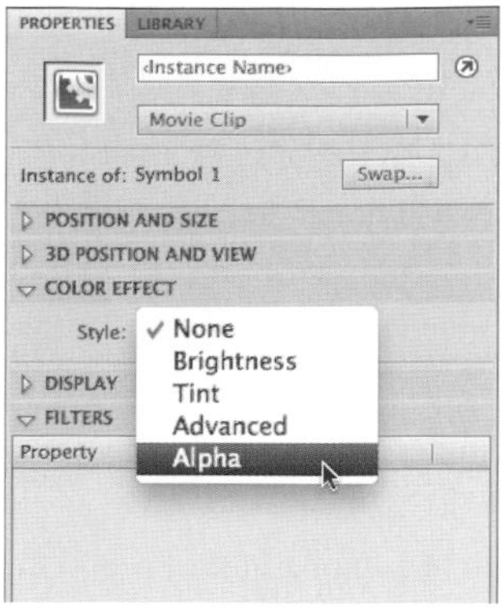

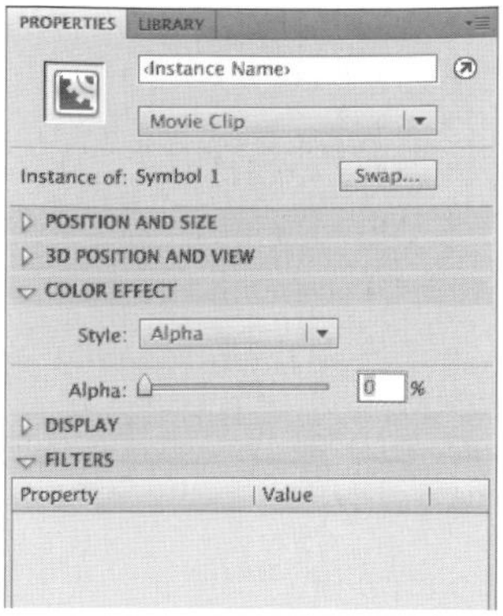

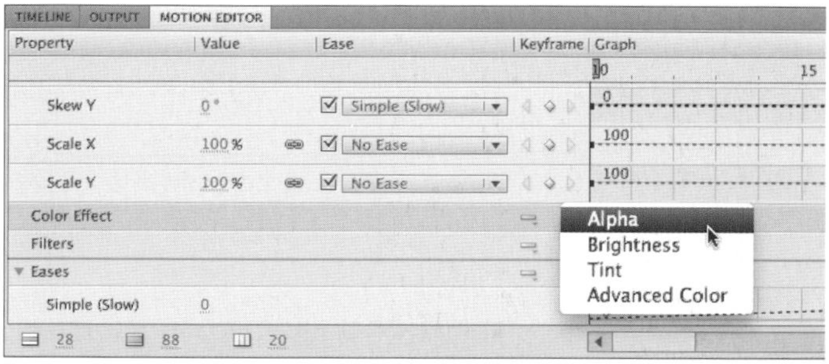

● **Note:** You can also apply a Color Effect through the Motion Editor, as explained later in this lesson. Click the Motion Editor tab next to the Timeline. Click the plus sign next to Color Effect and select Alpha.

The cityscape instance on the Stage becomes totally transparent.

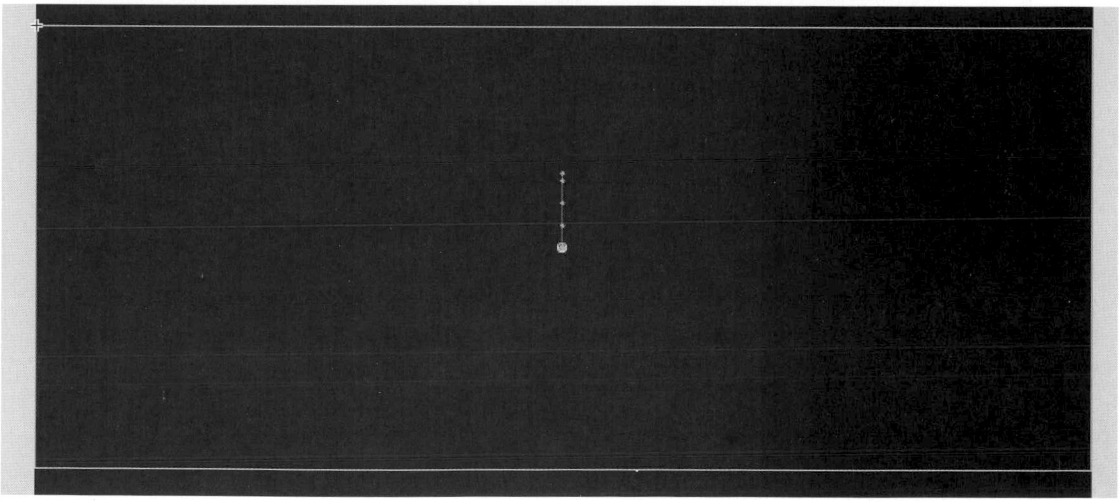

5 Move the red playhead to the last keyframe of the motion tween (frame 40).

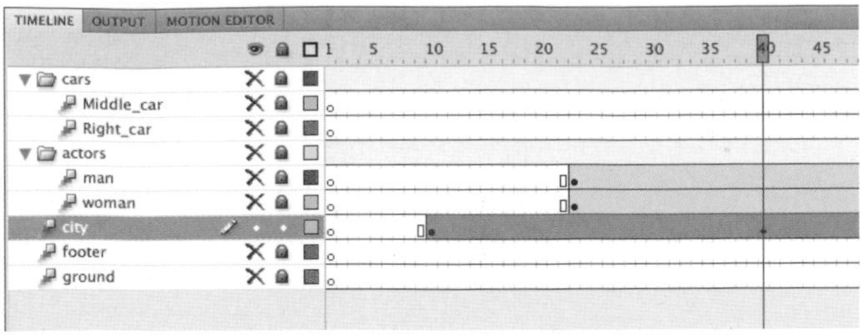

6 Select the cityscape instance on the Stage.

7 In the Properties inspector, under Color Effect, set the Alpha value to **100**%.

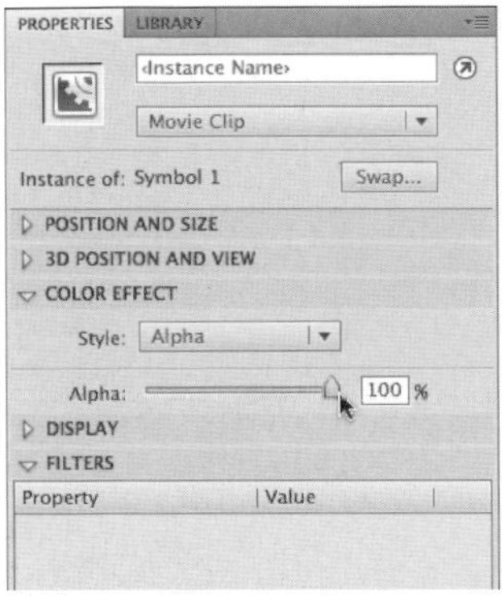

The cityscape instance on the Stage becomes totally opaque.

8 Preview the effect by choosing Control > Play (Enter).

Flash interpolates the changes in both position and transparency between the two keyframes.

Animating Filters

Filters, which give instances special effects such as blurs and drop shadows, can also be animated. You'll refine the motion tween of the actors next by applying a blur filter to one of them to make it appear as if the camera changes focus. Animating filters is no different from animating changes in position or changes in color effect. You simply set the values for a filter at one keyframe and set different values for the filter at another keyframe, and Flash creates a smooth transition.

1 Make the actors layer folder on the Timeline visible.

2 Lock all the layers on the Timeline except the woman layer.

3 Move the red playhead to the beginning keyframe of the motion tween in the woman layer—at frame 23.

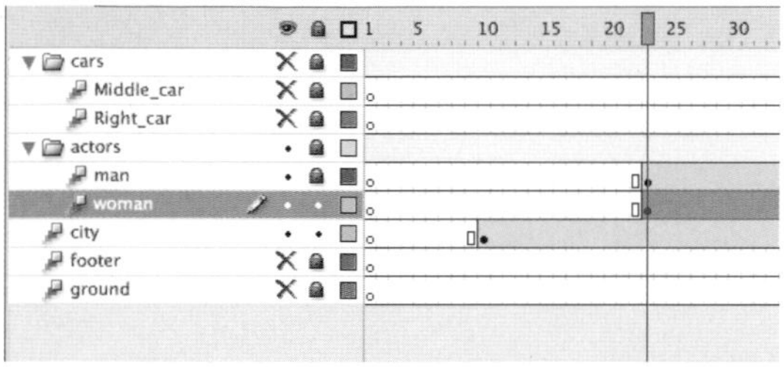

4 Select the instance of the woman on the Stage. You won't be able to see her because she has an alpha value of 0% (totally transparent), but if you click on the top-right side of the Stage, the transparent instance will be selected.

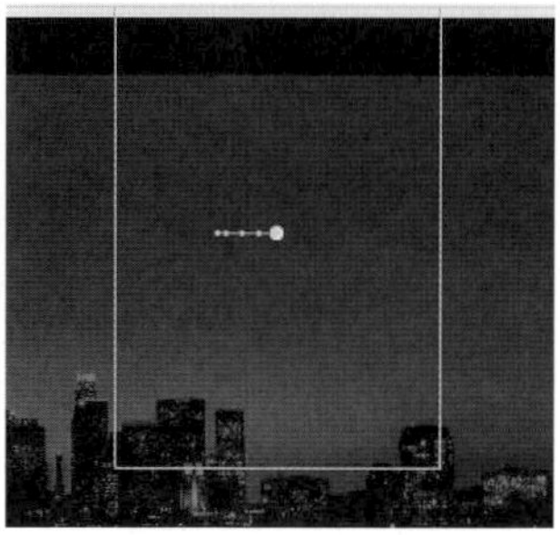

5 In the Properties inspector, expand the Filters section.

6 Click the Add filter button at the bottom of the Filters section and select Blur.

The Blur filter is applied to the instance.

Note: You can also apply a Filter through the Motion Editor, as explained later in this lesson. Click the Motion Editor tab next to the Timeline. Click the plus sign next to Filters and select Blur.

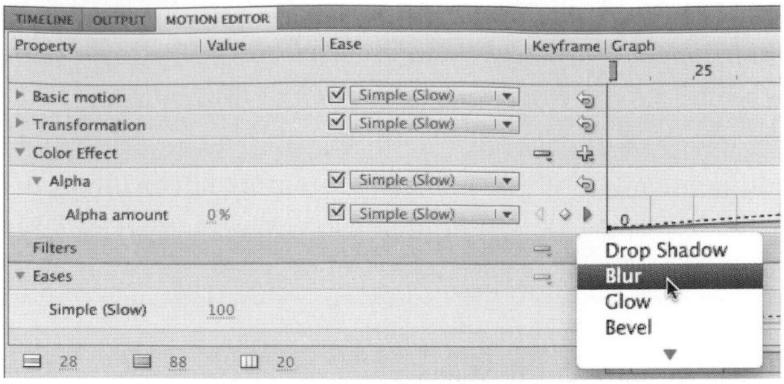

7 In the Filters section of the Properties inspector, click the link icon to constrain the blur values to both the *x* and *y* directions equally. Set the X and Y Blur values to **20** pixels.

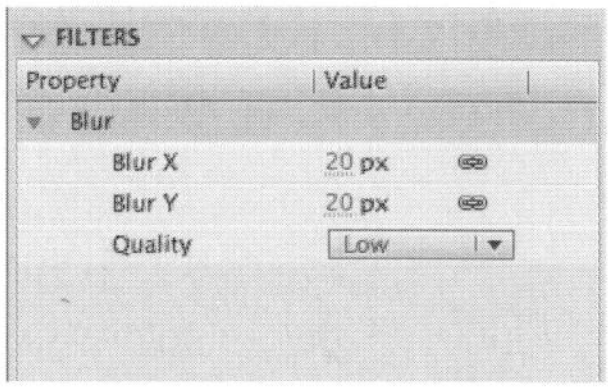

8 Move the red playhead across the entire Timeline to preview the animation.

The 20-pixel Blur filter is applied to the woman instance throughout the motion tween.

9 Position the playhead at frame 140 and right-click/Ctrl-click on the woman layer there. Then choose Insert Keyframe > Filter.

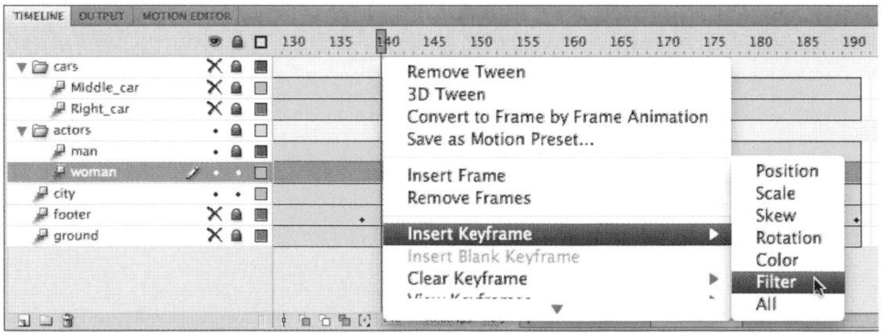

A keyframe for filters is established at frame 140.

10 Move the red playhead to frame 160.

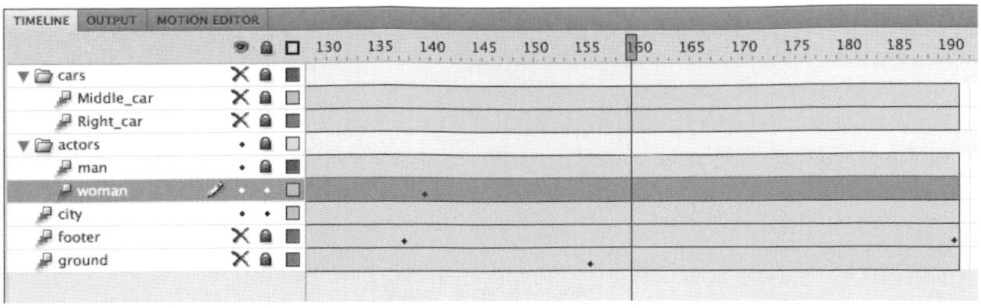

11 Select the instance of the woman on the Stage.

12 In the Properties inspector, change the value of the Blur filter to X=**0** and Y=**0**.

The Blur filter changes from the keyframe at frame 140 to the keyframe at 160. Flash creates a smooth transition from a blurry instance to an in-focus instance.

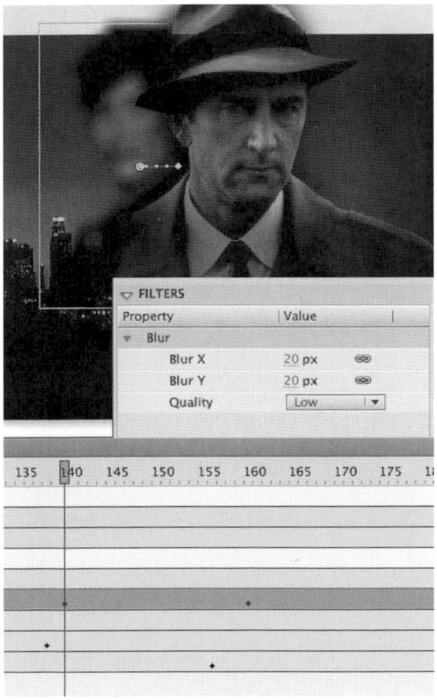

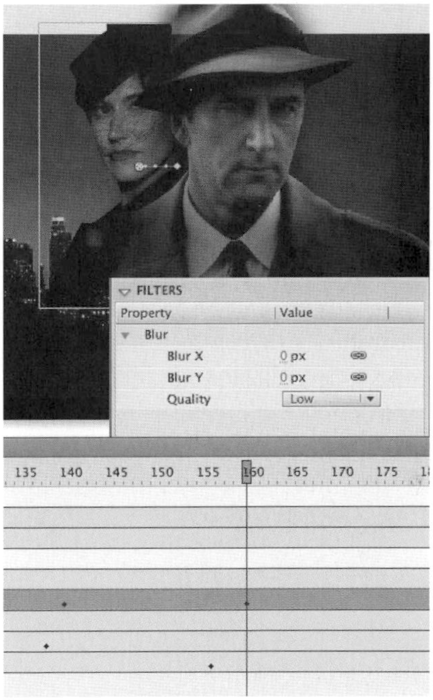

Understanding Property Keyframes

Changes in properties are independent of one another and do not need to be tied to the same keyframes. That is, you can have a keyframe for position, a different keyframe for the color effect, and yet another keyframe for a filter. Managing many different kinds of keyframes can become overwhelming, especially if you want different properties to change at different times during the motion tween. Fortunately, Flash Professional CS6 provides a few helpful tools for keyframe management.

When viewing the tween span, you can choose to view the keyframes of only certain properties. For example, you can choose to view only the position keyframes to see when your object moves. Or, you can choose to view only the filter keyframes to see when there is a filter change. Right-click/Ctrl-click on a motion tween in the Timeline, choose View Keyframes, and then select the desired property among the list. You can also choose All or None to see all the properties or none of the properties.

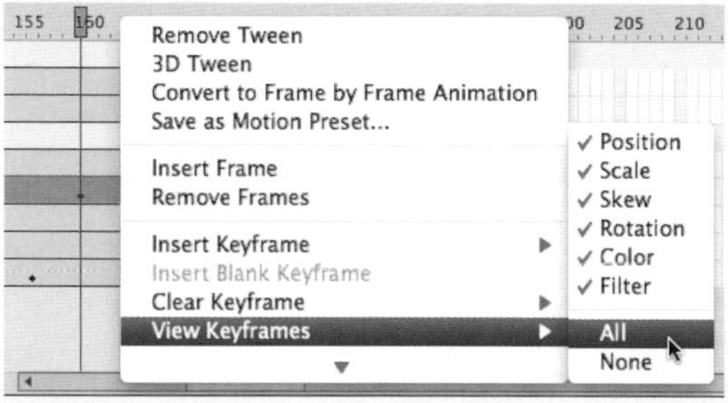

When inserting a keyframe, you can also insert a keyframe specific to the property you want to change. Right-click/Ctrl-click on a motion tween in the Timeline, choose Insert Keyframes, and then select the desired property.

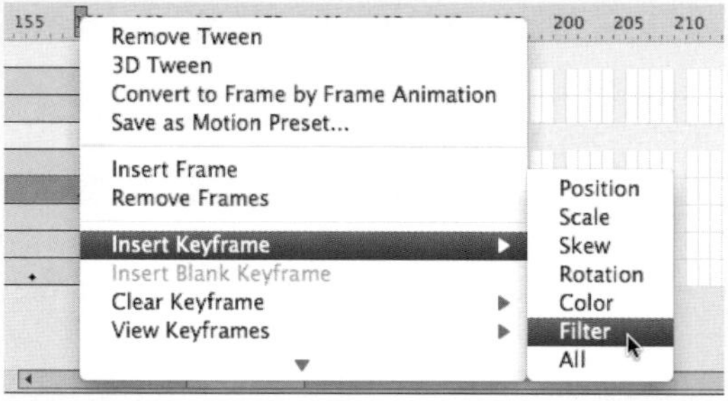

The Motion Editor is a special panel that displays all the properties of your motion tween visually as lines on a graph. The Motion Editor is helpful when multiple properties are changing at different times. For example, the Motion Editor for the woman is shown in the screenshot below, and shows changes in the *x*-position and Alpha values in the first few frames, and changes in the Blur filter in the last few frames.

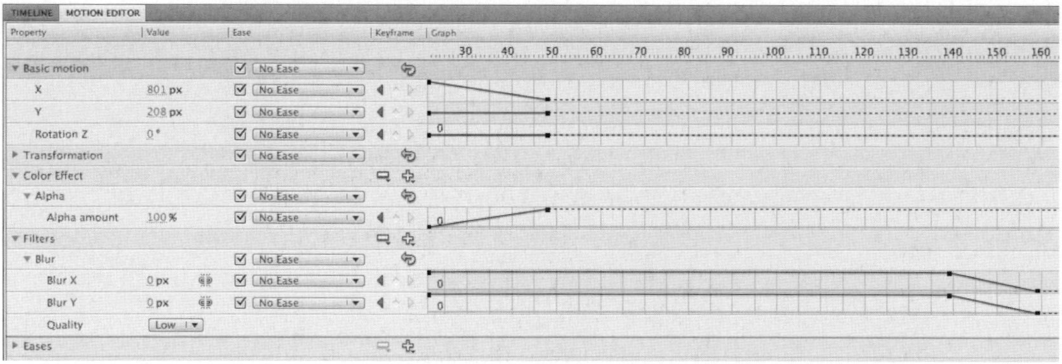

You'll learn more about how to use the Motion Editor later in this lesson.

Animating Transformations

Now you'll learn how to animate changes in scale or rotation. These kinds of changes are made with the Free Transform tool or with the Transform panel. You'll add a third car to the project. The car will start small, and then become larger as it appears to move forward toward the viewer.

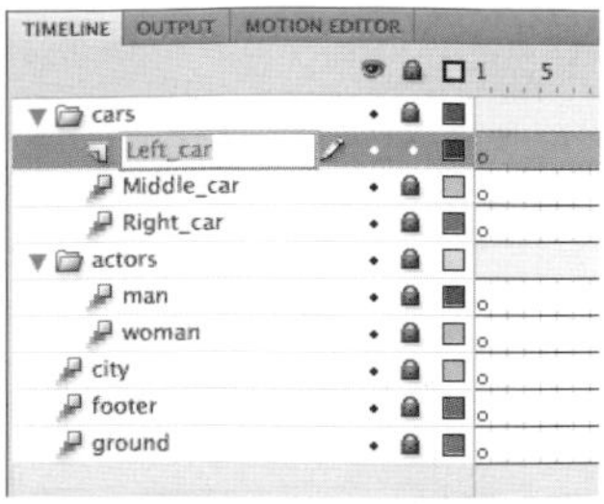

1 Lock all the layers on the Timeline.

2 Insert a new layer inside the Cars folder and rename it **Left_car**.

3 Select frame 75 and insert a new keyframe (F6).

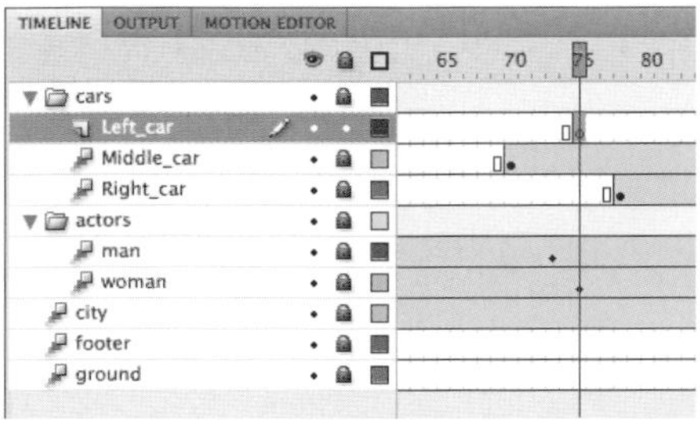

4 Drag the movie clip symbol called carLeft from the Library panel to the Stage at frame 75.

5 Select the Free Transform tool.

The transformation handles appear around the instance on the Stage.

6 While holding down the Shift key, click and drag the corner handle inward to make the car smaller.

7 In the Properties inspector, make sure that the width of the car is about 400 pixels.

8 Alternatively, you can use the Transform panel (Window > Transform) and change the scale of the car to about **29.4**%.

9 Move the car to its starting position at about X=710 and Y=488.

10 In the Properties inspector, select Alpha for the Color Effect.

11 Set the value of the Alpha to **0**%.

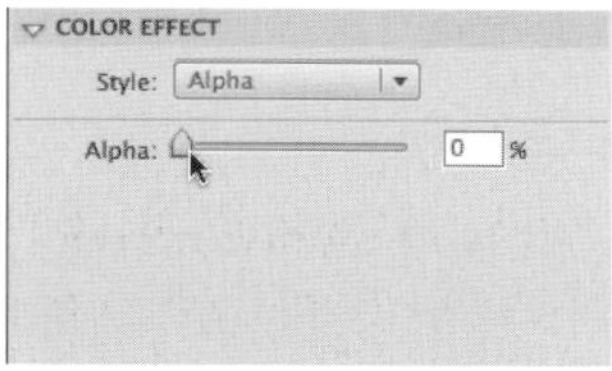

The car becomes totally transparent.

12 Right-click/Ctrl-click on the car on the Stage and select Create Motion Tween.

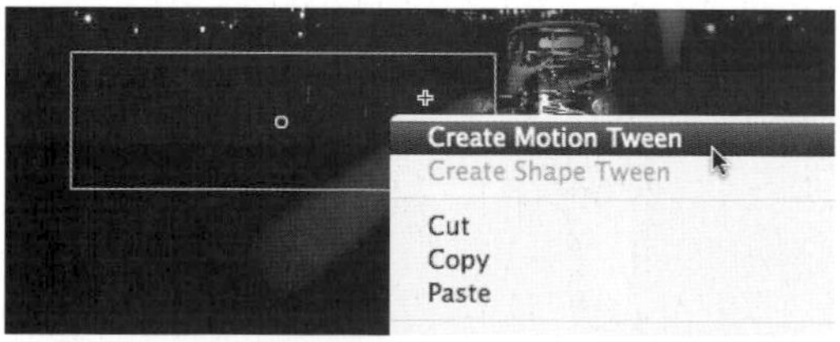

The current layer becomes a Tween layer.

13 Move the red playhead on the Timeline to frame 100.

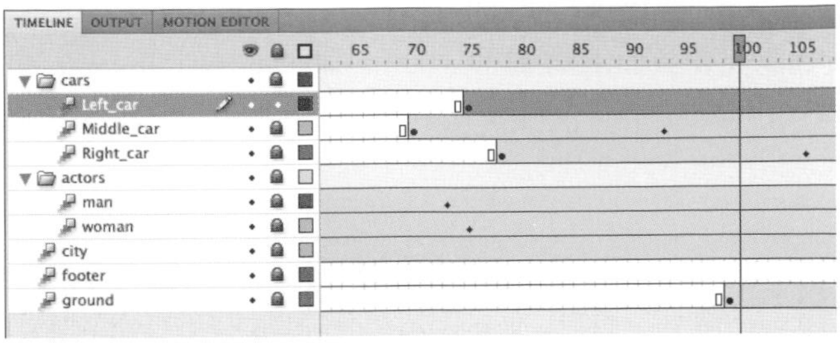

14 Select the transparent instance of the car, and in the Properties inspector, change the Alpha value to **100**%.

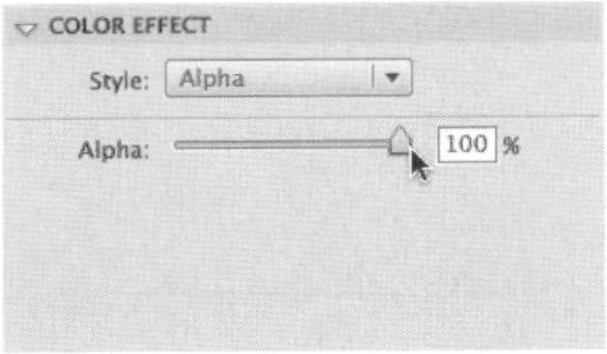

A new keyframe is automatically inserted at frame 100 to indicate the change in transparency.

15 Select the Free Transform tool if it's not already selected.

16 While holding down the Shift key, click and drag the corner handle outward to make the car larger. For more precision, use the Properties inspector and set the dimensions of the car to width=**1379.5** pixels and height=**467.8** pixels.

17 Position the car at X=607 and Y=545.

18 Move the Left_car layer in between the Middle_car and Right_car layers so that the car in the center overlaps the cars on the side.

Flash tweens the change in position and the change in scale from frame 75 to frame 100. Flash also tweens the change in transparency from frame 75 to frame 100.

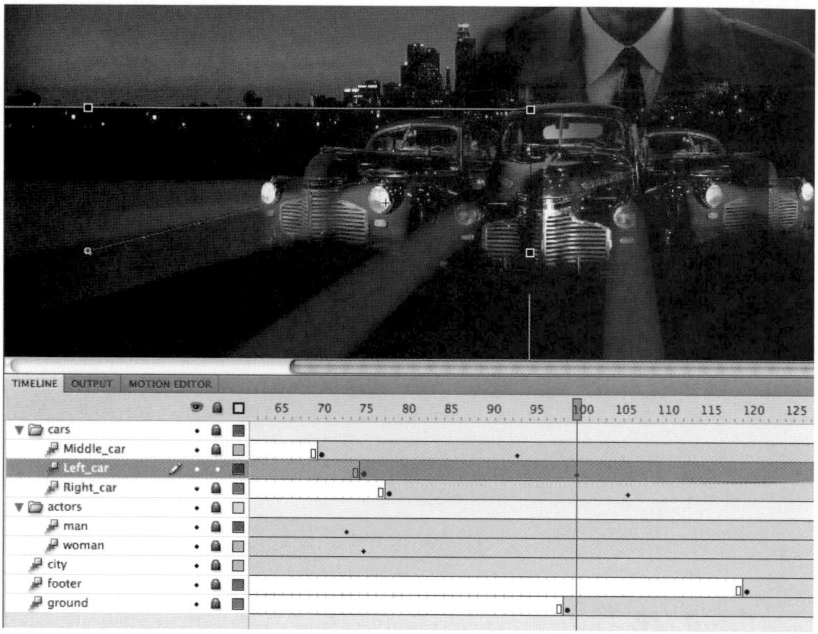

Motion Presets

If your project involves creating identical motion tweens repeatedly, Flash provides a panel called Motion Presets that can help. The Motion Presets panel (Window > Motion Presets) can store any motion tween so you can apply it to different instances on the Stage.

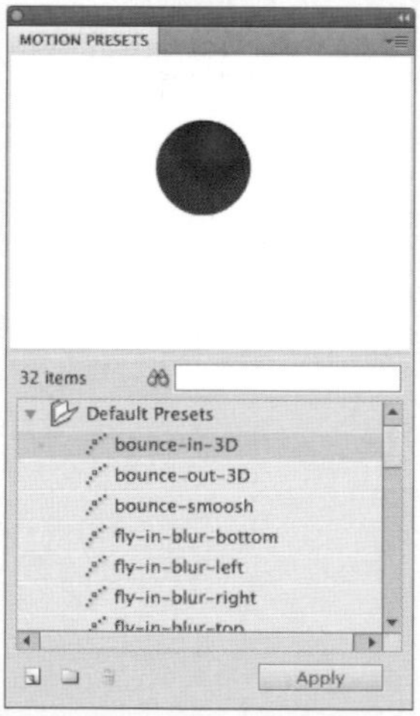

For example, if you want to build a slide show where each image fades out in the same manner, you can save that transition to the Motion Presets panel.

1. Select the first motion tween on the Timeline or the instance on the Stage.
2. In the Motion Presets panel, click the Save selection as preset button at the bottom of the panel.
3. Name your motion preset, and it will be saved in the Motion Presets panel.
4. Select a new instance on the Stage and choose the motion preset.
5. Click Apply and your saved motion preset will be applied to the new instance.

Flash provides a number of motion presets that you can use to quickly build sophisticated animations without much effort.

Changing the Path of the Motion

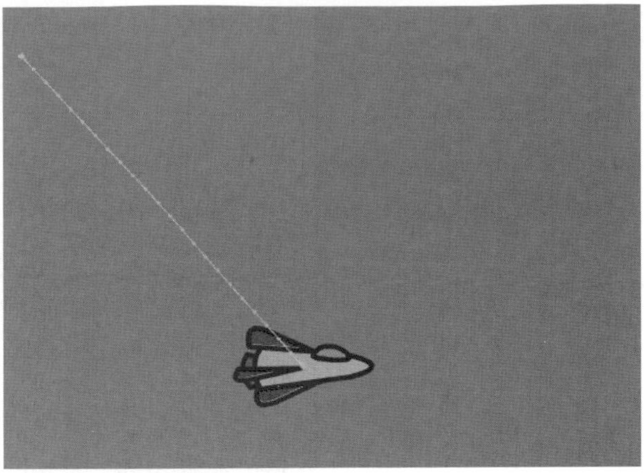

The motion tween of the left car that you just animated shows a colored line with dots indicating the path of the motion. The path of the motion can be edited easily so that the car travels in a curve, or the path can be moved, scaled, or even rotated just like any other object on the Stage.

To better demonstrate how you can edit the path of the motion, open the sample file 04MotionPath.fla in the 04Start folder. The file contains a single Tween layer with a rocket ship moving from the top left of the Stage to the bottom right.

Moving the path of the motion

You will move the path of the motion so the relative movement of the rocket ship remains the same but its starting and ending positions change.

1 Choose the Selection tool.

2 Click on the path of the motion to select it.

The path of the motion becomes highlighted when it is selected.

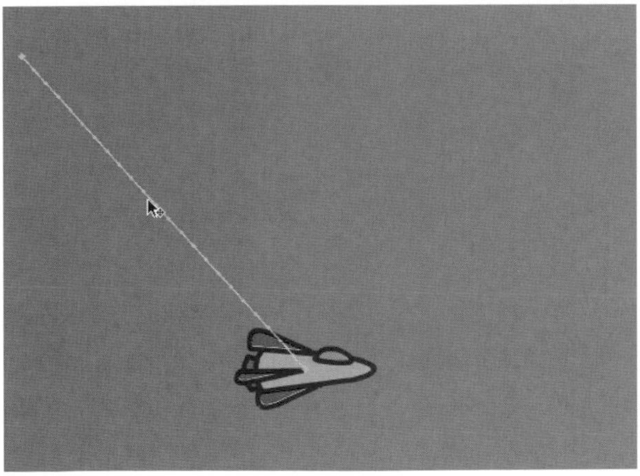

3 Click and drag the motion path to move it to a different place on the Stage.

The relative motion and timing of the animation remain the same, but the starting and ending positions are relocated.

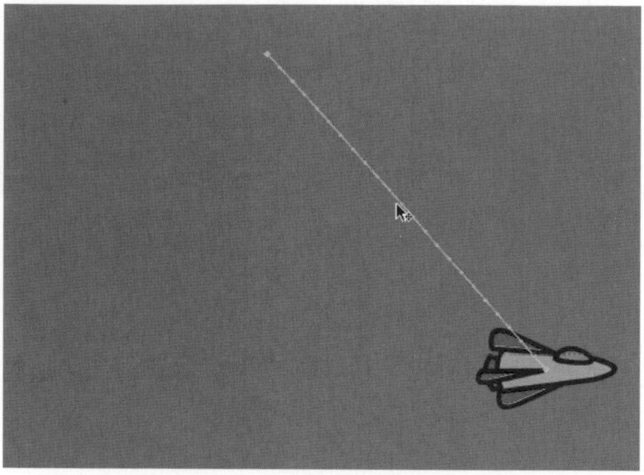

Changing the scale or rotation of the path

The path of the motion can also be manipulated with the Free Transform tool.

1 Select the path of the motion.

2 Choose the Free Transform tool.

Transformation handles appear around the path of the motion.

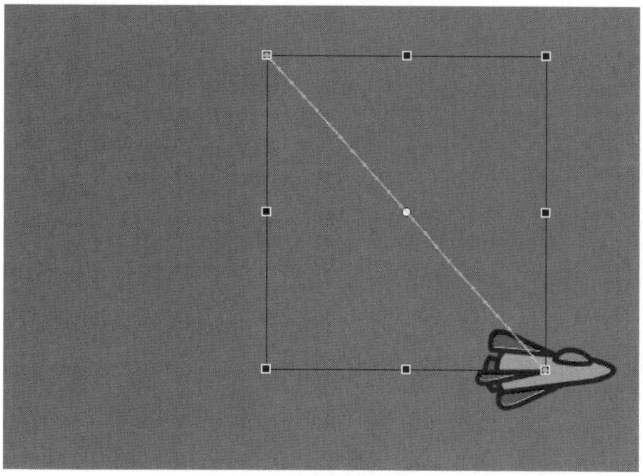

3 Scale or rotate the path of the motion as desired. You can make the path smaller or larger, or rotate the path so the rocket ship starts from the bottom left of the Stage and ends at the top right.

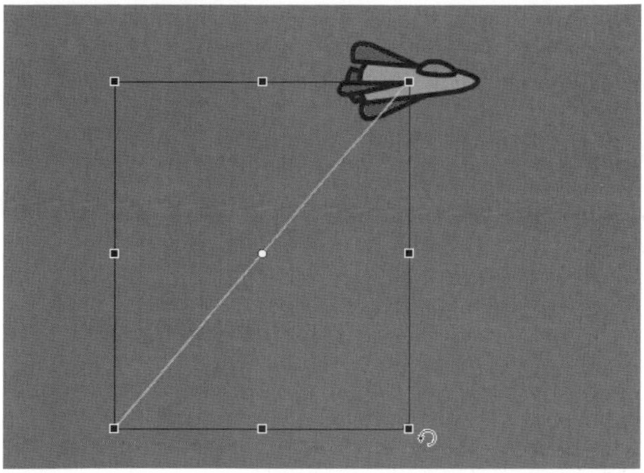

Editing the path of the motion

Making your objects travel on a curved path is a simple matter. You can either edit the path with Bézier precision using anchor point handles, or you can edit the path in a more intuitive manner with the Selection tool.

1 Choose the Convert Anchor Point tool, which is hidden under the Pen tool.

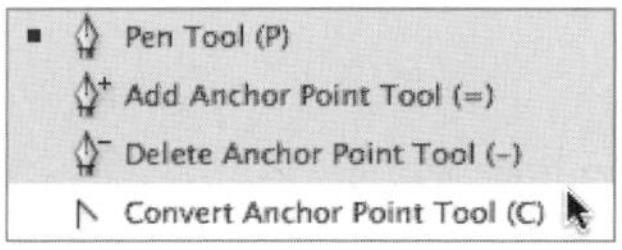

2 Click on the starting point or the ending point of the motion path on the Stage and drag the control handle out from the anchor point.

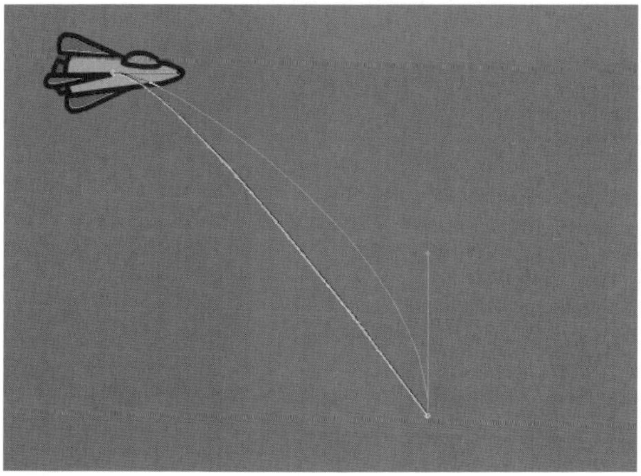

The handle on the anchor point controls the curvature of the path.

3 Choose the Subselection tool.

4 Click and drag the handle to edit the curve of the path. Make the rocket ship travel in a wide curve.

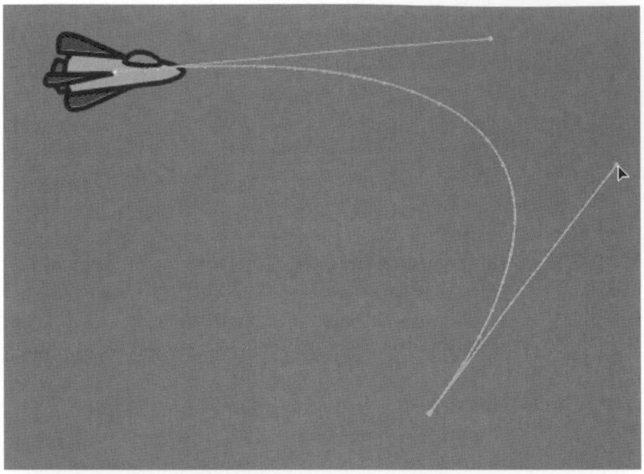

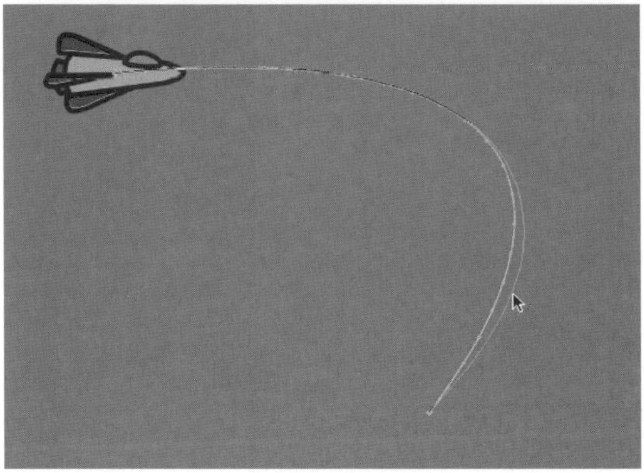

Note: The path of the motion can also be directly manipulated with the Selection tool. Choose the Selection tool and move it close to the path of the motion. A curved icon appears next to your cursor indicating that you can edit the path. Click and drag the path of the motion to change its curvature.

Orienting objects to the path

Sometimes the orientation of the object traveling along the path is important. In the motion picture splash page project, the orientation of the car is constant as it rumbles forward. However, in the rocket ship example, the rocket ship should follow the path with its nose pointed in the direction in which it is heading. The Orient to path option in the Properties inspector gives you this option.

1 Select the motion tween on the Timeline.

2 In the Properties inspector, under Rotation, select the Orient to path option.

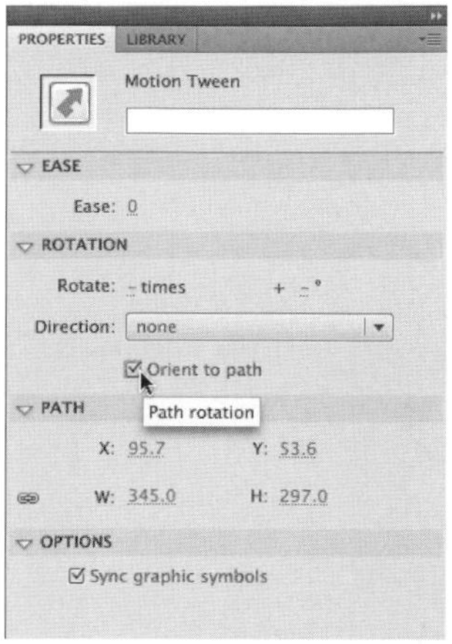

Flash inserts keyframes for rotation along the motion tween so that the nose of the rocket ship is oriented to the path of the motion.

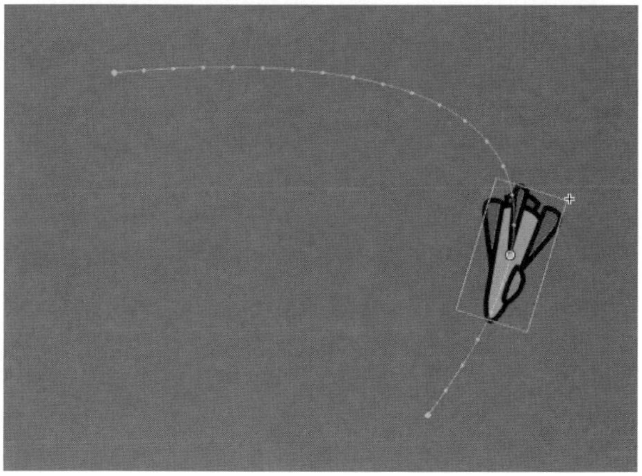

Note: To direct the nose of the rocket ship, or any other object, along the path of its motion, you must orient its position so that it is facing in the direction that you want it to travel. Use the Free Transform tool to rotate its initial position so that it is oriented correctly.

Swapping Tween Targets

The motion tween model in Flash Professional CS6 is object based. This means that an object and its motion are independent of each other, and you can easily swap out the target of a motion tween. If, for example, you'd rather see an alien moving around the Stage instead of a rocket ship, you can replace the target of the motion tween with an alien symbol from your Library panel and still preserve the animation.

1 Select the rocket ship on the Stage to select the motion tween.

2 Drag the movie clip symbol of the alien from the Library panel onto the rocket ship.

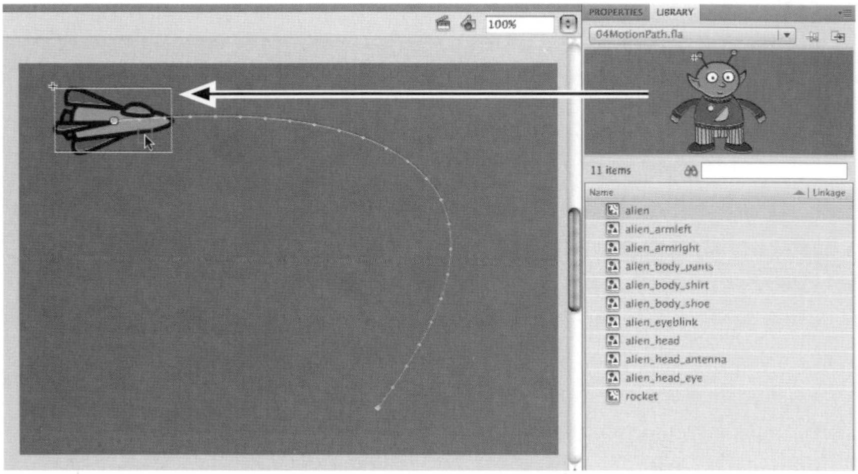

Flash asks you if you want to replace the existing tween target object with a new object.

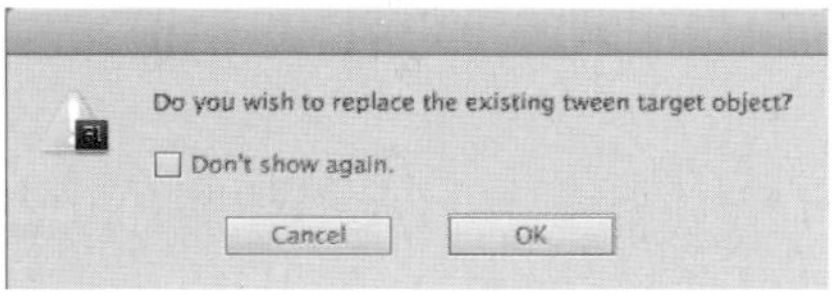

3 Click OK.

Flash replaces the rocket ship with the alien. The motion remains the same, but the target of the motion tween has been swapped.

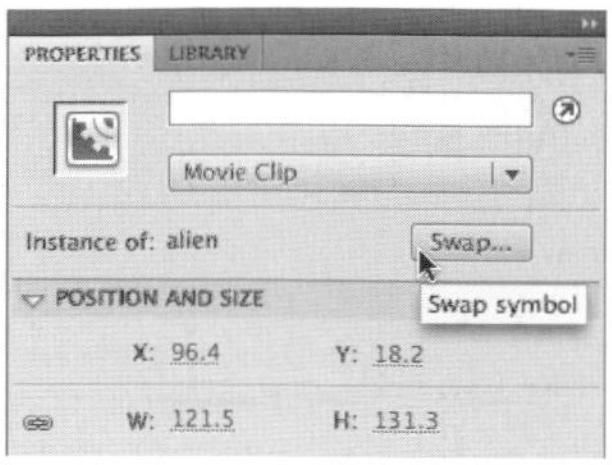

Note: You can also swap instances in the Properties inspector. Select the object that you want to swap on the Stage. In the Properties inspector, click the Swap button. In the dialog box that appears, choose a new symbol and click OK. Flash will swap the target of the motion tween.

Creating Nested Animations

Often, an object that is animated on the Stage will have its own animation. For example, a butterfly moving across the Stage will have an animation of its wings flapping as it moves. Or the alien that you swapped with the rocket ship could be waving his arms. These kinds of animations are called *nested animations*, because they are contained inside the movie clip symbols. Movie clip symbols have their own Timeline that is independent of the main Timeline.

In this example, you'll make the alien wave his arms inside the movie clip symbol, so he'll be waving as he moves across the Stage.

Creating animations inside movie clip symbols

1 In the Library panel, double-click the alien movie clip symbol icon.

You are now in symbol-editing mode for the alien movie clip symbol. The alien is in the middle of the Stage. In the Timeline, the parts of the alien are separated in layers.

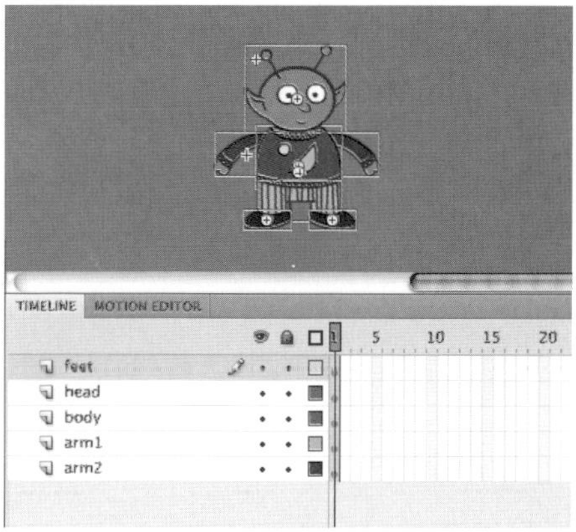

2 Choose the Selection tool.

3 Right click/Ctrl-click on the alien's left arm and choose Create Motion Tween.

Flash converts the current layer to a Tween layer and inserts one second worth of frames so you can begin to animate the instance.

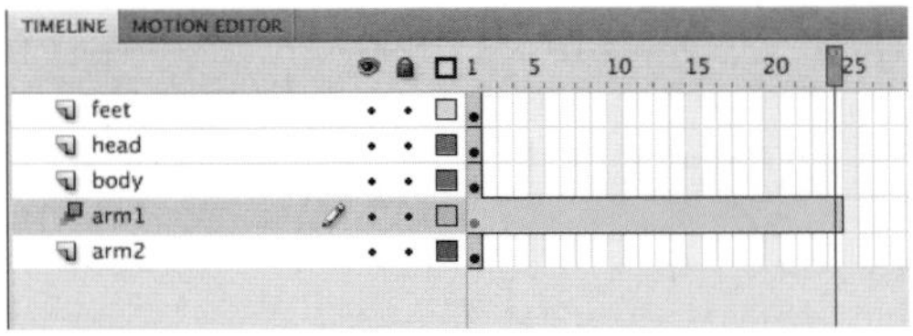

4 Choose the Free Transform tool.

5 Drag the corner rotation control points to rotate the arm upward to the alien's shoulder height.

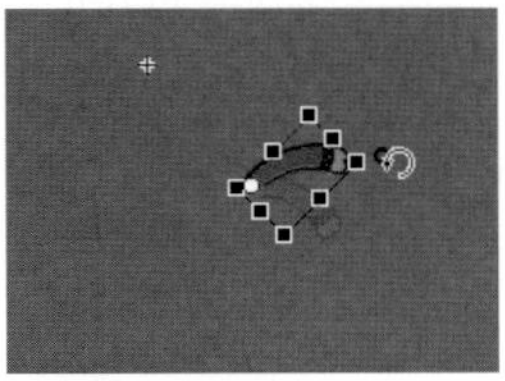

A keyframe is inserted at the end of the motion tween. The right arm rotates smoothly from the resting position to the outstretched position.

6 Move the red playhead back to frame 1.

7 Now create a motion tween for the alien's other arm. Right-click/Ctrl-click on his right arm and choose Create Motion Tween.

Flash converts the current layer to a Tween layer and inserts one second worth of frames so you can begin to animate the instance.

8 Choose the Free Transform tool.

9 Drag the corner rotation control points to rotate the arm upward to the alien's shoulder height.

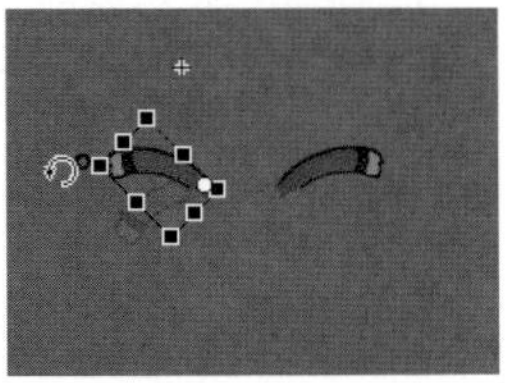

A keyframe is inserted at the end of the motion tween. The arm rotates smoothly from the resting position to the outstretched position.

10 Select the last frame in all the other layers and insert frames (F5) so that the head, body, and feet all remain on the Stage for the same amount of time as the moving arms.

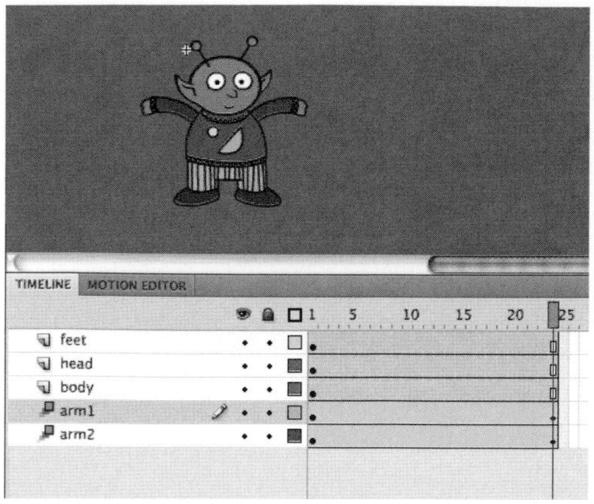

11 Exit symbol-editing mode by clicking the Scene 1 button at the top left of the Stage.

Your animation of the alien raising his arms is complete. Wherever you use the movie clip symbol, the alien will continue to play its nested animation.

12 Preview the animation by choosing Control > Test Movie > in Flash Professional.

Flash opens a window showing the exported animation. The alien moves along the motion path while the nested animation of his arms moving plays and loops.

Note: Animations inside of movie clip symbols won't play on the main timeline. Choose Control > Test Movie > in Flash Professional to preview nested animations.

Note: Animations inside movie clip symbols will loop automatically. To prevent the looping, you need to add ActionScript to tell the movie clip Timeline to stop on its last frame. You'll learn more about ActionScript in Lesson 6, "Creating Interactive Navigation."

Using the Motion Editor

The Motion Editor panel provides in-depth information and editing capabilities for all the properties of a motion tween. The Motion Editor is located behind the Timeline and can be accessed by clicking the top tab or by choosing Window > Motion Editor. The animated object on the Stage or the tween on the Timeline must be selected in order for the Motion Editor to display its information.

On the left side of the Motion Editor, an expandable list of properties is displayed along with those properties' values and easing options. On the right side, a timeline shows various lines and curves representing how those properties change.

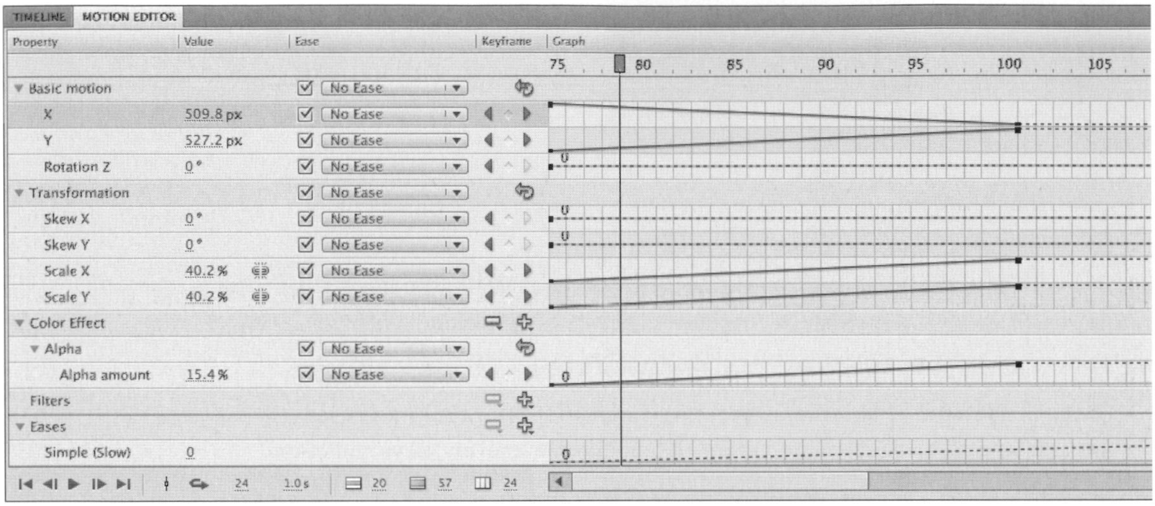

Setting the Motion Editor display options

Options for displaying the Motion Editor are listed at the bottom of the panel.

1 Select the alien on the Stage.

2 Open the Motion Editor panel if it is not already visible.

3 Move your cursor over the gray horizontal bar separating the Motion Editor from the Stage.

   Your cursor changes to a double-headed arrow indicating that you can increase or decrease the height of the Motion Editor panel.

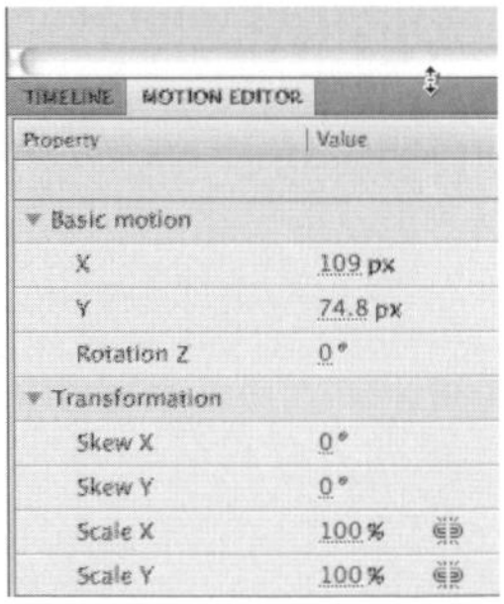

4 Click and drag the horizontal bar to increase the height of the Motion Editor panel.

5 Click the triangles to collapse all the properties categories on the left. You can expand or collapse the categories to see only those categories you are interested in.

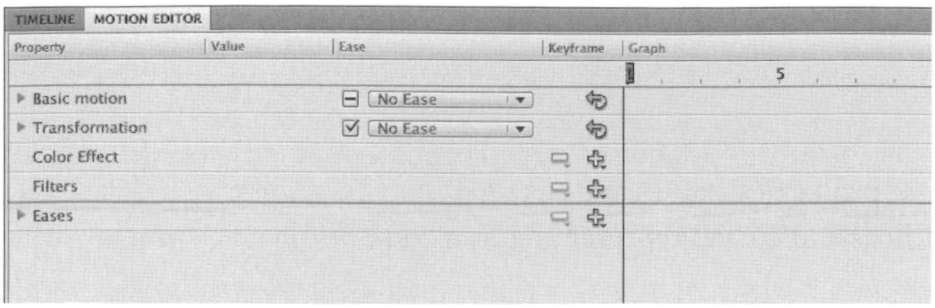

6 Click and drag the number next to the Viewable Frames icon at the bottom of the Motion Editor to change the number of frames that appear in the graph. Set the Viewable Frames value to the maximum to see the entire motion tween.

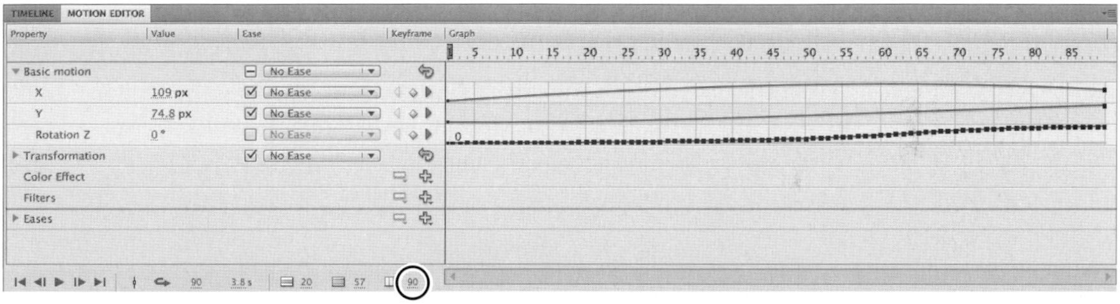

7 Click and drag the number next to the Graph Size icon at the bottom of the Motion Editor to change the vertical height of each property that is listed on the left.

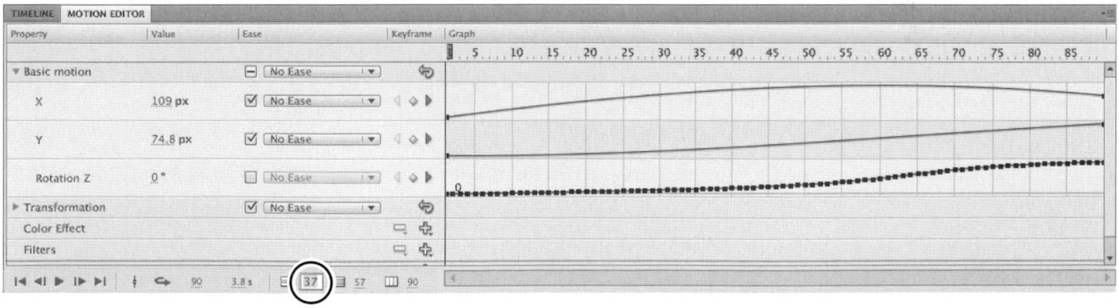

8 Click and drag the number next to the Expanded Graph Size icon at the bottom of the Motion Editor to change the vertical height of each selected property.

To see how the Expanded Graph Size option affects the display, click the X property under Basic motion. The larger the Expanded Graph Size value, the more of the selected property you can view.

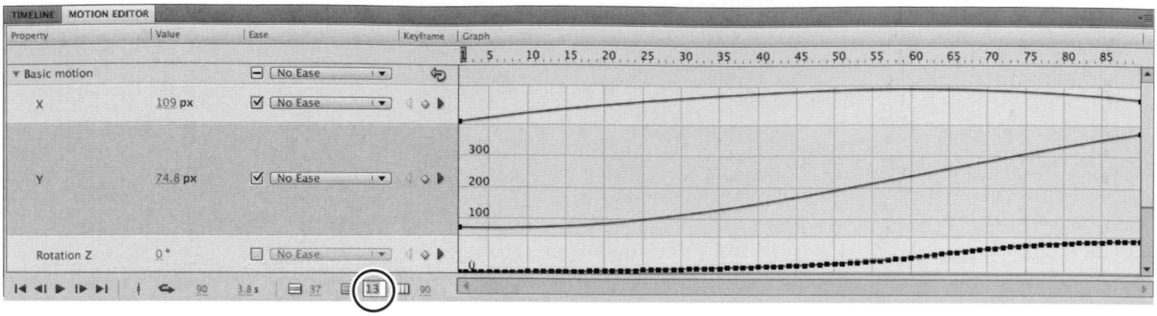

Changing property values

You will change another property of your flapping alien with the Motion Editor and see how easy it is to animate multiple properties independently. For this example, you'll create a fade-in effect by changing the Alpha property.

1 Next to the Color Effect property, click the Plus icon and choose Alpha.

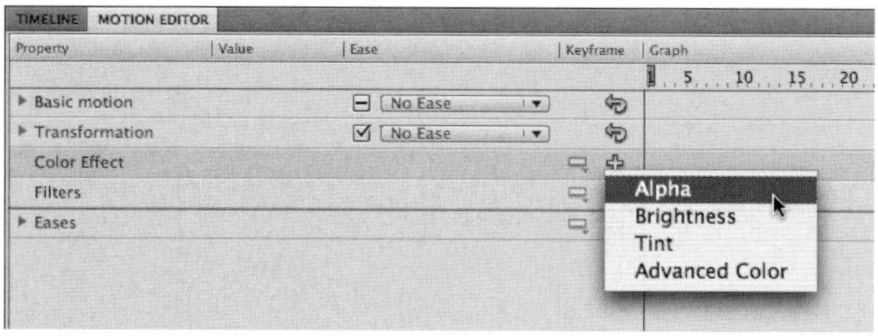

The Alpha property appears in the Motion Editor under the Color Effect category.

2 Select the Alpha amount.

The Alpha property expands, displaying a black-dotted horizontal line at 100% extending from frame 1 to the end of the timeline. This line represents the opacity of the alien throughout the motion tween.

3 Click on the first keyframe, which is indicated by a black square, and drag it down to 0%. You can also change the Alpha value by clicking and dragging the value next to the Alpha amount.

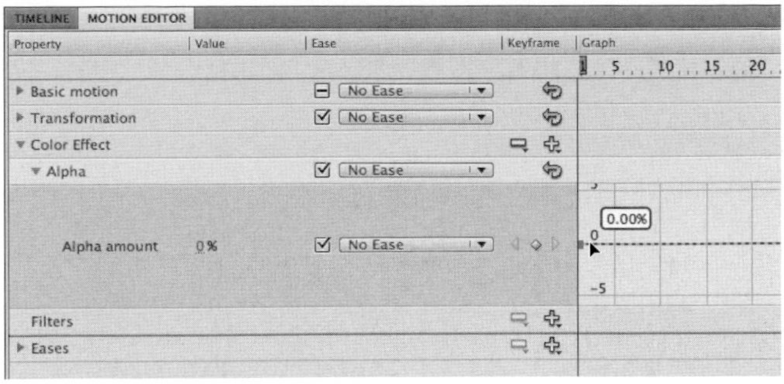

The alien becomes transparent beginning at frame 1.

Inserting keyframes

Inserting keyframes is easy.

1 In the Motion Editor, move the red playhead to frame 20.

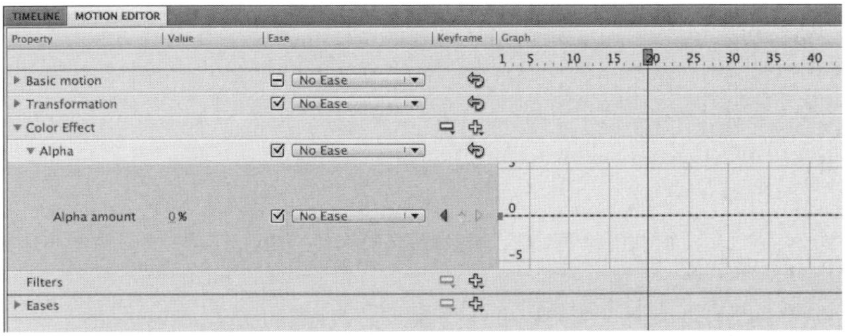

2 Click the diamond icon to add a keyframe at that point in time for the Alpha property. You can also right-click/Ctrl-click on the graph and choose Insert Keyframe.

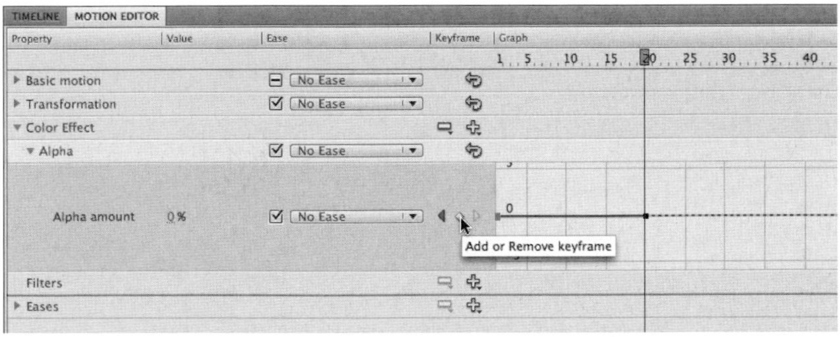

A new keyframe for the Alpha property is inserted at frame 20 indicated by a black square on the graph.

3 Click on the second keyframe.

The selected keyframe becomes highlighted.

4 Drag the second keyframe up to change the Alpha value to 100%.

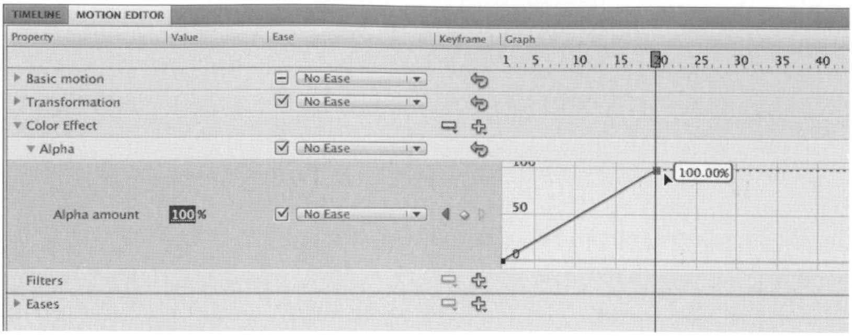

Flash animates the smooth transition of transparency from frame 1 to frame 20.

Editing keyframes

You can easily navigate keyframes and remove them, and you can move keyframes to control the precise timing of each of your transitions.

- Click the left or right arrow beside the diamond-shaped icon to move quickly between keyframes.
- Right-click/Ctrl-click on any keyframe and choose Remove Keyframe to delete a keyframe.
- Select a keyframe and click the yellow diamond to delete the keyframe.
- Shift-click to select multiple contiguous keyframes and move them together.

Resetting values and deleting properties

If you've made a mistake in setting a property, you can easily reset its value or delete it from the Motion Editor entirely so the property won't be animated.

1 Click the Reset Values button to reset the property to its default values.

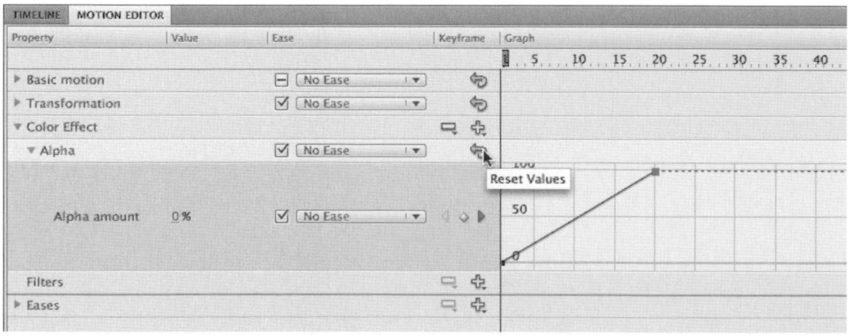

2 Click the Minus button and select Alpha to delete the property from the Motion Editor.

Choose Edit > Undo (Ctrl-Z/Cmd-Z) to restore the Alpha property because you'll be working with it in the next section.

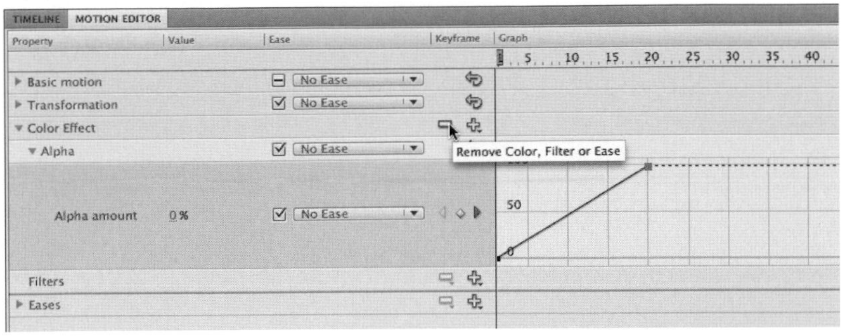

Easing

Easing refers to the way in which a motion tween proceeds. In the most basic sense, it can be thought of as acceleration or deceleration. An object that moves from one side of the Stage to the other side can start off slowly, then build up momentum, and then stop suddenly. Or, the object can start off quickly, and then gradually come to a halt. But easing can also be more complicated. It can describe motion that oscillates, bounces, and does other complex patterns. Your keyframes still indicate the beginning and end points of the motion, but the easing determines how your object gets from one keyframe to the next.

Easing is best visualized in the Motion Editor. The graphs that connect one keyframe to another are usually straight lines, which indicate that the change from one value to the next value proceeds linearly. However, if you want a more gradual change from the starting position (known as an ease-in), the line would be curved near the beginning keyframe, indicating a slower start. A gradual slowdown (known as an ease-out) would be represented by a curve near the ending keyframe.

Setting eases of a motion tween

You can create an ease by customizing the curvature of the property graph in the Motion Editor.

1 In the Motion Editor, right-click/Ctrl-click the second keyframe in the Alpha property and choose Smooth point.

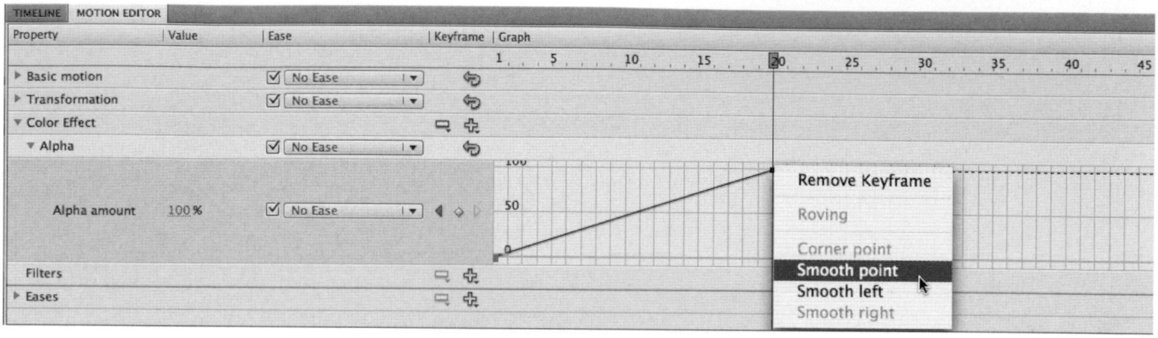

Control handles appear from the keyframe, which you can move to change the curvature of the line.

2 Click and drag the control handle to create a smooth curve approaching the 100% Alpha value.

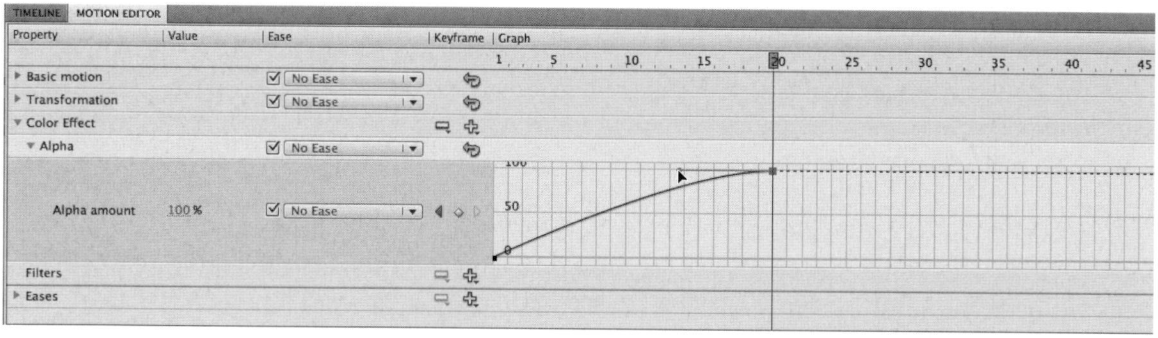

The transition from 0% to 100% Alpha slows down as it approaches 100% (ease-out).

3 Right-click/Ctrl-click the first keyframe in the Alpha property and choose Smooth point.

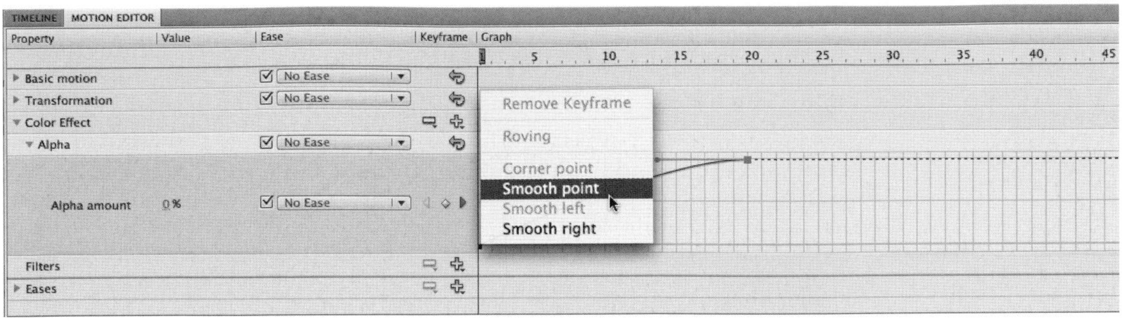

Control handles appear from the keyframe, which you can move to change the curvature of the line.

4 Click and drag the control handle to create a smooth curve as the line begins from 0%.

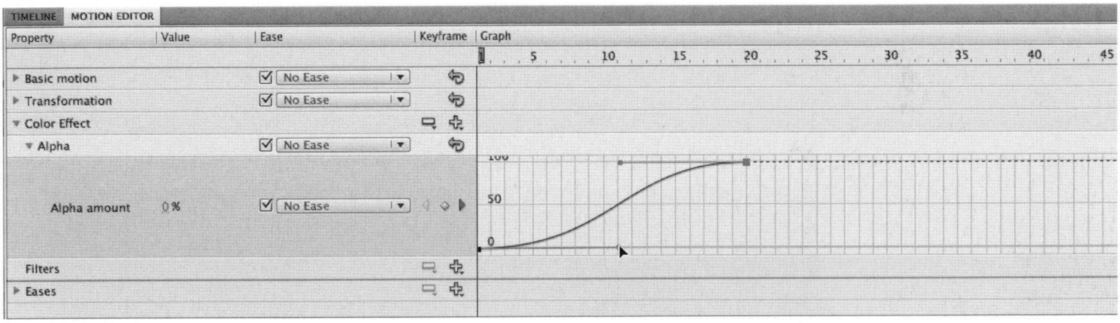

The transition from 0% to 100% Alpha begins gradually from 0% in addition to slowing down. The total effect of the S-shaped curve is both an ease-in and an ease-out effect.

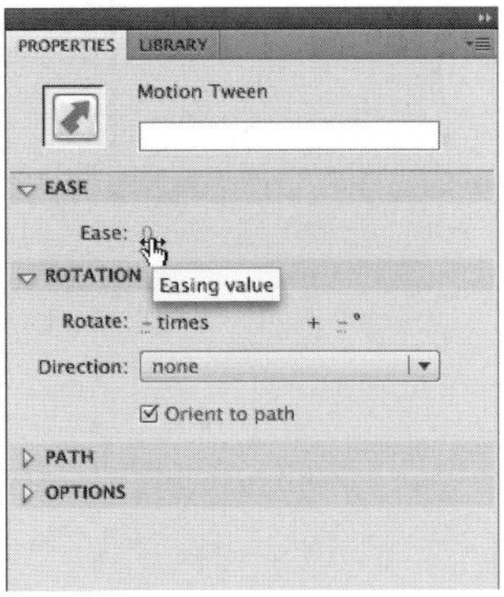

Note: You can also apply ease-in and ease-out effects from the Properties inspector. In the Timeline (not the Motion Editor), select the motion tween. In the Properties inspector, enter an easing value between –100 (ease-in) to 100 (ease-out).

Note: Easing values applied via the Properties inspector will be applied globally to all the properties throughout the entire motion tween. With the Motion Editor, you have precise control over individual properties and eases between keyframes.

Using preset eases

Easing can be very powerful and can be used to create many specialized motions. For example, a bouncing motion can be created with just two positional keyframes and an ease that moves the object back and forth between the two positions.

For the next example, you'll return to the motion picture project and add a preset ease to the motion of the car. You'll make the car shudder up and down to mimic the motion of an idling car. The motion tween will be created inside the movie clip symbol of the car.

1 Continue with your Flash project in progress, 04_workingcopy.fla.

2 In the Library panel, double-click the movie clip symbol called carLeft.

   Flash takes you to symbol-editing mode for the movie clip symbol. Two layers are inside this symbol: the top layer called lights, and the bottom layer called smallRumble.

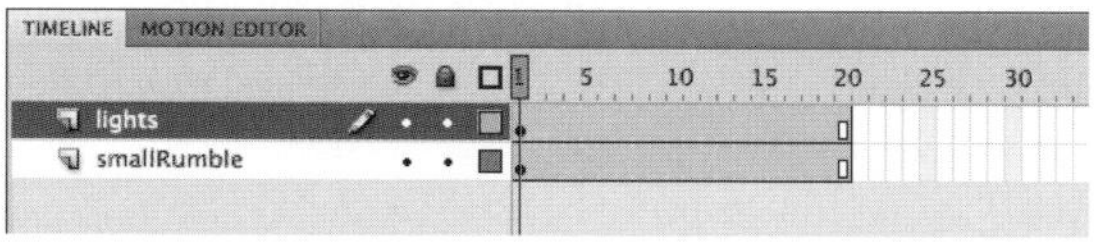

3 Lock the top lights layer.

4 Right-click/Ctrl-click on the car and choose Create Motion Tween.

   Flash converts the current layer to a Tween layer so you can begin to animate the instance.

5 Move the red playhead to the end of the Timeline.

6 Choose the Selection tool.

7 Move the car down about 5 pixels.

Flash creates a smooth animation of the car moving down slightly.

8 Click on the motion tween in the Timeline and open the Motion Editor.

9 Click the Plus icon on the Eases category and choose Random.

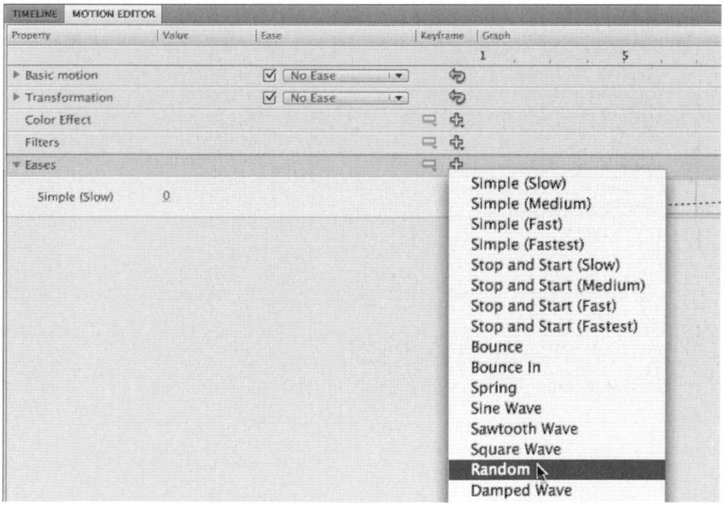

The Random preset ease appears.

10 Select the Random ease.

The Random ease jumps from one value to the next in random intervals. This is shown graphically as a series of abrupt stair steps.

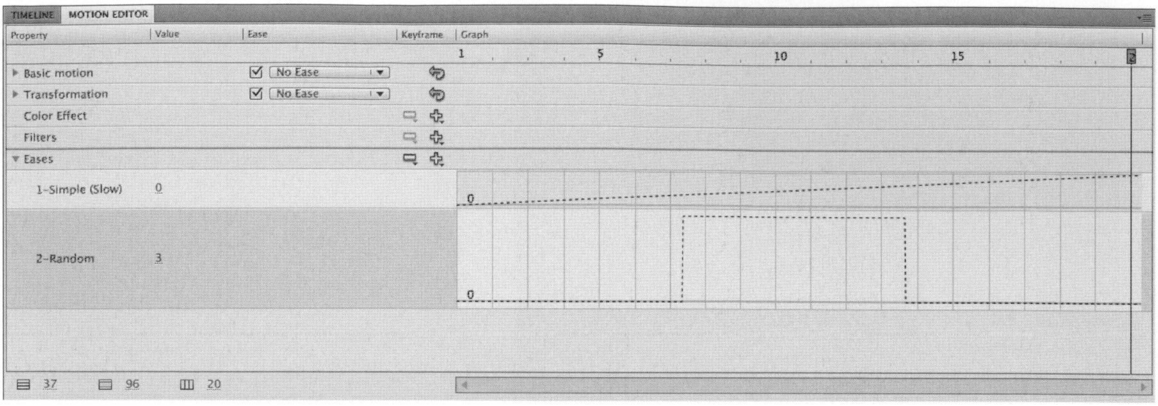

11 Change the Random value to **15**.

The frequency of random jumps increases based on the Random value.

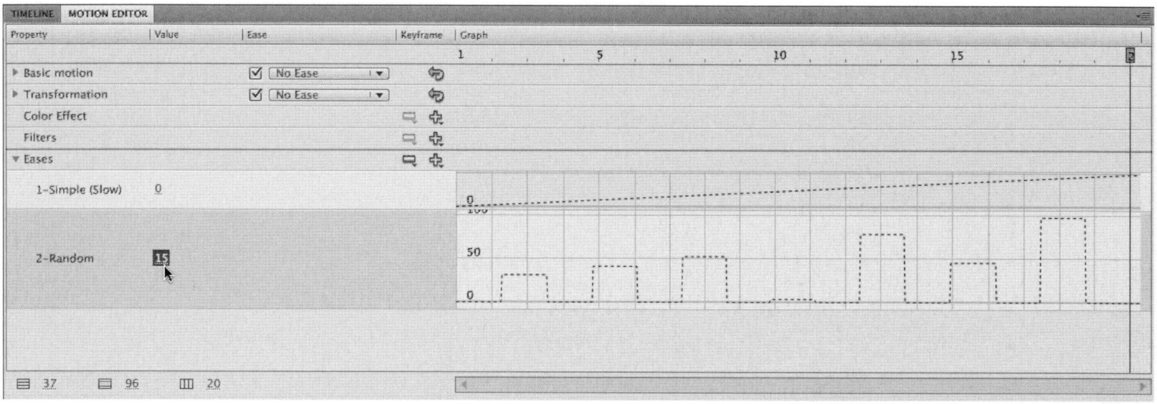

12 Select the Basic motion category.

13 In the Ease pull-down menu next to the Basic motion category, choose 2-Random.

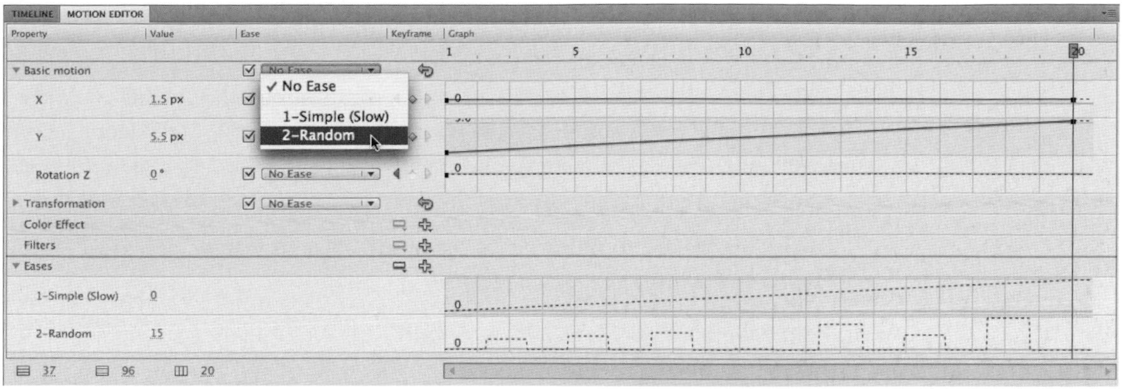

Flash applies the Random ease to the positional changes of the motion tween. Instead of a smooth change in the *y*-position, Flash makes the car jerk up and down randomly between the values of the keyframes, simulating a rumbling, idling car. Since the animation is nested in a movie clip, choose Control > Test Movie > in Flash Professional to preview the motion.

Classic Tween Model

In previous versions of Flash Professional (CS3 and earlier), motion tweens were created by first establishing keyframes in the Timeline, then changing one or more of the properties of the instance, and then applying a motion tween between the two keyframes. If you're more comfortable working with this older way of animating, you can do so by relying on the Classic Tween option.

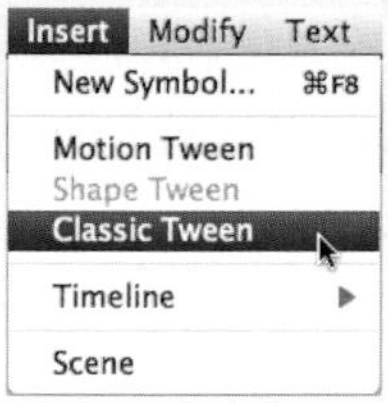

Select the first keyframe containing your instance, and then choose Insert > Classic Tween. Flash applies a classic motion tween to your Timeline.

The Motion Editor is not available for classic tweens.

Animating 3D Motion

Finally, you'll add a title and animate it in 3D space. Animating in 3D presents the added complication of a third (*z*) axis. When you choose the 3D Rotation or 3D Translation tool, you need to be aware of the Global Transform option at the bottom of the Tools panel. The Global Transform option toggles between a global option (button depressed) and a local option (button raised). Moving an object with the global option on makes the transformations relative to the global coordinate system, whereas moving an object with the local option on makes the transformations relative to itself.

1 Click on Scene 1 to return to the main timeline and insert a new layer at the top of the layer stack and rename it **title**.

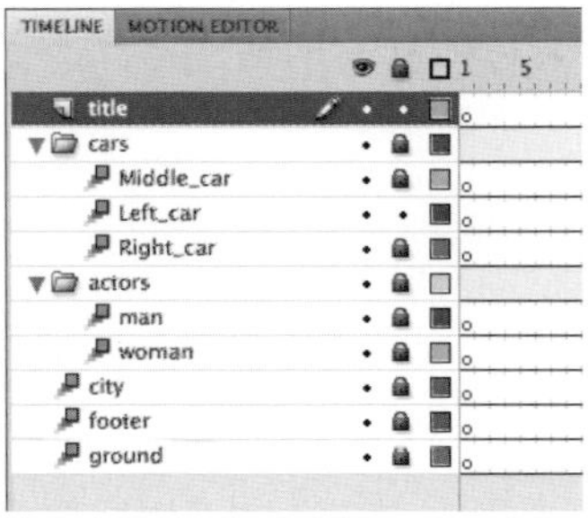

2 Lock all the other layers.

3 Insert a new keyframe at frame 120.

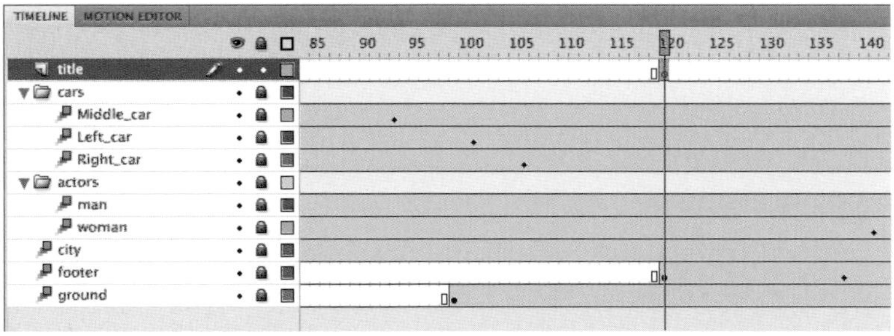

4 Drag the movie clip symbol called movietitle from the Library panel onto the Stage.

The movie title instance appears in your new layer in the keyframe at frame 120.

5 Position the title at x=**180** and y=**90**.

6 Right-click/Ctrl-click on the movie title and choose Create Motion Tween.

Flash converts the current layer to a Tween layer so you can begin to animate the instance.

7 Move the red playhead to frame 140.

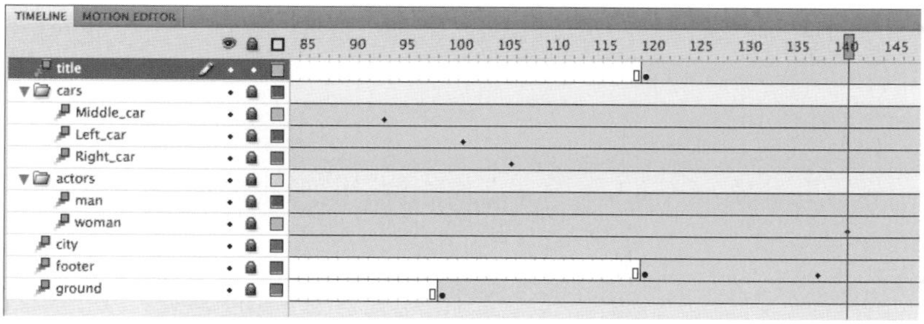

8 Select the 3D Rotation tool.

9 Deselect the Global Transform option at the bottom of the Tools panel.

10 Click and drag the title to rotate it around the *y*-axis (green) so that its angle is at about –50 degrees. You can check the rotation values in the Transform panel (Window > Transform).

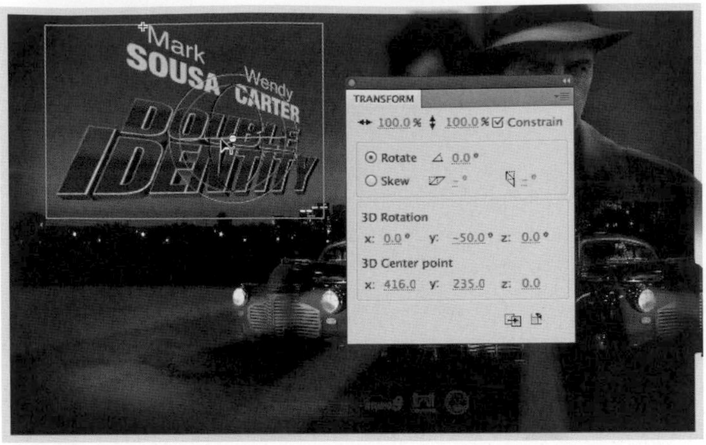

11 Move the red playhead to the first keyframe at frame 120.

12 Click and drag the title to rotate it around the *y*-axis in the opposite direction so that the instance looks like just a sliver.

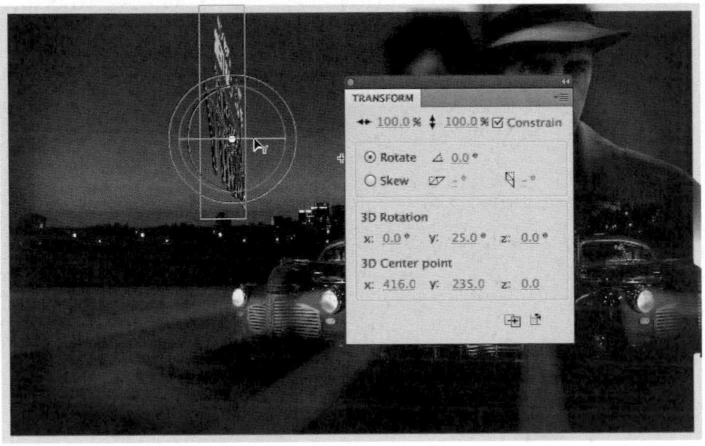

Flash motion tweens the change in the 3D rotation, so the title appears to swing in three dimensions.

Testing Your Movie

You can quickly preview your animation by "scrubbing" the red playhead back and forth on the Timeline or by choosing Control > Play. You can also use the integrated controller at the bottom of the Timeline or choose Window > Toolbars > Controller to display a separate controller panel.

However, to preview your animation as your audience will see it and to preview any nested animations within movie clip symbols, you should test your movie. Choose Control > Test Movie > in Flash Professional.

Flash exports a SWF file and saves it in the same location as your FLA file. The SWF file is the compressed, final Flash media that you would embed in an HTML page to play in a browser. Flash displays the SWF file in a new window with the exact Stage dimensions and plays your animation.

To exit Test Movie mode, click the Close window button.

You can also preview your animation by choosing Control > Test Movie > in Browser, and Flash will export a SWF file and open it automatically in your default browser.

Note: The exported SWF in Test Movie mode will loop automatically. To prevent the looping in Test Movie mode, choose Control > Loop to deselect the loop option.

Note: If you've targeted a different publishing platform in the Publish Settings (such as Adobe AIR), those options will be available for you in the Control > Test Movie menu.

Generating PNG Sequences and Sprite Sheets

While you can create sophisticated animations to play as a SWF file with the Flash Player, you can also use Flash's powerful tools to create your animation and export it as a series of images for use in other environments. For example, animations with HTML5 or on mobile devices rely on sequential PNG files or a single file that packs all the images organized in rows and columns known as a sprite sheet. The sprite sheet is accompanied by a data file that describes the position of each image, or sprite, in the file.

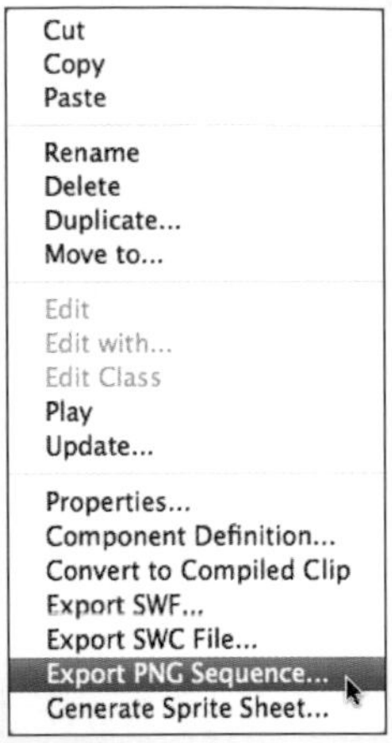

Generating either PNG sequences or a sprite sheet of your animation is easy. First, your animation must be within a Movie Clip symbol. In the Library panel, right-click/Ctrl-click the symbol and choose Export PNG Sequence.

Select the destination on your hard drive for your images.

For a sprite sheet, right-click/Ctrl-click the symbol and choose Generate sprite sheet. The Generate Sprite Sheet dialog box that appears provides different options such as sizing, background color, and the particular data format.

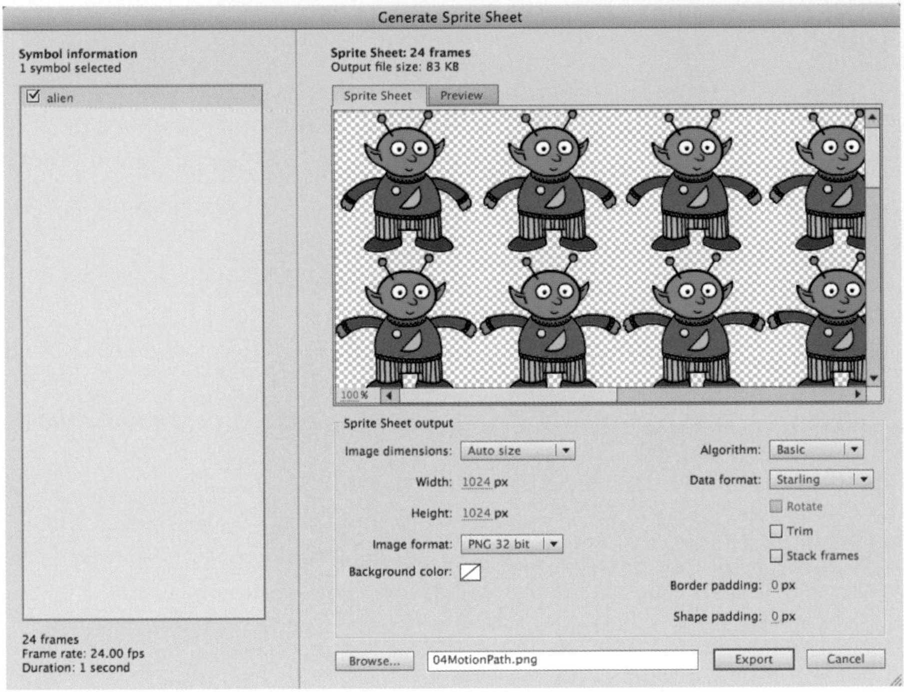

Click Export to output the sprite sheet and data file.

Review Questions

1 What are two requirements of a motion tween?

2 What kinds of properties can a motion tween change?

3 What are property keyframes, and why are they important?

4 How can you edit the path of an object's motion?

5 What are three ways to add easing to a motion tween?

Review Answers

1 A motion tween requires a symbol instance on the Stage and its own layer, which is called a Tween layer. No other tween or drawing object can exist on the Tween layer.

2 A motion tween creates smooth transitions between different keyframes of an object's location, scale, rotation, transparency, brightness, tint, filter values, or 3D rotation or translation.

3 A keyframe marks a change in one or more of an object's properties. Keyframes are specific to each property, so that a motion tween can have keyframes for position that are different from keyframes for transparency.

4 To edit the path of an object's motion, choose the Selection tool and click and drag directly on the path to bend it. You can also choose the Convert Anchor Point tool and Subselection tool to pull out handles at the anchor points. The handles control the curvature of the path.

5 Three ways to add easing to a motion tween include the following:

- Select the motion tween on the Timeline and change the Ease value in the Properties inspector.
- In the Motion Editor, right-click/Ctrl-click on any keyframe to pull out control handles and change the curvature of the graph.
- Add a preset ease to the Ease category of the Motion Editor and apply it to a property.

5 ARTICULATED MOTION AND MORPHING

Lesson Overview

In this lesson, you'll learn how to do the following:

- Animate armatures with multiple linked movie clips
- Constrain and pin the joints
- Animate armatures with shapes
- Morph organic shapes with shape tweens
- Simulate physics with the spring feature
- Use shape hints to refine shape tweens

This lesson will take approximately two and a half hours to complete. If needed, remove the previous lesson folder from your hard drive and copy the Lesson05 folder onto it.

You can easily create complex motion with articulations—joints between linked objects—using a feature called inverse kinematics. You can also morph—create organic changes in—your shapes with shape tweens.

Getting Started

You'll start the lesson by viewing the animated crane and floating buoy that you'll create as you learn about articulated motion and morphing in Flash. You'll also be animating a tentacle of an octopus.

1 Double-click the **05end.html** file in the Lesson05/05End folder to play the animation. Double-click the 05ShapeIK_End.html to play that animation as well.

The first project is an animation depicting a crane working at the seaside dock and a buoy floating along the gentle undulations of the water. In this lesson, you'll animate the crane arm, the buoy, and the smooth motion of the waves. The other project is an animation showing an octopus curling one of its tentacles.

2 Double-click the 05Start.fla file in the Lesson05/05Start folder to open the initial project file in Flash.

3 Choose File > Save As. Name the file **05_workingcopy.fla**, and save it in the 05Start folder. Saving a working copy ensures that the original start file will be available if you want to start over.

Articulated Motion with Inverse Kinematics

When you want to animate an articulated object (one that has multiple joints), such as a walking person, or as in this example, a moving crane, Flash Professional CS6 makes it easy to do so with inverse kinematics. Inverse kinematics is a mathematical way to calculate the different angles of a jointed object to achieve a certain configuration. You can pose your object in a beginning keyframe, and then set a different pose at a later keyframe. Flash will use inverse kinematics to figure out the different angles for all the joints to get from the first pose to the next pose.

Inverse kinematics makes animating easy because you don't have to worry about animating each segment of an object or limb of a character. You just focus on the overall poses.

Defining the bones

The first step to create articulated motion is to define the bones of your object. You use the Bone tool ( ) to do that. The Bone tool tells Flash how a series of movie clip instances are connected. The connected movie clips are called the *armature*, and each movie clip is called a *node*.

1 In your 05working_copy.fla file, select the crane layer. Lock all the other layers.

2 Drag the cranearm1 movie clip symbol from the Library panel onto the Stage. Place the instance right above the rectangular crane base.

3 Drag the cranearm2 movie clip symbol from the Library panel onto the Stage. Place the instance next to the tip of the cranearm1 movie clip instance.

4 Drag another instance of the cranearm2 movie clip symbol from the Library panel onto the Stage. Place this instance next to the free tip of the first cranearm2 instance.

You'll have two cranearm2 instances next to each other.

5 Drag the cranerope movie clip symbol from the Library panel onto the Stage. Place the instance so it hangs down from the last cranearm2 instance.

Your movie clip instances are now in place and ready to be connected with bones.

6 Select the Bone tool.

7 Click on the base of the cranearm1 instance and drag the Bone tool to the base of the cranearm2 instance. Release the mouse button.

Your first bone is defined. Flash shows the bone as a skinny triangle with a round joint at its base and a round joint at its tip. Each bone is defined from the base of the first node to the base of the next node. For example, to build an arm, you would click on the shoulder side of the upper arm and drag it to the elbow side of the lower arm.

8 Click on the base of the cranearm2 instance and drag it to the base of the next cranearm2 instance. Release the mouse button.

Your second bone is defined.

9 Click on the base of the second cranearm2 instance and drag it to the base of the cranerope instance. Release the mouse button.

Your third bone is defined. Note that the four movie clip instances, which are now connected with bones, have been separated to a new layer with a new icon and name. The new layer is a Pose layer, which keeps your armatures separate from other objects on the Timeline such as graphics or motion tweens.

10 Rename the Pose layer **cranearmature** and delete the empty crane layer that contained the initial movie clip instances.

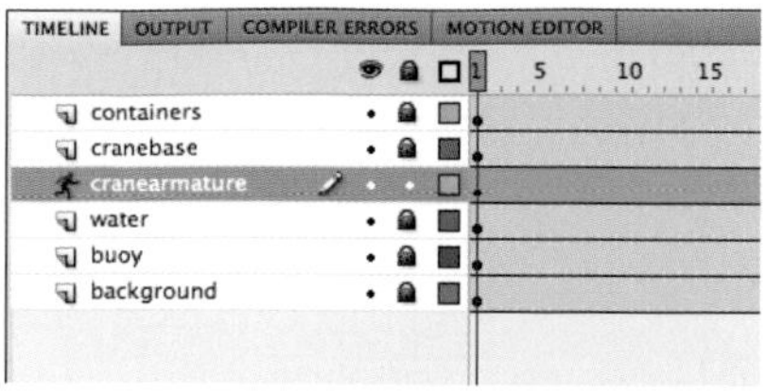

Armature Hierarchy

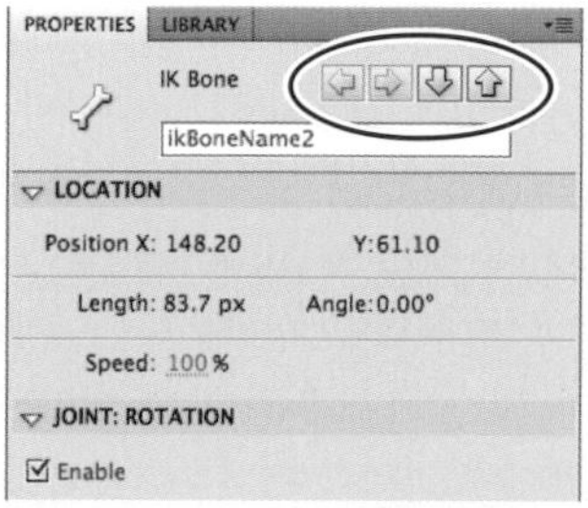

The first bone of an armature is referred to as the *parent*, and the bone that is linked to it is called the *child*. A bone can actually have more than one child attached to it as well. For example, an armature of a puppet would have a pelvis connected to two thighs, which in turn are attached to two lower legs of their own. The pelvis is the parent, each thigh is a child, and the thighs are siblings to each other. As your armature becomes more complicated, you can use the Properties inspector to navigate up and down the hierarchy using these relationships.

When you select a bone in an armature, the top of the Properties inspector displays a series of arrows.

You can click the arrows to move through the hierarchy and quickly select and view the properties of each node. If the parent bone is selected, you can click the down arrow to select the child. If a child bone is selected, you can click the up arrow to select its parent, or click the down arrow to select its own child if it has one. The sideways arrows navigate between sibling nodes.

Inserting poses

Think of poses as keyframes for your armature. You have an initial pose for your crane in frame 1. You will insert two additional poses for the crane. The next pose will position the crane down as if it were picking something up from the ocean. The last pose will position the crane back up to lift up the object.

1 Move the red playhead to frame 50.

2 Using the Selection tool, click on the hook at the end of the cranerope instance and drag it down to the water.

A new pose is automatically inserted at frame 50. As you drag the cranerope instance, notice how the entire armature moves along with it. The bones keep all the different nodes connected.

3 Move the red playhead to frame 100 (the last frame).

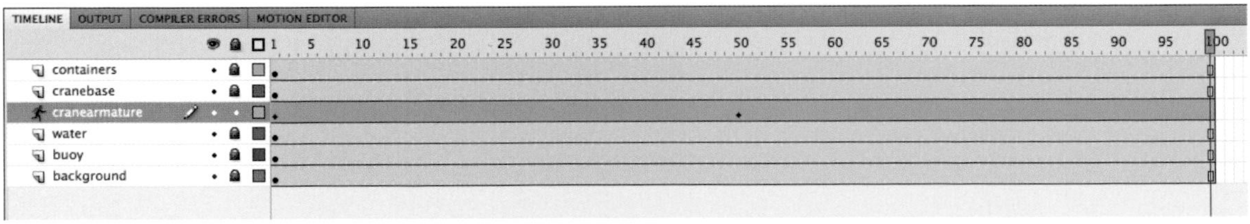

4 Click on the hook at the end of the cranerope instance and drag it up out of the water.

A new pose is automatically inserted at frame 100.

Note: You can edit poses on the Timeline just as you can with keyframes of a motion tween. Right-click/Ctrl-click along the Timeline and choose Insert Pose to insert a new pose. Right-click/Ctrl-click on any pose and select Clear Pose to remove the pose from the layer. Ctrl-click/Command-click on a pose to select it. Click and drag the pose to move it to a different position along the Timeline.

5 Preview the animation by choosing Control > Test Movie > in Flash Professional.

The crane animates, moving all its crane segments from one pose to the next.

Isolating the rotation of individual nodes

As you pull and push on the armature to create your pose, you may find it difficult to control the rotation of individual nodes because of their linkages. Holding down the Shift key as you move individual nodes will isolate their rotation.

1 Select the third pose at frame 100.

2 Holding down the Shift key, click and drag on the second node in the armature to rotate it so that it points downward.

The second node of the crane rotates, but the first node does not.

3 Holding down the Shift key, click and drag on the third node in the armature to rotate it so that it points upward.

The third node of the crane rotates, but the first and second nodes do not.

4 Holding down the Shift key, click and drag on the last node in the armature (the cranerope instance) so that it points straight down.

Holding down the Shift key helps you isolate the rotations of the individual nodes so that you can position your poses exactly as you want them. The crane now retracts by collapsing its different arm segments.

Pinning individual nodes

Another way you can more precisely control the rotation or position of your armature is to fix individual nodes in place, leaving the child nodes free to move in a different pose. You do this by using the Pin option in the Properties inspector.

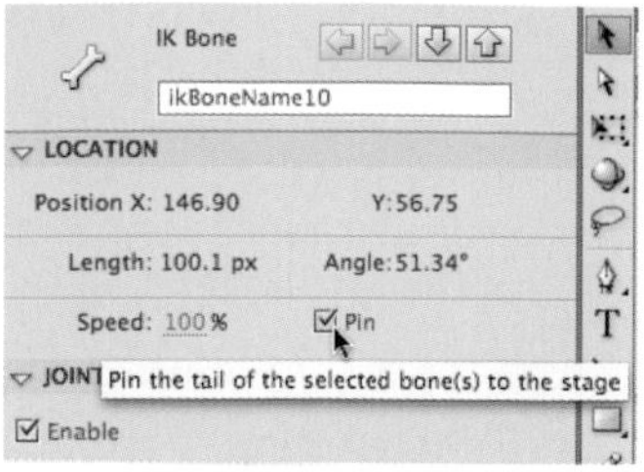

1 Choose the Selection tool.

2 Select the second node of the crane armature.

3 In the Properties inspector, check the Pin option.

The tail, or end of the selected node, is fixed to the Stage in the current position. An "X" appears on the joint to indicate that it is pinned.

4 Drag the last node in the armature.

Only the last two nodes move. Note how the armature motion is different when using the Pin option versus using the Shift key. The Shift key isolates an individual node and all the rest of the nodes connected to it. When you pin a node, the pinned node remains fixed, but you're free to move all the child nodes.

Note: You can also select a node and click on its tail when the icon of a pushpin appears as your cursor. That selected node will be pinned. Click again to unpin the node.

Editing Armatures

You can easily edit the armature by repositioning the nodes or by deleting and adding new bones. If one of the nodes of your armature is slightly off, for example, you can use the Free Transform tool to rotate it or move it into a new position. This does not change the bones, however.

You can also move nodes into new positions by holding down the Alt/Option key while dragging the node to a different location.

If you want to remove bones, simply click on the bone that you want to delete and press the Delete key on the keyboard. The selected bone and all the bones connected to it down the chain will be removed. You can then add new bones if desired.

Constraining Joints

The various joints of the crane can freely rotate, which isn't particularly realistic. Many armatures in real life are constrained to certain angles of rotation. For example, your forearm can rotate up toward your bicep, but it can't rotate in the other direction beyond your bicep. When working with armatures in Flash Professional CS6, you can choose to constrain the rotation for various joints or even constrain the translation (movement) of the various joints.

Next, you'll constrain the rotation and translation of the various joints of the crane so they move more realistically.

Constraining the rotation of joints

By default, the rotation of joints have no constraints, which means they can rotate in a full circle, or 360 degrees. If you want a certain joint to rotate only in a quarter circle arc, constrain the joint to 90 degrees.

1 Make sure that none of the nodes in your armature are pinned.

2 Click the second pose at frame 50 in the cranearmature layer, right-click/Ctrl-click, and select Clear Pose.

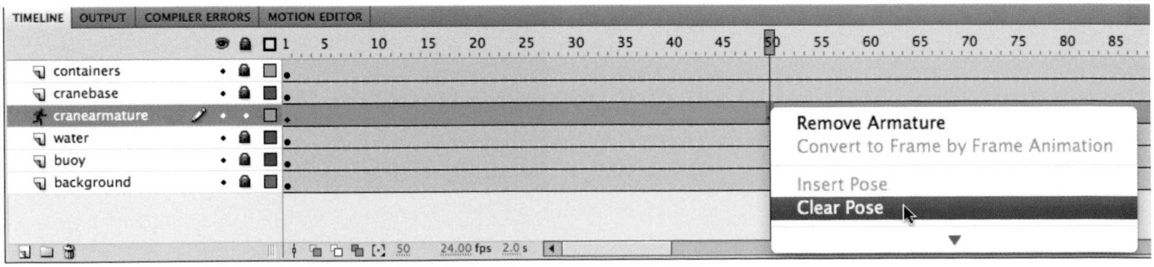

3 Click the third pose at frame 100 in the cranearmature layer, right-click/Ctrl-click, and select Clear Pose.

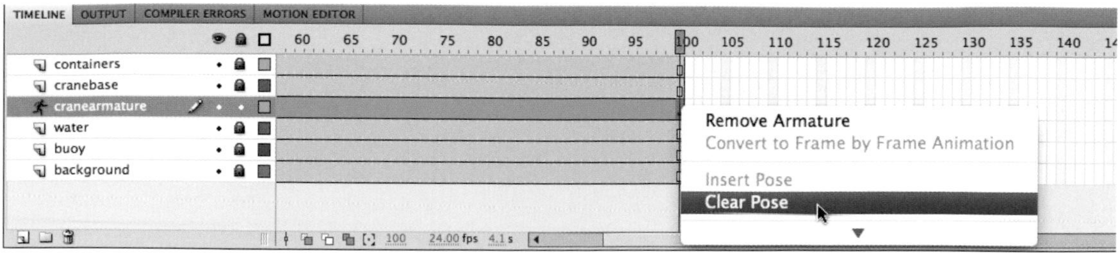

Your armature now has only a single pose at frame 1.

4 Move the red playhead to frame 1.

5 Choose the Selection tool.

6 Click on the second bone in the crane armature.

The bone becomes highlighted, indicating that it is selected.

7 In the Properties inspector, select the Constrain option in the Joint: Rotation section.

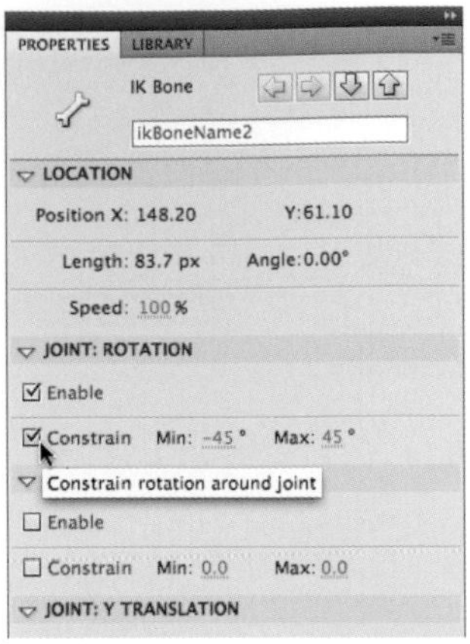

An angle indicator appears on the joint, showing the minimum and maximum allowable angles and the current position of the node.

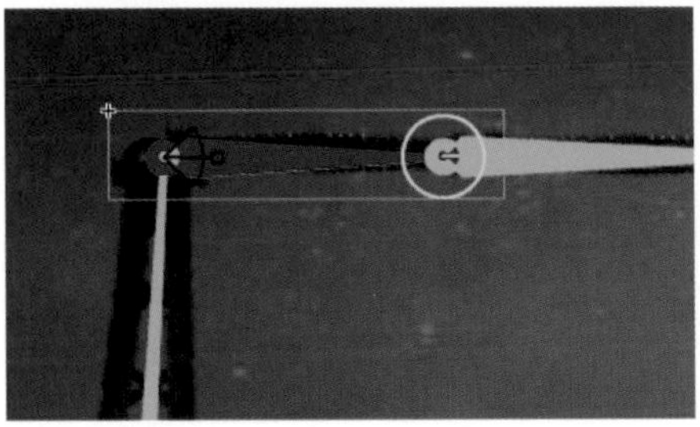

8 Set the minimum joint rotation angle to **0** degrees and the maximum joint rotation angle to **90** degrees.

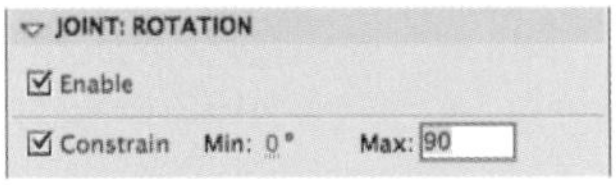

The angle indicator changes on the joint, showing the allowable angles. In this example, the second segment of the crane can only bend downward or rise up to be level with the horizon.

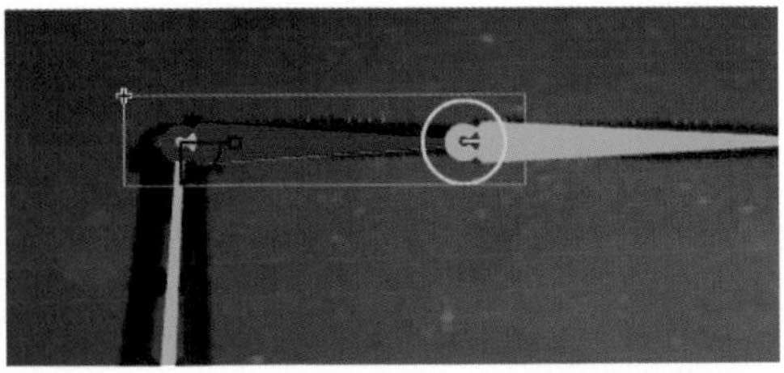

9 Click on the third bone in the crane armature.

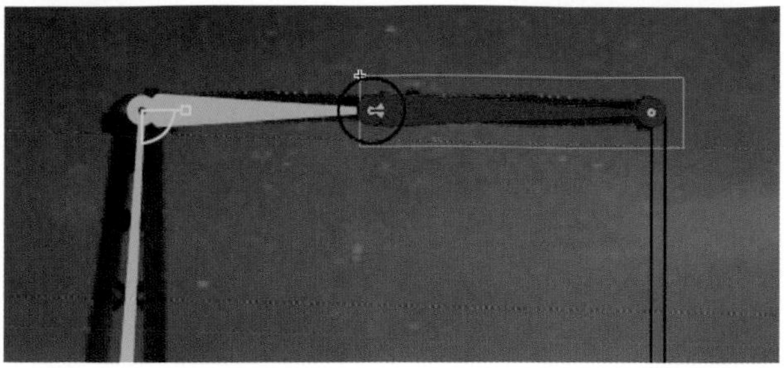

The bone becomes highlighted, indicating that it is selected.

10 In the Properties inspector, select the Constrain option in the Joint: Rotation section.

An angle indicator appears on the joint, showing the minimum and maximum allowable angles and the current position of the node.

11 Set the minimum joint rotation angle to **-90** degrees and the maximum joint rotation angle to **0** degrees.

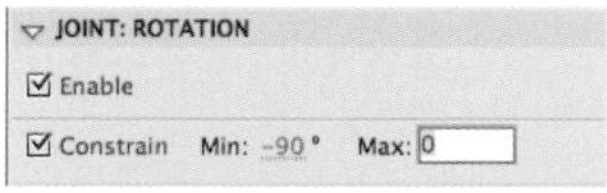

The angle indicator changes on the joint, showing the allowable angles. In this example, the third segment of the crane can bend only from a level position to a vertical position. Each joint in an armature can have its own rotation constraints.

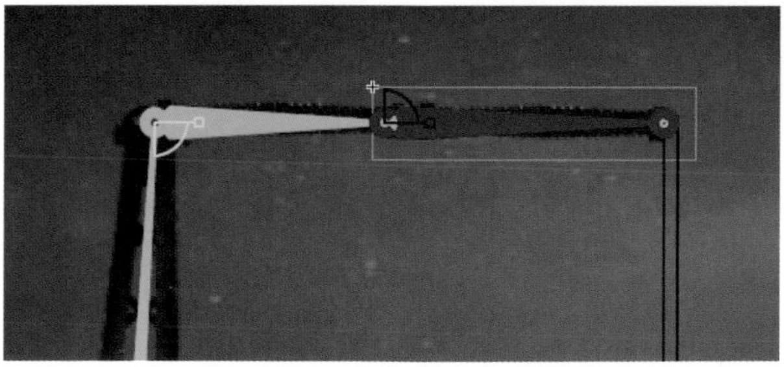

Constraining the translation of joints

You don't normally think of joints that can move positions. However, in Flash Professional CS6, you can allow joints to actually slide in either the *x* (horizontal) or the *y* (vertical) direction, and set the limits on how far those joints can travel.

In this example, you'll allow the first node (the tall first segment of the crane) to move back and forth as if it were on a track. This will give it the capability to pick up any sort of cargo from the ocean and place it on the dock.

1 Click on the first node in the crane armature.

2 Deselect the Enable option in the Joint: Rotation section of the Properties inspector.

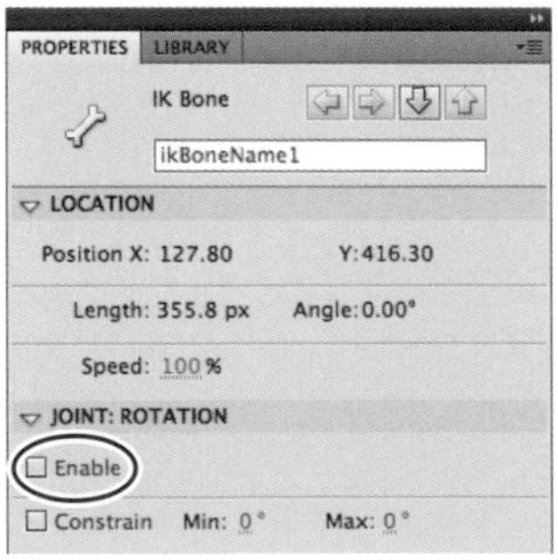

The circle around the joint disappears, indicating that it can no longer rotate.

3 Select the Enable option in the Joint: X Translation section of the Properties inspector.

Arrows appear from the joint, indicating that the joint can travel in that direction.

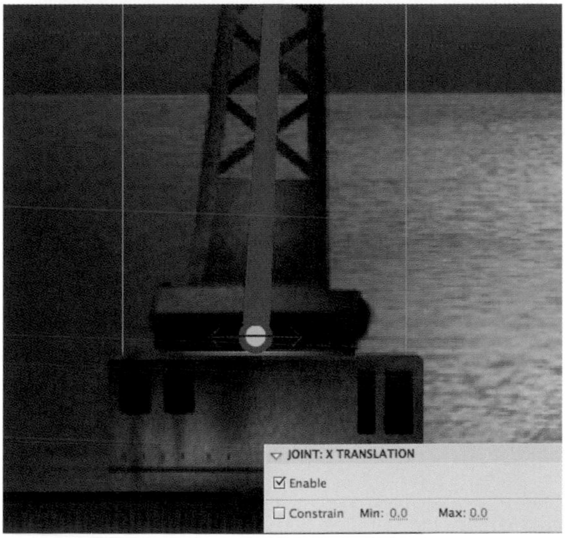

4 Select the Constrain option in the Joint: X Translation section of the Properties inspector.

The arrows turn into straight lines, indicating that the translation is limited.

5 Set the minimum X translation to **-50** and the maximum X translation to **50**.

The bars indicate how much translation in the *x* direction the first bone can do.

6 Grab the hook and pose the crane in the first keyframe so that the first node is close to the edge of the water and the hook is lowered.

7 Move the red playhead on the Timeline to the last frame.

8 Move the hook out of the water and the crane back from the edge of the water, creating a new pose.

The constraints on joint rotation and joint translation impose limits on the poses that help you create more realistic animations.

9 Watch your animation by choosing Control > Test Movie > in Flash Professional.

Changing Joint Speed

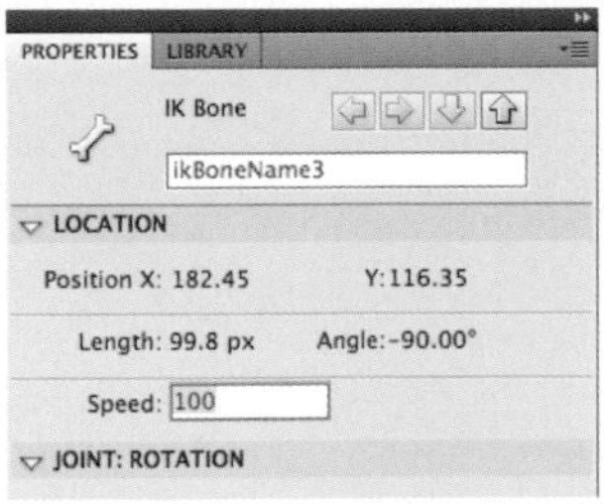

Joint speed refers to the stickiness, or stiffness, of a joint. A joint with a low joint speed value will be sluggish. A joint with a high joint speed value will be more responsive. You can set the joint speed value for any selected joint in the Properties inspector.

The joint speed is apparent when you drag the very end of an armature. If there are slow joints higher up on the armature chain, those particular joints will be less responsive and will rotate to a lesser degree than the others.

To change the joint speed, click on a bone to select it. In the Properties inspector, set the joint Speed value from 0% to 100%.

Inverse Kinematics with Shapes

The crane is an armature made with various movie clip symbols. You can also create armatures with shapes, which are useful for animating objects without obvious joints and segments but can still have an articulated motion. For example, the arms of an octopus have no actual joints, but you can add bones to a smooth tentacle to animate its undulating motion.

Defining bones inside a shape

You'll add bones to an octopus—perhaps one that was picked up by the crane from the ocean depths—and animate one of its tentacles.

1 Open the file 05ShapeIK_Start.fla. Choose File > Save As. Name the file **05ShapeIK_workingcopy.fla**.

The file contains an illustration of an octopus. One arm is separated on its own layer called arm1.

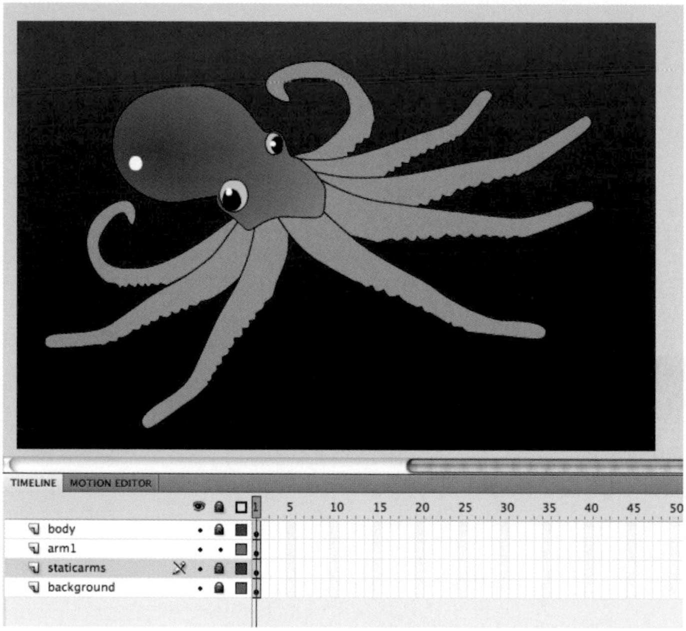

2 Lock all the layers except for the arm1 layer and select the contents of the arm1 layer.

3 Choose the Bone tool.

4 Click on the base of the tentacle in the arm1 layer and drag out the first bone a little ways down toward the tip of the tentacle.

The first bone is defined. The contents of the arm1 layer are separated to a new Pose layer.

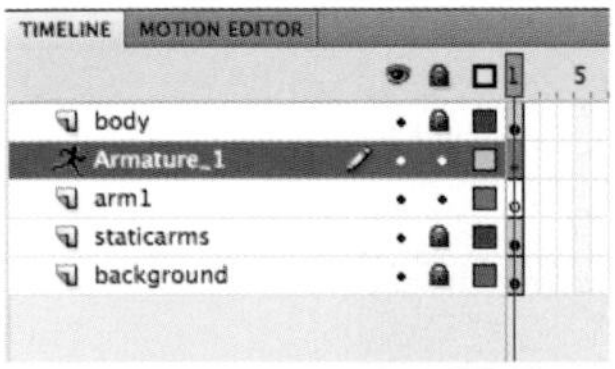

5 Click on the end of the first bone and drag out the next bone a little farther down toward the tip of the tentacle.

The second bone is defined.

6 Continue building the armature with a total of four bones.

7 When the armature is complete, use the Selection tool to click and drag the last bone to see how the deformation of the tentacle follows the bones of the armature.

Editing the shape

You don't need any special tools to edit the shape that contains bones. Many of the same drawing and editing tools in the Tools panel, such as the Paint Bucket, the Ink Bottle, and the Subselection tools, are available to you to edit the fill, the stroke, or the contours.

1 Choose the Paint Bucket tool.

2 Choose a dark peach color for the Fill.

3 Click on the shape in the Pose layer.

   The fill color of the tentacle changes.

4 Choose the Ink Bottle tool.

5 Choose a dark red color for the stroke.

6 Click on the shape in the Pose layer.

   The outline of the tentacle changes color.

7 Choose the Subselection tool.

8 Click on the contour of the shape.

The anchor points and the control handles appear around the contour of the shape.

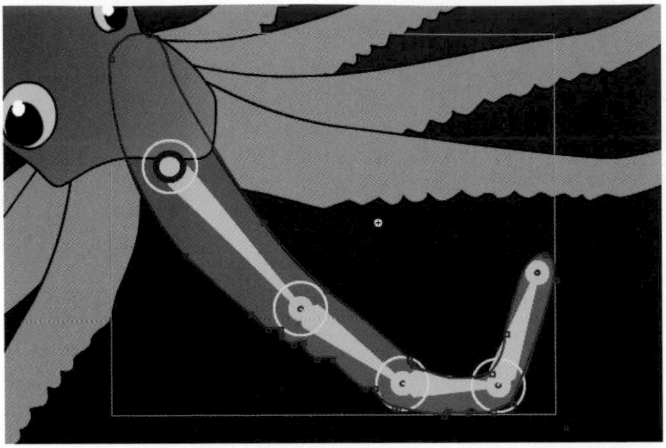

> **Note:** Add new points on the contour of the shape with the Add Anchor Point tool. Delete points on the contour of the shape with the Delete Anchor Point tool. Both the Add Anchor Point and Delete Anchor Point tools are located under the Pen tool.

9 Drag the anchor points to new locations or click and drag the handles to make edits to the tentacle shape.

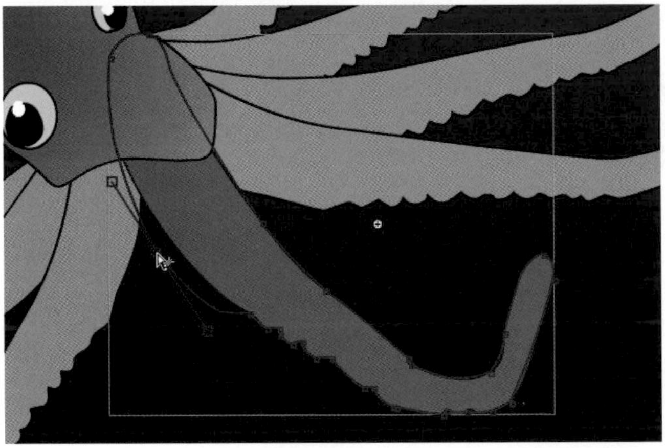

Editing the bones and armature

The Subselection tool can move the joints within a shape. However, the location of the joints within the shape can be edited only when you have a single pose for your armature. After your armature has been repositioned in later frames of the Pose layer, changes to the bone structure cannot be made.

Use the Selection tool if you want to move the entire armature to a different location but keep the bone structure unchanged.

1 Choose the Subselection tool.

2 Click on a joint.

3 Click and drag the joint within the shape to a new location.

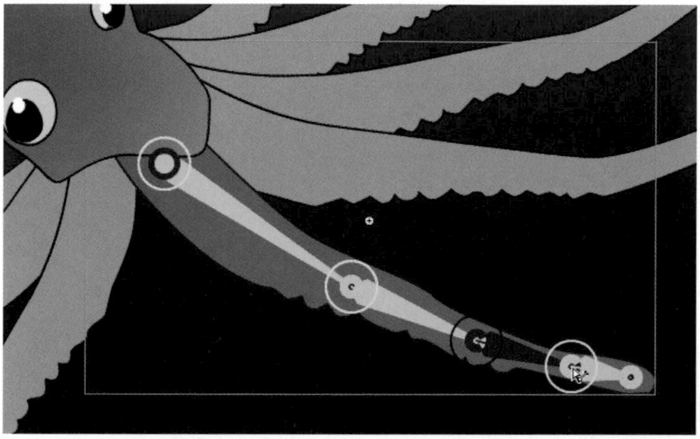

4 Choose the Selection tool. Hold down the Alt/Option key and drag the entire armature (and the shape around it) to a new location.

Note: You can easily remove bones or add more bones to your armature. Choose the Selection tool and click on the bone you want to delete. Press the Delete key to remove the selected bone; all the child bones will be removed as well. Add new bones by choosing the Bone tool and clicking on the armature.

Refining Shape Behavior with the Bind Tool

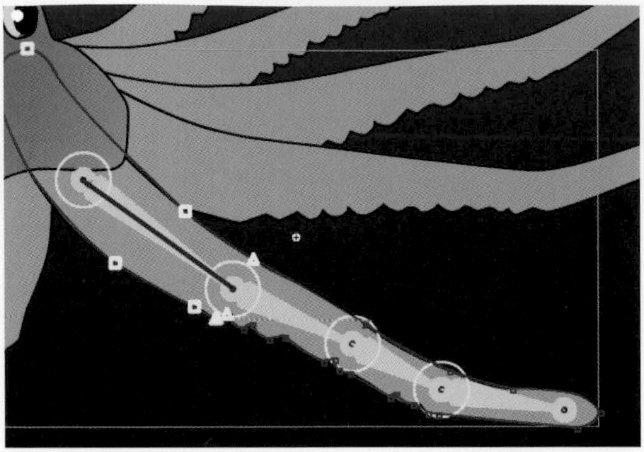

The organic control of a shape by its armature is a result of a mapping between the anchor points along the shape and its bones. The points along the tip of the tentacle, for example, are mapped to the very last bone, whereas the points farther up the tentacle are mapped to the bones farther up the tentacle. Hence, where the bones rotate, the shape follows.

You can edit the connections between the bones and their control points with the Bind tool ( ). The Bind tool is hidden under the Bone tool. The Bind tool displays which control points are connected to which bones and lets you break those connections and make new ones.

Choose the Bind tool and click on any bone in the shape. The selected bone is highlighted in red, and all the connected control points on the shape are highlighted in yellow.

If you want to redefine which control points are connected to the selected bone, you can do the following:

- Shift-click to add additional associations to control points.
- Ctrl-click/Command-click to remove associations to control points.
- Drag a connection line between the bone and the control point. In the following figure, a line is being dragged from the selected bone to a point on the left to make the association.

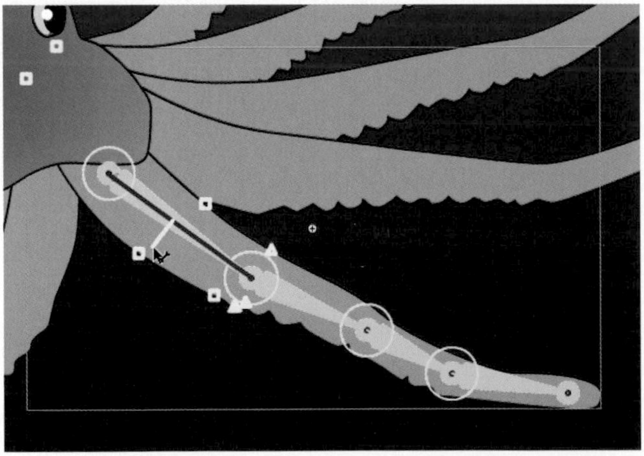

Click on any control point on the shape. The selected control point is highlighted in red, and all the connected bones are highlighted in yellow. In the following figure, the red highlighted point is associated with the first bone.

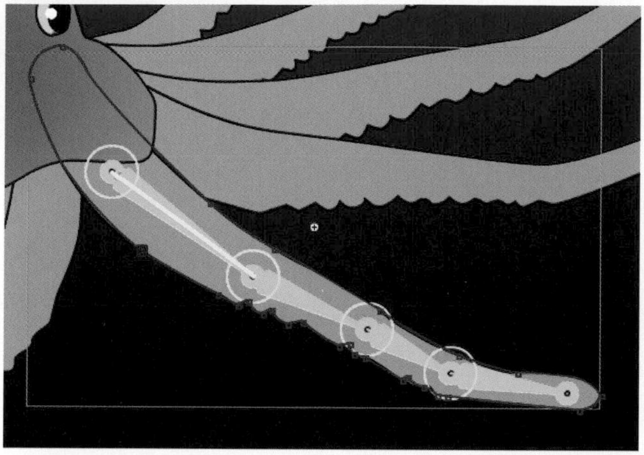

If you want to redefine which bones are connected to the selected control point, you can do the following:

- Shift-click to add additional associations to bones.
- Ctrl-click/Command-click to remove associations to bones.
- Drag a connection line between the control point and the bone. In the following figure, another control point farther down the tentacle is being associated with the first bone.

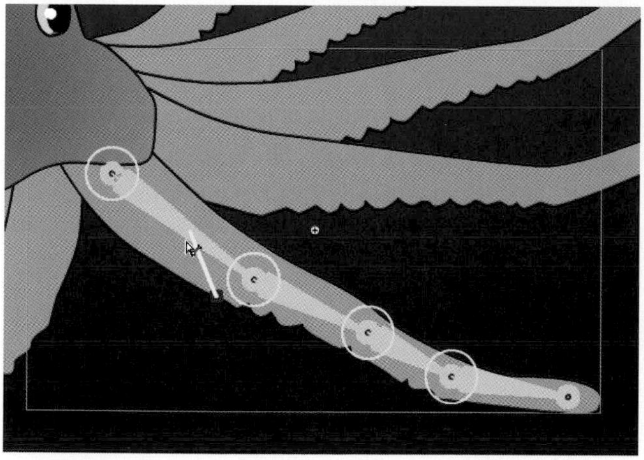

Armature Options

Many settings are available through the Properties inspector that can help you make your armature interactive or help you apply easing to your armature motion. You can also choose different viewing options for your armature to suit your working style.

Authortime and runtime armatures

Authortime armatures are those that you pose along the Timeline and play as straightforward animations. Runtime armatures refer to armatures that are interactive and allow the user to move your armature. You can make any of your armatures—whether they are made with a series of movie clips such as the crane or made with a shape such as the octopus tentacle—into an authortime or a runtime armature. Runtime armatures, however, are restricted to armatures that have only a single pose.

1 Continue with the file 05ShapeIK_workingcopy.fla.

2 Select the layer containing the tentacle armature.

3 In the Properties inspector, select Runtime from the Type option.

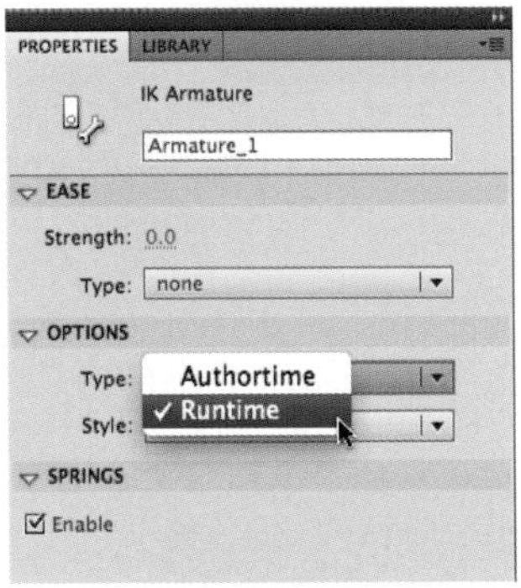

The armature becomes a runtime armature, allowing the user to directly manipulate the octopus tentacle. The first frame of the Pose layer displays the armature icon to indicate that the runtime option is selected and no additional poses can be added.

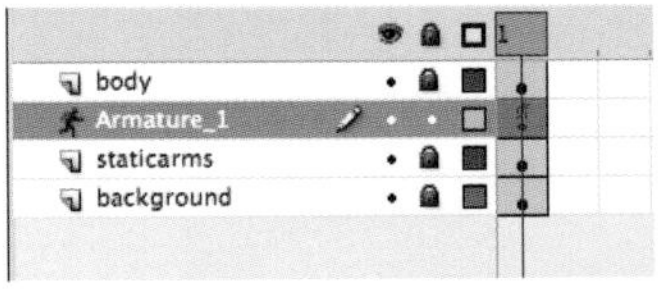

4 Test your movie by choosing Control > Test Movie > in Flash Professional.

The user can click and drag the tentacle and interactively move it on the Stage.

Controlling easing

The Motion Editor and its sophisticated controls for easing cannot be used with armatures. However, there are a few standard eases available from the Properties inspector that you can apply to your armatures. Easing can make your armature move with a sense of gravity due to acceleration or deceleration of its motion.

1 Select the layer containing the tentacle armature.

2 In the Properties inspector, select Authortime for Type in the Options section.

The armature becomes an authortime armature again.

3 Select frame 40 for all the layers and choose Insert > Timeline > Frame.

Frames are inserted in all the layers, giving you room on the Timeline to create additional poses for the tentacle.

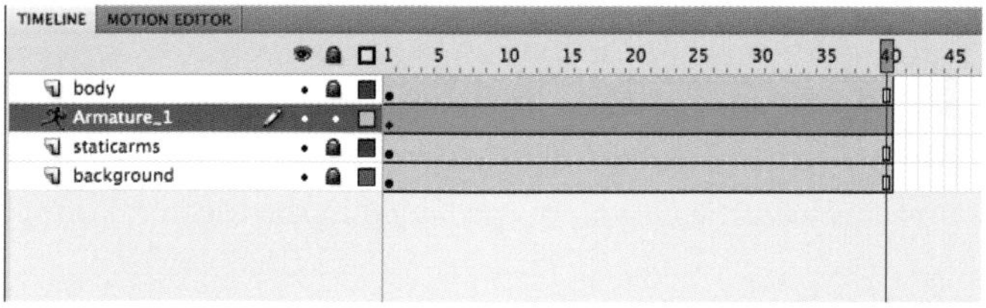

4 Move the red playhead to frame 40.

5 With the Selection tool, grab the tip of the tentacle, curl it upward, and move it to one side.

A new pose is inserted in frame 40 for the tentacle armature.

6 Select the first pose in frame 1 of the Armature layer.

7 In the Properties inspector, select Simple (Medium) for the Type under the Ease section.

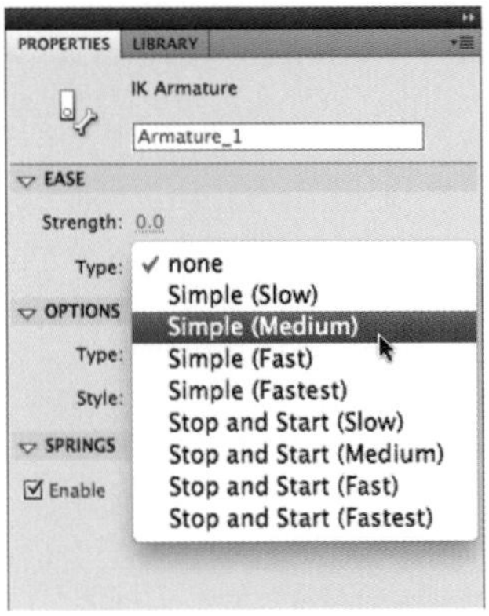

The variations of Simple eases (from Slow to Fastest) represent the severity of the ease. They represent the same curvatures provided in the Motion Editor for motion tweens.

8 Set the Strength to **100**.

The Strength represents the direction of the ease. A negative value is an ease-in and a positive value is an ease-out.

9 Choose Control > Test Movie > in Flash Professional to preview your animation.

The tentacle curls up, easing out of its motion gradually.

10 Close the Test Movie window.

11 Select the first pose in frame 1.

12 Change the Strength setting to **-100** and test your movie again.

The tentacle curls up, but the motion now eases in, starting slowly and gradually speeding up.

13 Close the Test Movie window.

14 Select the first pose in frame 1.

15 In the Properties inspector under the Ease section, select Start and Stop (Medium) for Type.

The variations of Stop and Start eases (from Slow to Fastest) represent the severity of the ease. The Stop and Start eases have curves on both ends of the motion, so the easing values affect the start of the motion and the end of the motion.

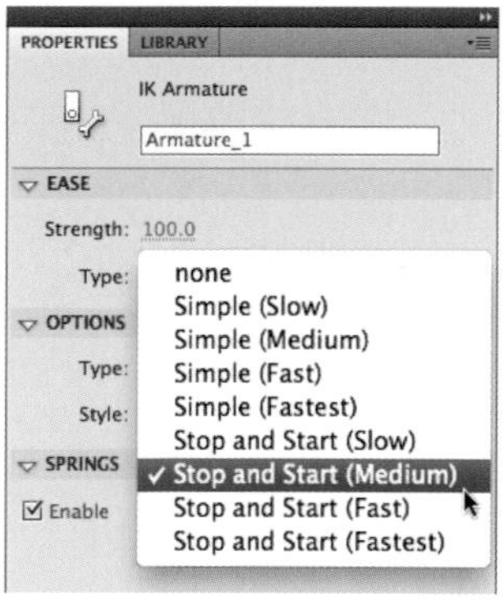

16 Set the Strength to **-100**.

17 Choose Control > Test Movie > in Flash Professional to preview your animation.

The tentacle curls up, easing into its motion gradually and also easing out of its motion gradually.

Morphing with Shape Tweens

Shape tweening is a technique for interpolating amorphous changes between shapes in different keyframes. Shape tweens make it possible to smoothly morph one thing into another. Any kind of animation that requires that the contours of a shape change—for example, animation of clouds, water, or fire—is a perfect candidate for shape tweening.

Both the fill and the stroke of a shape can be smoothly animated. Because shape tweening only applies to shapes, you can't use groups, symbol instances, or bitmap images.

Establish keyframes containing different shapes

In the following steps, you'll animate the gently undulating surface of the ocean beneath the crane with a shape tween.

1 Continue with the file of the crane animation called 05_workingcopy.fla.

2 Lock and hide all the layers except for the water layer. The water layer contains a transparent blue shape at the bottom of the Stage.

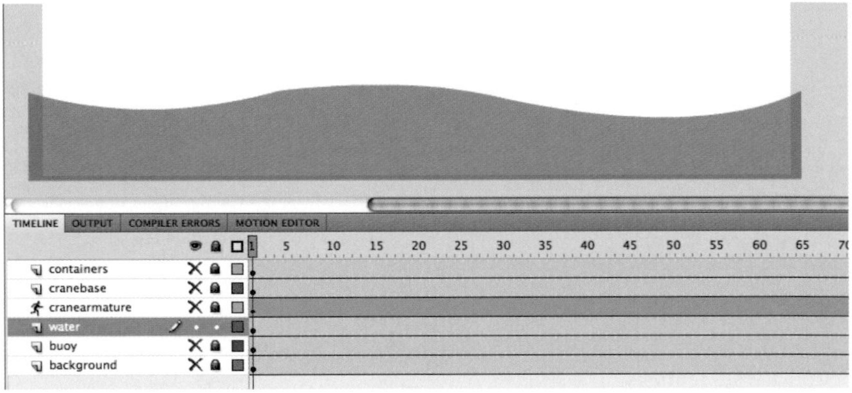

3 Move the red playhead to frame 50 in the water layer.

4 Right-click/Ctrl-click on frame 50 in the water layer and select Insert Keyframe. Or, choose Insert > Timeline > Keyframe (F6).

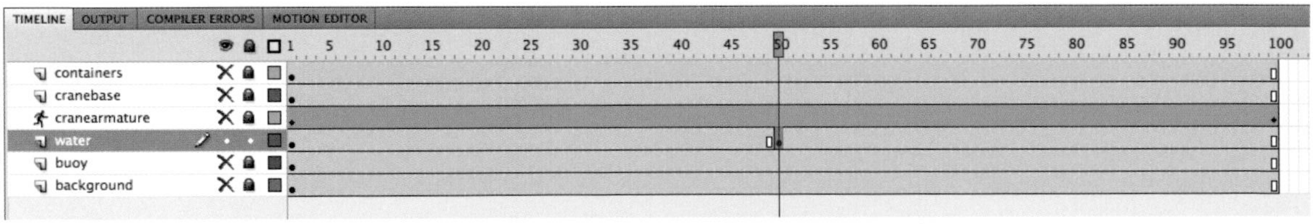

A new keyframe is inserted at frame 50. The contents of the previous keyframe are copied into the second keyframe.

5 Move the red playhead to frame 100.

6 Right-click/Ctrl-click on frame 100 in the water layer and select Insert Keyframe. Or, choose Insert > Timeline > Keyframe (F6).

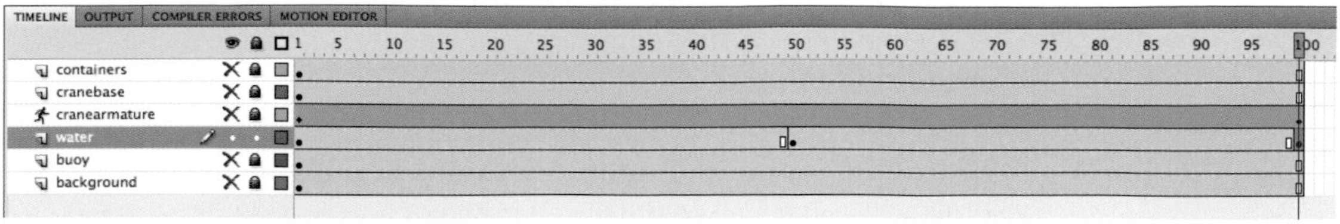

A new keyframe is inserted at frame 100. The contents of the previous keyframe are copied into this keyframe. You now have three keyframes on the Timeline in the water layer: one at frame 1, a second at frame 50, and a third at frame 100.

7 Move the red playhead back to frame 50.

Next, you'll change the shape of the water in the second keyframe.

8 Choose the Selection tool.

9 Deselect the water shape. Click and drag the contours of the water shape so that the crests become dips and the dips become crests.

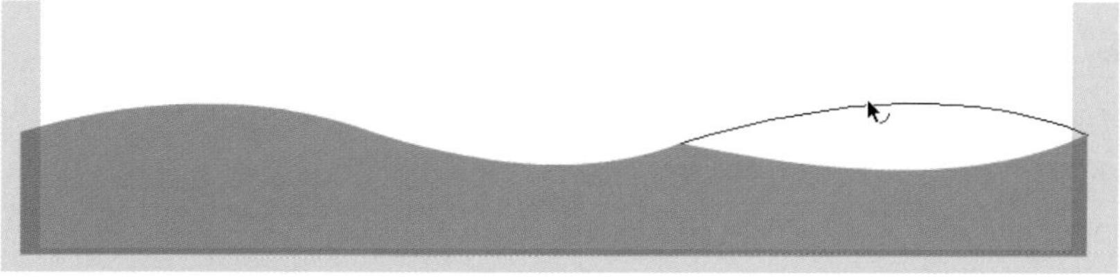

Each subsequent keyframe in the water layer contains a different shape.

Apply the shape tween

The next step is to apply a shape tween between the keyframes to create the smooth transitions.

1 Click on any frame between the first keyframe and the second keyframe in the water layer.

2 Right-click/Ctrl-click and select Create Shape Tween. Or, from the top menu choose Insert > Shape Tween.

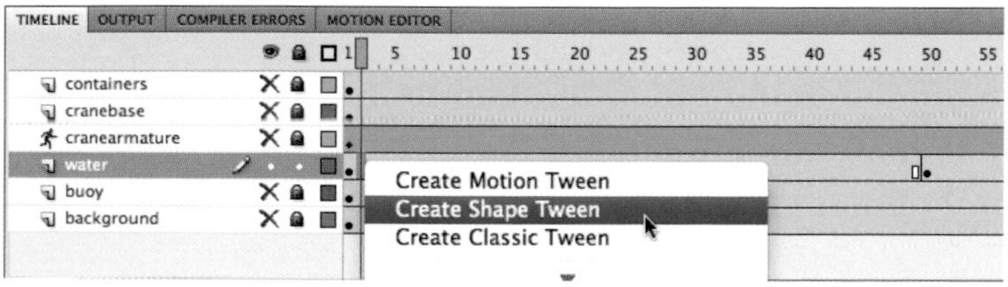

Flash applies a shape tween between the two keyframes, which is indicated by a black forward-pointing arrow.

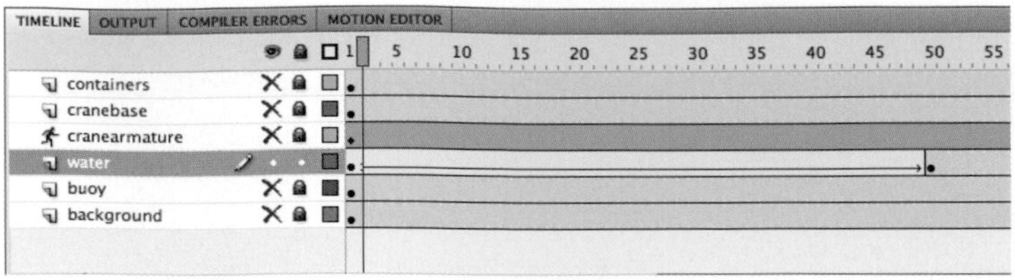

3 Click on any frame between the second keyframe and the last keyframe in the water layer.

4 Right-click/Ctrl-click and select Create Shape Tween. Or, choose Insert > Shape Tween.

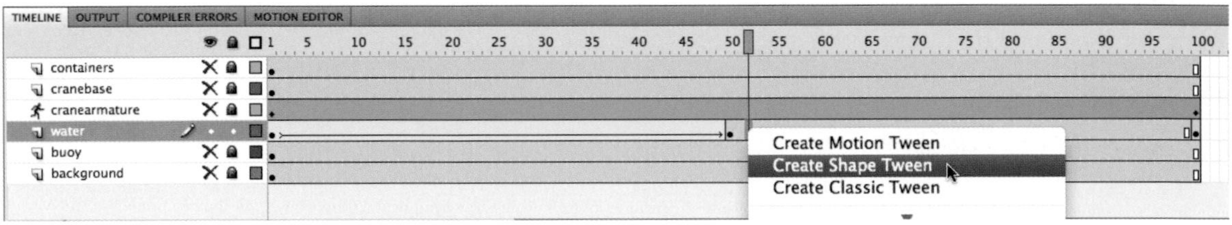

Flash applies a shape tween between the last two keyframes, which is indicated by a black forward-pointing arrow.

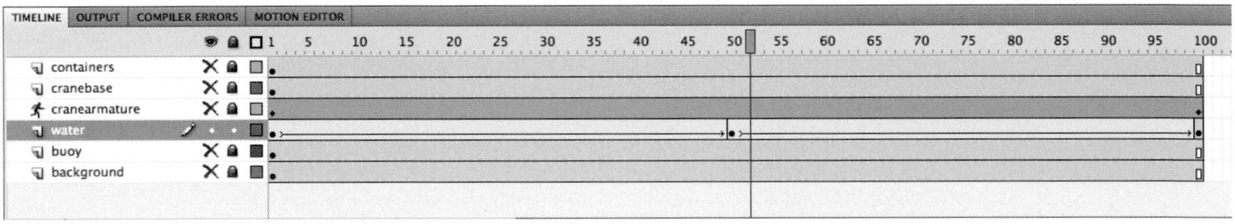

Note: The Motion Editor is not available for shape tweens.

5 Watch your animation by choosing Control > Test Movie > in Flash Professional. Flash creates a smooth animation between the keyframes in the water layer, morphing the shape of the ocean surface.

Using Shape Hints

Shape hints force Flash to map points on the first shape to corresponding points on the second shape. By placing multiple shape hints, you can control more precisely how a shape tween animates from one shape to the next.

Adding shape hints

Now you'll add shape hints to the shape tween of the wave to modify the way it morphs from one shape to the next.

1 Select the first keyframe of the shape tween in the water layer.

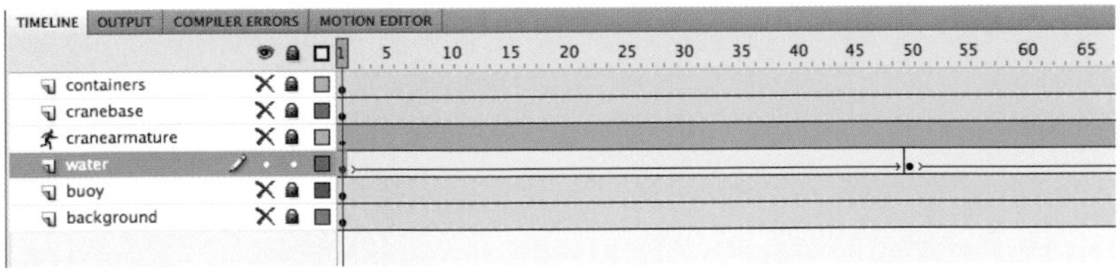

2 Choose Modify > Shape > Add Shape Hint (Ctrl+Shift+H/Command+Shift+H).

A red circled letter "a" appears on the Stage. The circled letter represents the first shape hint.

3 Drag the circled letter to the top-left corner of the ocean shape.

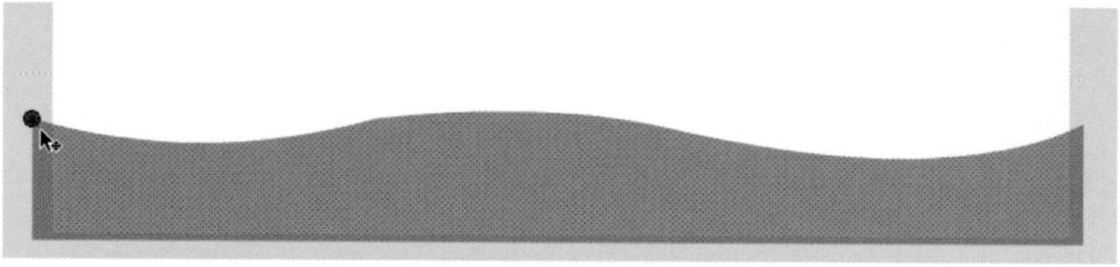

Shape hints should be placed on the contours of shapes.

4 Choose Modify > Shape > Add Shape Hint again to create a second shape hint.

A red circled "b" appears on the Stage.

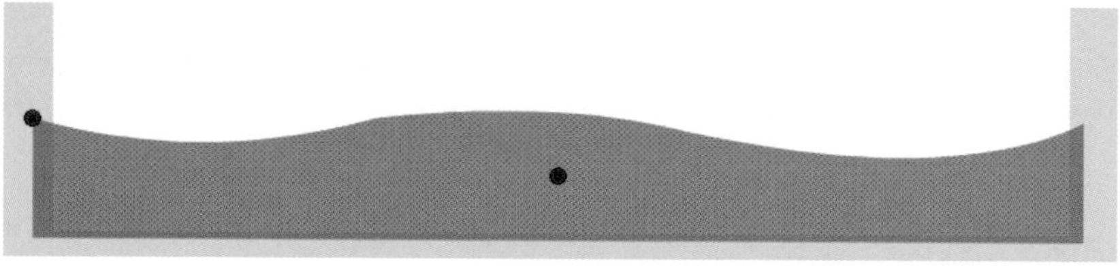

5 Drag the "b" shape hint to the top edge of the ocean shape at the bottom of a dip of the wave.

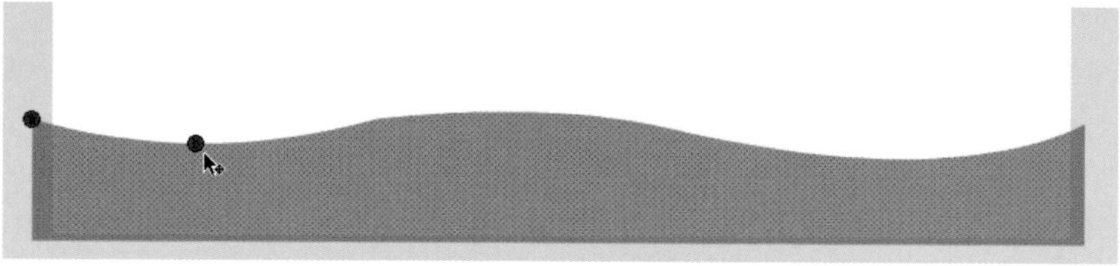

6 Add a third shape hint.

A red circled "c" appears on the Stage.

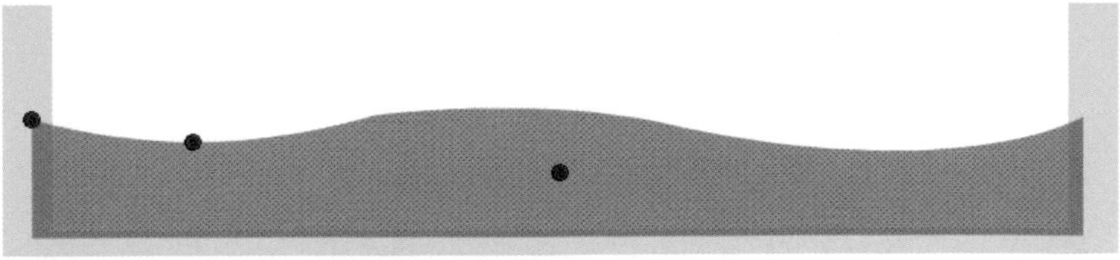

7 Drag the "c" shape hint to the far top-right corner of the ocean shape.

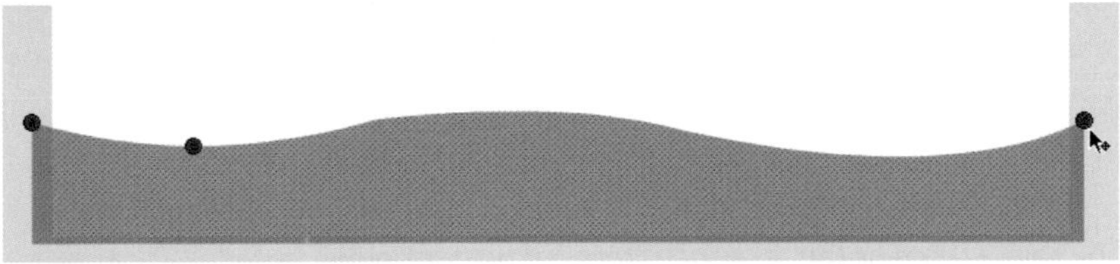

You have three shape hints mapped to different points on the shape in the first keyframe.

8 Select the next keyframe of the water layer (frame 50).

A corresponding circled "c" appears on the Stage, although an "a" and a "b" shape hint are directly under it.

9 Drag the circled letters to corresponding points on the shape in the second keyframe. The "a" hint goes on the top-left corner, the "b" hint goes on the bottom of the wave, and the "c" hint goes on the top-right corner.

The shape hints are green, indicating that you've correctly placed the shape hint.

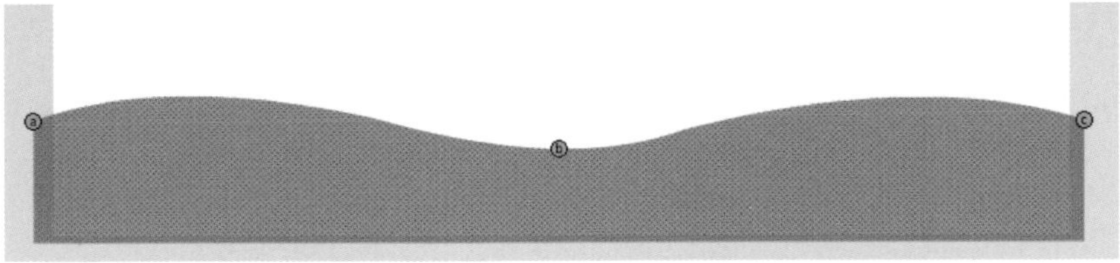

10 Select the first keyframe.

Note that the initial shape hints are yellow, indicating that they are correctly placed.

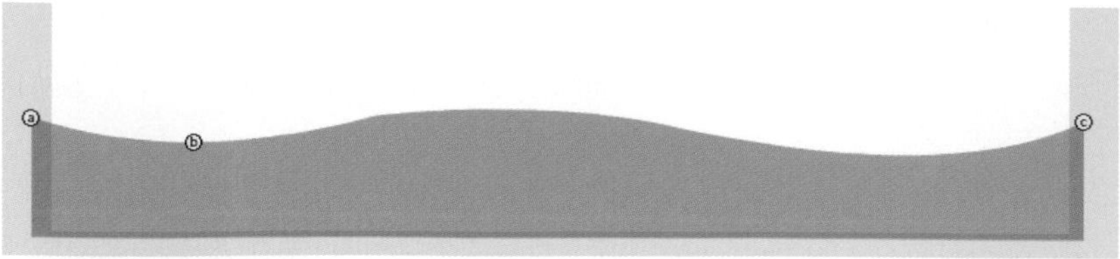

11 Choose Control > Test Movie > in Flash Professional to see the effects of the shape hints on the shape tween.

The shape hints force the dip of the first shape to map to the dip of the second shape, causing the shape tween to appear more like a traveling wave instead of an up-and-down bobbing motion. Use shape hints to lock down certain parts of the shape (such as the "a" and "c" hints in this example), or to tell Flash where to move the shape (such as the "b" hint).

Note: You can add a maximum of 26 shape hints to any shape tween. Be sure to add them in a clockwise or counterclockwise direction for best results.

Removing shape hints

If you've added too many shape hints, you can easily delete the unnecessary ones. Removing a shape hint in one keyframe will remove its corresponding shape hint in the other keyframe.

- Drag an individual shape hint entirely off the Stage and Pasteboard.
- Choose Modify > Shape > Remove All Hints to delete all the shape hints.

Simulating Physics with Inverse Kinematics

Now that you've animated the undulating water beneath the crane, it would be nice to see the red buoy bob up and down along the surface as well. You could create a motion tween so it floats along the water. However, since the buoy has a flexible flag attached, it'll be more realistic to see the flag and the pole wave and bend as the buoy moves. The Spring feature helps you do this easily.

The Spring feature simulates physics in any animated armature. A flexible object (like a flag or a flag pole) normally would have some "springiness" that would cause it to jiggle on its own as it moves, and continue to jiggle even after motion of the entire body stops. The amount of springiness can be set for each bone in an armature to help you get the exact amount of rigidity or flexibility in your animation.

Define bones for your armature

In the following steps, you'll animate the buoy bobbing along the water and set the strength of the spring in each of the bones in the armature of the buoy. The first step is to add bones to the shape of the buoy.

1 Lock and hide all the layers except for the buoy layer and select the contents of the buoy layer.

2 Choose the Bone tool.

3 Click on the base of the buoy and drag out the first bone to the tip of the triangular support at the bottom of the flag pole.

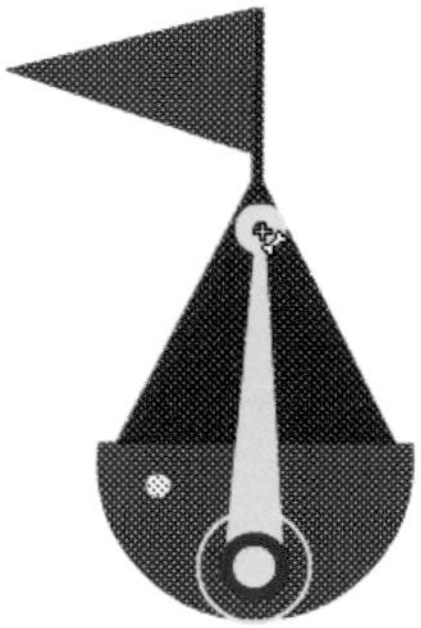

The first bone is defined. The contents of the buoy layer are separated to a new Pose layer.

4 Click on the end of the first bone and drag out the next bone a little farther up the flag pole.

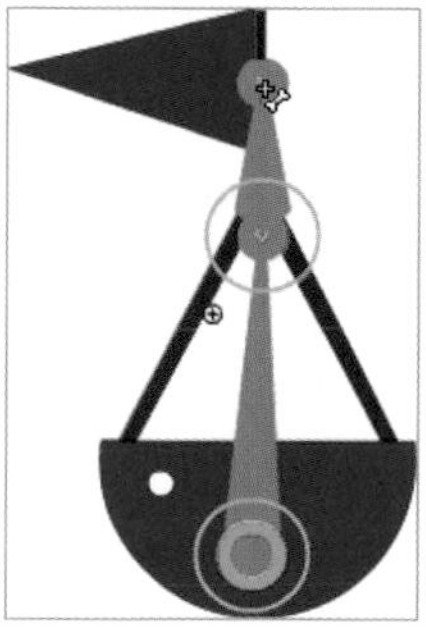

The second bone is defined.

5 Click on the end of the second bone and drag out the next bone to the left into the flag.

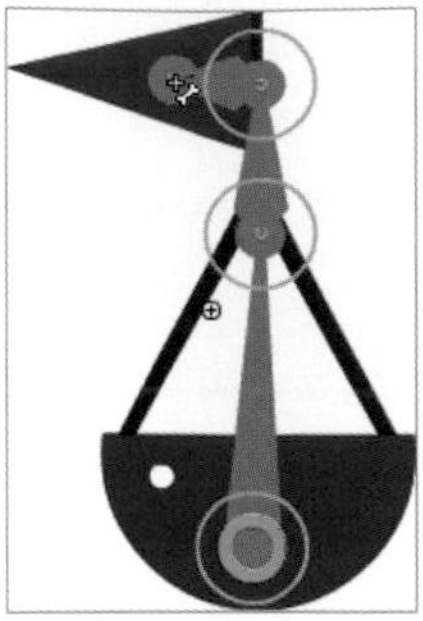

> **Note:** The Spring feature for inverse kinematics works for both armatures in shapes and armatures with movie clips.

6 Define two more bones to extend the armature to the tip of the flag.

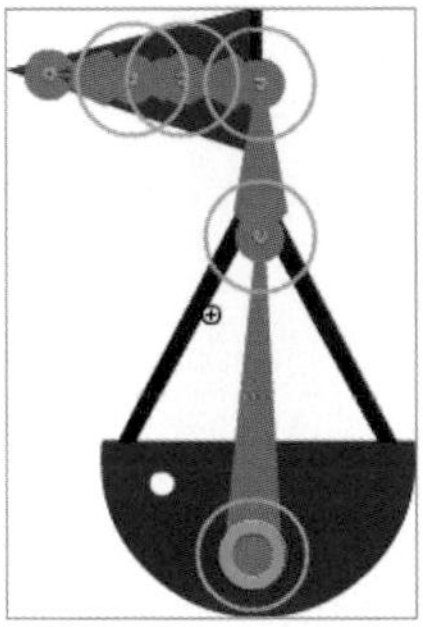

The bones in the flag will help the flag wave realistically. The bone in the flag pole will help the pole bend separately from the floating bottom.

Setting the spring strength for each bone

Next, you'll set the strength value for the spring for each bone. The strength value can range from 0 (no spring) to 100 (maximum spring).

1 Select the last bone (at the tip of the flag) of the armature in the buoy.

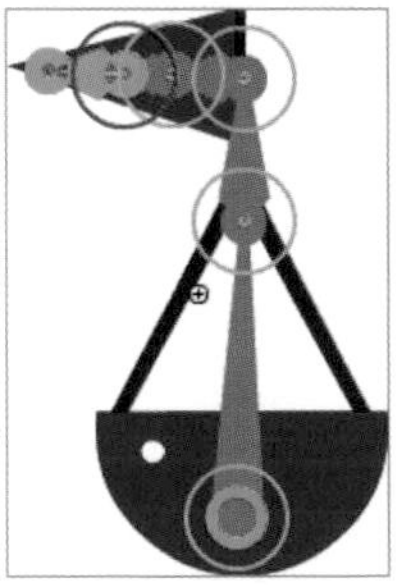

2 In the Properties inspector, in the Spring section, enter **100** for the Strength.

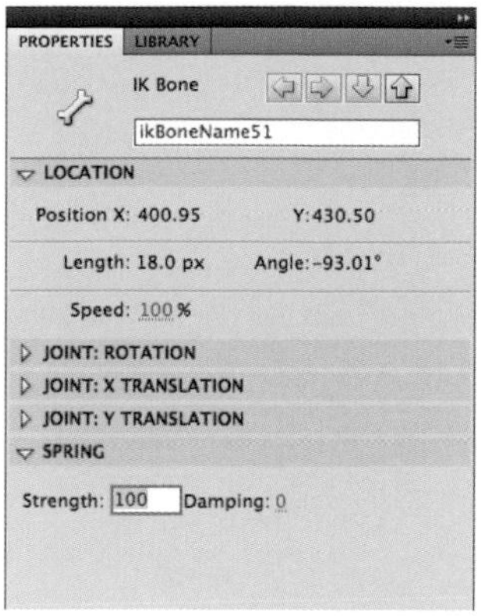

The last bone has the maximum spring strength since the flag tip is the most flexible part of the whole buoy and would have the most independent motion.

3 Select the next bone in the armature hierarchy. It may be difficult to select the next adjacent bone if they are too crowded together, so you can choose the Parent button in the Properties inspector to move up the hierarchy.

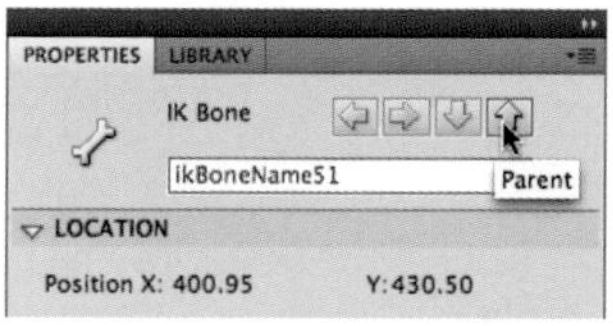

4 In the Properties inspector, in the Spring section, enter **60** for the Strength.

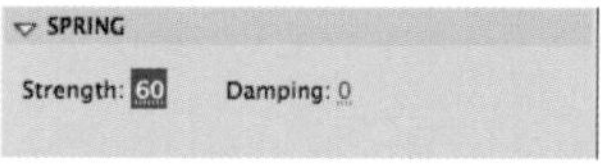

The middle of the flag is a little less flexible than the tip, so it has a smaller strength value.

5 Select the next adjacent bone, and in the Properties inspector, in the Spring section, enter **40** for the Strength.

The base of the flag is even less flexible than the middle of the flag, so it has an even smaller strength value.

6 Select the next adjacent bone (the bone within the pole), and in the Properties inspector, in the Spring section, enter **50** for the Strength.

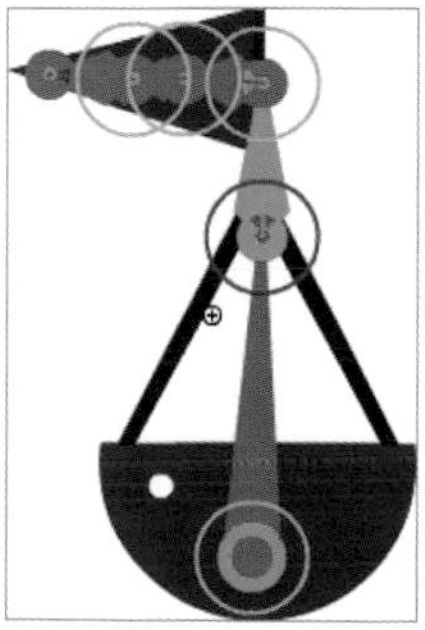

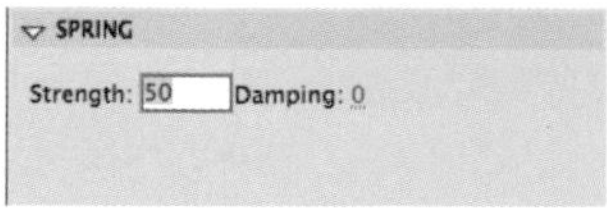

Giving the pole a medium amount of spring strength will make the pole bend back and forth on the buoy.

7 Select the next adjacent bone (the parent bone), and in the Properties inspector, in the Spring section, enter **20** for the Strength.

Insert the next pose

Next, you'll make the buoy float atop the water and watch how its motion affects the movement of the individual bones in the armature.

1 Unhide all the layers so you can see where the buoy is located on the scene.

2 Select frame 35 of the armature layer, which contains your buoy.

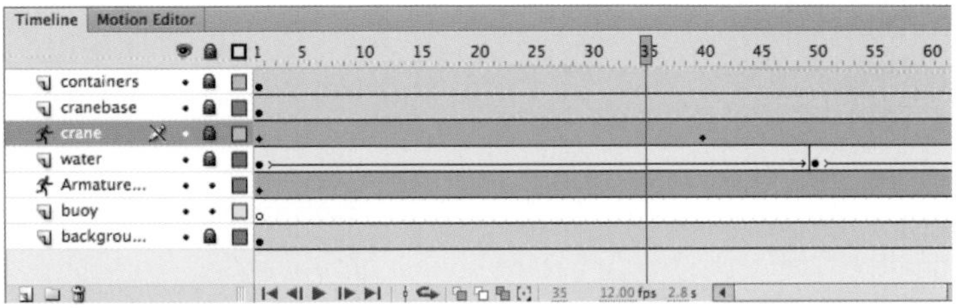

3 Rotate the first bone of the buoy to the left to make it rock slightly on the surface of the water.

4 Rotate the second bone (the flag pole) just a bit to the right to bend it.

5 Choose Control > Test Movie > in Flash Professional to see the motion of the buoy and its attached flag.

The buoy sways to the left. At the same time, the flag pole bends and the flag jiggles slightly. Even after the keyframe at frame 35, the buoy continues to rock back and forth slightly.

6 Move the playhead to frame 75.

7 Rotate the first bone of the buoy back to the right to make it sway in the other direction.

8 Test your movie again to see the complete motion.

The back-and-forth rotation of the buoy affects the lingering springing motion throughout the armature and makes the animation more realistic and much simpler to animate.

Note: The effects of the Spring feature are more apparent when there are additional frames on the Timeline after the armature's final pose, as in this lesson. The additional frames allow you to see the residual bouncing effect after the motion stops.

Adding damping effects

Damping refers to how much the spring effect decreases with time. It wouldn't be realistic if the rocking of the buoy or the swaying of the flag and the flag pole continues indefinitely. Over time, the swaying should lessen and eventually stop. You can set a damping value from 0 (no damping) to 100 (maximum damping) to control how rapidly these effects diminish.

1 Select the first bone of the buoy (in the floating part), and in the Properties inspector, in the Spring section, enter **100** for the Damping.

The maximum damping value will decrease the rocking of the buoy over time.

2 Continue to select each of the bones of the armature and enter the maximum value (**100**) for Damping.

3 Choose Control > Test Movie > in Flash Professional to see the effects that the damping values have on the motion of your floating buoy.

The buoy and the flag and flag pole still sway, but their motion quickly subsides after the initial starting motion and after the last keyframe. The damping values help add a sense of weight to the armature. Experiment with both the strength and damping values in the Spring section of your armature to get the most realistic motion.

Review Questions

1 What are the two ways of using the Bone tool?

2 What is the Bind tool used for?

3 Define and differentiate these terms: a bone, a node, a joint, and an armature.

4 What is a shape tween, and how do you apply it?

5 What are shape hints, and how do you use them?

6 What does strength and damping refer to in the Spring feature?

Review Answers

1 The Bone tool can connect movie clip instances together to form an articulated object that can be posed and animated with inverse kinematics. The Bone tool can also create an armature wtihin a shape, which can be posed and animated with inverse kinematics as well.

2 The Bind tool can redefine the connections between the control points of a shape and the bones of an armature. The connections between the control points and the bones determine how the shape reacts to the bending and rotations of the armature.

3 Bones are the objects that connect individual movie clips together or that make up the internal structure of a shape for motion with inverse kinematics. A node is one of the movie clip instances that have been linked with the Bone tool. A node can be described in terms of its relationship with other nodes, such as parent, child, or sibling. Joints are the articulations between bones. Joints can rotate as well as translate (slide in both the *x* and *y* directions). Armatures refer to the complete articulated object. Armatures are separated on a special Pose layer on the Timeline where poses can be inserted for animation.

4 A shape tween creates smooth transitions between keyframes containing different shapes. To apply a shape tween, create different shapes in an initial keyframe and in a final keyframe. Then select any frame between the keyframes in the Timeline, right-click/Ctrl-click, and select Create Shape Tween.

5 Shape hints are labeled markers that indicate how one point on the initial shape of a shape tween will map to a corresponding point on the final shape. Shape hints help refine the way the shapes will morph. To use shape hints, first select the initial keyframe of a shape tween. Choose Modify > Shape > Add Shape Hint. Move the first shape hint to the edge of the shape. Move the playhead to the final keyframe, and move the corresponding shape hint to a matching edge of the shape.

6 Strength is the amount of springiness of any individual bone in an armature. Add springiness with the Spring feature to simulate the way different parts of a flexible object jiggle when the entire object moves and continue to jiggle when the object stops. Damping refers to how quickly the springiness effect subsides over time.

6 CREATING INTERACTIVE NAVIGATION

Lesson Overview

In this lesson, you'll learn how to do the following:

- Create button symbols
- Add sound effects to buttons
- Duplicate symbols
- Swap symbols and bitmaps
- Name button instances
- Write ActionScript 3.0 to create nonlinear navigation
- Use the Code Snippets panel to quickly add interactivity
- Create and use frame labels
- Create animated buttons

This lesson will take approximately three hours to complete. If needed, remove the previous lesson folder from your hard drive and copy the Lesson06 folder onto it.

Let your viewers explore your project and become active participants. Button symbols and ActionScript work together to create engaging, user-driven, interactive experiences.

Getting Started

To begin, view the interactive restaurant guide that you'll create as you learn to make interactive projects in Flash.

1 Double-click the 06End.html file in the Lesson06/06End folder to play the animation.

   The project is an interactive restaurant guide for an imaginary city. Viewers can click any button to see more information about a particular restaurant. In this lesson, you'll create interactive buttons and structure the Timeline properly. You'll learn to write ActionScript to provide instructions for what each button will do.

2 Close the 06End.html file.

3 Double-click the 06Start.fla file in the Lesson06/06Start folder to open the initial project file in Flash. The file includes several assets already in the Library panel, and the Stage has already been sized properly.

4 Choose File > Save As. Name the file **06_workingcopy.fla** and save it in the 06Start folder. Saving a working copy ensures that the original start file will be available if you want to start over.

Note: Flash warns you if your computer doesn't have the same fonts contained in a FLA file. Choose substitute fonts, or simply click Use Default to have Flash automatically make the substitutions.

About Interactive Movies

Interactive movies change based on the viewer's actions. For example, when the viewer clicks a button, a different graphic with more information is displayed. Interactivity can be simple, such as a button click, or it can be complex, receiving inputs from a variety of sources, such as the movements of the mouse, keystrokes from the keyboard, or even data from databases.

In Flash, you use ActionScript to achieve most interactivity. ActionScript provides the instructions that tell each button what to do when the user clicks one of them. In this lesson, you'll learn to create a nonlinear navigation—one in which the movie doesn't have to play straight from the beginning to the end. ActionScript can tell the Flash playhead to jump around and go to different frames of the Timeline based on which button the user clicks. Different frames on the Timeline contain different content. The user doesn't actually know that the playhead is jumping around the Timeline; the user just sees (or hears) different content appear as the buttons are clicked on the Stage.

Creating Buttons

A button is a basic visual indicator of what the user can interact with. The user usually clicks a button, but many other types of interactions are possible. For example, something can happen when the user rolls the mouse over a button.

Buttons are a kind of symbol that have four special states, or keyframes, that determine how the button appears. Buttons can look like virtually anything—an image, graphic, or a bit of text—they don't have to be those typical pill-shaped, gray rectangles that you see on many Web sites.

Creating a button symbol

In this lesson, you'll create buttons with small thumbnail images and restaurant names. A button symbol's four special states include the following:

- **Up state.** Shows the button as it appears when the mouse is not interacting with it.
- **Over state.** Shows the button as it appears when the mouse is hovering over it.
- **Down state.** Shows the button as it appears when the mouse button is depressed.
- **Hit state.** Indicates the clickable area of the button.

You'll understand the relationship between these states and the button appearance as you work through this exercise.

1 Choose Insert > New Symbol.

2 In the Create New Symbol dialog box, select Button and name the symbol **gabel loffel button**. Click OK.

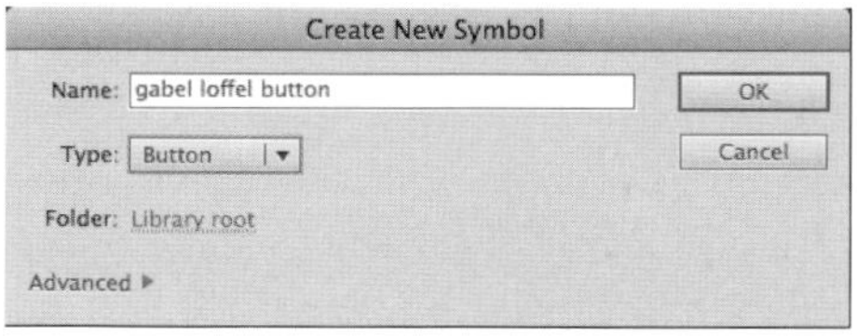

Flash brings you to symbol-editing mode for your new button.

3 In the Library panel, expand the folder called restaurant thumbnails and drag the graphic symbol gabel loffel thumbnail to the middle of the Stage.

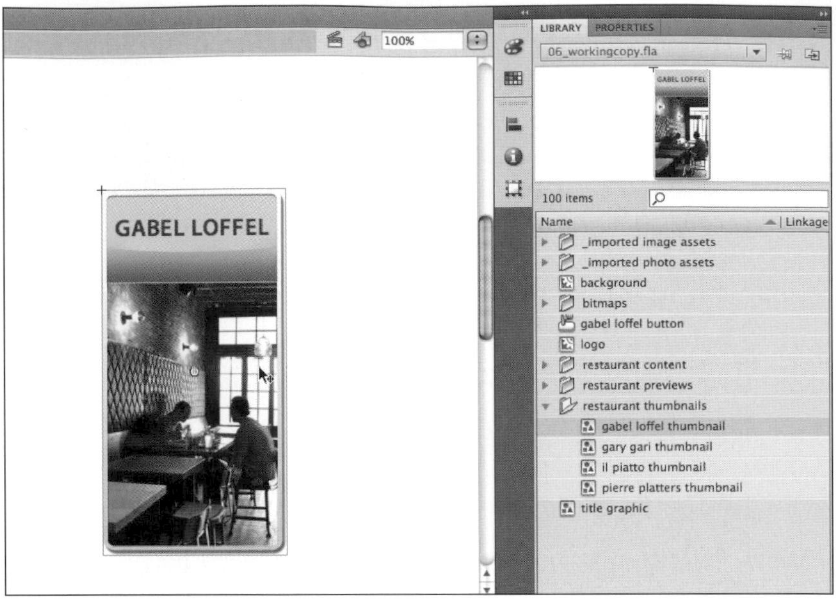

4 In the Properties inspector, set the X value to **0** and the Y value to **0**.

The upper-left corner of the small gabel loffel restaurant image is now aligned to the registration point of the symbol.

5 Select the Hit frame in the Timeline and choose Insert > Timeline > Frame to extend the Timeline.

The gabel loffel image now extends through the Up, Over, Down, and Hit states.

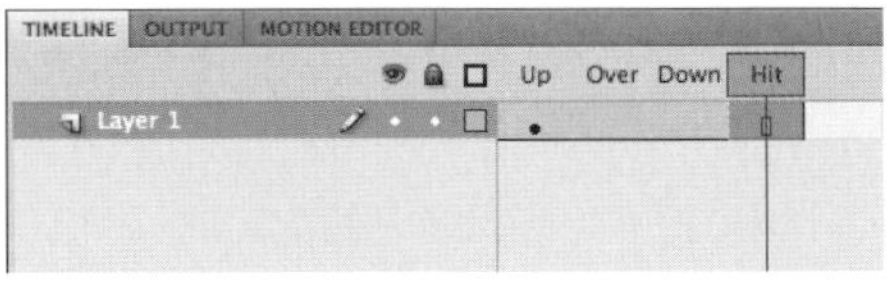

6 Insert a new layer.

7 Select the Over frame and choose Insert > Timeline > Keyframe.

A new keyframe is inserted in the Over state of the top layer.

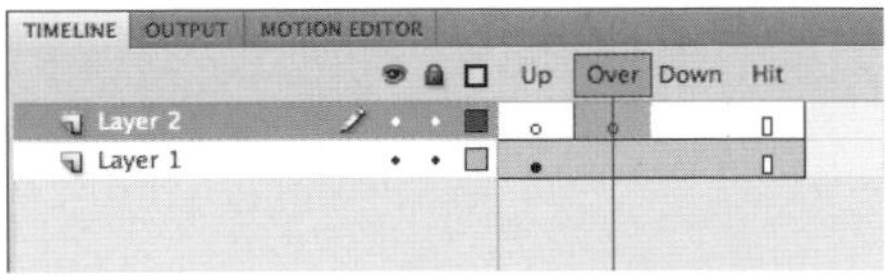

8 In the Library panel, expand the folder called restaurant previews, and drag the movie clip symbol called gabel loffel over info to the Stage.

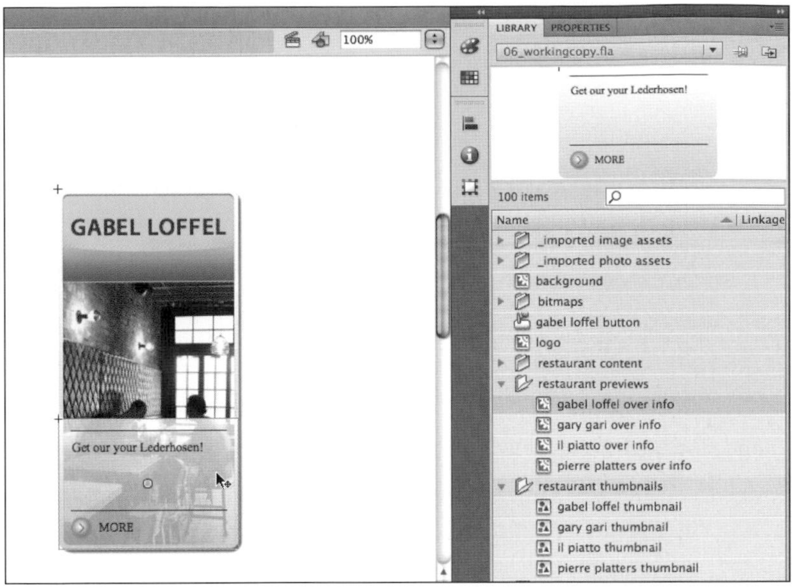

9 In the Properties inspector, set the X value to **0** and the Y value to **215**.

The gray information box will appear over the restaurant image whenever the mouse cursor rolls over the button.

10 Insert a third layer above the first two.

11 Select the Down frame on the new layer and choose Insert > Timeline > Keyframe.

A new keyframe is inserted in the Down state of the new layer.

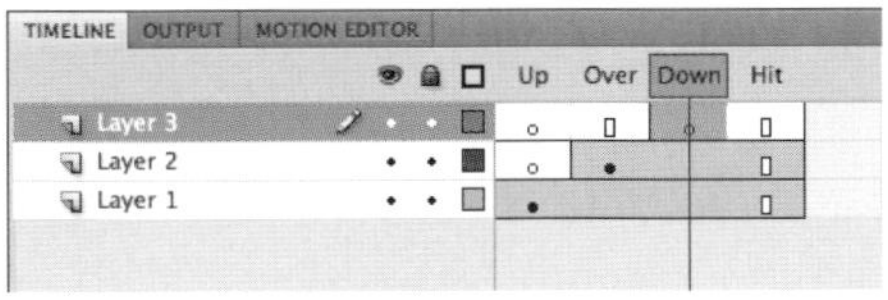

12 Drag the sound file called clicksound.mp3 from the Library panel to the Stage.

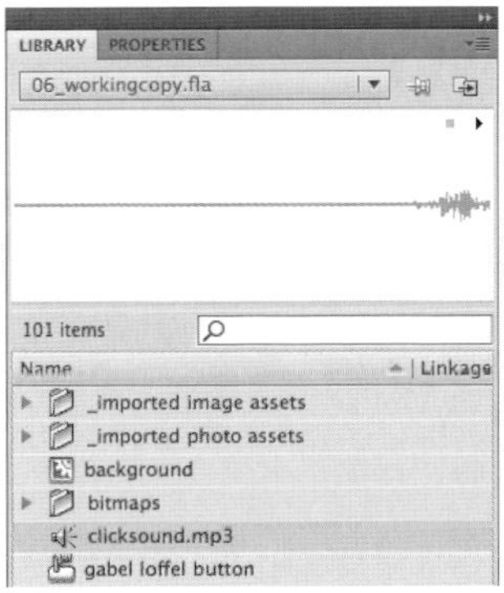

Note: You'll learn more about sound in Lesson 8, "Working with Sound and Video."

13 Select the Down keyframe where the sound form appears, and in the Properties inspector, make sure that Sync is set to Event.

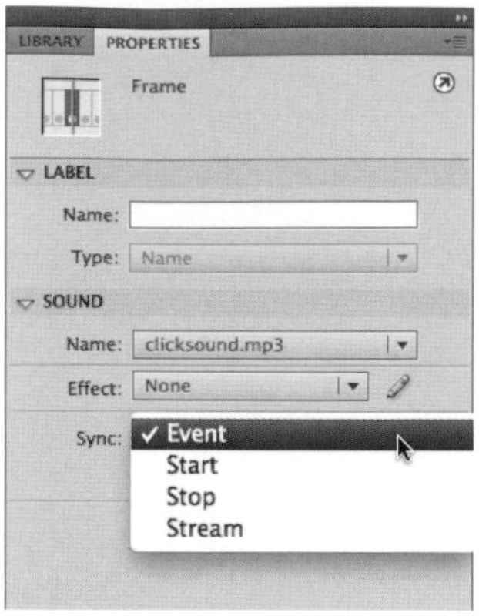

A clicking sound will play only when a viewer depresses the button.

14 Click Scene 1 above the Stage to exit symbol-editing mode and return to the main Timeline. Your first button symbol is complete! Look in your Library panel to see the new button symbol stored there.

Invisible Buttons and the Hit Keyframe

Your button symbol's Hit keyframe indicates the area that is "hot," or clickable, to the user. Normally, the Hit keyframe contains a shape that is the same size and location as the shape in your Up keyframe. In most cases, you want the graphics that users see to be the same area where they click. However, in certain advanced applications, you may want the Hit keyframe and the Up keyframe to be different. If your Up keyframe is empty, the resulting button is known as an invisible button.

Users can't see invisible buttons, but because the Hit keyframe still defines a clickable area, invisible buttons remain active. So, you can place invisible buttons over any part of the Stage and use ActionScript to program them to respond to users.

Invisible buttons are useful for creating generic hotspots. For example, placing them on top of different photos can help you make each photo respond to a mouse click without having to make each photo a different button symbol.

Duplicating buttons

Now that you've created one button, you'll be able to create others more easily. You'll duplicate one button here, change the image in the next section, and then continue to duplicate buttons and modify images for the remaining restaurants.

1 In the Library panel, right-click/Ctrl-click the gabel loffel button symbol and select Duplicate. You can also click the options menu at the top-right corner of the Library panel and select Duplicate.

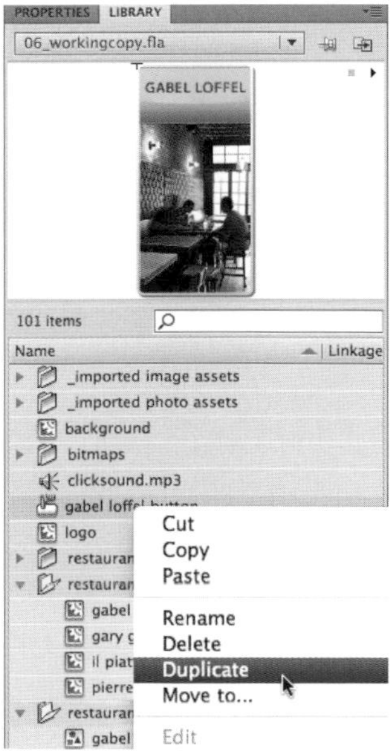

2 In the Duplicate Symbol dialog box, select Button, and name it **gary gari button**. Click OK.

Swapping bitmaps

Bitmaps and symbols are easy to swap on the Stage and can significantly speed up your workflow.

1 In the Library panel, double-click the icon for your newly duplicated symbol (gary gari button) to edit it.

2 Select the restaurant image on the Stage.

3 In the Properties inspector, click Swap.

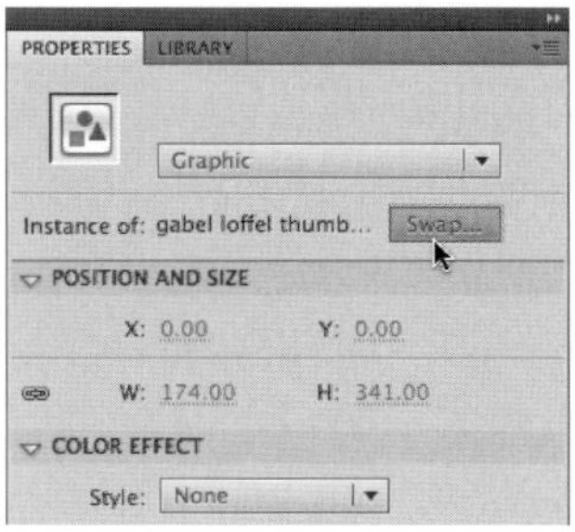

4 In the Swap Symbol dialog box, select the next thumbnail image, called gary gari thumbnail, and click OK.

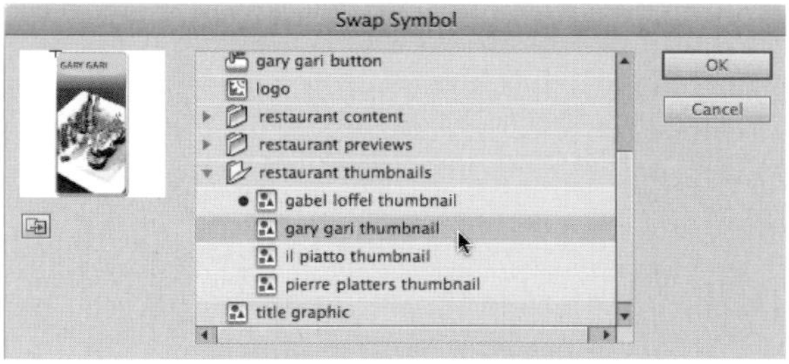

The original thumbnail (shown with a black dot next to the symbol name) is swapped for the one you selected. Because they are both the same size, the replacement is seamless.

5 Now select the Over keyframe and click the gray information box on the Stage.

6 In the Properties inspector, click Swap and swap the selected symbol with the symbol called gary gari over info.

The instance in the Over keyframe of your button is replaced with one that is appropriate for the second restaurant. Since the symbol was duplicated, all other elements, such as the sound in the top layer, remain the same.

7 Continue duplicating your buttons and swapping the two instances inside them until you have four different button symbols in your Library panel, each representing a different restaurant. When you're done, it's a good idea to organize all your restaurant buttons in a folder in your Library panel.

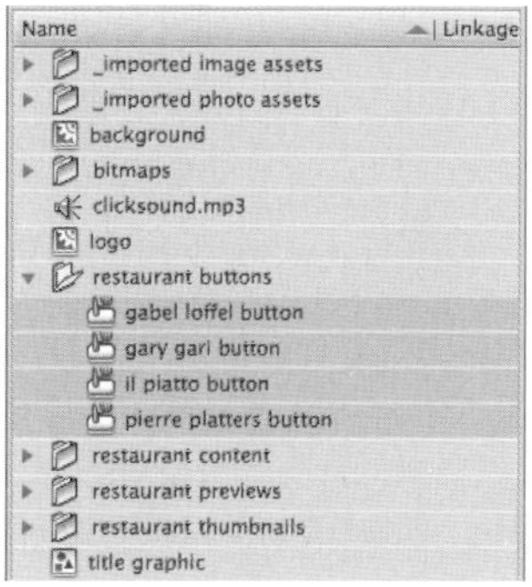

Placing the button instances

The buttons need to be put on the Stage and given names in the Properties inspector so that ActionScript can identify them.

1 On the main Timeline, insert a new layer and rename it **buttons**.

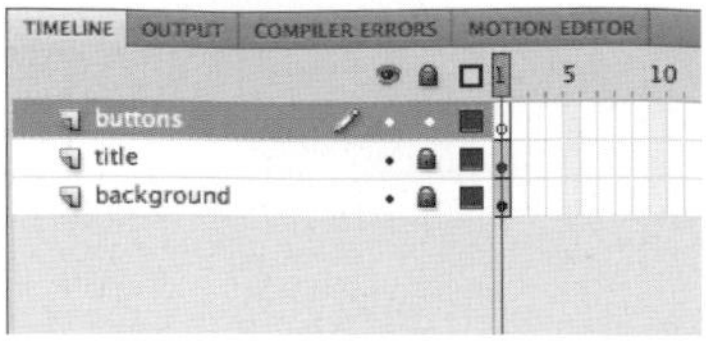

2 Drag each of your buttons from the Library panel to the middle of the Stage, placing them in a horizontal row. Don't worry about their exact position because you'll align them nicely in the next few steps.

3 Select the first button, and in the Properties inspector, set the X value to **100**.

4 Select the last button, and in the Properties inspector, set the X value to **680**.

5 Select all four buttons. In the Align panel (Window > Align), deselect the Align to stage option, click the Space Evenly Horizontally button, and then click the Align Top Edge button.

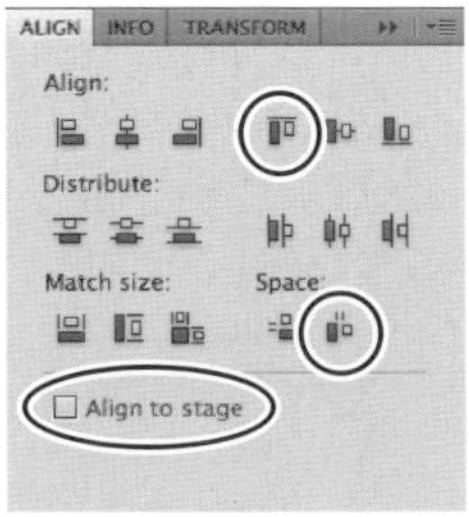

All four buttons are now evenly distributed and aligned horizontally.

6 With all the buttons still selected, in the Properties inspector, enter **170** for the Y value.

All four buttons are positioned on the Stage correctly.

7 You can now test your movie to see how the buttons behave. Choose Control > Test Movie > in Flash Professional. Note how the gray information box in the Over keyframe appears when your mouse hovers over each button, and how the clicking sound is triggered when you depress your mouse over each button. At this point, however, you haven't provided any instructions for the buttons to actually do anything. That part comes after you name the buttons and learn a little about ActionScript.

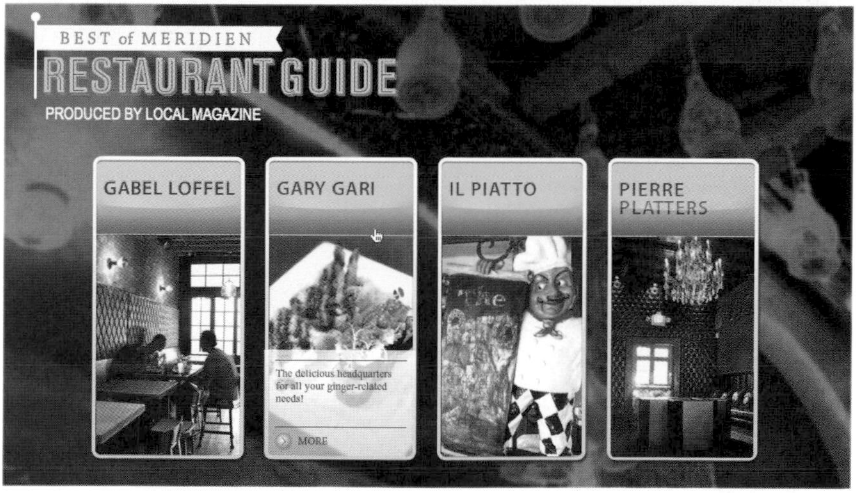

Naming the button instances

Name each button instance so that it can be referenced by ActionScript. This is a crucial step that many beginners forget to do.

1 Click on an empty part of the Stage to deselect all the buttons, and then select just the first button.

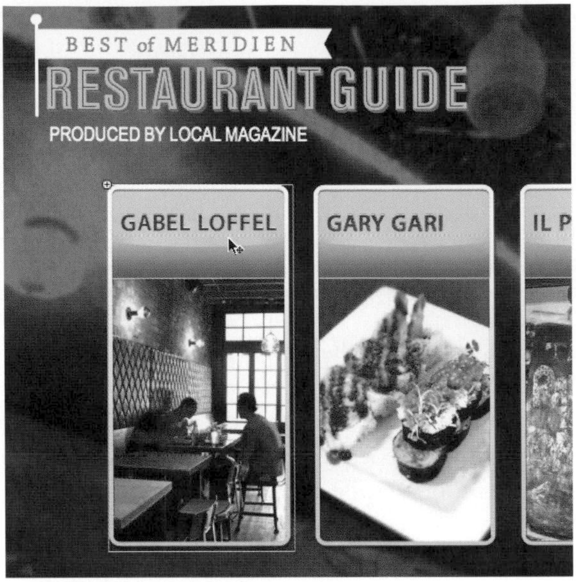

2 Type **gabelloffel_btn** in the Instance Name field in the Properties inspector.

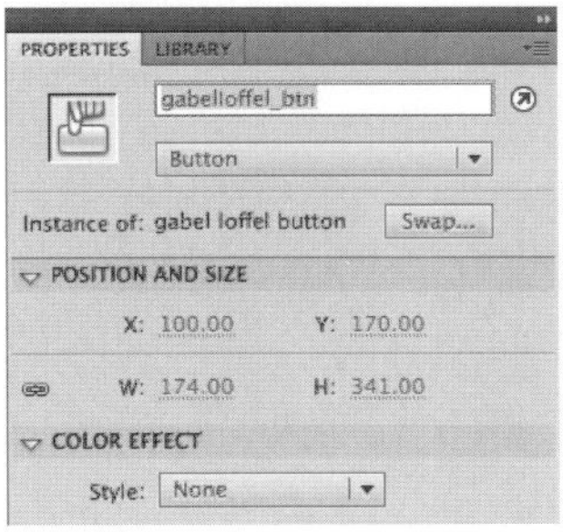

3 Name each of the other buttons **garygari_btn**, **ilpiatto_btn**, and **pierreplatters_btn**.

Make sure that you use all lowercase letters, leave no spaces, and double-check the spelling of each button instance. Flash is very picky and one typo will prevent your entire project from working correctly!

4 Lock all the layers.

Naming Rules

Naming instances is a critical step in creating interactive Flash projects. The most common mistake made by novices is not to name, or to incorrectly name, a button instance.

The instance names are important because ActionScript uses the names to reference those objects. Instance names are not the same as the symbol names in the Library panel. The names in the Library panel are simply organizational reminders.

Instance naming follows these simple rules:

1. Do not use spaces or special punctuation. Underscores are okay to use.
2. Do not begin a name with a number.
3. Be aware of uppercase and lowercase letters. Instance names are case-sensitive.
4. End your button name with _btn. Although it is not required, it helps identify those objects as buttons.
5. Do not use any word that is reserved for a Flash ActionScript command.

Understanding ActionScript 3.0

Adobe Flash Professional CS6 uses ActionScript 3.0, a robust scripting language, to extend the functionality of Flash. Although ActionScript 3.0 may seem intimidating to you if you're new to scripting, you can get great results with some very simple scripts. As with any language, it's best if you take the time to learn the syntax and some basic terminology.

About ActionScript

ActionScript, which is similar to JavaScript, lets you add more interactivity to Flash animations. In this lesson, you'll use ActionScript to attach behaviors to buttons. You'll also learn how to use ActionScript for such simple tasks as stopping an animation.

You don't have to be a scripting expert to use ActionScript. In fact, for common tasks, you may be able to copy script that other Flash users have shared. And you can also use the Code Snippets panel, which provides an easy, visual way to add ActionScript to your project or share ActionScript code among developers.

However, you'll be able to accomplish much more in Flash—and feel more confident using the application—if you understand how ActionScript works.

This lesson isn't designed to make you an ActionScript expert. Instead, it introduces common terms and syntax, walks you through a simple script, and provides an introduction to the ActionScript language.

If you've used scripting languages before, the documentation included in the Flash Help menu may provide additional guidance you need to use ActionScript proficiently. If you're new to scripting and want to learn ActionScript, you may find an ActionScript 3.0 book for beginners helpful.

Understanding scripting terminology

Many of the terms used in describing ActionScript are similar to terms used for other scripting languages. The following terms are used frequently in ActionScript documentation.

Variable

Note: Variable names must be unique, and they are case-sensitive. The variable mypassword is not the same as the variable MyPassword. Variable names can contain only numbers, letters, and underscores; they cannot begin with a number. These are the same naming rules that apply to instances. (In fact, variables and instances are conceptually the same.)

A *variable* represents a specific piece of data that may or may not be constant. When you create, or *declare*, a variable, you also assign a data type, which determines what kind of data the variable can represent. For example, a String variable holds any string of alphanumeric characters, whereas a Number variable must contain a number.

Keyword

In ActionScript, a *keyword* is a reserved word that is used to perform a specific task. For example, *var* is a keyword that is used to create a variable.

You can find a complete list of keywords in Flash Help. Because these words are reserved, you can't use them as variable names or in other ways. ActionScript always uses them to perform their assigned tasks. As you enter ActionScript in the Actions panel, keywords will turn a different color. This is a great way to know if a word is reserved by Flash.

Arguments

Arguments provide specific details for a particular command and are the values between parentheses () in a line of code. For example, in the code `gotoAndPlay(3);` the argument instructs the script to go to frame 3.

Function

A *function* is a group of statements that you can refer to by name. Using a function makes it possible to run the same set of statements without having to type them repeatedly.

Objects

In ActionScript 3.0, you work with objects, which are abstract types of data that help you do certain tasks. A Sound object, for example, helps you control sound, and a Date object can help you manipulate time-related data. The button symbols that you created earlier in this lesson are also objects—they are called SimpleButton objects.

Every object should be named. An object that has a name can be referenced and controlled with ActionScript. Buttons on the Stage are referred to as instances, and in fact, *instances* and *objects* are synonymous.

Methods

Methods are commands that result in action. Methods are the doers of ActionScript, and each kind of object has its own set of methods. Understanding ActionScript involves learning the methods for each kind of object. For example, two methods associated with a MovieClip object are `stop()` and `gotoAndPlay()`.

Properties

Properties describe an object. For example, the properties of a movie clip include its height and width, *x* and *y* coordinates, and horizontal and vertical scale. Many properties can be changed, whereas other properties can only be "read," meaning they simply describe an object.

Using proper scripting syntax

If you're unfamiliar with program code or scripting, you may find ActionScript code challenging to decipher. Once you understand the basic *syntax*, which is the grammar and punctuation of the language, you'll find it easier to follow a script.

- The *semicolon* at the end of the line tells ActionScript that it has reached the end of the code line.
- As in English, every open *parenthesis* must have a corresponding close parenthesis, and the same is true for *brackets* and *curly brackets*. If you open something, you must close it. Very often, the curly brackets in ActionScript code will be separated on different lines. This makes it easier to read what's inside the curly brackets.
- The *dot* operator (.) provides a way to access the properties and methods of an object. Type the instance name, followed by a dot, and then the name of the property or method. Think of the dot as a way to separate objects, methods, and properties.
- Whenever you're entering a string, use *quotation marks*.
- You can add *comments* to remind you or others of what you are accomplishing with different parts of the script. To add a comment for a single line, start it with two slashes (//). To type a multiline comment, start it with /* and end it with */. Comments are ignored by Flash and won't affect your code at all.

Flash provides assistance in the following ways as you write scripts in the Actions panel:

- Words that have specific meanings in ActionScript, such as keywords and statements, appear in blue as you type them in the Actions panel. Words that are not reserved in ActionScript, such as variable names, appear in black. Strings appear in green. Comments, which ActionScript ignores, appear in gray.
- As you work in the Actions panel, Flash detects the action you are entering and displays a code hint. There are two types of code hints: a tooltip that contains the complete syntax for that action and a pop-up menu that lists possible ActionScript elements.
- To check the syntax of a script you've completed, click the Check Syntax icon ( ). Syntax errors are listed in the Compiler Errors panel.

  You can also click the AutoFormat icon ( ) (which will also format the script according to conventions to make it easier for others to read).

Navigating the Actions panel

The Actions panel is where you write all your code. Open the Actions panel by choosing Window > Actions or by selecting a keyframe on the Timeline and clicking the ActionScript panel icon ( ) on the top right of the Properties inspector. You can also right-click/Ctrl-click on any keyframe and select Actions.

The Actions panel gives you quick access to the core elements of ActionScript as well as provides you with different options to help you write, debug, format, edit, and find your code.

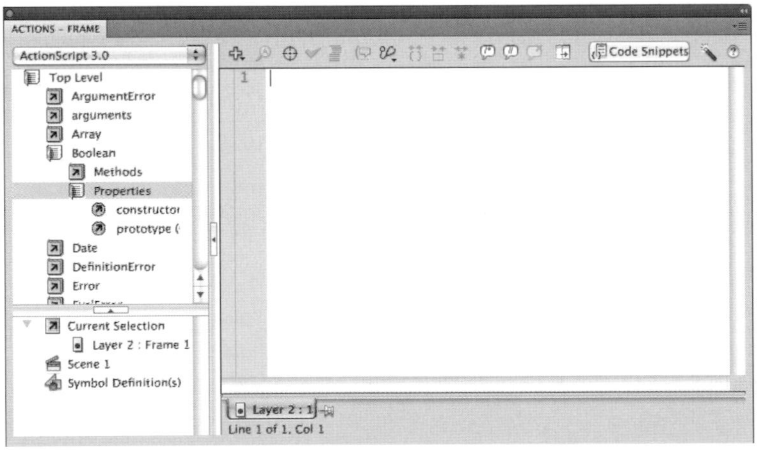

The Actions panel is divided into several panes. At the top-left corner is the Actions toolbox, which contains categories that organize all the ActionScript code. At the top of the Actions toolbox is a pull-down menu that displays only the code for the version of ActionScript you select. You should select ActionScript 3.0, the latest version. At the very bottom of the Actions toolbox categories is a yellow Index category that lists, in alphabetical order, all the language elements. You don't need to use the toolbox to add code to your script, but it can help to ensure that you're using the code correctly.

At the top right of the Actions panel is the Script pane—the blank slate in which all your code appears. You enter ActionScript in the Script pane just as you would in a text-editing application.

At the bottom left of the Actions panel is the Script navigator, which can help you find a particular piece of code. ActionScript is placed on keyframes on the Timeline, so the Script navigator can be particularly useful if you have lots of code scattered in different keyframes and on different Timelines.

All the panes in the Actions panel can be resized to suit your working style. They can even be collapsed completely to maximize the pane that you are working in. To resize a pane, click and drag the horizontal or vertical dividers.

Preparing the Timeline

Every new Flash project begins with just a single frame. To create room on the Timeline to add more content, you'll have to add more frames to all your layers.

1 Select a later frame in the top layer. In this example, select frame 50.

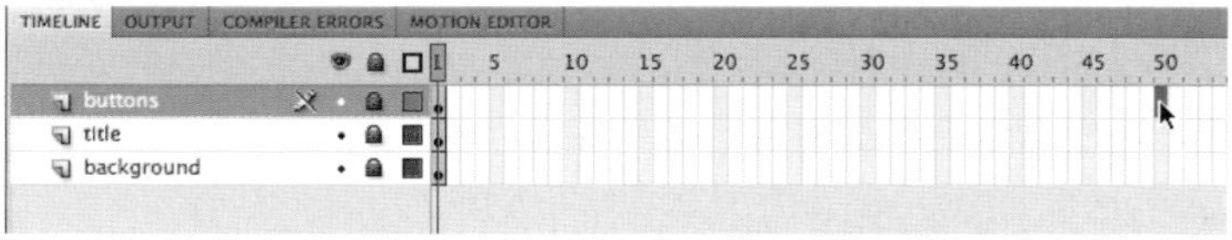

2 Choose Insert > Timeline > Frame (F5). You can also right-click/Ctrl-click and choose Insert Frame.

Flash adds frames in the top layer up to the selected point, frame 50.

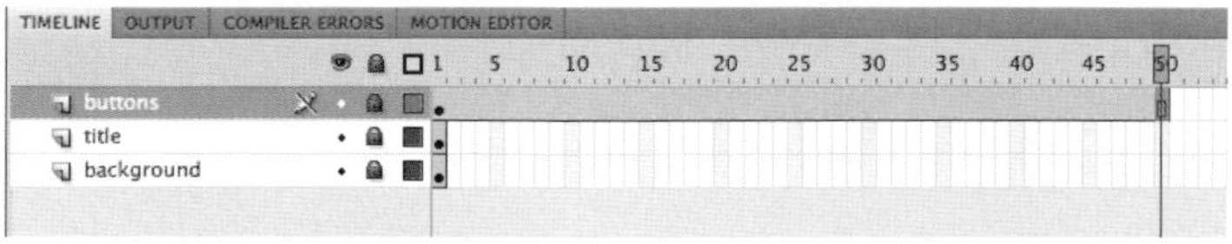

3 Select frame 50 in the other two layers and insert frames up to the selected frame.

All your layers have 50 frames on the Timeline.

Adding a Stop Action

Now that you have frames on the Timeline, your movie will play linearly from frame 1 to frame 50. However, with this interactive restaurant guide, you'll want your viewers to choose a restaurant to see in whichever order they choose. So you'll need to pause the movie at the very first frame to wait for your viewer to click a button. You use a stop action to pause your Flash movie. A stop action simply stops the movie from continuing by halting the playhead.

1 Insert a new layer at the top and rename it **actions**.

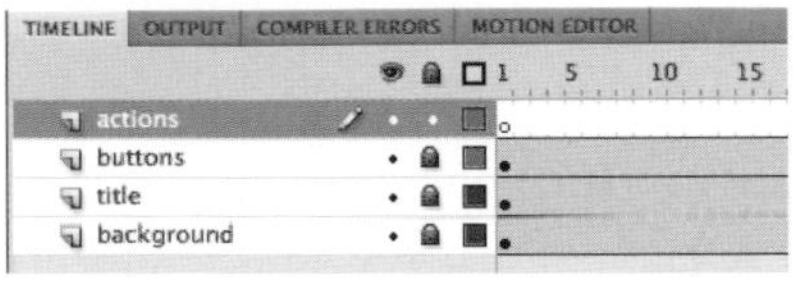

2 Select the first keyframe of the actions layer and open the Actions panel (Window > Actions).

3 In the Script pane, type `stop();`

The code appears in the Script pane and a tiny lowercase "a" appears in the first keyframe of the actions layer to indicate it contains some ActionScript. The movie will now stop at frame 1.

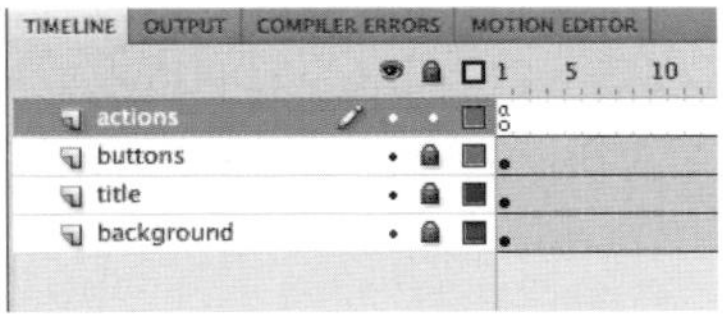

Creating Event Handlers for Buttons

Events are occurrences that happen in the Flash environment that Flash can detect and respond to. For example, a mouse click, a mouse movement, and a key press on the keyboard are all events. A pinch and a swipe gesture on mobile devices are also events. These events are produced by the user, but some events can happen independently of the user, like the successful loading of a piece of data or the completion of a sound. With ActionScript, you can write code that detects events and respond to them with an event handler.

The first step in event handling is to create a listener that will detect the event. A listener looks something like this:

```
wheretolisten.addEventListener(whatevent, responsetoevent);
```

The actual command is `addEventListener()`. The other words are placeholders for objects and parameters for your situation. *Wheretolisten* is the object where the event occurs (often a button), *whatevent* is the specific kind of event (such as a mouse click), and *responsetoevent* is the name of a function that is triggered when the event happens. So if you want to listen for a mouse click over a button called `btn1_btn`, and the response is to trigger a function called `showimage1`, the code would look like this:

```
btn1_btn.addEventListener(MouseEvent.CLICK, showimage1);
```

The next step is to create the function that will respond to the event—in this case, the function called `showimage1`. A *function* simply groups a bunch of actions together; you can then trigger that function by referencing its name. A function looks something like this:

```
function showimage1 (myEvent:MouseEvent){ };
```

Function names, like button names, are arbitrary. You can name functions whatever makes sense to you. In this particular example, the name of the function is `showimage1`. It receives one parameter (within the parentheses) called `myEvent`, which is an event that involves the mouse. The item following the colon indicates what type of object it is. If this function is triggered, all the actions between the curly brackets are executed.

Adding the event listener and function

You'll add ActionScript code to listen for a mouse click on each button. The response will make Flash go to a particular frame on the Timeline to show different content.

1 Select the first frame of the actions layer.

2 Open the Actions panel.

3 In the Script pane of the Actions panel, beginning on the second line, type

```
gabelloffel_btn.addEventListener(MouseEvent.CLICK,
restaurant1);
```

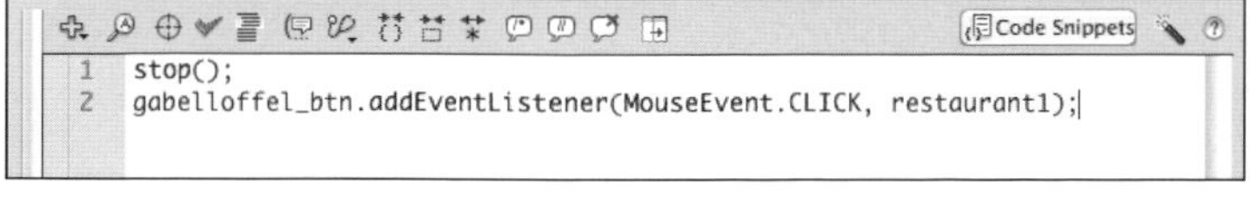
ACTIONS - FRAME
Code Snippets
1 stop();
2 gabelloffel_btn.addEventListener(MouseEvent.CLICK, restaurant1);

The listener listens for a mouse click over the gabelloffel_btn object on the Stage. If the event happens, the function called restaurant1 is triggered.

Mouse Events

The following list contains the ActionScript codes for common mouse events for the desktop. Use these codes when you create your listener, and make sure that you pay attention to lowercase and uppercase letters. For most users, the first event (`MouseEvent.CLICK`) will be sufficient for all projects. That event happens when the user presses and releases the mouse button.

- `MouseEvent.CLICK`
- `MouseEvent.MOUSE_MOVE`
- `MouseEvent.MOUSE_DOWN`
- `MouseEvent.MOUSE_UP`
- `MouseEvent.MOUSE_OVER`
- `MouseEvent.MOUSE_OUT`

For a complete list of all the events available for a button, check out the Flash Help files and look for the Events of the SimpleButton class.

Note: The void term refers to the data type that is returned by the function. Void means that nothing is returned. Sometimes, after functions are executed, they "return" data, such as doing some calculations and returning an answer.

4 On the next line of the Script pane, type

```
function restaurant1(event:MouseEvent):void {
 gotoAndStop(10);
}
```

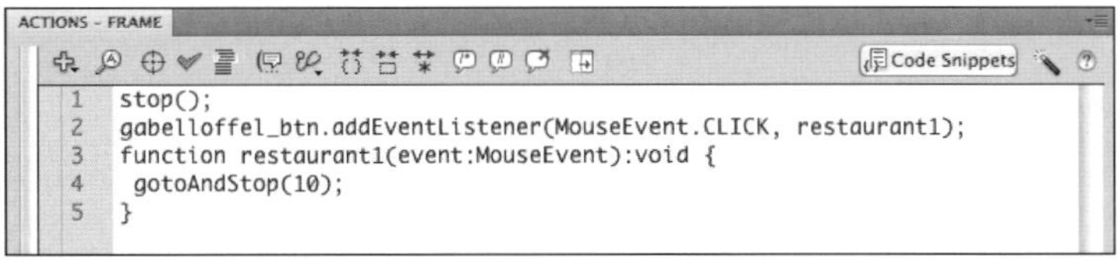

The function called restaurant1 contains instructions to go to frame 10 and stop there. The code for your button called gabelloffel_btn is complete.

Note: Be sure to include the final curly bracket for each function, or the code won't work.

5 On the next line of the Script pane, enter additional code for the remaining three buttons. You can copy and paste lines 2 through 5, and simply change the names of the button, the name of the function (in two places), and the destination frame. The full script should be as follows:

```
stop();
gabelloffel_btn.addEventListener(MouseEvent.CLICK,
restaurant1);
function restaurant1(event:MouseEvent):void {
 gotoAndStop(10);
}
```

```
garygari_btn.addEventListener(MouseEvent.CLICK, restaurant2);
function restaurant2(event:MouseEvent):void {
 gotoAndStop(20);
}
ilpiatto_btn.addEventListener(MouseEvent.CLICK, restaurant3);
function restaurant3(event:MouseEvent):void {
 gotoAndStop(30);
}
pierreplatters_btn.addEventListener(MouseEvent.CLICK,
restaurant4);
function restaurant4(event:MouseEvent):void {
 gotoAndStop(40);
}
```

ActionScript Commands for Navigation

The following list contains the ActionScript codes for common navigation commands. Use these codes when you create buttons to stop the playhead, start the playhead, or move the playhead to different frames on the Timeline. The `gotoAndStop` and `gotoAndPlay` commands require additional information, or arguments, within their parentheses as indicated.

- `stop();`
- `play();`
- `gotoAndStop(framenumber or "framelabel");`
- `gotoAndPlay(framenumber or "framelabel");`
- `nextFrame();`
- `prevFrame();`

Checking syntax and formatting code

ActionScript can be very picky, and a single misplaced period can cause your entire project to grind to a halt. Fortunately, the Actions panel provides a few tools to help you identify errors and fix them.

1 Select the first frame of your actions layer and open the Actions panel if it is not already open.

Note: Change the automatic formatting by selecting Preferences from the upper-right options menu. Choose Auto Format from the left menu and select the various options for formatting your code.

2 Click the Check Syntax button at the top of the Actions panel.

Flash checks the syntax of your ActionScript code. In the Compiler Errors panel (Window > Compiler Errors), Flash notifies you if there are errors or if your code is error-free. You should get 0 Errors and 0 Warnings if your code is correct.

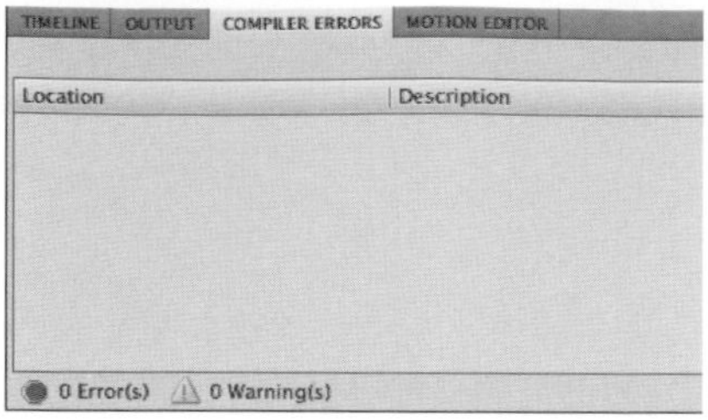

3 Click the AutoFormat icon at the top of the Actions panel.

Flash formats your code so it conforms to standard spacing and line breaks.

Creating Destination Keyframes

When the user clicks each button, Flash moves the playhead to a new spot on the Timeline according to the ActionScript instructions you just programmed. However, you haven't yet placed anything different at those particular frames. That's the next step.

Inserting keyframes with different content

You will create four keyframes in a new layer and place information about each of the restaurants in the new keyframes.

1 Insert a new layer at the top of the layer stack but below the actions layer and rename it **content**.

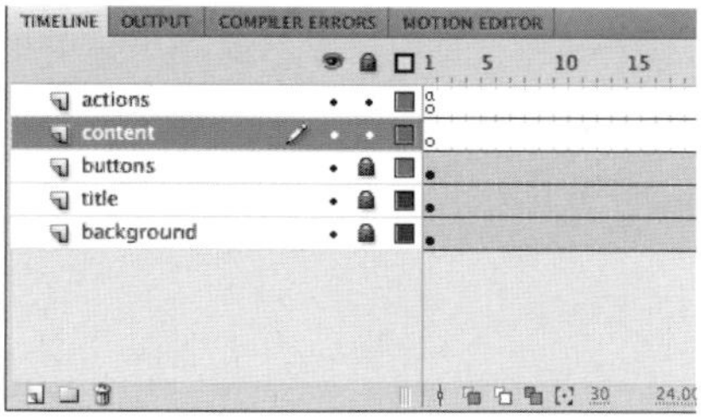

2 Select frame 10 of the content layer.

3 Insert a new keyframe at frame 10 (Insert > Timeline > Keyframe, or F6).

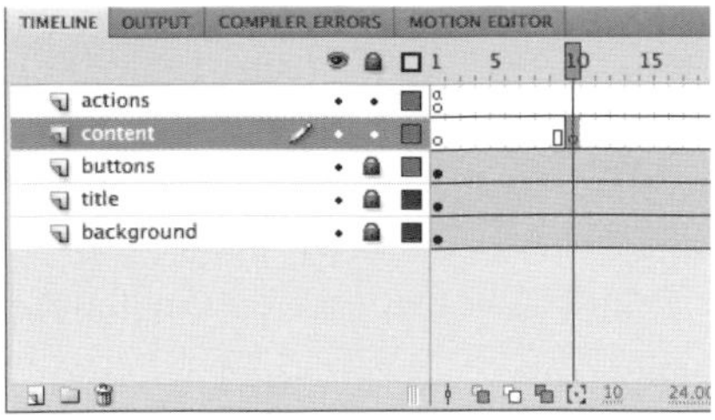

4 Insert new keyframes at frames 20, 30, and 40.

Your Timeline has four empty keyframes in the content layer.

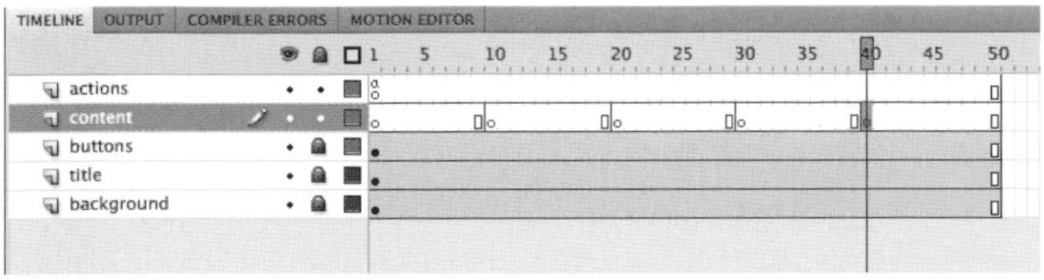

5 Select the keyframe at frame 10.

6 In the Library panel, expand the folder called restaurant content. Drag the symbol called gabel and loffel from the Library panel to the Stage. The symbol named gabel and loffel is a movie clip symbol that contains a photo, graphics, and text about the restaurant.

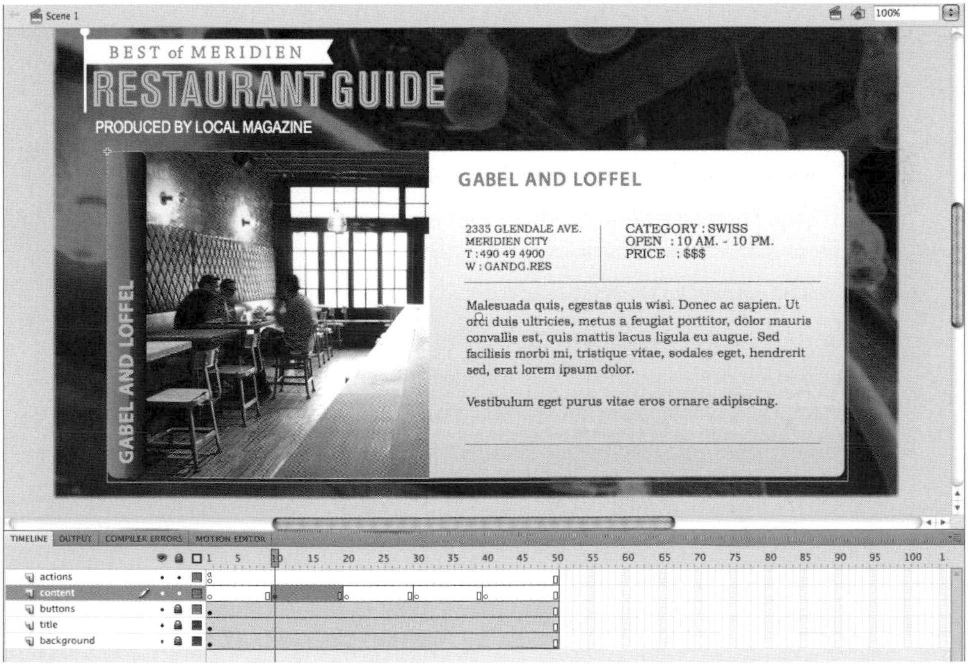

7 In the Properties inspector, set the X value to **60** and the Y value to **150**.

The restaurant information about gabel and loffel is centered on the Stage and covers all the buttons.

8 Select the keyframe at frame 20.

9 Drag the symbol called gary gari from the Library panel to the Stage. The symbol named gary gari is another movie clip symbol that contains a photo, graphics, and text about this restaurant.

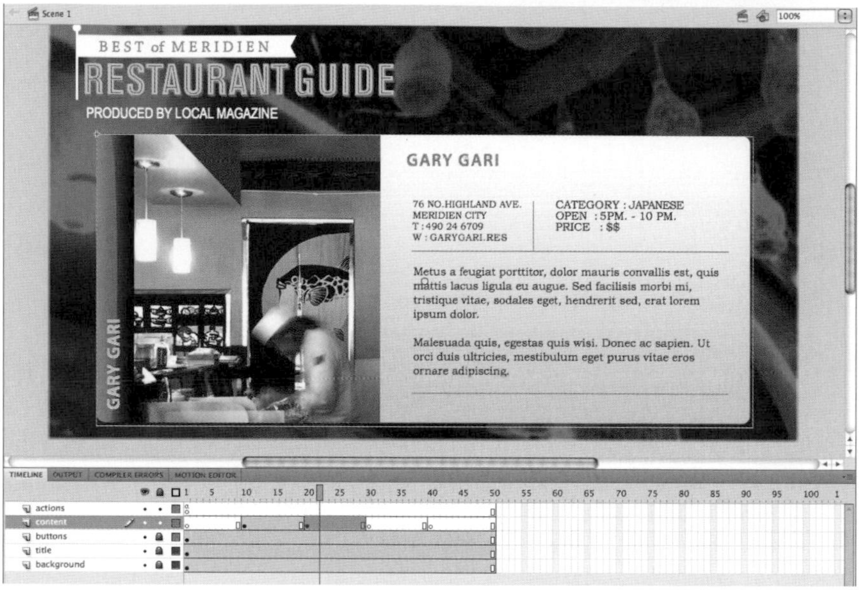

10 In the Properties inspector, set the X value to **60** and the Y value to **150**.

11 Place each of the movie clip symbols from the restaurant content folder in the Library panel to the corresponding keyframes in the content layer.

Each keyframe should contain a different movie clip symbol about a restaurant.

Using labels on keyframes

Your ActionScript code tells Flash to go to a different frame number when the user clicks each of the buttons. However, if you decide to edit your Timeline and add or delete a few frames, you'll need to go back into your ActionScript and change your code so the frame numbers match.

An easy way to avoid this problem is to use frame labels instead of fixed frame numbers. *Frame labels* are names that you give to keyframes. Instead of referring to keyframes by their frame number, you refer to them by their label. So, even if you move your destination keyframes as you edit, the labels remain with their keyframes. To reference frame labels in ActionScript, you must enclose them in quotation marks. The command `gotoAndStop("label1")` makes the playhead go to the keyframe with the label called label1.

1 Select frame 10 on the content layer.

2 In the Properties inspector, enter **label1** in the Label Name field.

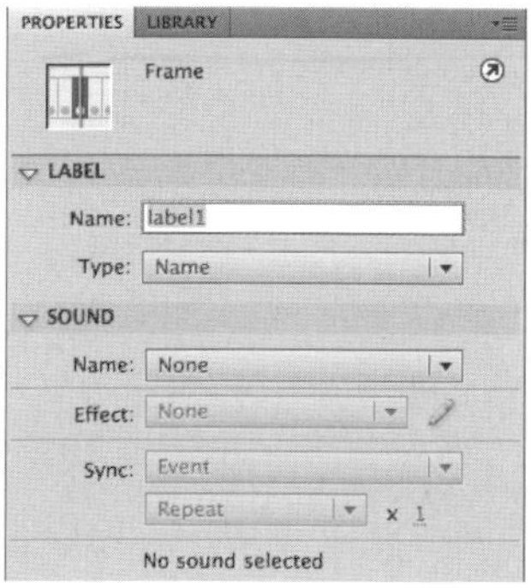

A tiny flag icon appears on each of the keyframes that have labels.

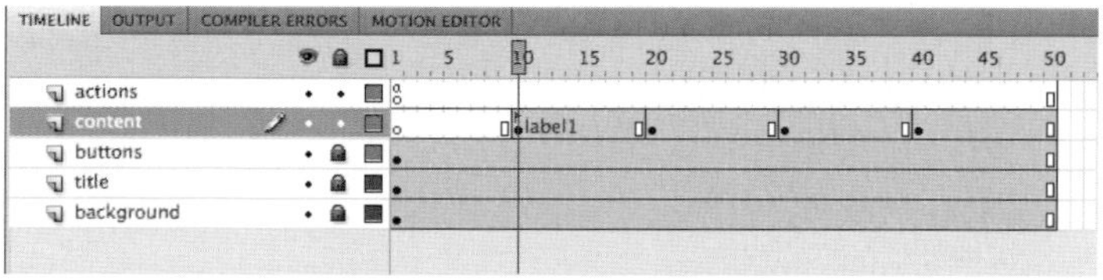

3 Select frame 20 on the content layer.

4 In the Properties inspector, enter **label2** in the Label Name field.

5 Select frames 30 and 40, and in the Properties inspector, enter corresponding names in the Label Name field: **label3** and **label4**.

A tiny flag icon appears on each of the keyframes that have labels.

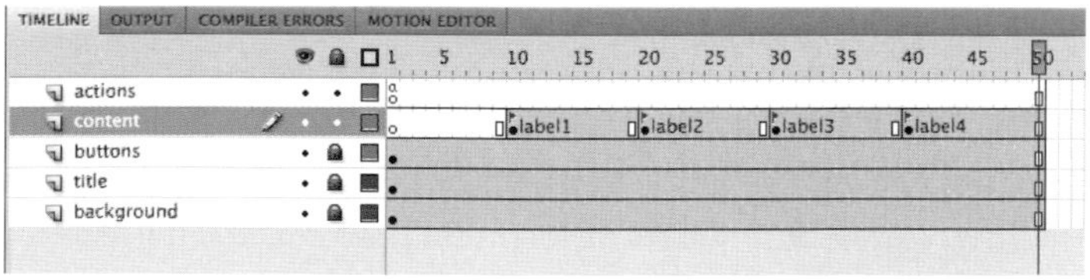

6 Select the first frame of the actions layer and open the Actions panel.

7 In your ActionScript code, change all the fixed frame numbers in each of the `gotoAndStop()` commands to the corresponding frame labels:

- `gotoAndStop(10);` should be changed to `gotoAndStop("label1");`
- `gotoAndStop(20);` should be changed to `gotoAndStop("label2");`
- `gotoAndStop(30);` should be changed to `gotoAndStop("label3");`
- `gotoAndStop(40);` should be changed to `gotoAndStop("label4");`

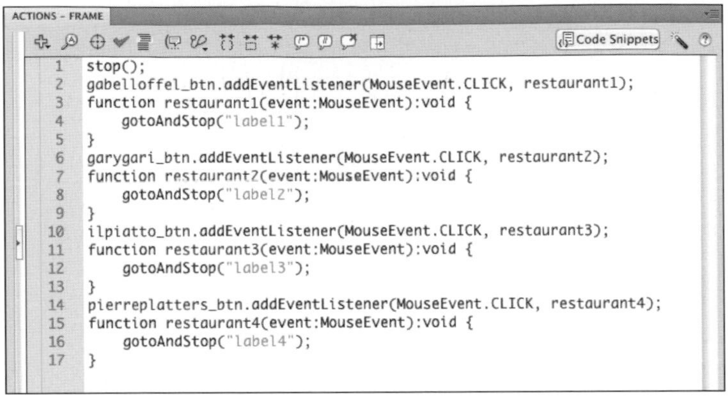
ACTIONS - FRAME
Code Snippets
```
stop();
gabelloffel_btn.addEventListener(MouseEvent.CLICK, restaurant1);
function restaurant1(event:MouseEvent):void {
    gotoAndStop("label1");
}
garygari_btn.addEventListener(MouseEvent.CLICK, restaurant2);
function restaurant2(event:MouseEvent):void {
    gotoAndStop("label2");
}
ilpiatto_btn.addEventListener(MouseEvent.CLICK, restaurant3);
function restaurant3(event:MouseEvent):void {
    gotoAndStop("label3");
}
pierreplatters_btn.addEventListener(MouseEvent.CLICK, restaurant4);
function restaurant4(event:MouseEvent):void {
    gotoAndStop("label4");
}
```


The ActionScript code now directs the playhead to a particular frame label instead of a particular frame number.

8 Test your movie by choosing Control > Test Movie > in Flash Professional.

Each button moves the playhead to a different labeled keyframe on the Timeline, where a different movie clip is displayed. The user can choose to see any restaurant in any order. However, since the restaurant information covers the buttons, you can't return to the original menu screen to choose another restaurant. You'll need to provide another button to return to the first frame, which you'll do in the next section.

Creating a Home Button with Code Snippets

A *home button* simply makes the playhead go back to the first frame of the Timeline, or to a keyframe where an original set of choices, or the main menu, are presented to the viewer. Creating a button that goes to frame 1 is the same process as creating the four restaurant buttons. However, in this section, you'll learn to use the Code Snippets panel to add ActionScript to your project.

Adding another button instance

A home, or main menu, button is provided for you in the Library panel.

1 Select the Buttons layer and unlock it if it is locked.

2 Drag the button called mainmenu from the Library panel to the Stage. Position the button instance at the top-right corner.

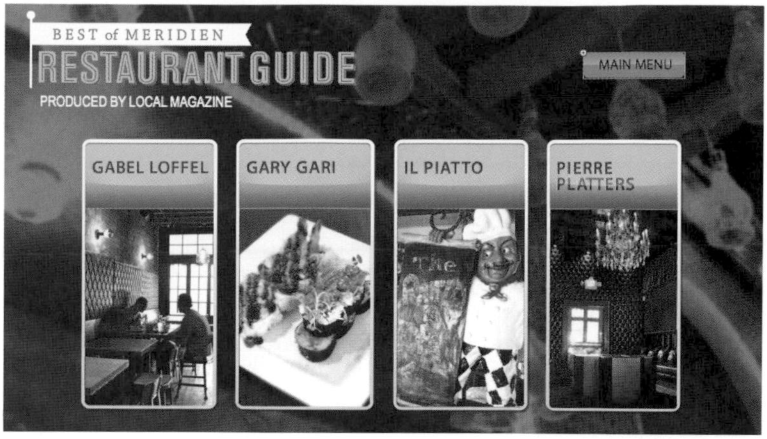

3 In the Properties inspector, set the X value to **726** and the Y value to **60**.

Using the Code Snippets panel to add ActionScript

The Code Snippets panel provides common ActionScript code that makes it easy for you to add interactivity to your Flash project, and simplifies the process. If you are unsure of your ability to code your own buttons, you can use the Code Snippets panel to learn how to add interactivity. The Code Snippets panel gives you a preview of the actual code, allows you to modify the critical parameters of the code, and use a visual pointer, called the pick whip, to point to objects on the Stage.

You can also save, import, and share code between a team of developers to make the development and production process more efficient.

1 Select the first frame of the actions layer in your Timeline. Choose Window > Code Snippets, or if your Actions panel is already open, click the Code Snippets button (Code Snippets) at the top right of the Actions panel.

   The Code Snippets panel appears. The code snippets are organized in folders that describe their function.

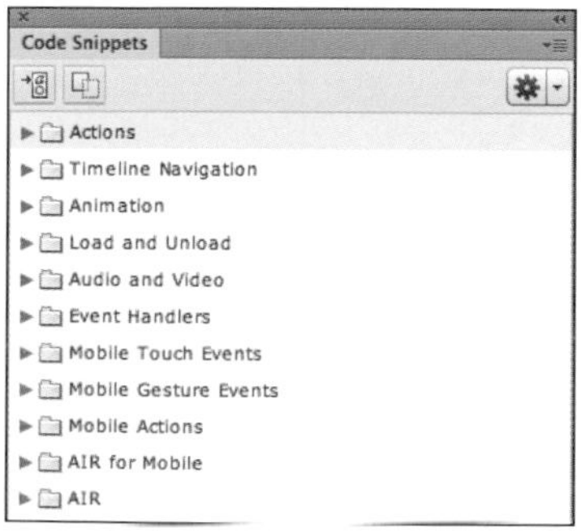

2 In the Code Snippets panel, expand the folder called Timeline Navigation and select Click to Go to Frame and Stop.

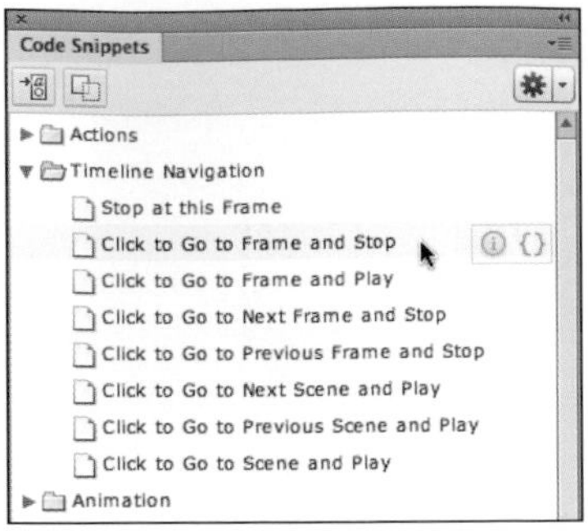

Immediately to the right of the code snippet name you'll find a description button and a code button.

3 Click the description button.

A brief description of the selected code appears.

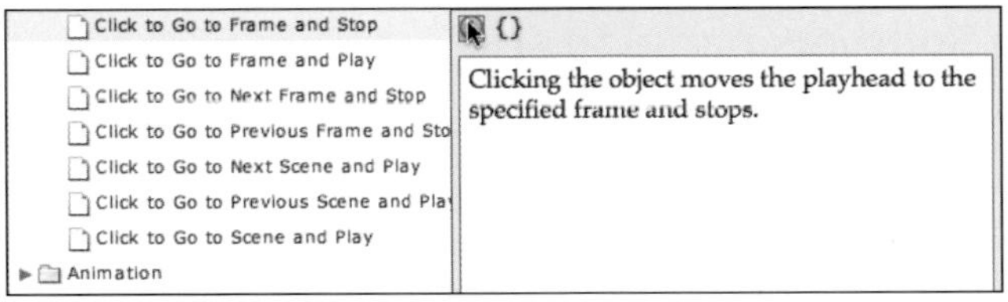

4 Click the code button.

The actual code appears. There is a commented portion of the code that describes the function of the code and the different parameters. The colored parts of the code are the parts that you need to change.

5 Move your mouse over the blue words **instance_name_here**.

6 Click and drag your cursor from the blue code words to the Home button on the Stage.

A purple line extends from the Code Snippets panel to the Home button. The Home button becomes highlighted with a yellow border, indicating that the selected code snippet will be applied to it.

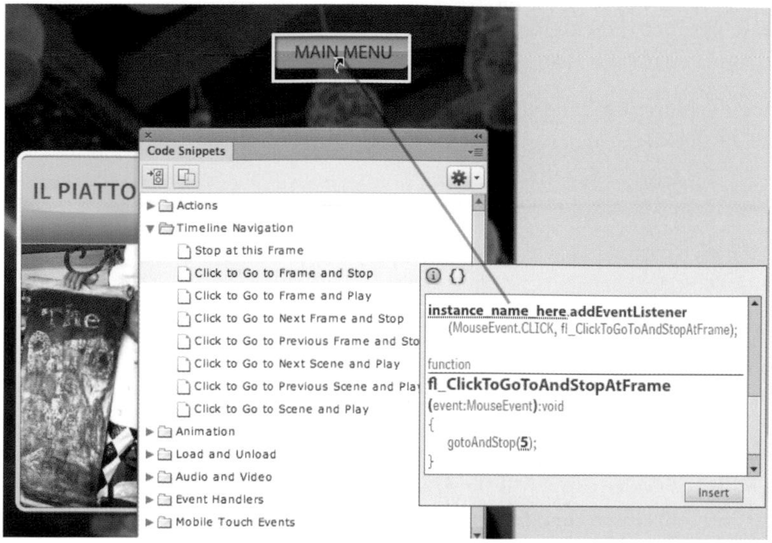

If you point your pick whip to an object that doesn't support the particular code snippet, a circular icon with a diagonal line appears (the international "no" symbol).

7 Release your mouse cursor.

Since you have not yet named the Home button, a dialog box appears to allow you to give a name to the instance. Enter *home_btn* for the instance name and click OK.

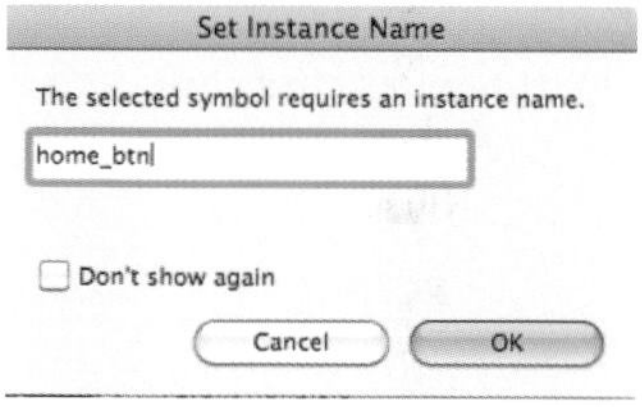

The instance name of the Home button is added to the code.

If you pointed your pick whip to an object that doesn't support the particular code snippet, your pick whip will rebound and the code snippet will remain unmodified.

8 Highlight the blue number within the parentheses in the code.

The blue number indicates which frame of the Timeline that Flash will display when you click on the Home button.

9 Replace the blue number with the number **1**.

home_btn.addEventListener(MouseEvent.CLICK,
fl_ClickToGoToAndStopAtFrame);
function
fl_ClickToGoToAndStopAtFrame
(event:MouseEvent):void
{
gotoAndStop(1);
}
Insert

10 Click Insert.

Flash adds the code snippet to the current keyframe on the Timeline. A flag appears on the Timeline to let you know that the code has been added, and to indicate where on the Timeline it's been placed.

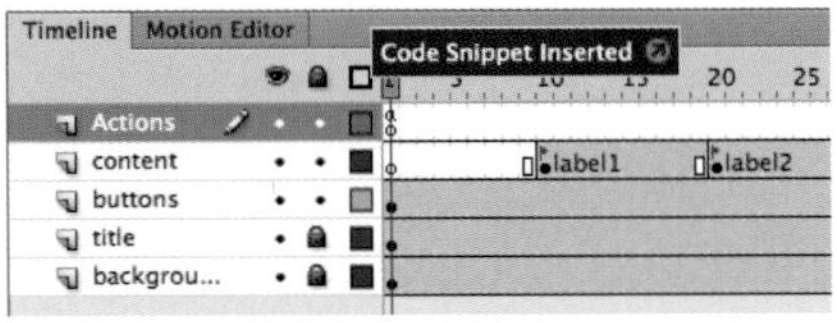

Click on the flag to open the Actions panel to view the code. You should be familiar with the syntax since you hand-coded your restaurant buttons earlier in this lesson. The Code Snippets panel, however, can make adding code quick and easy.

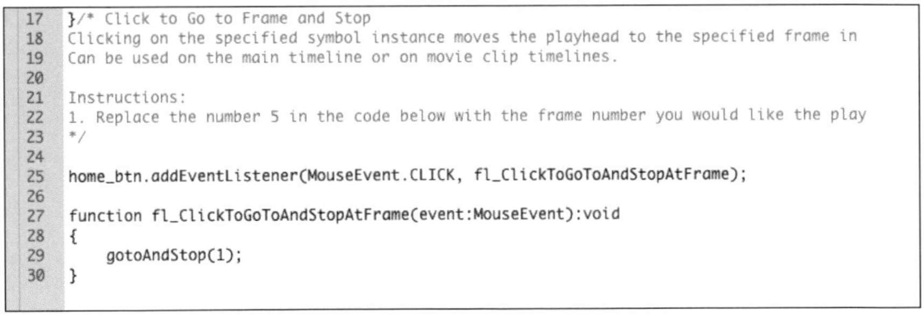

Code Snippets Options

Using the Code Snippets panel not only makes adding interactivity quick and learning code easy, but it can help organize frequently used code for yourself and for a team working on the same project. There are additional options in the Code Snippets panel for saving your own code and sharing your code with others.

Creating your own code snippet

If you have your own ActionScript code that you'll use repeatedly, you can store it in the Code Snippets panel and apply it in other projects easily.

1 Open the Code Snippets panel, if it isn't already open.

2 From the Options menu at the upper right of the panel, choose Create New Code Snippet.

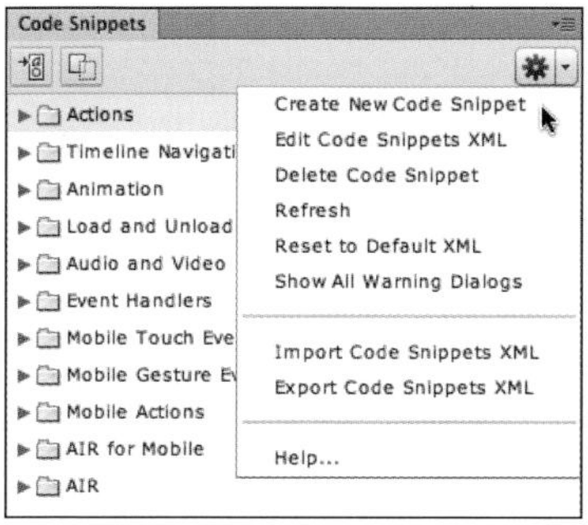

The Create New Code Snippet dialog box appears.

3 Enter a title in the Title field and a description in the Description field for your new code snippet. In the Code field, enter the ActionScript you want to save. Use the term **instance_name_here** for any placeholder instance names and be sure to check the option below the Code field.

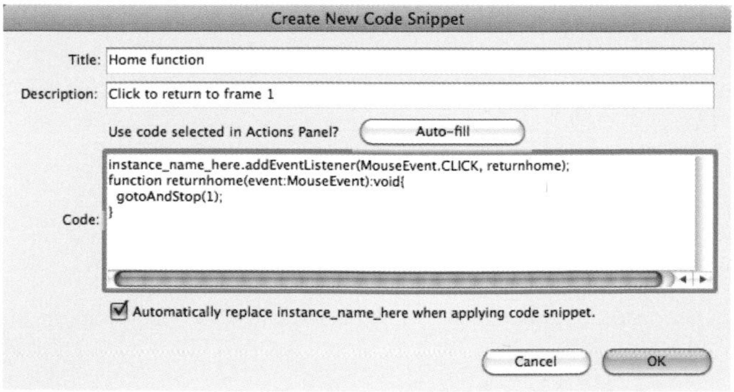

4 Click OK.

Your code is saved in the Code Snippets panel under a Custom folder. You can now access your code and apply it to future projects.

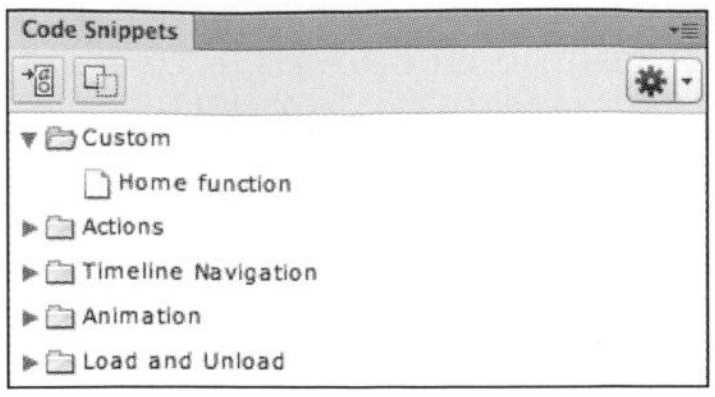

Sharing your code snippet

Soon, you may accumulate a large library of useful code snippets that you want to share with other developers. It's easy to export your custom code snippets and enable other Flash developers to import them into their own Code Snippets panel.

1 Open the Code Snippets panel, if it isn't already open.

2 From the Options menu at the upper right of the panel, choose Export Code Snippets XML.

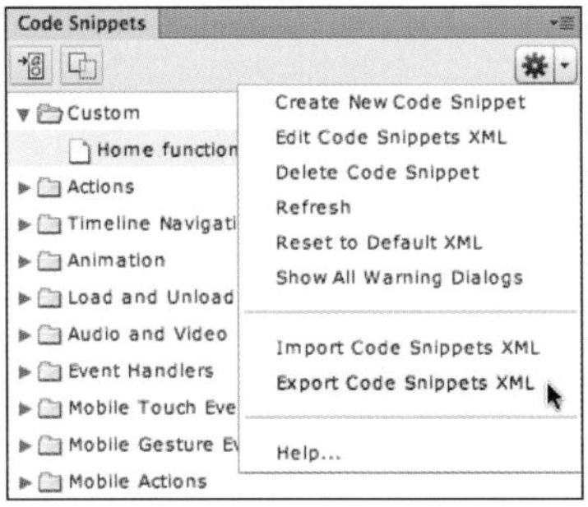

In the Save file dialog box that appears, choose a file name and a destination, and click OK. All the code snippets from your Code Snippets panel (the default ones as well as your own custom snippets) are saved in an XML file that can be distributed to other developers on your team.

3 To import custom code snippets, choose Import Code Snippets XML from the Options menu in the Code Snippets panel.

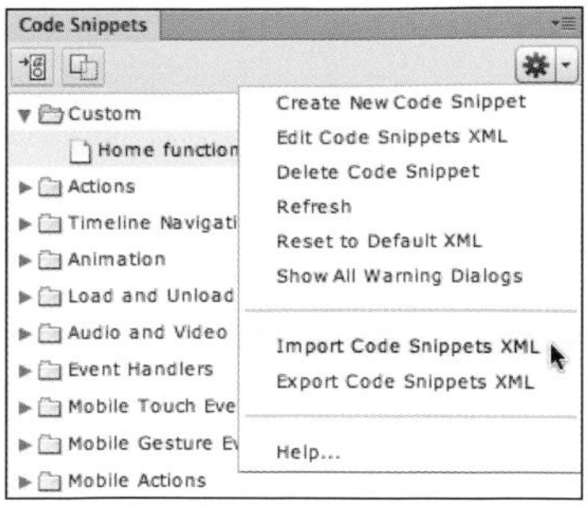

Choose the XML file that contains the custom snippets and click Open. Your Code Snippets panel will now contain all the snippets from the XML file.

Playing Animation at the Destination

So far, this interactive restaurant guide works by using the `gotoAndStop()` command to show information in different keyframes along the Timeline. But how would you play an animation after a user clicks a button? One way is to use the command `gotoAndPlay()`, which moves the playhead to the frame number or frame label specified by its parameter and plays from that point.

Creating transition animations

Next, you will create a short transition animation for each of the restaurant guides. Then you'll change your ActionScript code to direct Flash to go to each of the keyframes and play the animation.

1 Move the playhead to the label1 frame label.

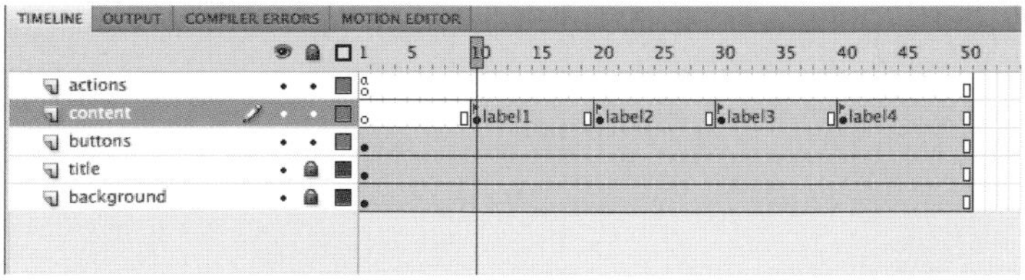

2 Right-click/Ctrl-click on the instance of the restaurant information on the Stage and choose Create Motion Tween.

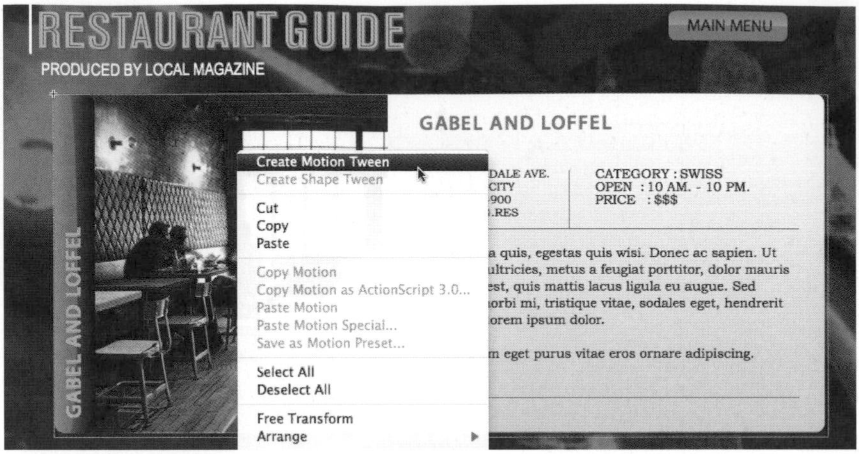

Flash creates a separate Tween layer for the instance so that it can proceed with the motion tween.

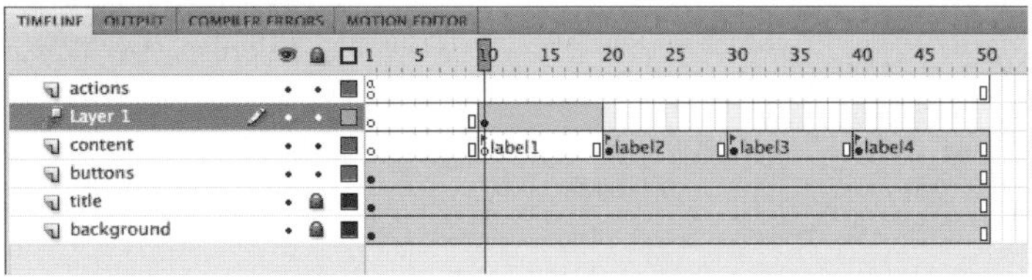

3 In the Properties inspector, select Alpha from the Style pull-down menu in the Color Effect section.

4 Set the Alpha slider to **0**%.

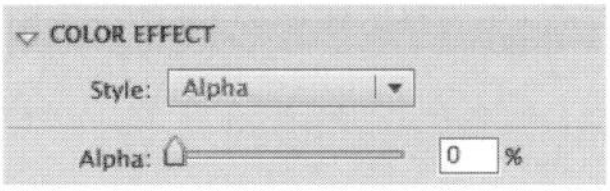

The instance on the Stage becomes totally transparent.

5 Move the playhead to the end of the tween span at frame 19.

6 Select the transparent instance on the Stage.

7 In the Properties inspector, set the Alpha slider to **100**%.

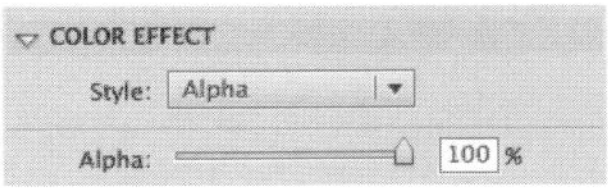

The instance is displayed at a normal opacity level. The motion tween from frame 10 to frame 19 shows a smooth fade-in effect.

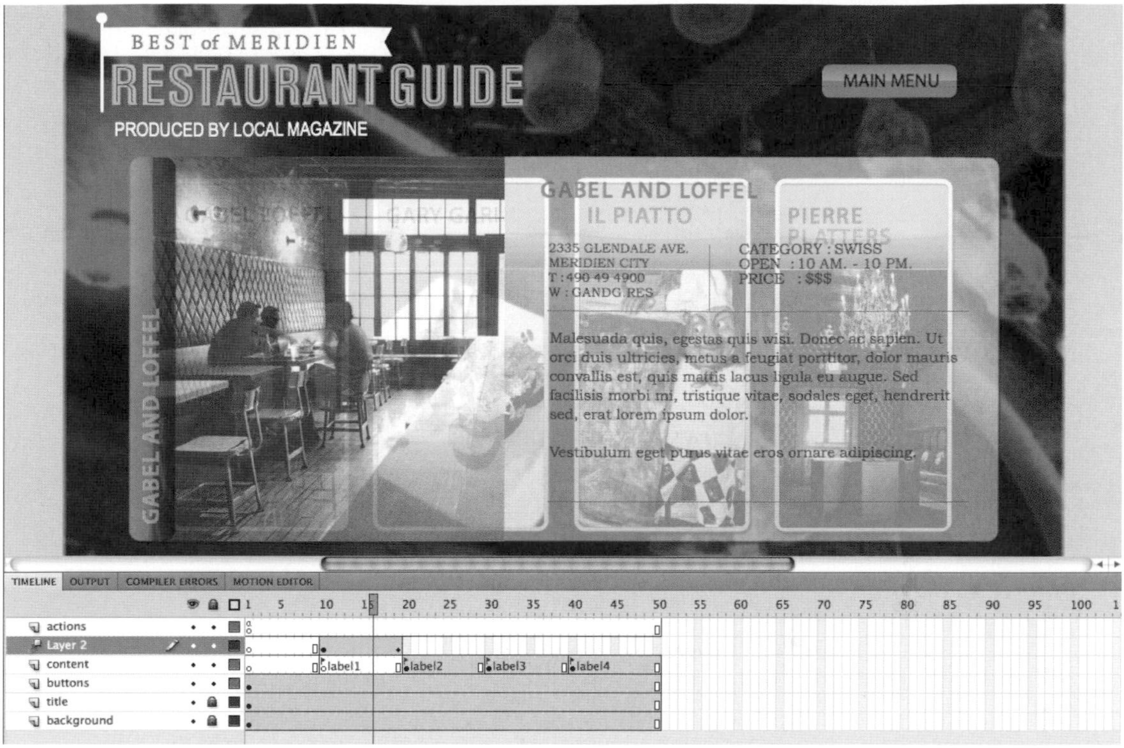

8 Create similar motion tweens for the remaining restaurants in the keyframes labeled label2, label3, and label4.

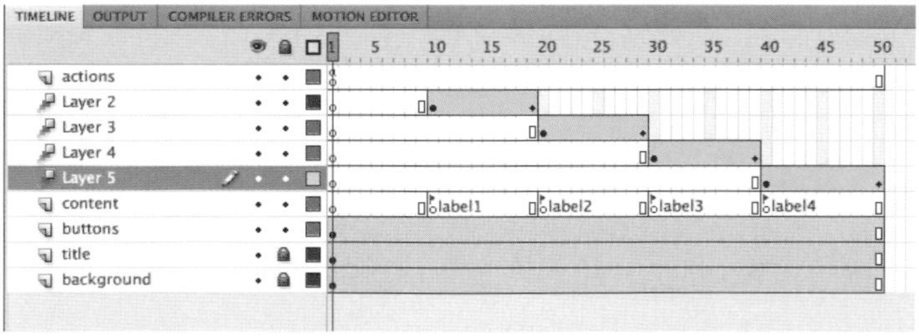

Note: Recall that you can use the Motion Presets panel to save a motion tween and apply it to other objects to save you time and effort. Select the first motion tween on the Timeline and click Save selection as preset. Once saved, you can apply the same motion tween to another instance.

Using the gotoAndPlay command

The gotoAndPlay command makes the Flash playhead move to a specific frame on the Timeline and begin playing from that point.

1 Select the first frame of the actions layer and open the Actions panel.

2 In your ActionScript code, change all the first four `gotoAndStop()` commands to `gotoAndPlay()` commands. Leave the parameter unchanged:

- `gotoAndStop("label1");` should be changed to `gotoAndPlay("label1");`
- `gotoAndStop("label2");` should be changed to `gotoAndPlay("label2");`
- `gotoAndStop("label3");` should be changed to `gotoAndPlay("label3");`
- `gotoAndStop("label4");` should be changed to `gotoAndPlay("label4");`

Note: A fast and easy way of doing multiple replacements is to use the Find and Replace command in the Actions panel. From the options menu in the upper-right corner, select Find and Replace.

```
stop();
gabelloffel_btn.addEventListener(MouseEvent.CLICK, restaurant1);
function restaurant1(event:MouseEvent):void {
    gotoAndPlay("label1");
}
garygari_btn.addEventListener(MouseEvent.CLICK, restaurant2);
function restaurant2(event:MouseEvent):void {
    gotoAndPlay("label2");
}
ilpiatto_btn.addEventListener(MouseEvent.CLICK, restaurant3);
function restaurant3(event:MouseEvent):void {
    gotoAndPlay("label3");
}
pierreplatters_btn.addEventListener(MouseEvent.CLICK, restaurant4);
function restaurant4(event:MouseEvent):void {
    gotoAndPlay("label4");
}

```

For each of the restaurant buttons, the ActionScript code now directs the playhead to a particular frame label and begins playing at that point.

Make sure you keep the function for your Home button unchanged. You'll want that function to remain a `gotoAndStop()` command.

Stopping the animations

If you test your movie now (Control > Test Movie > in Flash Professional), you'll see that each button goes to its corresponding frame label and plays from that point, but it keeps playing, showing all the remaining animations in the Timeline. The next step is to tell Flash when to stop.

1 Select frame 19 of the actions layer, the frame just before the label2 keyframe on the content layer.

2 Right-click/Ctrl-click and choose Insert Keyframe.

A new keyframe is inserted in frame 19 of the actions layer.

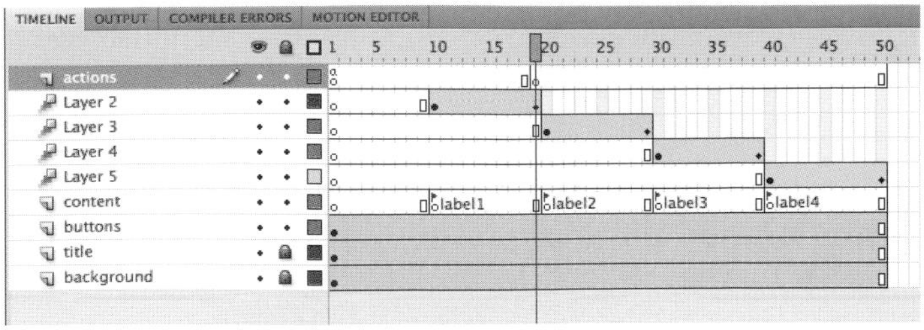

3 Open the Actions panel.

The Script pane in the Actions panel is blank. Don't panic! Your code has not disappeared. Your code for the event listeners is on the first keyframe of the actions layer. You have selected a new keyframe in which you will add a stop command.

4 In the Script pane, enter **stop();**

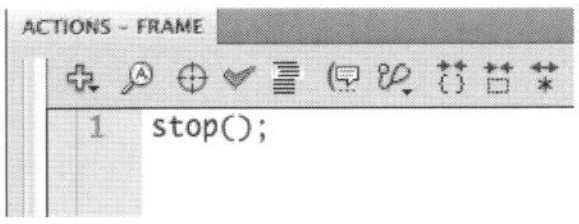

If you wish, you could also use the Code Snippets panel to add the stop command.

Flash will stop playing when it reaches frame 19.

5 Insert keyframes at frames 29, 39, and 50.

6 In each of those keyframes, add a stop command in the Actions panel.

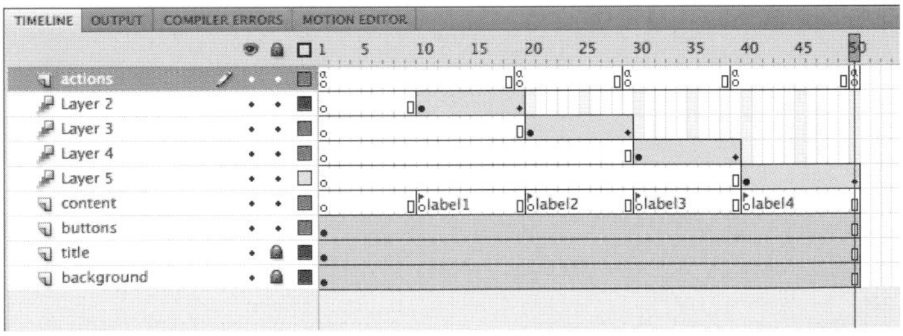

▶ **Tip:** If you want a quick and easy way to duplicate the keyframe containing the stop command, hold down the Alt/Option key while you move it to a new location on the Timeline.

7 Test your movie by choosing Control > Test Movie > in Flash Professional.

Each button takes you to a different keyframe and plays a short fade-in animation. At the end of the animation, the movie stops and waits for the viewer to click the Home button.

Animated Buttons

Currently, when you hover your mouse cursor over one of the restaurant buttons, the gray additional information box suddenly appears. But imagine if that gray information box were animated. It would give more life and sophistication to the interaction between the user and the button.

Animated buttons display an animation in the Up, Over, or Down keyframes. The key to creating an animated button is to create an animation inside a movie clip symbol, and then place that movie clip symbol inside the Up, Over, or Down keyframes of a button symbol. When one of those button keyframes is displayed, the animation in the movie clip plays.

Creating the animation in a movie clip symbol

Your button symbols in this interactive restaurant guide already contain a movie clip symbol of a gray information box in their Over states. You will edit each movie clip symbol to add an animation inside it.

1 In the Library panel, expand the restaurant previews folder. Double-click the movie clip symbol icon for gabel loffel over info.

   Flash puts you in symbol-editing mode for the movie clip symbol called gabel loffel over info.

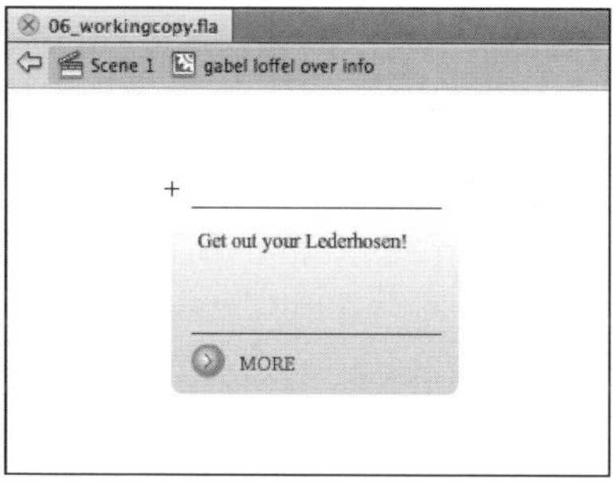

2 Select all the visual elements on the Stage (Ctrl/Command+A).

3 Right-click/Ctrl-click and choose Create Motion Tween.

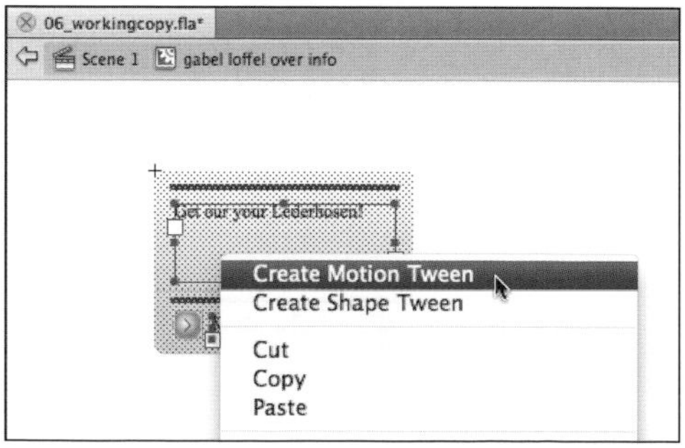

4 In the dialog box that appears asking for confirmation to convert the selection to a symbol, click OK.

Flash creates a Tween layer and adds one second worth of frames to the movie clip Timeline.

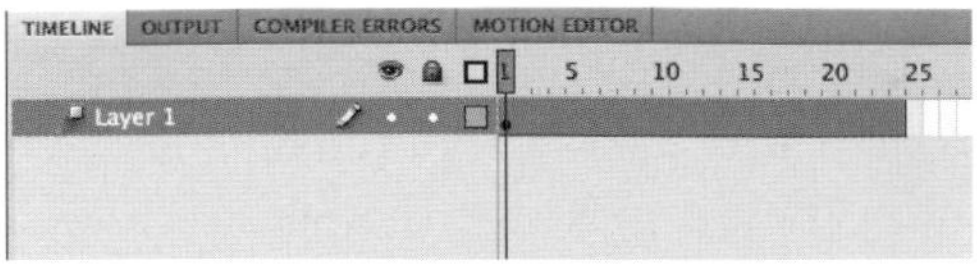

5 Drag the end of the tween span back so the Timeline only has 10 frames.

6 Move the playhead to frame 1 and select the instance on the Stage.

7 In the Properties inspector, select Alpha from the Style pull-down menu in the Color Effect section and set the Alpha slider to **0**%.

The instance on the Stage becomes totally transparent.

8 Move the playhead to the end of the tween span at frame 10.

9 Select the transparent instance on the Stage.

10 In the Properties inspector, set the Alpha slider to **100**%.

Flash creates a smooth transition between the transparent and opaque instance in the 10 frame tween span.

11 Insert a new layer and rename it **actions**.

12 Insert a new keyframe in the last frame (frame 10) of the actions layer.

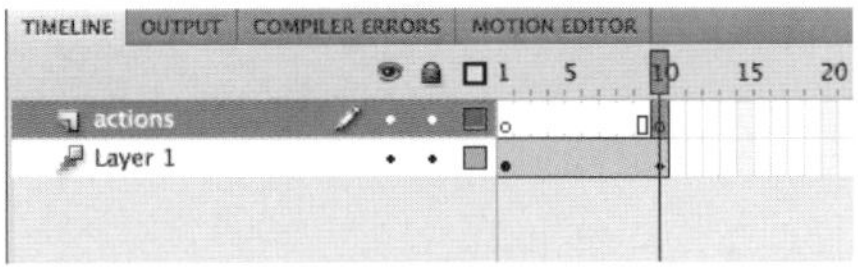

13 Open the Actions panel (Window > Actions) and enter **`stop();`** in the Script pane.

Adding the stop action in the last frame ensures that the fade-in effect plays only once.

14 Exit symbol-editing mode by clicking the Scene 1 button above the Stage.

Note: If you want an animated button to repeat its animation, leave out the stop command at the end of the movie clip's Timeline.

15 Choose Control > Test Movie > in Flash Professional.

When your mouse cursor hovers over the first restaurant button, the gray information box fades in. The motion tween inside the movie clip symbol plays the fade-in effect, and the movie clip symbol is placed in the Over state of the button symbol.

16 Create identical motion tweens for the other gray information box movie clips so that all the restaurant buttons are animated.

Review Questions

1 How and where do you add ActionScript code?

2 How do you name an instance, and why is it necessary?

3 How can you label frames, and when is it useful?

4 What is a function?

5 What is an event? What is an event listener?

6 How do you create an animated button?

Review Answers

1 ActionScript code resides in keyframes on the Timeline. Keyframes that contain ActionScript are indicated by a small lowercase "a." You add ActionScript through the Actions panel. Choose Window > Actions, or select a keyframe and click the ActionScript panel icon in the Properties inspector, or right-click/Ctrl-click and select Actions. You enter code directly in the Script pane in the Actions panel, or you can select commands from the categories in the Actions toolbox. You can also add ActionScript through the Code Snippets panel.

2 To name an instance, select it on the Stage, and then type in the Instance Name field in the Properties inspector. You need to name an instance so that ActionScript can identify it with code.

3 To label a frame, select a keyframe on the Timeline, and then type a name in the Frame Label box in the Properties inspector. You can label frames in Flash to make it easier to reference frames in ActionScript and to give you more flexibility.

4 A function is a group of statements that you can refer to by name. Using a function makes it possible to run the same set of statements without having to type them repeatedly into the same script. When an event is detected, a function is executed in response.

5 An event is an occurrence that is initiated by a button click, a keystroke, or any number of inputs that Flash can detect and respond to. An event listener, also called an event handler, is a function that is executed in response to specific events.

6 Animated buttons display an animation in the Up, Over, or Down keyframes. To create an animated button, make an animation inside a movie clip symbol, and then place that movie clip symbol inside the Up, Over, or Down keyframes of a button symbol. When one of those button keyframes is displayed, the animation in the movie clip plays.

7 USING TEXT

Lesson Overview

In this lesson, you'll learn how to do the following:

- Understand the difference between Classic and TLF Text
- Add and edit text on the Stage
- Apply style and formatting options to text
- Create text with multiple columns
- Create text that wraps around objects
- Add hyperlinks to text
- Use editable text for user input
- Dynamically change text content
- Embed fonts and understand device fonts
- Load external text

This lesson will take approximately two and a half hours to complete. If needed, remove the previous lesson folder from your hard drive and copy the Lesson07 folder onto it.

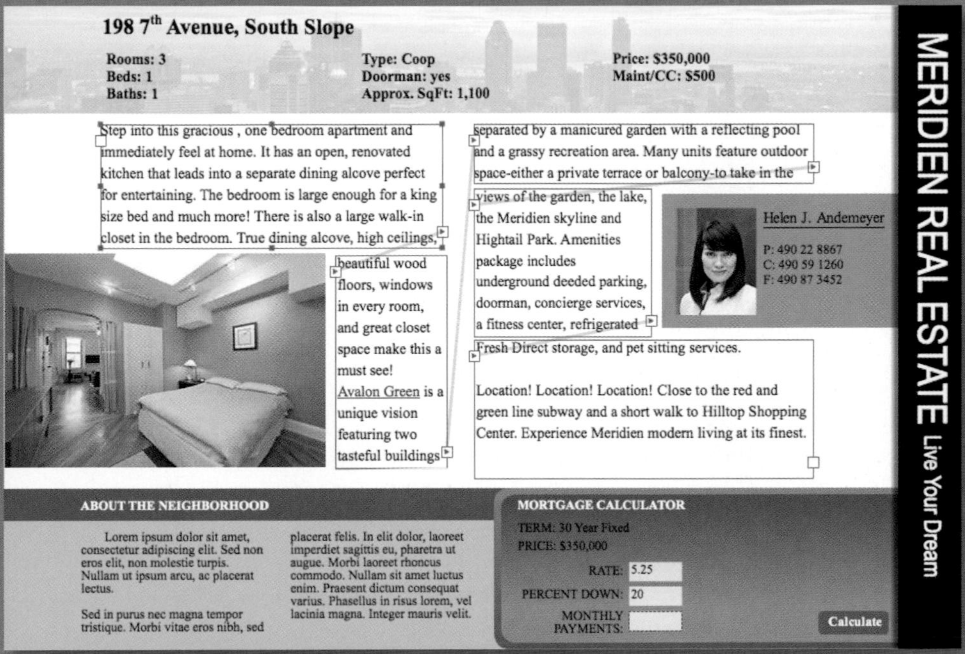

198 7th Avenue, South Slope
Rooms: 3
Beds: 1
Baths: 1
Type: Coop
Doorman: yes
Approx. SqFt: 1,100
Price: $350,000
Maint/CC: $500
Step into this gracious , one bedroom apartment and immediately feel at home. It has an open, renovated kitchen that leads into a separate dining alcove perfect for entertaining. The bedroom is large enough for a king size bed and much more! There is also a large walk-in closet in the bedroom. True dining alcove, high ceilings,
beautiful wood floors, windows in every room, and great closet space make this a must see! Avalon Green is a unique vision featuring two tasteful buildings
separated by a manicured garden with a reflecting pool and a grassy recreation area. Many units feature outdoor space-either a private terrace or balcony-to take in the
views of the garden, the lake, the Meridien skyline and Hightail Park. Amenities package includes underground deeded parking, doorman, concierge services, a fitness center, refrigerated
Fresh Direct storage, and pet sitting services.
Location! Location! Location! Close to the red and green line subway and a short walk to Hilltop Shopping Center. Experience Meridien modern living at its finest.
Helen J. Andemeyer
P: 490 22 8867
C: 490 59 1260
F: 490 87 3452
ABOUT THE NEIGHBORHOOD
Lorem ipsum dolor sit amet, consectetur adipiscing elit. Sed non eros elit, non molestie turpis. Nullam ut ipsum arcu, ac placerat lectus.
Sed in purus nec magna tempor tristique. Morbi vitae eros nibh, sed
placerat felis. In elit dolor, laoreet imperdiet sagittis eu, pharetra ut augue. Morbi laoreet rhoncus commodo. Nullam sit amet luctus enim. Praesent dictum consequat varius. Phasellus in risus lorem, vel lacinia magna. Integer mauris velit.
MORTGAGE CALCULATOR
TERM: 30 Year Fixed
PRICE: $350,000
RATE: 5.25
PERCENT DOWN: 20
MONTHLY PAYMENTS:
Calculate
MERIDIEN REAL ESTATE Live Your Dream

Words are integral to any Flash site. Learn how to use the Text Layout Framework to create titles, sophisticated layouts, and dynamic text content that can change to suit different situations.

Getting Started

To begin, view the finished project to see the different kinds of text elements that you'll create in this lesson.

1 Double-click the 07End.html file in the Lesson07/07End folder to play the animation.

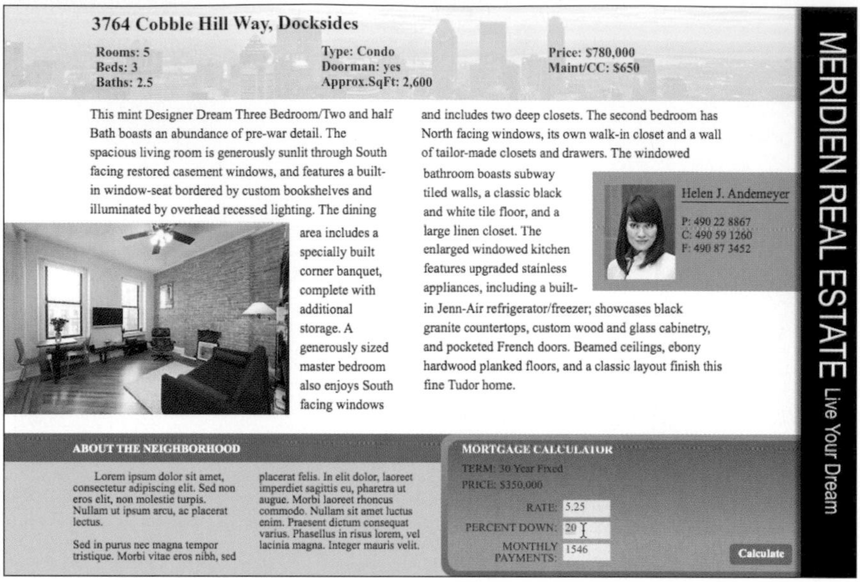

The finished project is an interactive real estate site for the imaginary city of Meridien, whose restaurant guide you completed in the previous lesson. Viewers can read about the featured property and its neighborhood or figure out how much they can afford to pay every month using the mortgage calculator at the bottom right. Enter a new rate, a new value for the percent down, and click the Calculate button to display the estimated monthly payment.

2 Close the 07End.html file.

3 Double-click the 07Start.fla file in the Lesson07/07Start folder to open the initial project file in Flash.

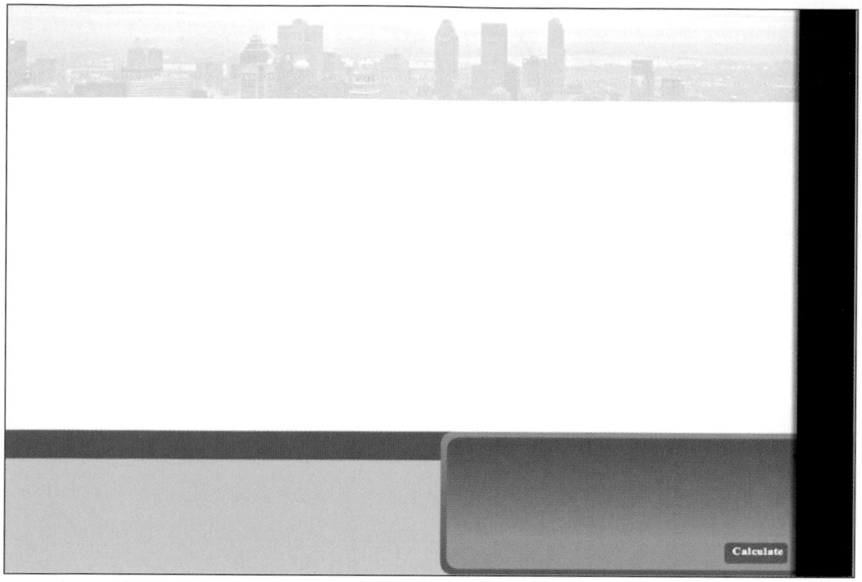

The Stage already includes some simple design elements to divide the space, with several assets already created and stored in the Library panel.

4 Choose File > Save As. Name the file **07_workingcopy.fla** and save it in the 07Start folder. Saving a working copy ensures that the original Start file will be available if you want to start over.

Understanding TLF Text

Flash Professional CS6 uses two different text options. When you choose the Text tool (T) in the Tools panel to add text to the Stage, you choose either TLF Text or Classic Text.

TLF text stands for Text Layout Framework, and is a more recent and more powerful text engine. Choose TLF Text when you want to use more sophisticated controls for text formatting such as multiple columns or wrap-around text. You'll learn many of the features unique to TLF Text in this lesson. Choose Classic Text when you don't need that degree of layout control or if you need to target an older version of the Flash Player.

TLF Text depends on a specific external ActionScript library to function properly. When you test a movie or publish a movie that contains TLF Text, an additional Text Layout SWZ file ( ) is created next to your SWF file. The SWZ file is the external ActionScript library that supports TLF Text.

When a SWF file that contains TLF Text is playing from the Web, the SWF looks for the library in a couple of different locations. The SWF looks for the library on the local computer it is playing on, where the library is usually cached from normal Internet usage. The SWF also looks on Adobe.com for the library file, and if that fails, looks in the same directory as the SWF.

You should always keep the SWZ file with your SWF file so the TLF Text features work properly when you test your movies locally. You should also have the SWZ file accompany your SWF file when you upload it to your Web server, just to be safe.

Merging the TLF Text library

If you don't want to maintain the separate SWZ file, you can merge the required ActionScript library with your SWF file. However, doing so adds substantially to the size of your published SWF file and is not recommended.

1 Choose File > Publish Settings. Click the Flash format from the left and choose Settings for ActionScript 3.0. You can also click the Edit button next to ActionScript settings in the Properties inspector.

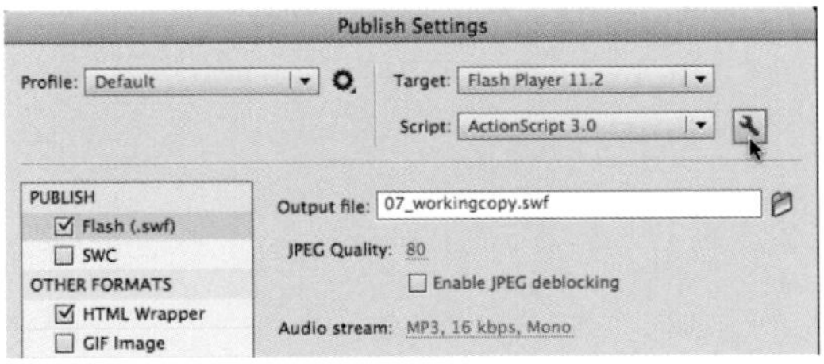

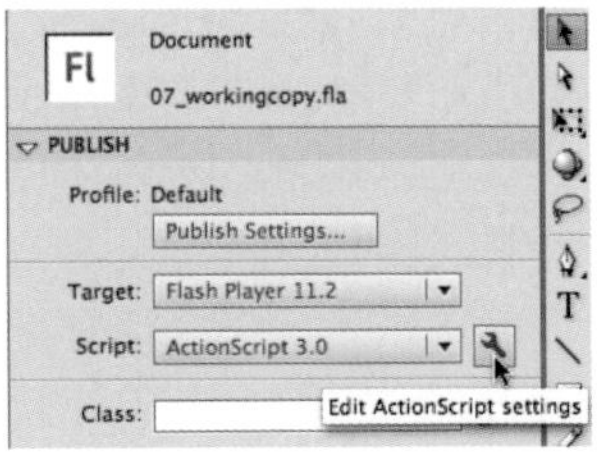

The Advanced ActionScript 3.0 Settings dialog box opens.

2 Click on the Library path tab.

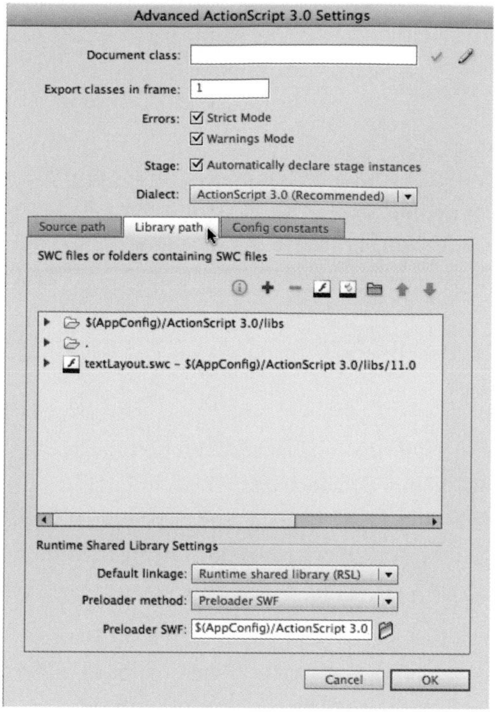

3 Click the arrow next to the textLayout.swc listing in the display window.

The arrow points downward, expanding the information about the TLF Text feature. Note that the Link Type shows that the file uses a runtime shared library, and the URL for the library is on Adobe.com.

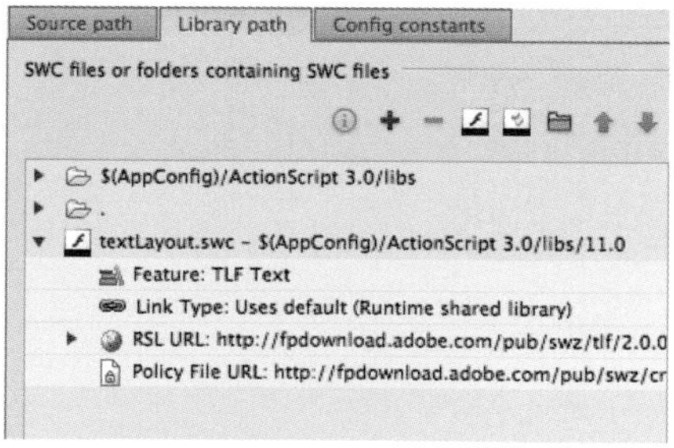

4 In the Runtime Shared Library Settings section, choose Merged into code for the Default linkage.

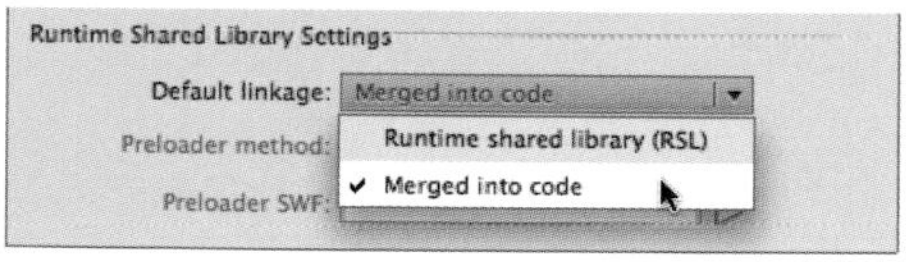

The Link Type changes to Merged into code.

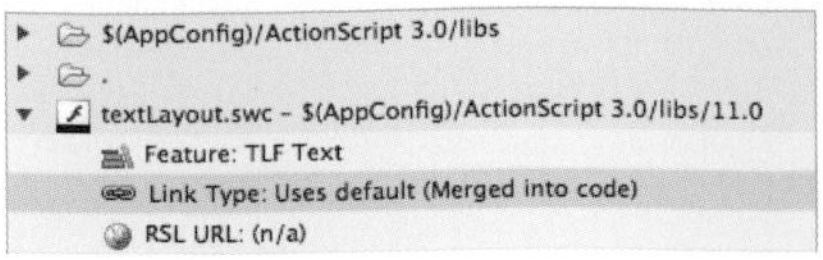

The current Flash file will merge the TLF Text ActionScript library into the published SWF if you click OK to accept these settings. For the project in this lesson, do *not* merge the code. Click Cancel to leave the default setting, Link Type as a Runtime Shared Library.

Adding Simple Text

● **Note:** You can break apart text (Modify > Break Apart) to convert each letter into separate drawing objects whose stroke and fill you can modify. However, once broken apart, your text will no longer be editable.

You'll start by adding simple, single lines of text for display. Add text to the Stage using the Text tool in the Tools panel. When you add text, whether TLF Text or Classic Text, the text remains fully editable. So at any point after you create your text, you can return to it and change it or any of its properties, such as its color, font, size, or alignment.

As with other Flash elements, it's best to separate text on its own layer to keep your layers organized. Having text on its own layer also makes it easy to select, move, or edit your text without disturbing the items in the layers below or above it.

Adding the titles

You'll add titles to various sections of the real estate site and learn about the different formatting and style options.

1 Select the banner layer and click the New Layer button. Rename it **text**.

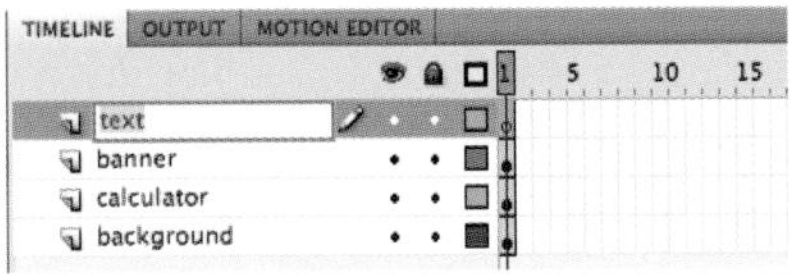

2 Select the Text tool.

3 In the Properties inspector, select TLF Text and Read Only. In the Character section, choose Times New Roman for Family, Bold for Style, 20.0 for Size, 14.0 pt for Leading, and black for Color.

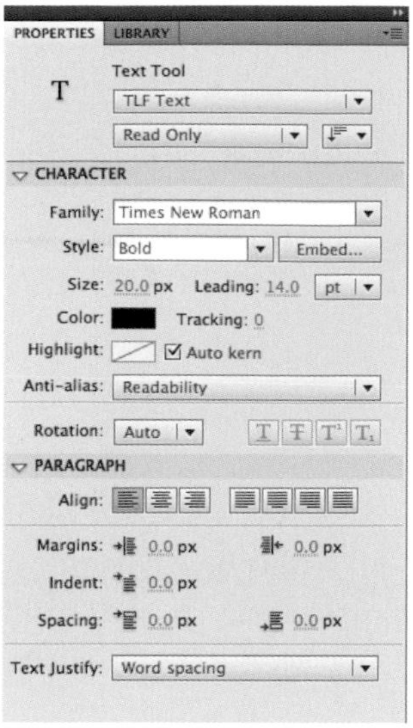

You may choose a similar font if Times New Roman is unavailable on your computer. For TLF Text, you have the option of choosing Read Only, Selectable, or Editable.

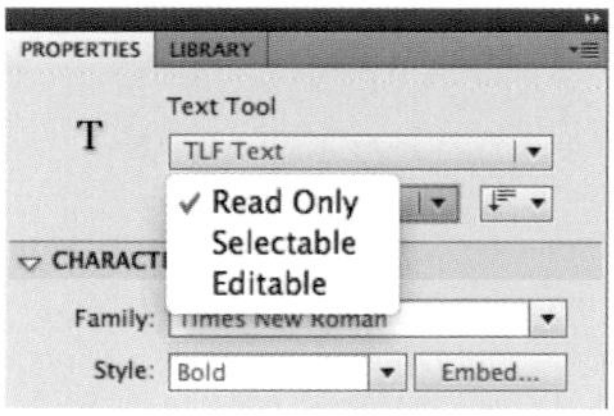

- **Read Only** displays text that can't be selected or edited by the end user.
- **Selectable** displays text that the user can select to copy.
- **Editable** displays text that the user can select and edit. Use the Editable option for text input fields, such as login and passwords. You'll use the Editable option later in this lesson to create the Mortgage Calculator.

4 Click the top-left corner of the Stage where you want to begin adding text. Begin entering the address of the featured property, **198 7th Avenue, South Slope**. Exit the Text tool by choosing the Selection tool.

● **Note:** The registration of text is at the top-left corner of the text box.

5 In the Properties inspector, position the text at X=**90** and Y=**10**.

6 Deselect the text by clicking on another part of the Stage and choose the Text tool again.

7 In the Properties inspector, select TLF Text and Read Only. In the Character section, choose Times New Roman for Family, Bold for Style, 12.0 for Size, 12.0 pt for Leading, and white for Color.

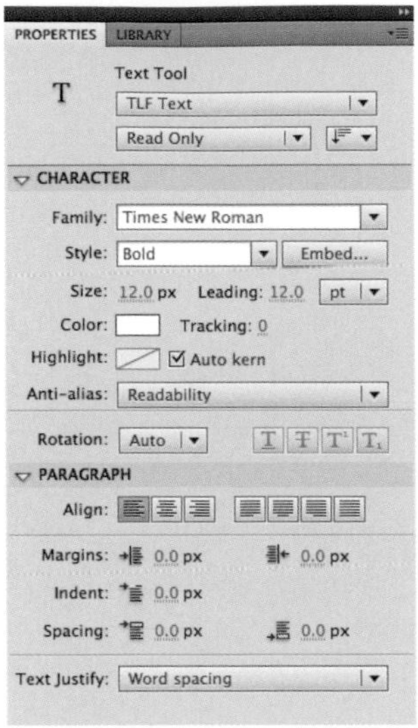

● **Note:** You can also click and drag with the Text tool to define a text box at a set width and height. You can always change the dimensions of the text box to accommodate your text.

8 Click on the dark green banner to place the beginning of your next piece of text and enter the section title **About the Neighborhood**.

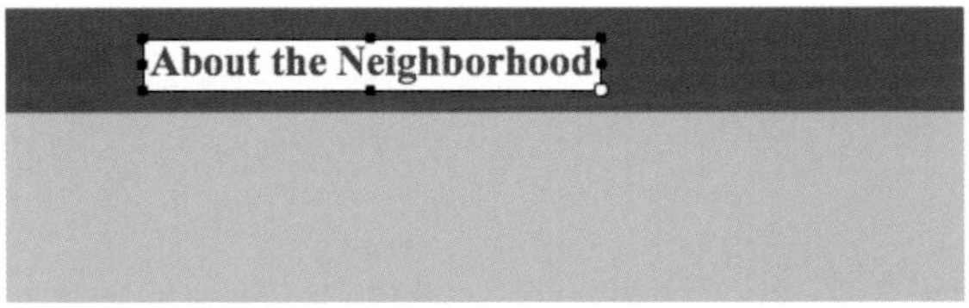

9 Create a third piece of text at the top of the dark brown area with the section title **Mortgage Calculator**.

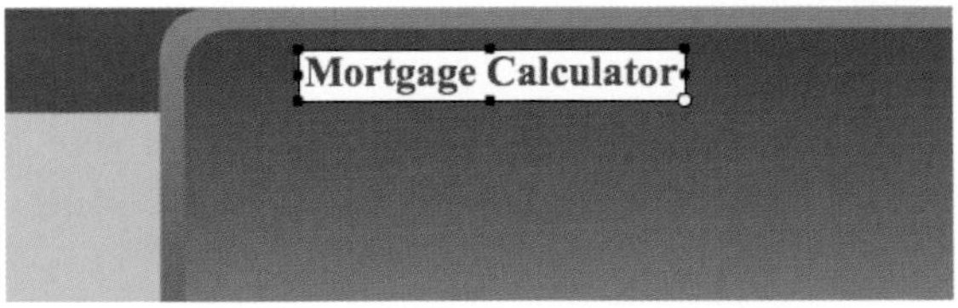

10 Position the About the Neighborhood title at X=**70** and Y=**460**. Position the Mortgage Calculator title at X=**480** and Y=**460**.

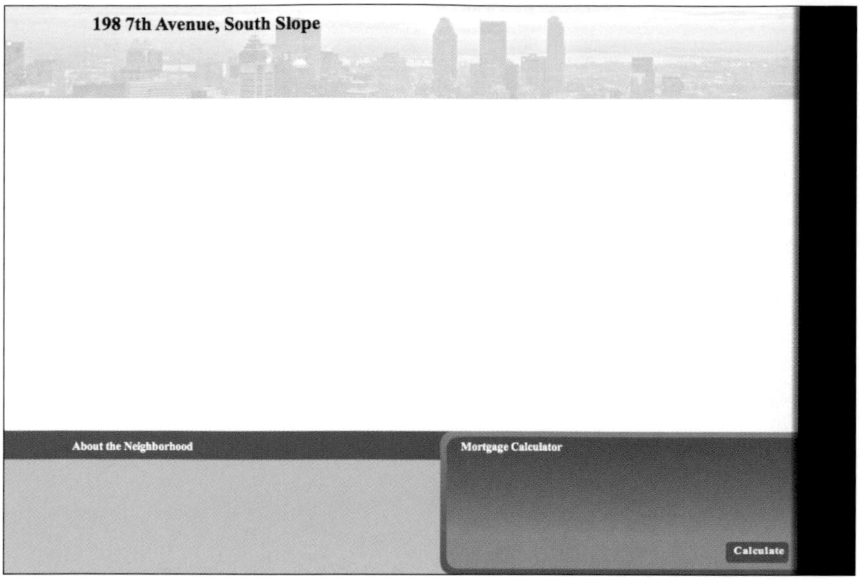

Creating vertical text

Although vertical text is not common, it can be useful for unusual displays. For many Asian languages, vertical text is essential to display them correctly. In this lesson, you'll use a vertical orientation for the overall banner title.

1 Deselect any selected text and choose the Text tool.

2 In the Properties inspector, select TLF Text and Read Only. In the Character section, choose Arial Narrow for Family, Regular for Style, 38.0 for Size, and white for Color.

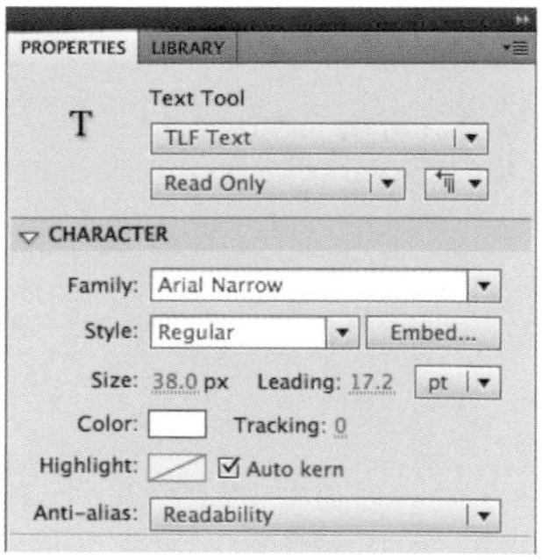

3 From the orientation pull-down menu, choose Vertical.

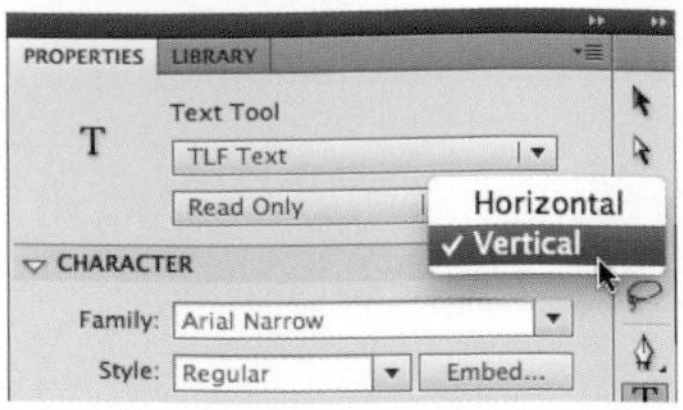

4 Click on the black vertical banner to place the beginning of your text and enter the banner title **Meridien Real Estate Live Your Dream**.

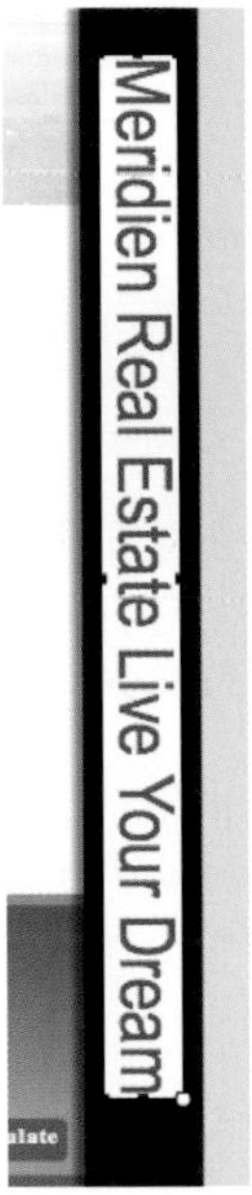

● **Note:** In the Character section of the Properties inspector, you can choose 270° to change the orientation of the individual characters as well as the lines of text.

Modifying characters

Use the Character and Advanced Character options in the Properties inspector to modify the way your text appears. You've already used different colors, font families, font sizes, and orientations. Now you'll explore some less obvious options.

1 Double-click the top address and select the "th" characters.

2 In the Character section of the Properties inspector, select the Superscript option.

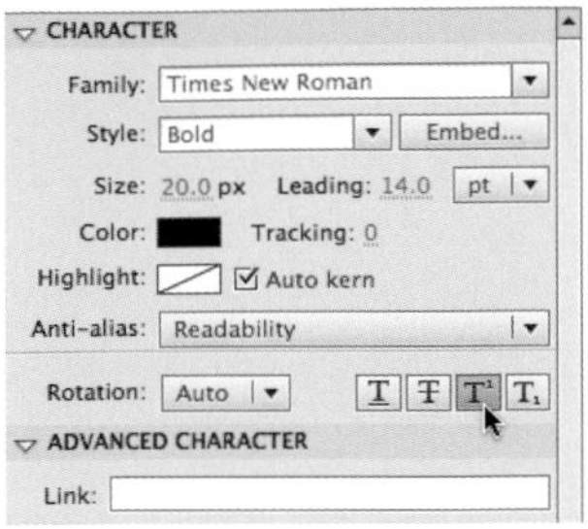

The "th" becomes smaller and is raised from the baseline as a superscript.

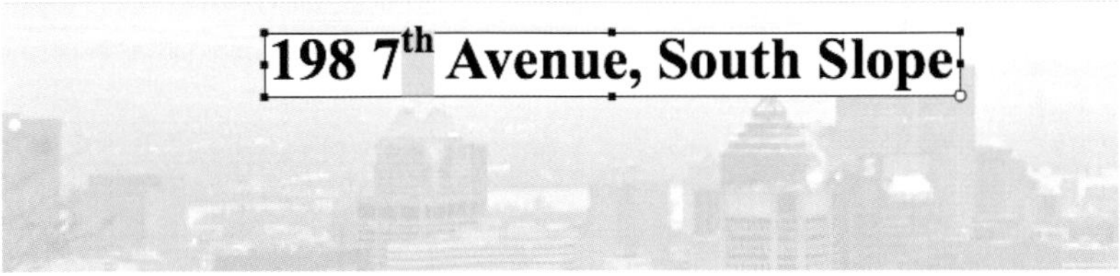

3 Exit the Text tool by selecting the Selection tool, and click an empty part of the Stage to deselect the text.

4 Hold down the Shift key and select the bottom two text titles, About the Neighborhood and Mortgage Calculator.

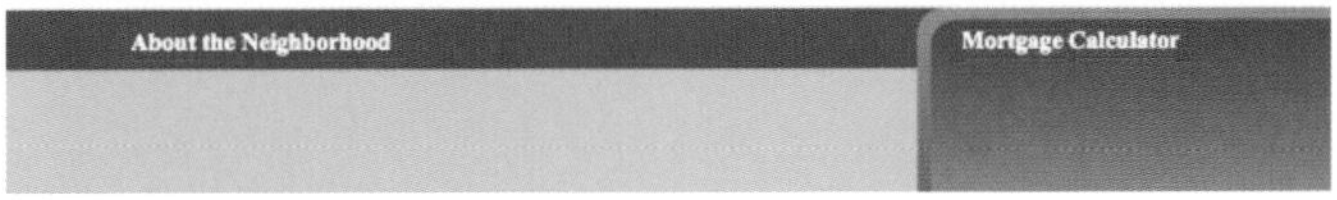

5 In the Advanced Character section of the Properties inspector, choose Upper Case from the Case menu.

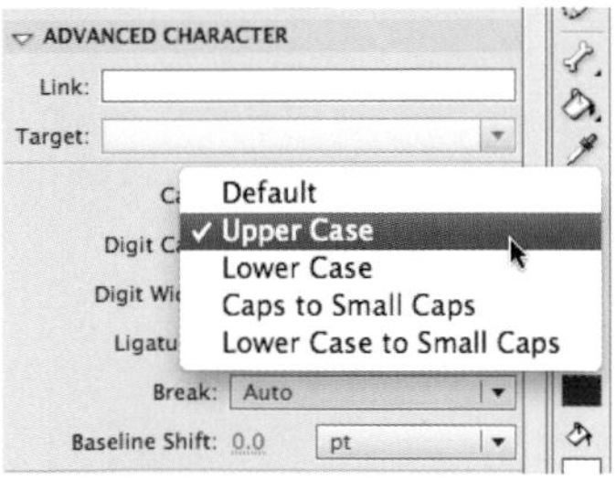

The characters in the two selected bottom titles change to all uppercase.

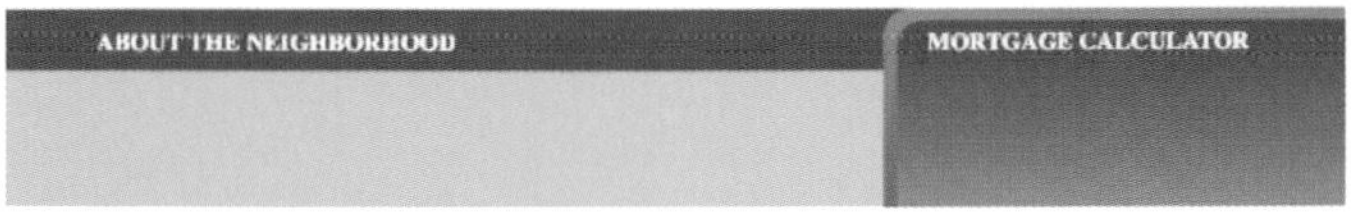

6 Double-click the vertical banner text and select the words Meridien Real Estate.

7 In the Advanced Character section of the Properties inspector, choose Upper Case from the Case menu.

The selected words in the banner title change to all uppercase.

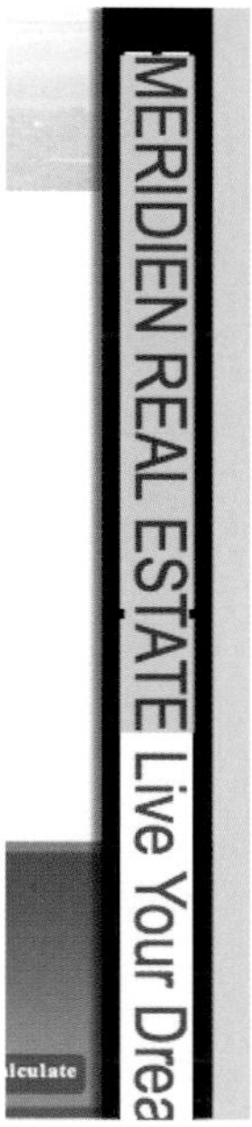

8 Select the last three words of the banner title, Live Your Dream.

9 In the Properties inspector, change the font size to 22 and Baseline Shift to 6.0.

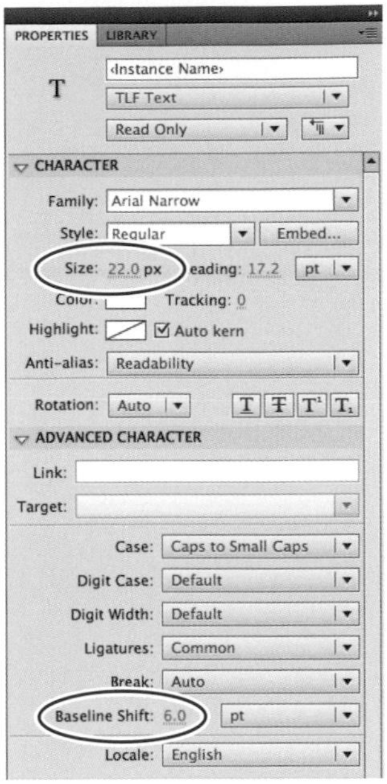

The selected words in the banner title become smaller and are shifted upward from their baseline. The variations in size and baseline shift in the banner title create a more pleasing design.

Adding Multiple Columns

Now you'll add the text description of the property and some details about the neighborhood. The text will appear in different columns. For the property details, you'll add a three-column text description, and for the neighborhood, you'll add a two-column text description.

1 Deselect any selected text and choose the Text tool.

2 In the Properties inspector, select TLF Text and Read Only. In the Character section, choose Times New Roman for Family, Bold for Style, 14.0 for Size, 16.0 pt for Leading, and black for Color. Make sure you switch back to horizontal text.

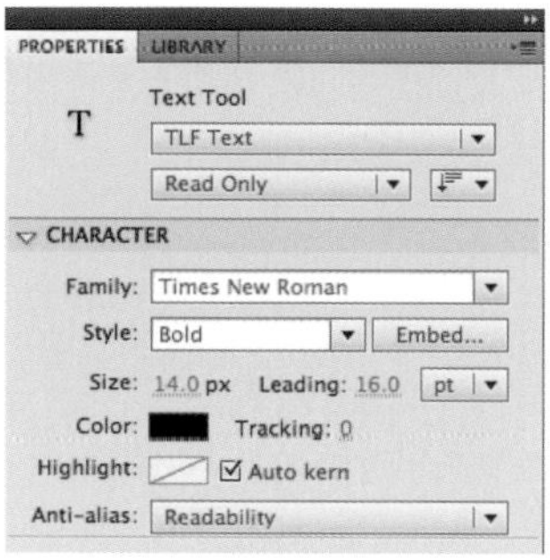

3 Click on the top horizontal banner below the address and drag out a long text box to define the width and height of the text.

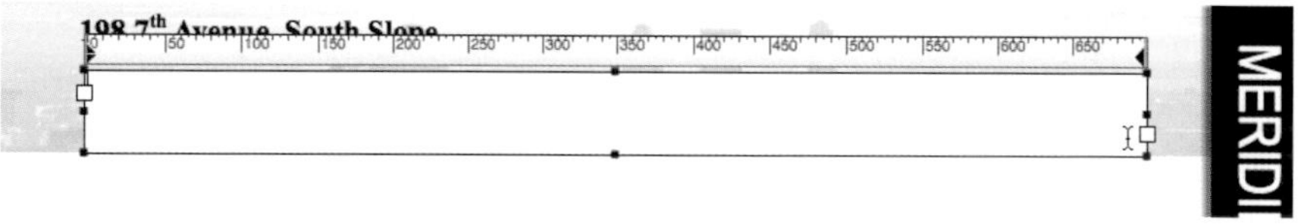

4 In the Container and Flow section of the Properties inspector, enter **3** for the Columns option.

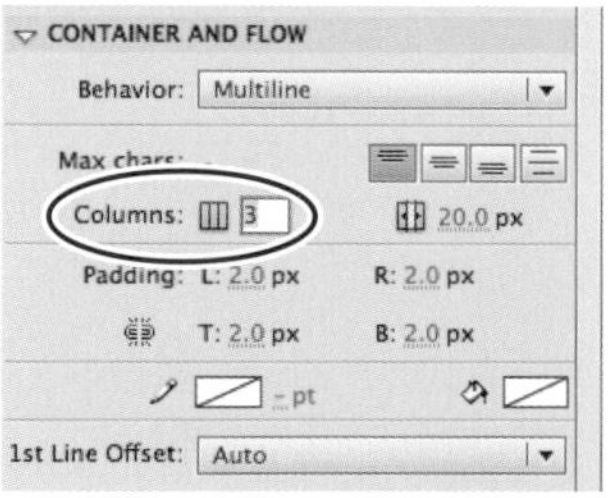

Your selected text box becomes enabled to display three columns.

5 Enter text in the text box that provides details of this hypothetical property, such as the number of rooms, number of beds, and so on. Press Return or Enter after each line. You can copy the information from the text file 07SampleRealEstateText1.txt in the 07Start folder.

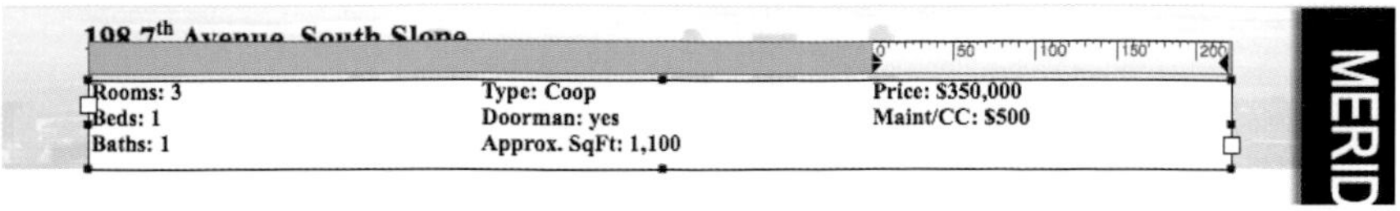

The text is displayed in three columns. As text in the first column reaches the bottom of the text box, the next line appears at the top of the next column.

6 Exit the Text tool by choosing the Selection tool, and click an empty part of the Stage to deselect the text.

7 Select the Text tool again. Now you'll create the text for the About the Neighborhood section.

8 In the Properties inspector, select TLF Text and Read Only. In the Character section, choose Times New Roman for Family, Regular for Style, 12.0 for Size, 12.0 pt for Leading, and black for Color.

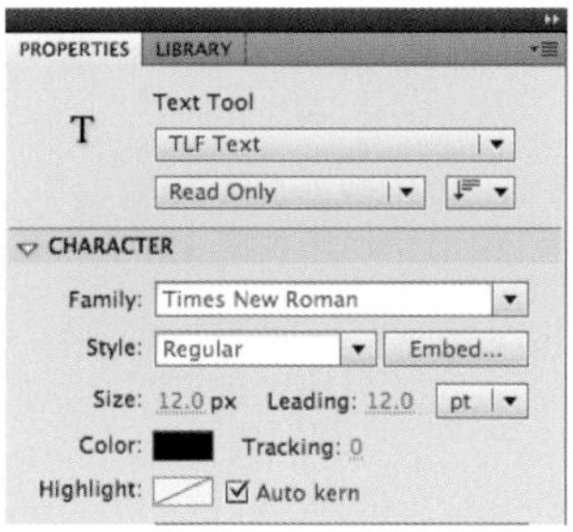

9 Click on the bottom green bar below the About the Neighborhood title and drag out a text box so that it takes up most of the light green space.

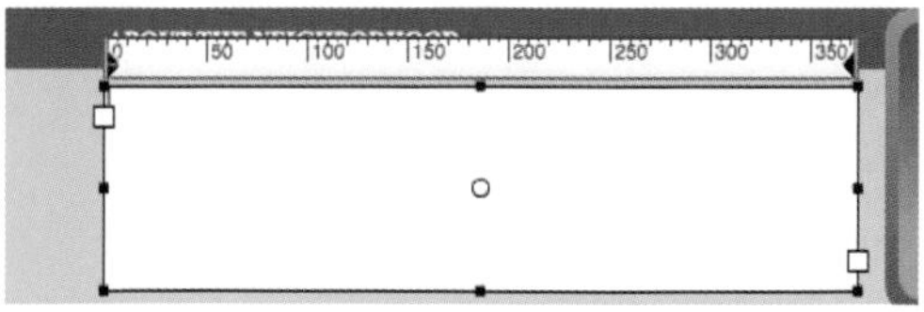

10 In the Container and Flow section of the Properties inspector, enter **2** for the Columns option.

Your selected text box becomes enabled to display two columns.

Note: In the Container and Flow section of the Properties inspector, you can also modify the gutter, the space between columns, and the padding between the text and the boundaries of the text box to help you get the exact text layout you desire.

11 Open the text file 07SampleRealEstateText1.txt in the 07Start folder if it's not already open. Copy the Latin placeholder text in the About the Neighborhood section and paste it into the two-column text box.

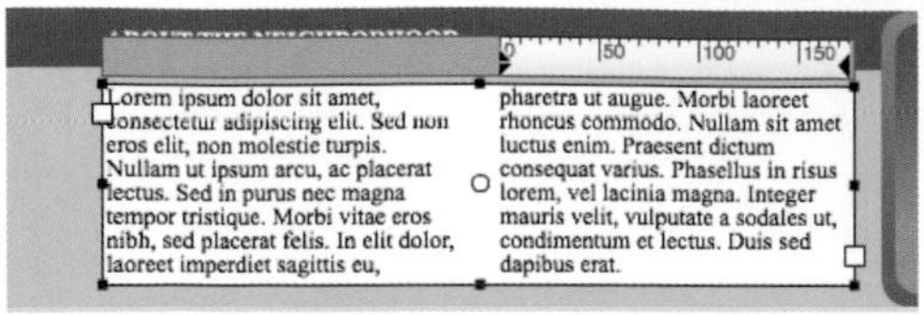
Lorem ipsum dolor sit amet,
consectetur adipiscing elit. Sed non
eros elit, non molestie turpis.
Nullam ut ipsum arcu, ac placerat
lectus. Sed in purus nec magna
tempor tristique. Morbi vitae eros
nibh, sed placerat felis. In elit dolor,
laoreet imperdiet sagittis eu,
pharetra ut augue. Morbi laoreet
rhoncus commodo. Nullam sit amet
luctus enim. Praesent dictum
consequat varius. Phasellus in risus
lorem, vel lacinia magna. Integer
mauris velit, vulputate a sodales ut,
condimentum et lectus. Duis sed
dapibus erat.

The text is displayed in two columns. As text in the first column reaches the bottom of the text box, the next line appears at the top of the next column.

Modifying the text box

If your text doesn't entirely fit in its text box, Flash displays a red cross at the bottom-right corner. The red cross means there is overflow text that is not visible.

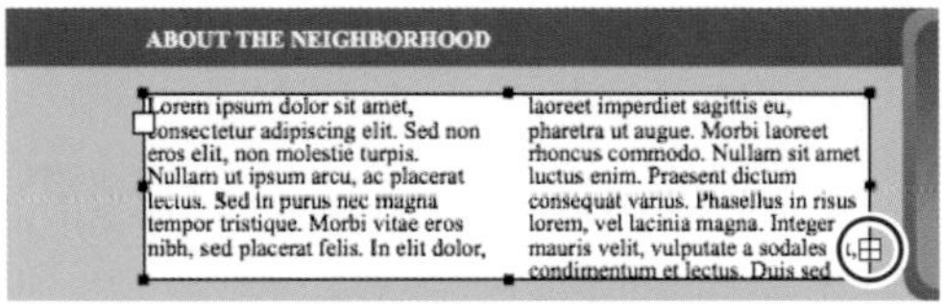
ABOUT THE NEIGHBORHOOD
Lorem ipsum dolor sit amet,
consectetur adipiscing elit. Sed non
eros elit, non molestie turpis.
Nullam ut ipsum arcu, ac placerat
lectus. Sed in purus nec magna
tempor tristique. Morbi vitae eros
nibh, sed placerat felis. In elit dolor,
laoreet imperdiet sagittis eu,
pharetra ut augue. Morbi laoreet
rhoncus commodo. Nullam sit amet
luctus enim. Praesent dictum
consequat varius. Phasellus in risus
lorem, vel lacinia magna. Integer
mauris velit, vulputate a sodales

To see more of the text, you can enlarge the text box.

1 Select the Text tool or the Selection tool.

2 Move your mouse cursor over one of the solid blue squares surrounding the text box.

   Your mouse cursor changes to a double-headed arrow, indicating the direction in which you can modify the size of the text box.

Note: You can also resize a text box by entering new Width and Height values in the Properties inspector. However, do not resize a text box with the Transform panel or the Free Transform tool. Doing so will squash or stretch the contents of the text box and distort the text.

3 Click and drag to make the text box wider or taller to fit the text.

ABOUT THE NEIGHBORHOOD
Lorem ipsum dolor sit amet,
consectetur adipiscing elit. Sed non
eros elit, non molestie turpis.
Nullam ut ipsum arcu, ac placerat
lectus. Sed in purus nec magna
tempor tristique. Morbi vitae eros
nibh, sed placerat felis. In elit dolor,
laoreet imperdiet sagittis eu,
pharetra ut augue. Morbi laoreet
rhoncus commodo. Nullam sit amet
luctus enim. Praesent dictum
consequat varius. Phasellus in risus
lorem, vel lacinia magna. Integer
mauris velit, vulputate a sodales ut,
condimentum et lectus. Duis sed
dapibus erat.

   The text box gets resized, and the text reflows to accommodate the new dimensions.

Using the Tab Ruler

All TLF text boxes that you place on the Stage include a ruler at their top edges. The ruler measures the left and right margins and indents, as well as tab stops. To view the ruler, double-click a TLF text box or select the Text tool and click in a TLF text box to begin editing. You can toggle to view or to hide the ruler by choosing Text > TLF Tab Ruler.

Next, you'll use the TLF Tab Ruler to modify margins, indents, and tab stops.

1 Double-click the text box if it isn't already selected.

   The TLF Tab Ruler is displayed at the top edge of the text box, above either the left or the right column, depending on where your mouse cursor is positioned. The TLF Tab Ruler measurements are in pixels.

2 Drag the left margin indicator (solid black triangle) along the TLF Tab Ruler.

   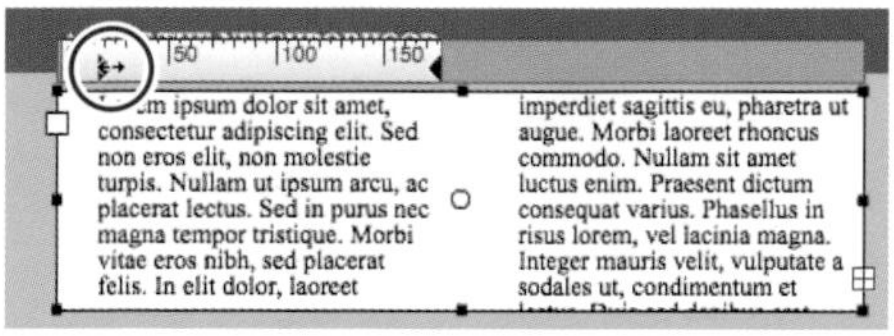

   The margins for the text increase. The margins are determined for each paragraph. If there were paragraph breaks in your text box, you'd see the margin for only the selected paragraph change.

   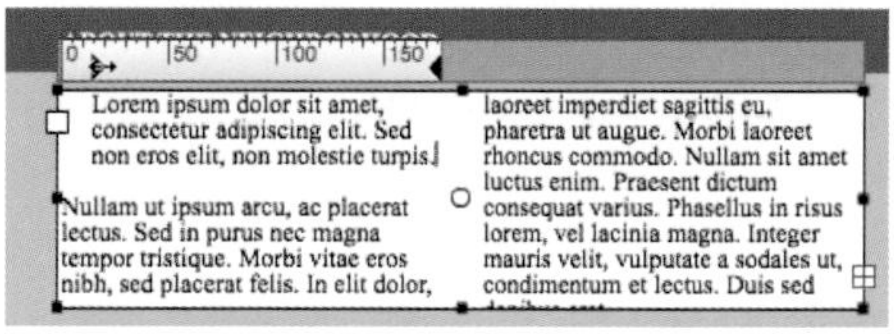

   Notice how the margin values change in the Properties inspector as well. Move the margin indicator back to its original position after you finish exploring how it works.

Note: If you have multiple paragraphs and you want to change the margins for the entire contents of the text box, choose Edit > Select All, or use the mouse to first select all the text before moving the margin indicator.

3 You can split the left margin indicator to establish the indent amount for the first line of new paragraphs. To see the indents, press the Return or Enter key to create a few new paragraphs in the text.

4 Click inside the TLF Tab Ruler.

   Flash creates a tab stop.

   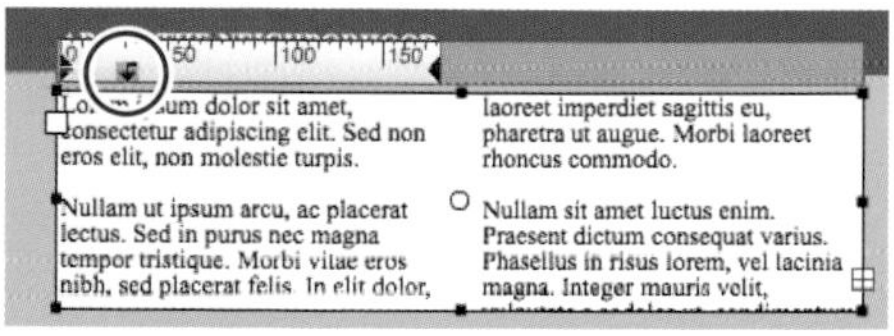

Note: Drag the tab stop off the ruler to delete it.

5 Drag the tab stop along the ruler to move the position of the tab.

6 To see the effects of the tab stop, press the Tab key when your cursor is in front of new paragraphs.

Flash indents the text to the next tab stop on the TLF Tab Ruler.

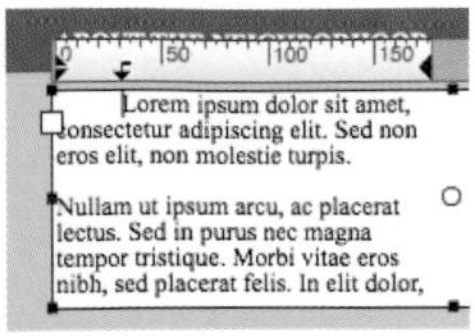

Wrapping Text

Long passages of text are visually boring. Instead, if you can wrap text around photographs or graphic elements, you create more visual interest and a more pleasing design. Take a look at any magazine in print or online, and you'll see how text flows around photos to help integrate the elements on the page.

Note: Linked text boxes are also referred to as "threaded text containers."

In this section, you'll add some graphic elements to the real estate site—an animated slide show and a photo of the real estate agent—and create text that wraps around them both. You create wrapping text by linking separate text boxes. Text will flow from one text box to another as if in a single container.

Adding the graphics

The animated slide show and the graphic of the real estate agent have already been created and are in the Library panel for you to use.

1 Insert a new layer and rename it **images**. Drag the images layer under the banner layer.

2 In the Library panel, select the photos movie clip symbol.

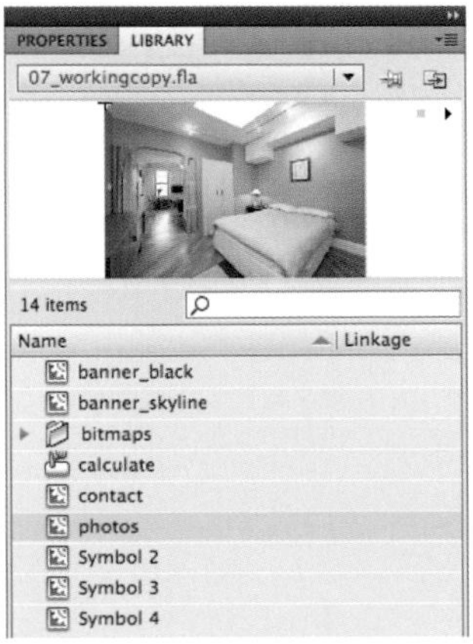

3 Drag the photos movie clip symbol from the Library panel to the Stage. Position the movie clip instance at X=**0** and Y=**230**.

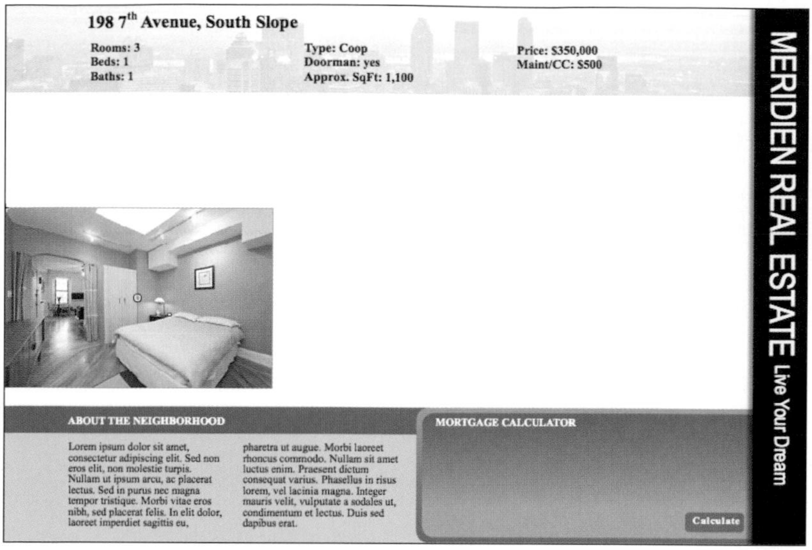

The movie clip contains motion tweens of several photographs fading in and out. A movie clip's animation is independent of the main Timeline and plays only when you test the movie (Control > Test Movie > in Flash Professional).

4 In the Library panel, drag the contact movie clip symbol from the Library panel to the Stage. Position the contact movie clip instance at X=**620** and Y=**175**.

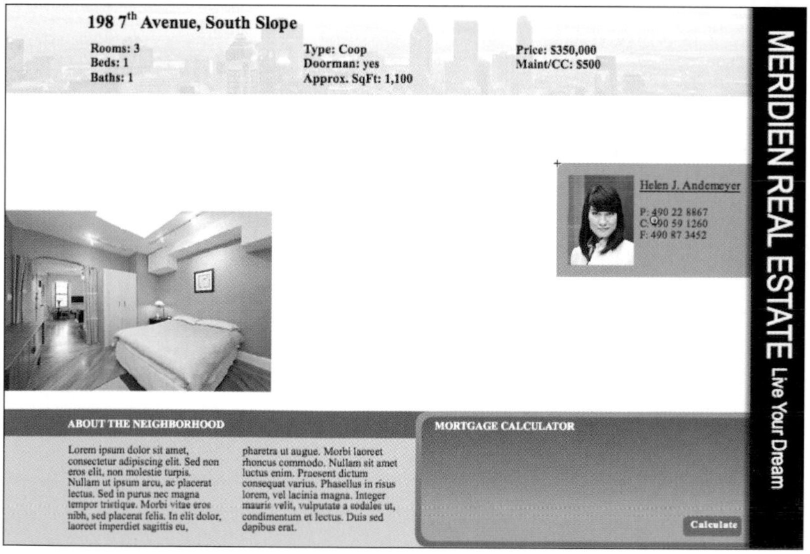

The movie clip of the real estate agent and her contact information is a simple static graphic.

Linking the text boxes

Now you'll arrange several linked text boxes around the graphic elements.

1 Select the Text tool.

2 In the Properties inspector, select TLF Text and Read Only. In the Character section, choose Times New Roman for Family, Regular for Style, 14.0 for Size, 20.0 pt for Leading, and black for Color.

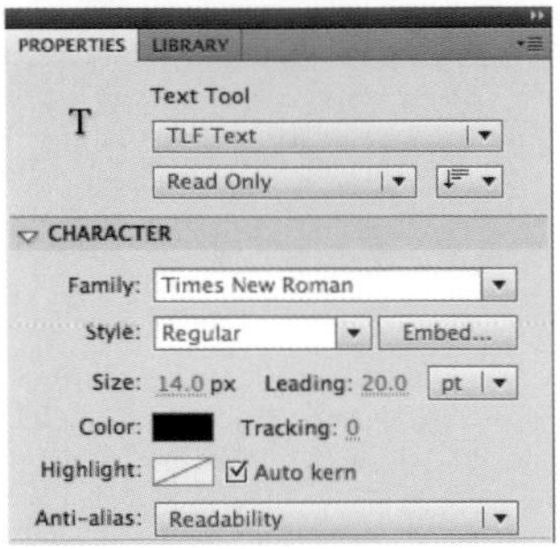

3 Click and drag out the first text box that takes up the space above the photo of the bedroom and whose right edge extends to about the middle of the Stage. Don't worry about precise placement at this point because you can always adjust the size and location of your text box.

Your first text box is created.

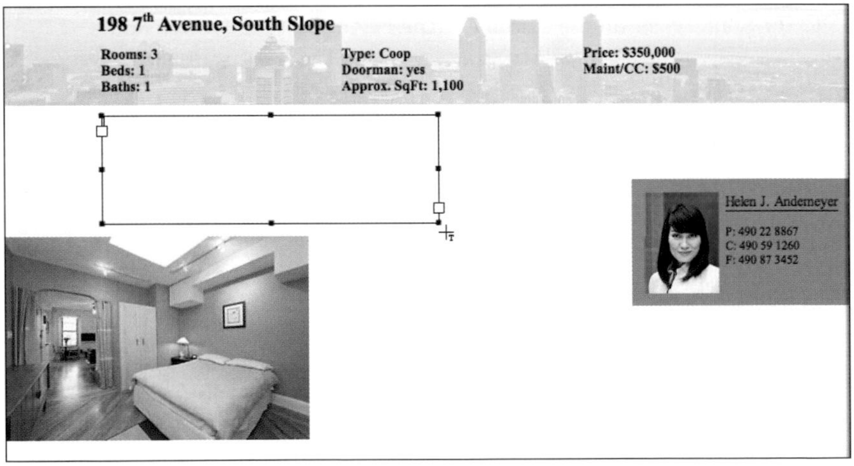

4 Click on the lower-right corner of your text box.

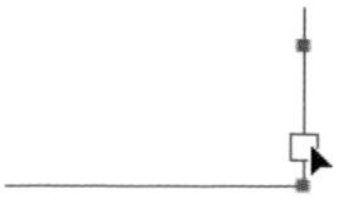

Your cursor changes to an icon of the corner of a text box ().

5 Click and drag out your second text box just to the right of the photos movie clip instance.

● **Note:** If you simply click on the Stage to define your next linked text box, Flash creates a text box that is identical in size to the previous text box.

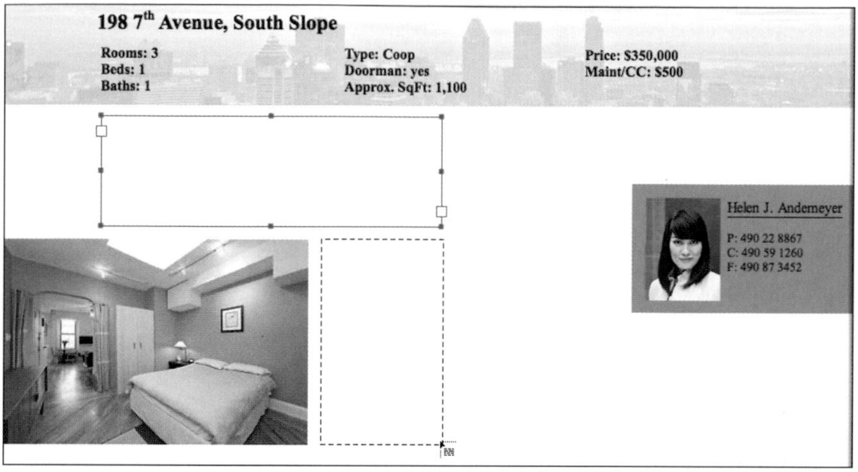

When you release your mouse cursor, your second text box becomes linked to the first text box. A blue line that connects the first to the second represents the linkage.

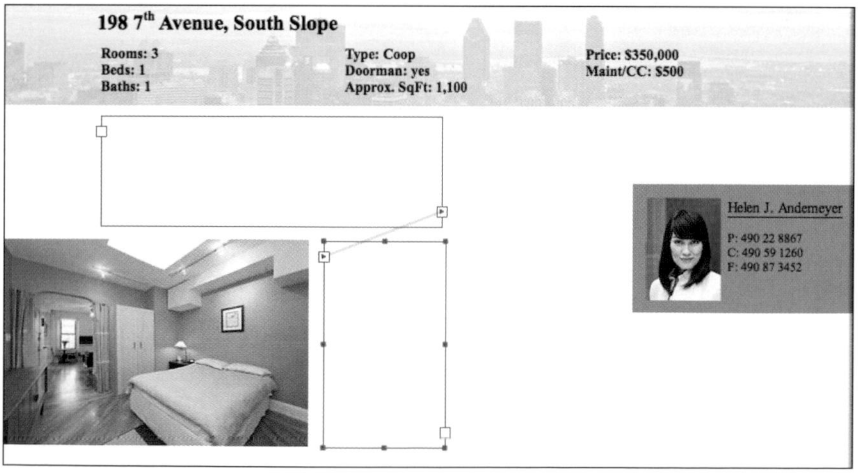

6 Click on the empty box on the lower-right corner of your second text box; then click and drag out your third text box above the real estate agent contact information.

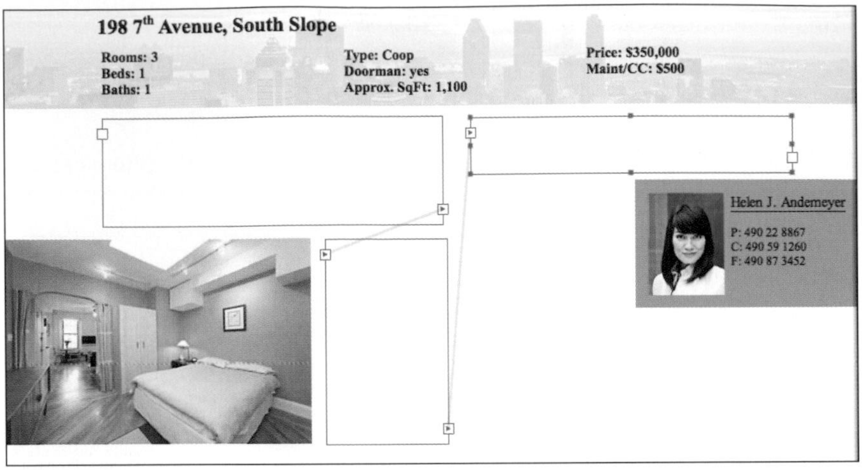

7 Continue creating linked text boxes until you have five boxes that flow around the photo and real estate agent.

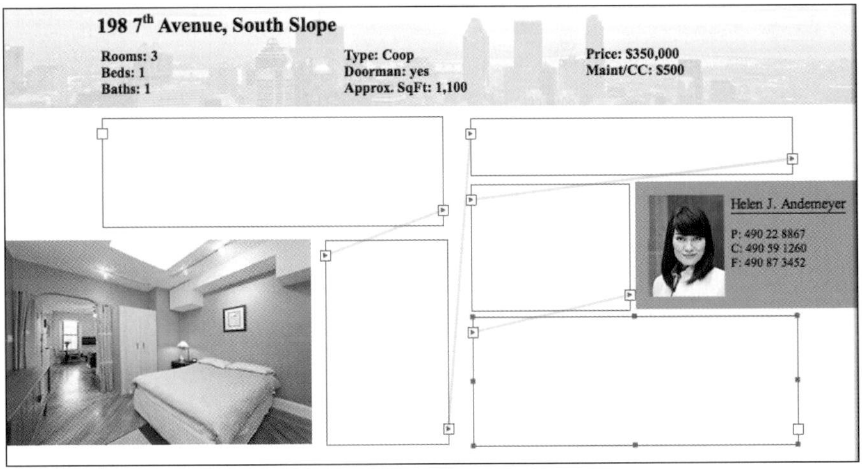

Adding content to the linked text boxes

Next, add text to your linked text boxes. Begin with the first text box, and as text reaches the limit of one box, it will automatically flow into the next.

1 Open the file 07SampleRealEstateText1.txt from the 07Start folder if it's not already open.

2 Copy the description of the property.

3 Double-click the first text box on the Stage and paste the text.

● **Note:** Treat the linked text boxes as if they were a single container. As you add, delete, and edit text, the contents reflow to fit. You can select all (Edit > Select All), and the contents of all the linked text boxes will be selected.

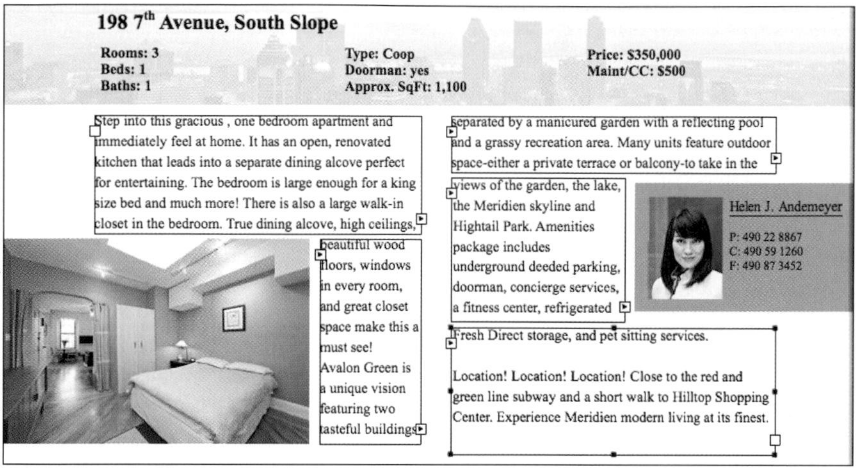

198 7th Avenue, South Slope
Rooms: 3
Beds: 1
Baths: 1
Type: Coop
Doorman: yes
Approx. SqFt: 1,100
Price: $350,000
Maint/CC: $500
Step into this gracious , one bedroom apartment and immediately feel at home. It has an open, renovated kitchen that leads into a separate dining alcove perfect for entertaining. The bedroom is large enough for a king size bed and much more! There is also a large walk-in closet in the bedroom. True dining alcove, high ceilings,
beautiful wood floors, windows in every room, and great closet space make this a must see!
Avalon Green is a unique vision featuring two tasteful buildings
separated by a manicured garden with a reflecting pool and a grassy recreation area. Many units feature outdoor space-either a private terrace or balcony-to take in the
views of the garden, the lake, the Meridien skyline and Hightail Park. Amenities package includes underground deeded parking, doorman, concierge services, a fitness center, refrigerated
Fresh Direct storage, and pet sitting services.
Location! Location! Location! Close to the red and green line subway and a short walk to Hilltop Shopping Center. Experience Meridien modern living at its finest.
Helen J. Andemeyer
P: 490 22 8867
C: 490 59 1260
F: 490 87 3452

Click on the Stage outside the text boxes to deselect them and view how your text appears as it wraps around the graphics. Adjust the size or location to finesse the way your text flows from one box to the next.

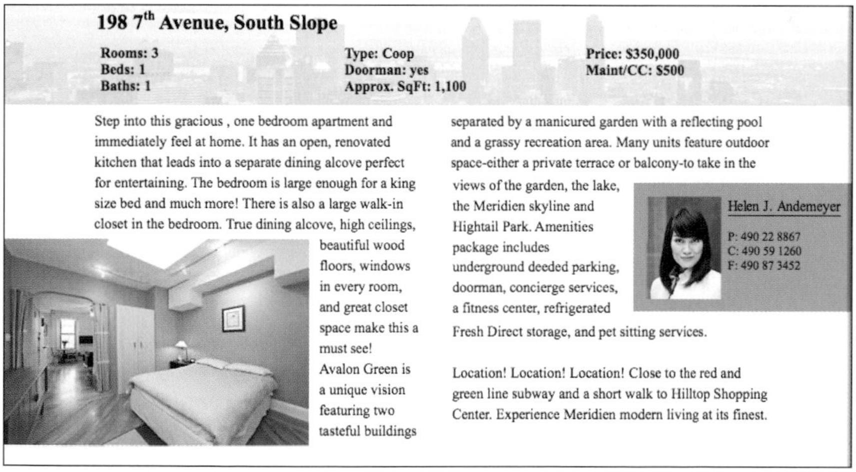

198 7th Avenue, South Slope
Rooms: 3
Beds: 1
Baths: 1
Type: Coop
Doorman: yes
Approx. SqFt: 1,100
Price: $350,000
Maint/CC: $500
Step into this gracious , one bedroom apartment and immediately feel at home. It has an open, renovated kitchen that leads into a separate dining alcove perfect for entertaining. The bedroom is large enough for a king size bed and much more! There is also a large walk-in closet in the bedroom. True dining alcove, high ceilings,
beautiful wood floors, windows in every room, and great closet space make this a must see!
Avalon Green is a unique vision featuring two tasteful buildings
separated by a manicured garden with a reflecting pool and a grassy recreation area. Many units feature outdoor space-either a private terrace or balcony-to take in the
views of the garden, the lake, the Meridien skyline and Hightail Park. Amenities package includes underground deeded parking, doorman, concierge services, a fitness center, refrigerated
Fresh Direct storage, and pet sitting services.
Location! Location! Location! Close to the red and green line subway and a short walk to Hilltop Shopping Center. Experience Meridien modern living at its finest.
Helen J. Andemeyer
P: 490 22 8867
C: 490 59 1260
F: 490 87 3452

Deleting and inserting text boxes

If you need to edit the way the text flows, you can always delete linked text boxes or add new ones, and the linkages between the existing ones will be maintained.

1 With the Selection tool, select the second linked text box.

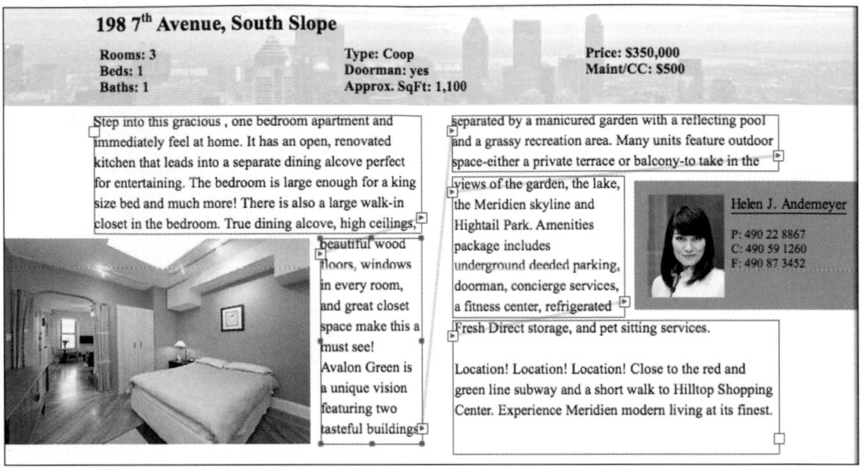
198 7th Avenue, South Slope
Rooms: 3
Beds: 1
Baths: 1
Type: Coop
Doorman: yes
Approx. SqFt: 1,100
Price: $350,000
Maint/CC: $500
Step into this gracious , one bedroom apartment and immediately feel at home. It has an open, renovated kitchen that leads into a separate dining alcove perfect for entertaining. The bedroom is large enough for a king size bed and much more! There is also a large walk-in closet in the bedroom. True dining alcove, high ceilings,
beautiful wood floors, windows in every room, and great closet space make this a must see!
Avalon Green is a unique vision featuring two tasteful buildings
separated by a manicured garden with a reflecting pool and a grassy recreation area. Many units feature outdoor space-either a private terrace or balcony-to take in the
views of the garden, the lake, the Meridien skyline and Hightail Park. Amenities package includes underground deeded parking, doorman, concierge services, a fitness center, refrigerated
Fresh Direct storage, and pet sitting services.
Location! Location! Location! Close to the red and green line subway and a short walk to Hilltop Shopping Center. Experience Meridien modern living at its finest.
Helen J. Andemeyer
P: 490 22 8867
C: 490 59 1260
F: 490 87 3452

2 Press the Delete key on the keyboard.

The second linked text box is deleted from the Stage, but the remaining text boxes maintain their linkages. The first text box is now linked to the third at the top of the second column. Notice that the last text box shows the red cross at its bottom-right corner, indicating overflow text that cannot be displayed.

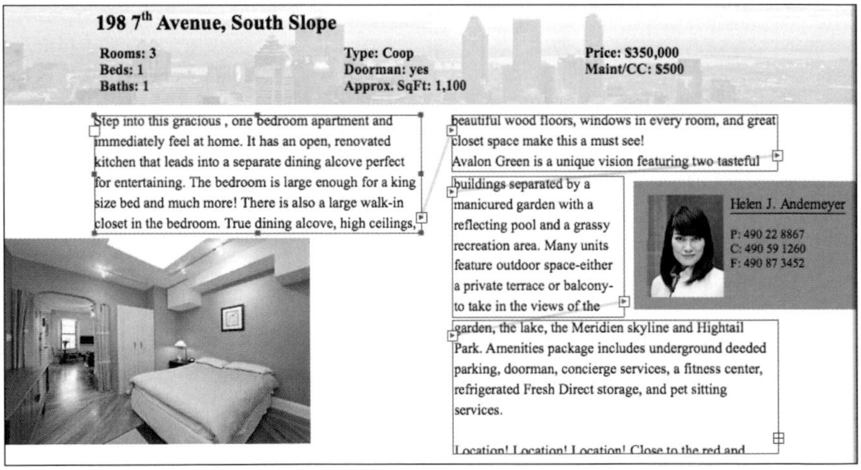
198 7th Avenue, South Slope
Rooms: 3
Beds: 1
Baths: 1
Type: Coop
Doorman: yes
Approx. SqFt: 1,100
Price: $350,000
Maint/CC: $500
Step into this gracious , one bedroom apartment and immediately feel at home. It has an open, renovated kitchen that leads into a separate dining alcove perfect for entertaining. The bedroom is large enough for a king size bed and much more! There is also a large walk-in closet in the bedroom. True dining alcove, high ceilings,
beautiful wood floors, windows in every room, and great closet space make this a must see!
Avalon Green is a unique vision featuring two tasteful
buildings separated by a manicured garden with a reflecting pool and a grassy recreation area. Many units feature outdoor space-either a private terrace or balcony-to take in the views of the
garden, the lake, the Meridien skyline and Hightail Park. Amenities package includes underground deeded parking, doorman, concierge services, a fitness center, refrigerated Fresh Direct storage, and pet sitting services.
Helen J. Andemeyer
P: 490 22 8867
C: 490 59 1260
F: 490 87 3452

3 Click on the box containing the small arrowhead on the lower-right corner of the first text box.

4 Click and drag out the text box to reestablish the one you just deleted.

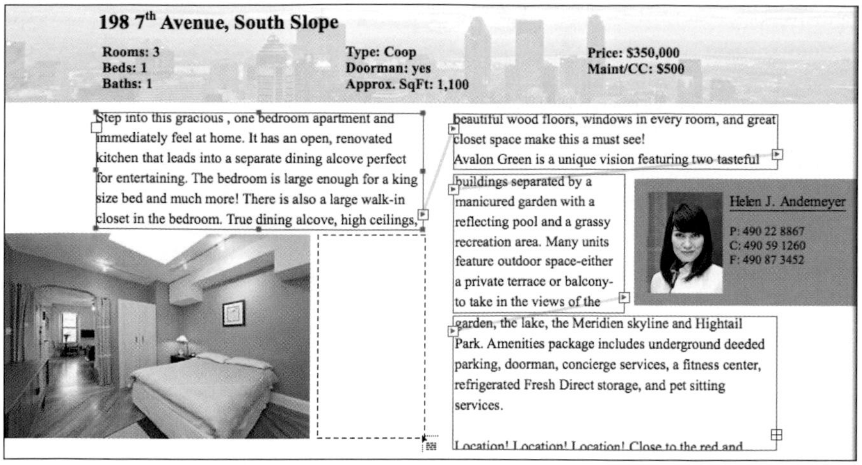
198 7th Avenue, South Slope
Rooms: 3
Beds: 1
Baths: 1
Type: Coop
Doorman: yes
Approx. SqFt: 1,100
Price: $350,000
Maint/CC: $500
Step into this gracious , one bedroom apartment and immediately feel at home. It has an open, renovated kitchen that leads into a separate dining alcove perfect for entertaining. The bedroom is large enough for a king size bed and much more! There is also a large walk-in closet in the bedroom. True dining alcove, high ceilings,
beautiful wood floors, windows in every room, and great closet space make this a must see!
Avalon Green is a unique vision featuring two tasteful
buildings separated by a manicured garden with a reflecting pool and a grassy recreation area. Many units feature outdoor space-either a private terrace or balcony-to take in the views of the
garden, the lake, the Meridien skyline and Hightail Park. Amenities package includes underground deeded parking, doorman, concierge services, a fitness center, refrigerated Fresh Direct storage, and pet sitting services.
Helen J. Andemeyer
P: 490 22 8867
C: 490 59 1260
F: 490 87 3452

A new text box is inserted between the existing linked text boxes, and the text reflows to fill the new container.

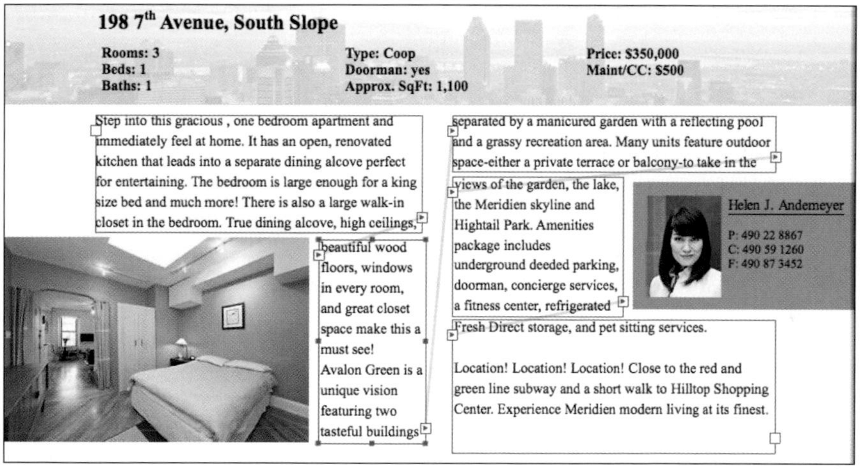
198 7th Avenue, South Slope
Rooms: 3
Beds: 1
Baths: 1
Type: Coop
Doorman: yes
Approx. SqFt: 1,100
Price: $350,000
Maint/CC: $500
Step into this gracious , one bedroom apartment and immediately feel at home. It has an open, renovated kitchen that leads into a separate dining alcove perfect for entertaining. The bedroom is large enough for a king size bed and much more! There is also a large walk-in closet in the bedroom. True dining alcove, high ceilings,
beautiful wood floors, windows in every room, and great closet space make this a must see!
Avalon Green is a unique vision featuring two tasteful buildings
separated by a manicured garden with a reflecting pool and a grassy recreation area. Many units feature outdoor space-either a private terrace or balcony-to take in the
views of the garden, the lake, the Meridien skyline and Hightail Park. Amenities package includes underground deeded parking, doorman, concierge services, a fitness center, refrigerated
Fresh Direct storage, and pet sitting services.
Location! Location! Location! Close to the red and green line subway and a short walk to Hilltop Shopping Center. Experience Meridien modern living at its finest.
Helen J. Andemeyer
P: 490 22 8867
C: 490 59 1260
F: 490 87 3452

Breaking and relinking text boxes

You can also break the links between text boxes and create new linkages.

1 Click on the box containing the small arrowhead on the lower-right corner of the first text box (ngs,).

2 Move your mouse cursor over the second text box.

Your cursor changes to a broken link icon ( ), indicating that you can break the link to the text box that is currently below your cursor.

3 Click on the second text box.

The link from the first text box to the second text box is broken. Your text now can't flow out of the first text box.

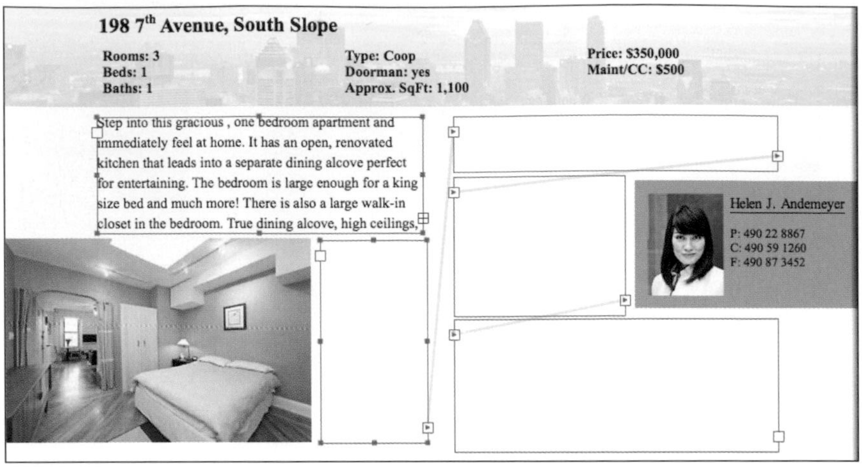
198 7th Avenue, South Slope
Rooms: 3
Beds: 1
Baths: 1
Type: Coop
Doorman: yes
Approx. SqFt: 1,100
Price: $350,000
Maint/CC: $500
Step into this gracious , one bedroom apartment and immediately feel at home. It has an open, renovated kitchen that leads into a separate dining alcove perfect for entertaining. The bedroom is large enough for a king size bed and much more! There is also a large walk-in closet in the bedroom. True dining alcove, high ceilings,
Helen J. Andemeyer
P: 490 22 8867
C: 490 59 1260
F: 490 87 3452

4 Let's reestablish the link. Click on the red cross on the lower-right corner of the first text box and move your cursor over the second text box.

Your cursor changes to a linked icon (), indicating that you can establish a link to the text box that is currently below your cursor.

5 Click on the second text box.

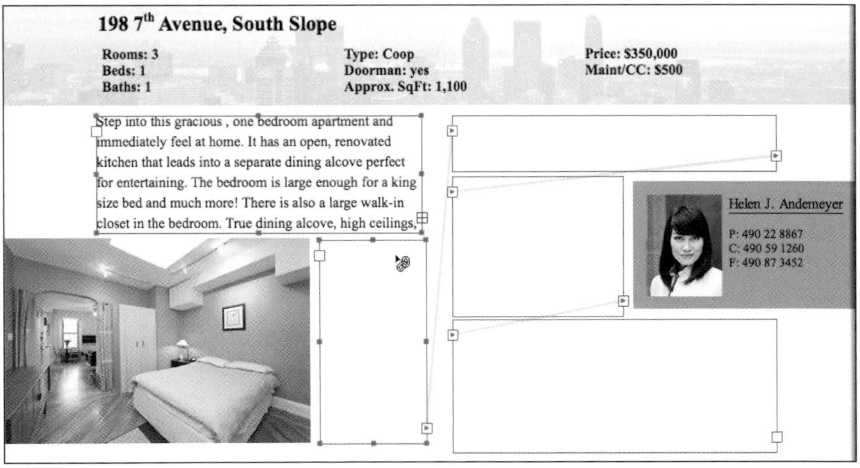
198 7th Avenue, South Slope
Rooms: 3
Beds: 1
Baths: 1
Type: Coop
Doorman: yes
Approx. SqFt: 1,100
Price: $350,000
Maint/CC: $500
Step into this gracious , one bedroom apartment and immediately feel at home. It has an open, renovated kitchen that leads into a separate dining alcove perfect for entertaining. The bedroom is large enough for a king size bed and much more! There is also a large walk-in closet in the bedroom. True dining alcove, high ceilings,
Helen J. Andemeyer
P: 490 22 8867
C: 490 59 1260
F: 490 87 3452

The first text box is again linked to the second text box. Your text now flows throughout the five text boxes.

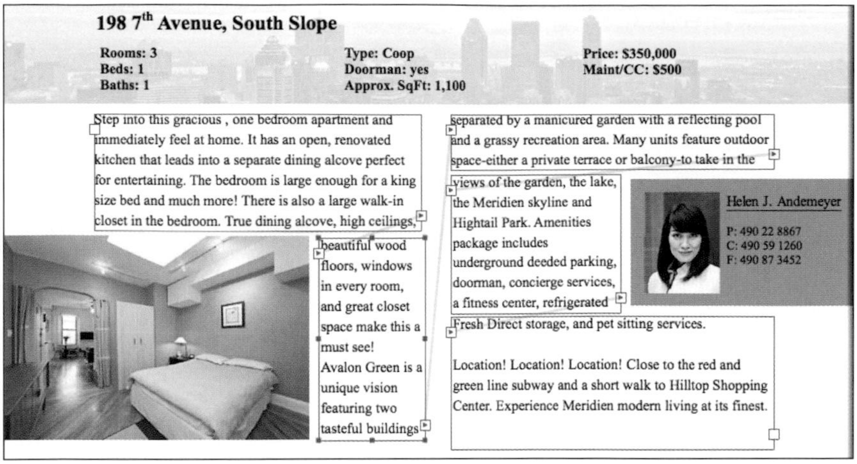
198 7th Avenue, South Slope
Rooms: 3
Beds: 1
Baths: 1
Type: Coop
Doorman: yes
Approx. SqFt: 1,100
Price: $350,000
Maint/CC: $500
Step into this gracious , one bedroom apartment and immediately feel at home. It has an open, renovated kitchen that leads into a separate dining alcove perfect for entertaining. The bedroom is large enough for a king size bed and much more! There is also a large walk-in closet in the bedroom. True dining alcove, high ceilings,
beautiful wood floors, windows in every room, and great closet space make this a must see! Avalon Green is a unique vision featuring two tasteful buildings
separated by a manicured garden with a reflecting pool and a grassy recreation area. Many units feature outdoor space-either a private terrace or balcony-to take in the
views of the garden, the lake, the Meridien skyline and Hightail Park. Amenities package includes underground deeded parking, doorman, concierge services, a fitness center, refrigerated
Fresh Direct storage, and pet sitting services.
Location! Location! Location! Close to the red and green line subway and a short walk to Hilltop Shopping Center. Experience Meridien modern living at its finest.
Helen J. Andemeyer
P: 490 22 8867
C: 490 59 1260
F: 490 87 3452

Finding the Next or Previous Link

Sometimes, if you have multiple linked text boxes, it may be confusing to see the linkages or difficult to select the boxes in succession. You can right-click/Ctrl-click over any text box and, if it is linked, you can choose Find Previous Link or Find Next Link. The previous or next linked text box will become selected.

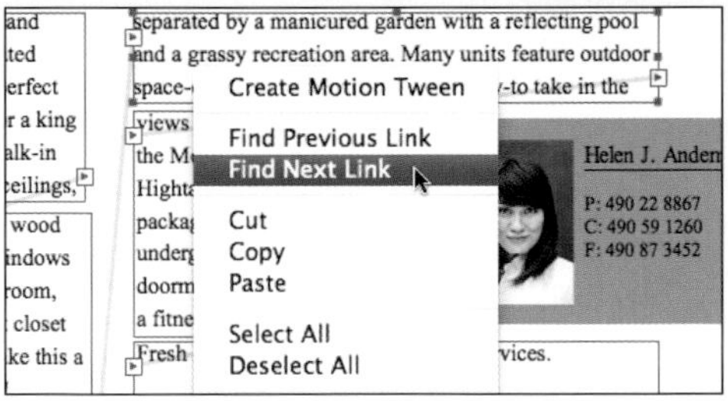
Create Motion Tween
Find Previous Link
Find Next Link
Cut
Copy
Paste
Select All
Deselect All

Hyperlinking Text

The description of the property on the real estate site contains references to several landmarks and destinations of interest in Meridien City. You'll add a hyperlink to one of those text references so your users can click it and be directed to a Web site with additional information. Hyperlinks are easy to add to text and don't require any HTML or ActionScript coding.

Adding a hyperlink

1 Double-click the second linked text box on the Stage and select the words **Avalon Green**.

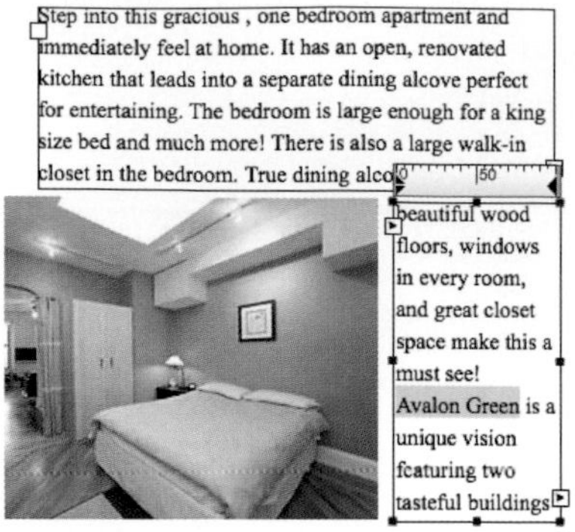

● **Note:** A _self Target loads the URL in the same browser window, taking over your Flash movie. A _top and _parent Target refers to the arrangement of a frameset, and loads the URL in a particular frame relative to the current frame.

2 In the Advanced Character section of the Properties inspector, enter **http://www.avalongreen.org** for the Link and choose _blank in the Target pull-down menu.

The selected words in your text box become underlined, indicating that it is hyperlinked.

The Web address is a fictional one. Be sure to include the protocol **http://** before any URL to choose a site on the Web. The Target field determines where the Web site loads. A _blank Target means that the Web site loads in a blank browser window.

3 Select the words Avalon Green, and in the Character section of the Properties inspector, change the color from black to blue.

The selected words become blue and remain underlined, which is the standard visual cue for a hyperlinked item in a browser. However, you are free to display your hyperlink in any fashion, just as long as your user can recognize it as a clickable item.

Step into this gracious , one bedroom apartment and immediately feel at home. It has an open, renovated kitchen that leads into a separate dining alcove perfect for entertaining. The bedroom is large enough for a king size bed and much more! There is also a large walk-in closet in the bedroom. True dining alcove, high ceilings, beautiful wood floors, windows in every room, and great closet space make this a must see! Avalon Green is a unique vision featuring two tasteful buildings

4 Choose Control > Test Movie > in Flash Professional. Click the hyperlink.

A browser opens and attempts to load the fictional Web site at www.avalongreen.org.

Creating User-input Text

Next, you'll create the mortgage calculator, which accepts input from the user through the keyboard and displays estimated monthly payments based on those inputs. You create user-input text with Editable TLF Text. User-input text can be used to create sophisticated customized interactions that gather information from the viewer and tailor the Flash movie based on that information. Examples include applications requiring a login and password, surveys and forms, or quizzes.

Adding the static text elements

Start by creating all the text that doesn't change or can't be edited—the static elements of the mortgage calculator.

1 Select the Text tool.

2 In the Properties inspector, select TLF Text and Read Only. In the Character section, choose Times New Roman for Family, Regular for Style, 12.0 for Size, 12.0 pt for Leading, and black for Color.

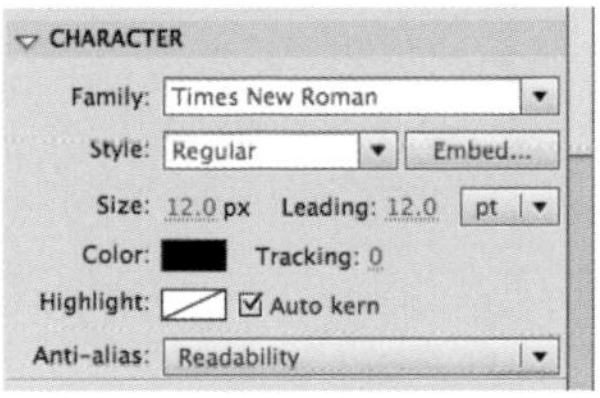

3 Click in the dark brown area under the Mortgage Calculator text and insert five separate lines of text for **TERM: 30 Year Fixed**, **PRICE: $350,000**, **RATE:**, **PERCENT DOWN:**, and **MONTHLY PAYMENTS:**.

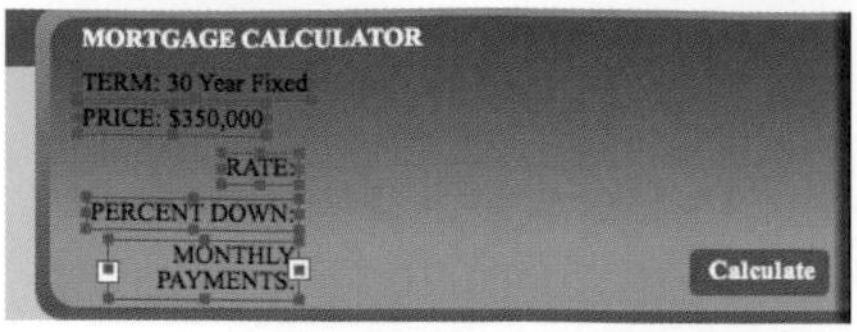

Adding the display fields

For RATE and PERCENT DOWN, you'll add Editable text boxes so your users can enter their own numbers and customize the mortgage calculations to evaluate their buying decisions.

1 Select the Text tool.

2 In the Properties inspector, select TLF Text and Editable. Keep the other font information the same as the previous text you created.

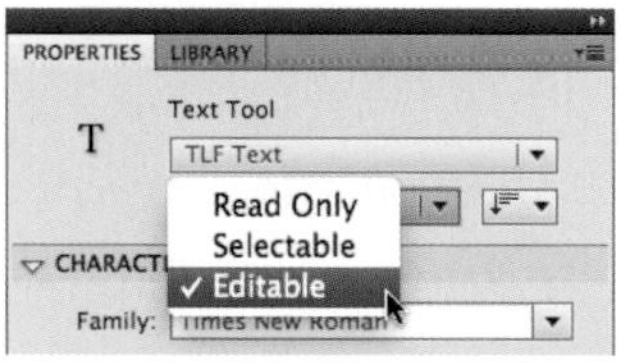

3 Click and drag out a small text box next to RATE.

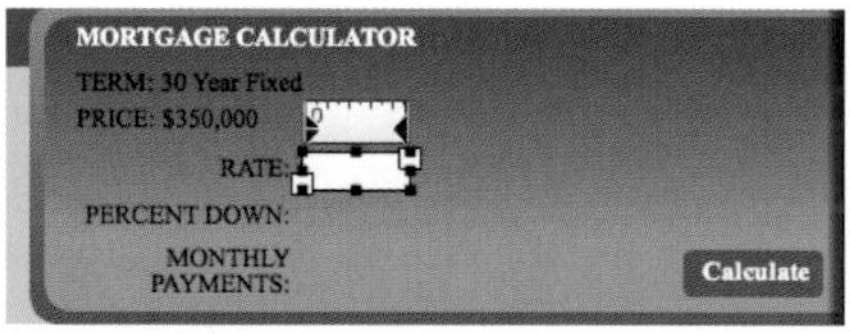

4 In the Container and Flow section of the Properties inspector, choose a white color and 75% Alpha value for the Fill.

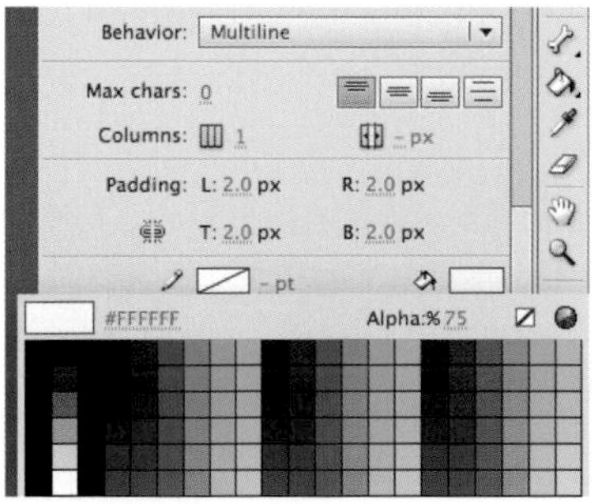

The Editable text box next to Rate displays a semitransparent white background. You can also add a stroke to the text box to give it more definition if you desire.

5 Create a second Editable text box next to PERCENT DOWN with the same semitransparent white background.

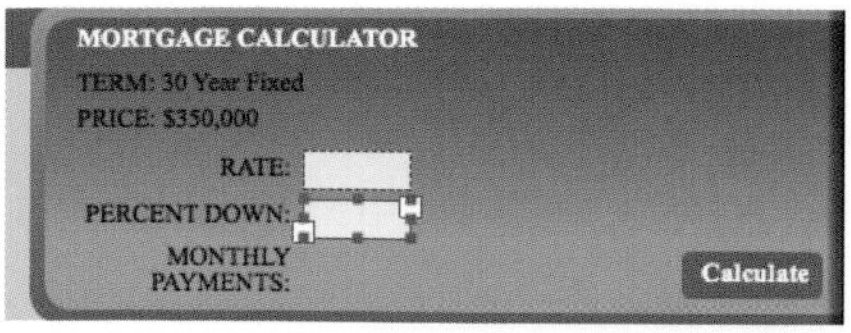

6 Create a third text box next to MONTHLY PAYMENTS with the same semitransparent white background, but make this text box Read Only.

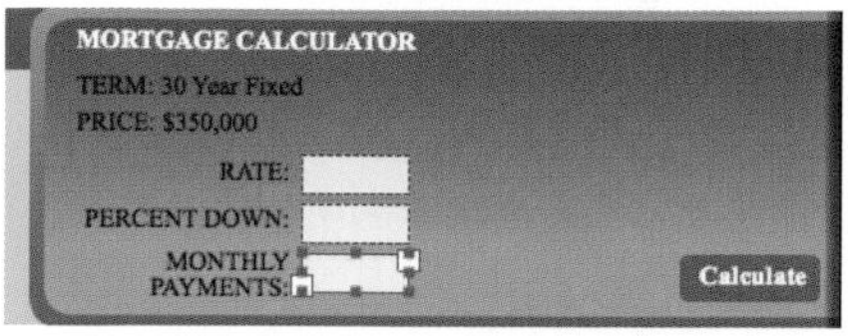

The text box next to MONTHLY PAYMENTS is Read Only because it will display a number calculated based on the user-inputted RATE and PERCENT DOWN. The user does not need to edit the information in that box.

7 In the Editable text box next to RATE, enter **5.25**. In the Editable text box next to PERCENT DOWN, enter **20**.

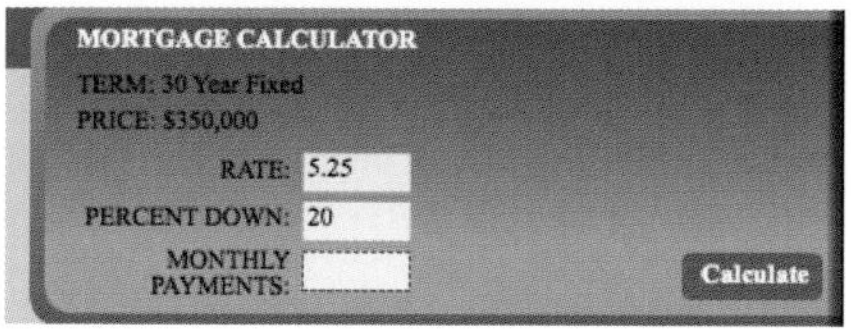

Entering initial text in Editable text boxes often guides users in knowing what kind of text is expected.

Embedding fonts

For any text that may be edited during runtime, you should embed the fonts. Since the user can enter any kind of text in Editable text boxes, you need to include those potential characters in the final SWF to ensure that text appears as you expect it, with the same font that you've chosen in the Properties inspector.

1 Select the first Editable text box next to Rate.

2 In the Character section of the Properties inspector, click the Embed button.

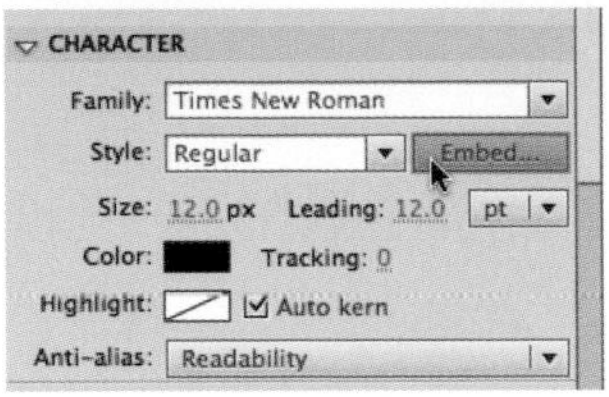

The Font Embedding dialog box appears. The font that is used in the selected text box appears on the left.

Note: Embedding fonts dramatically increases the size of your final SWF, so exercise caution when doing so, and limit the number of fonts and characters when possible.

3 In the Character ranges section, select Numerals. Click OK.

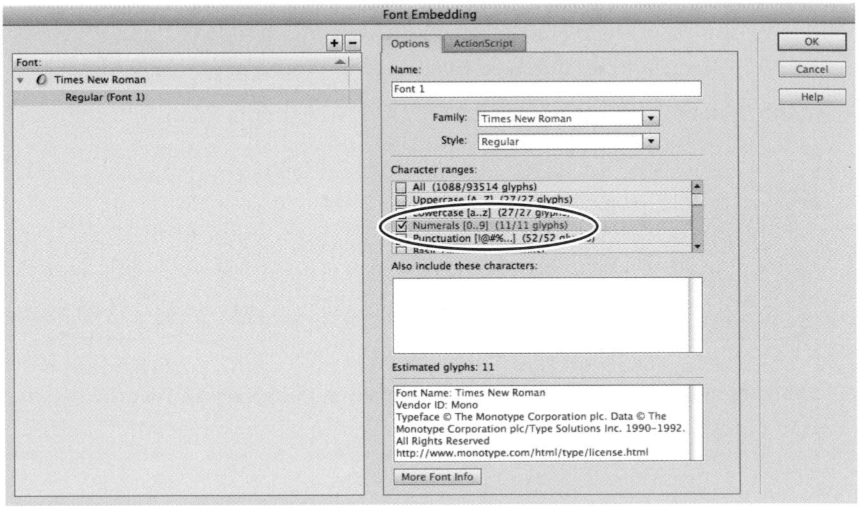

All the number characters of the current font, Times New Roman Regular, will be included in the published SWF.

Device Fonts

Use device fonts as an alternative to embedding fonts. Device fonts are three generic options grouped at the top of the Character Family pull-down menu. You can also choose the Use device fonts option from the Anti-alias pull-down menu.

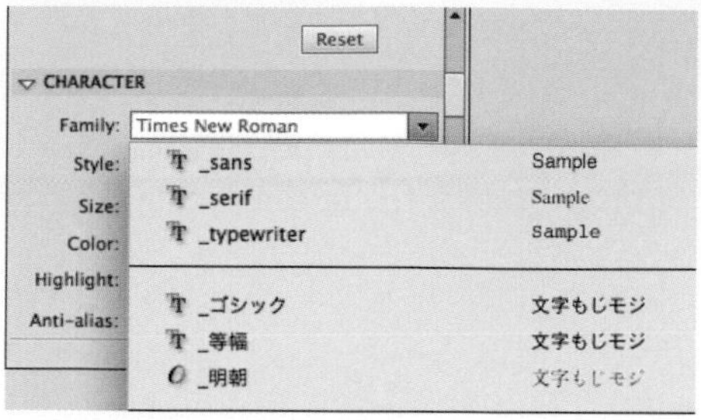

The three device fonts are _sans, _serif, and _typewriter. These options find and use the fonts on a user's computer that most closely resemble the specified device font. When you use device fonts, you don't have to worry about embedding fonts, and you can be assured that your viewer sees text that is similar to the text you see in the authoring environment.

Naming the text boxes

For Flash to control what text to display in a text box or to know what has been entered in an Editable text box, the text box must be given an instance name in the Properties inspector. Just as you named button instances in Lesson 6, "Creating Interactive Navigation," naming text boxes on the Stage allows ActionScript to identify them. The same naming rules apply for text boxes as they do for buttons.

1 Select the first Editable text box next to Rate.

2 In the Properties inspector, enter **rate_txt** for the instance name.

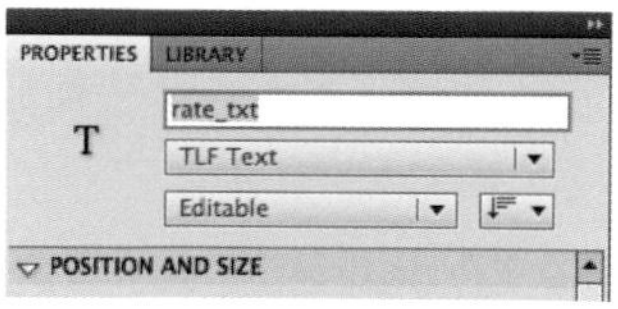

The suffix _txt is the convention for text boxes.

3 Select the next Editable text box next to Percent Down.

4 In the Properties inspector, enter **down_txt** for the instance name.

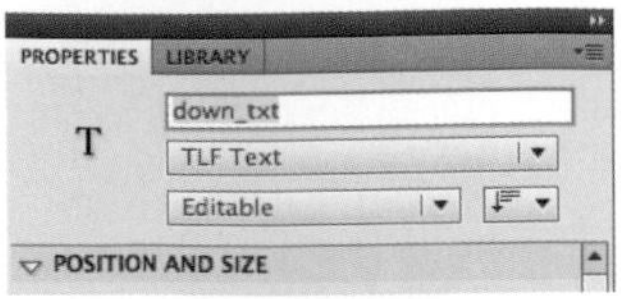

5 Select the Read Only text box next to Monthly Payments.

6 In the Properties inspector, enter **monthly_txt** for the instance name.

Changing the contents of text boxes

The contents of a text box are represented by its `text` property. You can dynamically change a text box's contents by assigning new text to the `text` property. In this section, you'll add ActionScript that reads the text entered in the Editable text boxes next to Rate and Percent Down, perform some mathematical calculations, and then display new text in the Read Only text box next to Monthly Payments.

1 Unlock the calculator layer, select the Calculate button on the Stage, and in the Properties inspector, enter **calculate_btn** for the instance name.

2 Insert a new layer and rename it **actionscript**.

3 Select the first keyframe of the actionscript layer and open the Actions panel.

4 You must first create a few variables to hold numerical information. The variables will help you make the mortgage calculations. Variables are created, or "declared," using the `var` keyword. Enter the code as follows:

```
var term:Number=360;
var price:Number=350000;
var monthlypayment:Number;
```

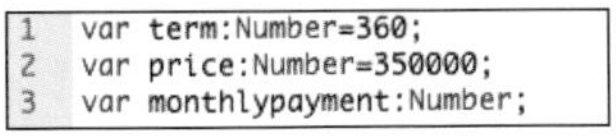

5 Create an event listener and function for the Calculate button. You should be familiar with event listeners from Lesson 6, but if not, you should review the concepts in that lesson before moving on. The event listener and function should appear as shown here:

```
var term:Number=360;
var price:Number=350000;
var monthlypayment:Number;
calculate_btn.addEventListener(MouseEvent.CLICK, calculatemonthlypayment);
function calculatemonthlypayment(e:MouseEvent):void {

}
```

6 Enter code within the function to make the mortgage calculations and display the results. The completed code for the event listener and function should be as follows:

```
calculate_btn.addEventListener(MouseEvent.CLICK, 
calculatemonthlypayment);

function calculatemonthlypayment(e:MouseEvent):void {

 var loan:Number=price-Number(down_txt.text)/100*price;

 var c:Number=Number(rate_txt.text)/1200;

 monthlypayment = loan*(c*(Math.pow((1+c),term)))/(Math.
pow((1+c),term)-1);

 monthly_txt.text=String(Math.round(monthlypayment));

}
```

```
var term:Number=360;
var price:Number=350000;
var monthlypayment:Number;
calculate_btn.addEventListener(MouseEvent.CLICK, calculatemonthlypayment);
function calculatemonthlypayment(e:MouseEvent):void {
    var loan:Number=price-Number(down_txt.text)/100*price;
    var c:Number=Number(rate_txt.text)/1200;
    monthlypayment = loan*(c*(Math.pow((1+c),term)))/(Math.pow((1+c),term)-1);
    monthly_txt.text=String(Math.round(monthlypayment));
}
```

Don't get too discouraged looking at the code! Take your time to copy it exactly, or you can copy and paste it from the 07End.fla file in the 07End folder.

It may look complicated, but there are only two important concepts to identify. First, the contents of text boxes are referenced by the `text` property. So `down_txt.text` refers to the contents in the text box named `down_txt`, and `rate_txt.text` refers to the contents in the text box named `rate_txt`.

Second, text boxes contain text, or String data. To make numeric calculations, you must first convert the text to a number using `Number()`. To convert a number back to text, use `String()`.

The rest of the surrounding code is algebraic manipulation using addition, subtraction, multiplication, division, and exponents according to a straightforward mortgage payment formula.

Testing the calculator

Now test your movie to see how Flash controls the contents of the named text boxes.

1 Choose Control > Test Movie > in Flash Professional.

2 In the preview movie that appears, enter new values in the text boxes next to RATE and PERCENT DOWN, and then click the Calculate button.

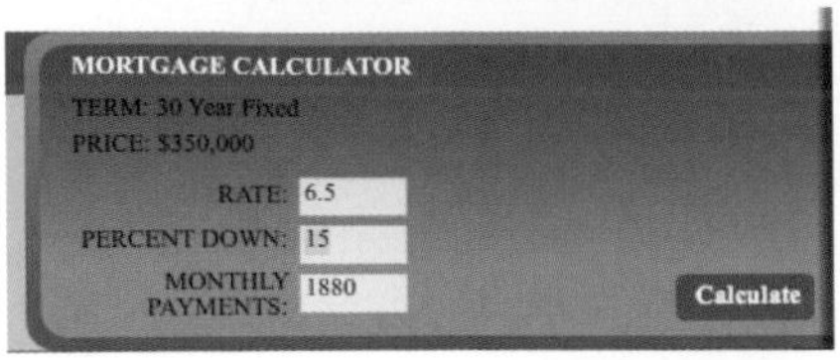

Flash reads the values in the text boxes next to Rate and Percent Down, calculates a monthly payment, and displays new text in the text box next to MONTHLY PAYMENTS. Try different values to see how much you can afford!

Loading External Text

So far, you've created an attractive layout with an interactive tool for this property listing for the real estate agent. However, the agent has many more listings, and it would be convenient to use the same layout to display the information without re-creating it for each property. Fortunately, you can load new text from an external file and display it in an existing text box, replacing its contents. To display additional listings, simply maintain additional text files and load them to be displayed as needed. This is an example of dynamic content—content that changes at runtime (in the SWF file) rather than being fixed during authortime (in the FLA file).

In this section, you'll load new content from external text files to replace the property address, information, and description.

Naming the text boxes

To change the contents of the text boxes, you first need to give them instance names so they can be referenced in ActionScript. You'll provide instance names for the address, information, and description of the property listing.

1 Select the text box at the top of the Stage that contains the address of the property listing.

2 In the Properties inspector, enter **address_txt** for the instance name.

PROPERTIES
LIBRARY
address_txt
TLF Text
Read Only

3 Select the text box below the address that contains the details of the property listing.

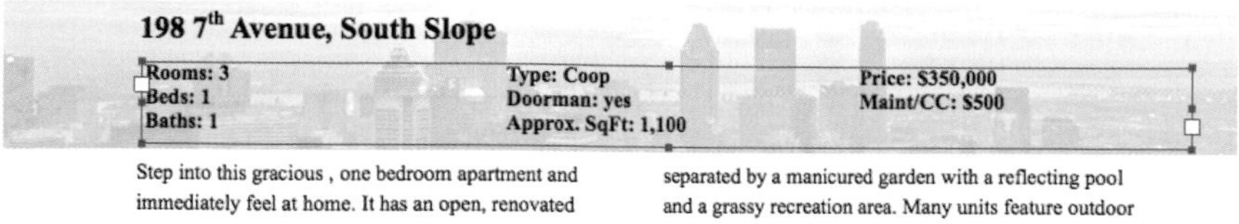
198 7th Avenue, South Slope
Rooms: 3
Beds: 1
Baths: 1
Type: Coop
Doorman: yes
Approx. SqFt: 1,100
Price: $350,000
Maint/CC: $500
Step into this gracious , one bedroom apartment and
immediately feel at home. It has an open, renovated
separated by a manicured garden with a reflecting pool
and a grassy recreation area. Many units feature outdoor

4 In the Properties inspector, enter **info_txt** for the instance name.

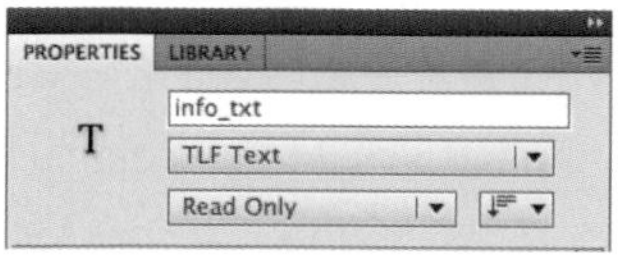
PROPERTIES
LIBRARY
info_txt
TLF Text
Read Only

5 Select the first linked text box of the description of the property.

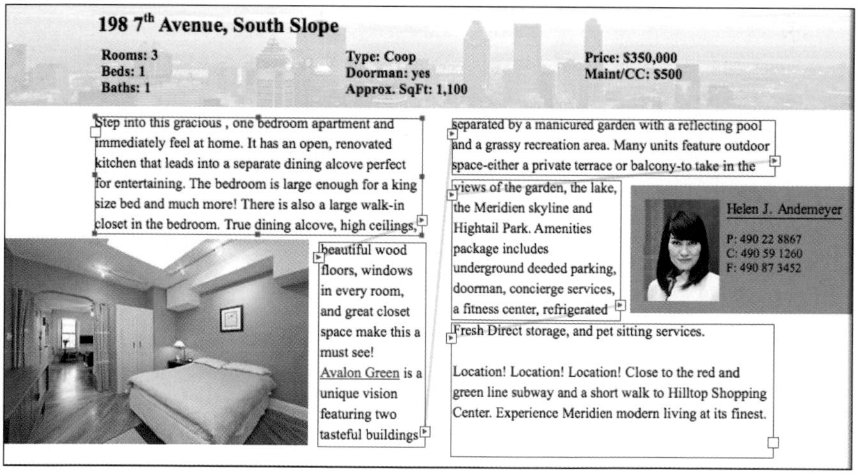
198 7th Avenue, South Slope
Rooms: 3
Beds: 1
Baths: 1
Type: Coop
Doorman: yes
Approx. SqFt: 1,100
Price: $350,000
Maint/CC: $500
Step into this gracious , one bedroom apartment and immediately feel at home. It has an open, renovated kitchen that leads into a separate dining alcove perfect for entertaining. The bedroom is large enough for a king size bed and much more! There is also a large walk-in closet in the bedroom. True dining alcove, high ceilings,
beautiful wood floors, windows in every room, and great closet space make this a must see! Avalon Green is a unique vision featuring two tasteful buildings
separated by a manicured garden with a reflecting pool and a grassy recreation area. Many units feature outdoor space-either a private terrace or balcony-to take in the
views of the garden, the lake, the Meridien skyline and Hightail Park. Amenities package includes underground deeded parking, doorman, concierge services, a fitness center, refrigerated
Fresh Direct storage, and pet sitting services.
Location! Location! Location! Close to the red and green line subway and a short walk to Hilltop Shopping Center. Experience Meridien modern living at its finest.
Helen J. Andemeyer
P: 490 22 8867
C: 490 59 1260
F: 490 87 3452

6 In the Properties inspector, enter **description_txt** for the instance name.

PROPERTIES
LIBRARY
description_txt
TLF Text
Read Only

Embedding the fonts

When text changes at runtime, you need to embed all the characters of the font that the text would potentially use to make sure that the text displays properly.

1 Select the first text box named address_txt.

2 In the Character section of the Properties inspector, click the Embed button.

The Font Embedding dialog box appears. You can also choose Text > Font Embedding to display the dialog box.

3 The font used in the selected text box appears on the left side of the dialog box (Times New Roman Bold). In the Character ranges section, select Uppercase, Lowercase, Numerals, and Punctuation. Click OK.

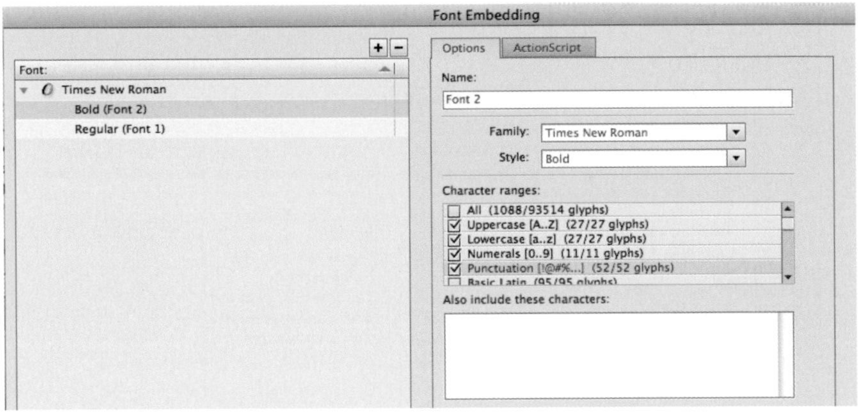

The character ranges that you've selected will be embedded in the final SWF file. Any of the characters in those ranges will display properly in your final Flash movie.

4 Select the first linked text box named description_txt.

5 In the Character section of the Properties inspector, click the Embed button.

The Font Embedding dialog box appears. The Numerals for Character range should already be selected since you embedded those characters for the mortgage calculator.

6 In the Character ranges section, select Uppercase, Lowercase, and Punctuation in addition to Numerals. Click OK.

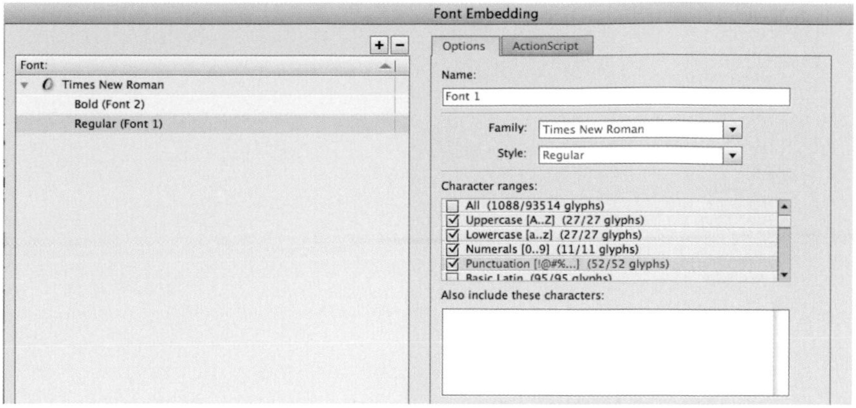

The character ranges that you've selected will be embedded in the final SWF file. Any of the characters in those ranges will display properly in your final Flash movie.

Loading and displaying external text

Information for a second property listing is saved in three additional text files in the 07Start folder. You'll add ActionScript to your movie that loads information from those text files.

1 Open the file in the 07Start folder called 07SampleRealEstate2-address.txt.

The file contains information about the address of another property listing.

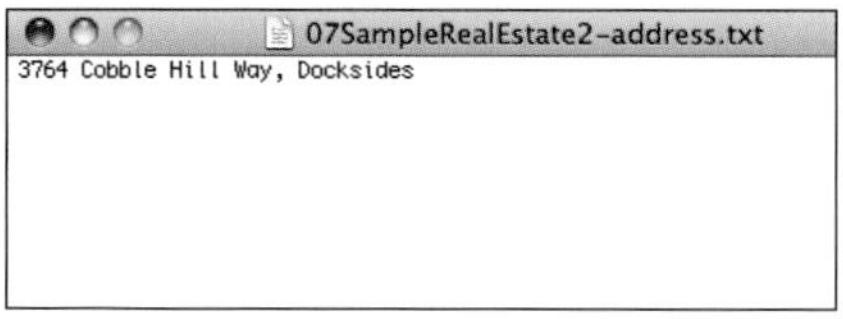

2 Choose Window > Code Snippets.

The Code Snippets panel appears.

Note: Make sure you save external text content as a text-only file in an application such as TextEdit (Mac) or Notepad (Windows). Do not use Microsoft Word, because Word adds unnecessary additional information to the file that interferes with its proper loading. If you use Word, always choose Save As Text Only.

3 Expand the Load and Unload folder and double-click the Load External Text option.

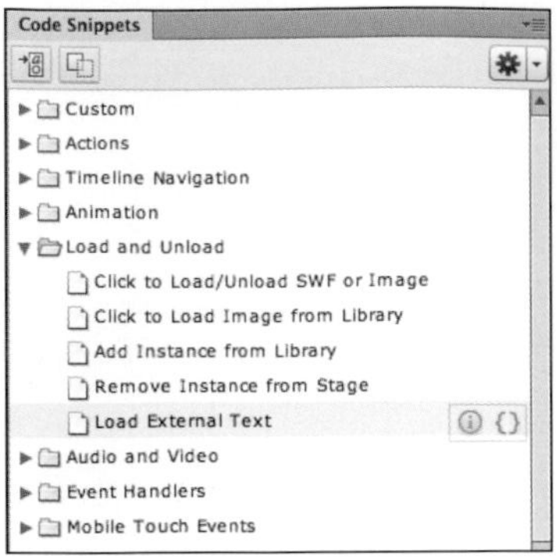

A new layer named Actions is automatically inserted in the Timeline, and the Actions panel opens to display the inserted code snippet. You'll need to customize some of the code for it to work in this particular project.

```
1
2  /* Load External Text
3  Loads an external text file and displays it in the Output panel.
4
5  Instructions:
6  1. Replace "http://www.helpexamples.com/flash/text/loremipsum.txt" with the URL address of the text
   file you would like to load.
7  The address can be a relative link or an "http://" link.
8  The address must be placed inside quotation marks ("").
9  */
10
11 var fl_TextLoader:URLLoader = new URLLoader();
12 var fl_TextURLRequest:URLRequest = new URLRequest(
   "http://www.helpexamples.com/flash/text/loremipsum.txt");
13
14 fl_TextLoader.addEventListener(Event.COMPLETE, fl_CompleteHandler);
15
16 function fl_CompleteHandler(event:Event):void
17 {
18     var textData:String = new String(fl_TextLoader.data);
19     trace(textData);
20 }
21
22 fl_TextLoader.load(fl_TextURLRequest);
23
```

4 Replace the URL in line 12 of the code snippet with the filename of the property address, 07SampleRealEstate2-address.txt. Make sure you keep the double quotation marks surrounding the filename.

```
10
11 var fl_TextLoader:URLLoader = new URLLoader();
12 var fl_TextURLRequest:URLRequest = new URLRequest("07SampleRealEstate2-address.txt");
13
```

The code loads the file 07SampleRealEstate2-address.txt.

5 Replace the `trace` command in line 19 of the code snippet with the following code that assigns the new text to the text box named address_txt:

```
address_txt.text = textData;
```

```
16   function fl_CompleteHandler(event:Event):void
17   {
18       var textData:String = new String(fl_TextLoader.data);
19 ▼     address_txt.text = textData;
20   }
```

The contents of the text file, 07SampleRealEstate2-address.txt, will be displayed in the text box named address_txt.

6 In the Code Snippets panel, double-click the Load External Text option again.

7 A second code snippet appears in the Actions panel that loads a second text file.

```
23
24 ▼ /* Load External Text
25   Loads an external text file and displays it in the Output panel.
26
27   Instructions:
28   1. Replace "http://www.helpexamples.com/flash/text/loremipsum.txt" with the URL address of the text
     file you would like to load.
29   The address can be a relative link or an "http://" link.
30   The address must be placed inside quotation marks ("").
31   */
32
33   var fl_TextLoader_2:URLLoader = new URLLoader();
34   var fl_TextURLRequest_2:URLRequest = new URLRequest(
     "http://www.helpexamples.com/flash/text/loremipsum.txt");
35
36   fl_TextLoader_2.addEventListener(Event.COMPLETE, fl_CompleteHandler_2);
37
38   function fl_CompleteHandler_2(event:Event):void
39   {
40       var textData:String = new String(fl_TextLoader_2.data);
41       trace(textData);
42   }
43
44 ▲ fl_TextLoader_2.load(fl_TextURLRequest_2);
45
```

8 Replace the URL in line 34 with the filename of the property details, 07SampleRealEstate2-info.txt, and replace the trace command in line 41 with the following code that assigns the new text to the text box named info_txt:

```
info_txt.text = textData;
```

```
23
24   /* Load External Text
25   Loads an external text file and displays it in the Output panel.
26
27   Instructions:
28   1. Replace "http://www.helpexamples.com/flash/text/loremipsum.txt" with the URL address of the text
     file you would like to load.
29   The address can be a relative link or an "http://" link.
30   The address must be placed inside quotation marks ("").
31   */
32
33   var fl_TextLoader_2:URLLoader = new URLLoader();
34   var fl_TextURLRequest_2:URLRequest = new URLRequest("07SampleRealEstate2-info.txt");
35
36   fl_TextLoader_2.addEventListener(Event.COMPLETE, fl_CompleteHandler_2);
37
38   function fl_CompleteHandler_2(event:Event):void
39   {
40       var textData:String = new String(fl_TextLoader_2.data);
41       info_txt.text = textData;
42   }
43
44   fl_TextLoader_2.load(fl_TextURLRequest_2);
45
```

9 In the Code Snippets panel, double-click the Load External Text option a third time and make the code replacements to load 07SampleRealEstate2-description.txt and display the text in `description_txt`.

```
/* Load External Text
Loads an external text file and displays it in the Output panel.

Instructions:
1. Replace "http://www.helpexamples.com/flash/text/loremipsum.txt" with the URL address of the text file you would like to load.
The address can be a relative link or an "http://" link.
The address must be placed inside quotation marks ("").
*/

var fl_TextLoader_3:URLLoader = new URLLoader();
var fl_TextURLRequest_3:URLRequest = new URLRequest("07SampleRealEstate2-description.txt");

fl_TextLoader_3.addEventListener(Event.COMPLETE, fl_CompleteHandler_3);

function fl_CompleteHandler_3(event:Event):void
{
    var textData:String = new String(fl_TextLoader_3.data);
    description_txt.text = textData;
}

fl_TextLoader_3.load(fl_TextURLRequest_3);
```

The three large blocks of code snippets appear in the Actions panel one after the other.

10 Choose Control > Test Movie > in Flash Professional.

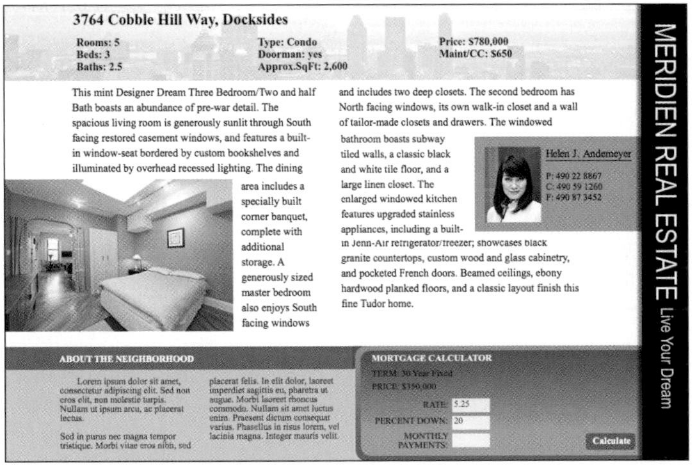

Flash loads the three external text files and displays the contents of the text files in the targeted text boxes. The listing now displays details for a property on Cobble Hill Way instead of 7th Avenue.

The photos and mortgage calculator still refer to the previous listing, so the update to the new property is unfinished. However, you can still see in this incomplete example how flexible it is to develop a template that loads external text content and displays it in text boxes on the Stage. Many professional Flash projects rely on dynamic content fed from external assets such as text files.

Review Questions

1 What is the extra SWZ file that is required for TLF Text?

2 What is the difference between Read Only, Selectable, and Editable TLF Text?

3 When do you need to embed fonts, and how do you do it?

4 How do you make text wrap around objects in a layout?

5 How do you change or read the contents of a text box?

Review Answers

1 The SWZ file is an external ActionScript library that contains information that supports TLF Text. If your Flash movie contains TLF Text, it needs the SWZ file to function properly. Flash automatically generates the additional file, which should always accompany your SWF file.

2 Read Only text is for display purposes and doesn't allow the user to select or edit the text. Selectable text allows the user to select and copy text. Editable text allows the user to select, copy, delete, and edit the text. The contents of all three kinds of text can be changed dynamically with ActionScript.

3 Fonts should be embedded for any text that may be edited or changed at runtime, which means any Editable text box or any text box whose contents dynamically changes, except for text that uses device fonts. Choose Text > Font Embedding or click the Embed button in the Properties inspector to display the Font Embedding dialog box. In the Font Embedding dialog box, you can choose which font, style, and range of characters to embed in your Flash movie.

4 You can wrap text around objects such as photos or graphic elements in a layout by creating a series of linked text boxes, sometimes called threaded text containers. The links establish how overflow text from one text box flows into the next text box. Create the first text box, and then click on the small white box in its lower-right corner. After the mouse cursor changes to a text box icon, click and drag to add the next linked text box.

5 A text box's contents are determined by its `text` property, which accepts String values. To change or access the contents of a text box, you must first give the text box an instance name in the Properties inspector. Then, in ActionScript, you can reference the contents of the text box with its instance name, followed by a dot, followed by the keyword `text`.

8 WORKING WITH SOUND AND VIDEO

Lesson Overview

In this lesson, you'll learn how to do the following:

- Import sound files
- Edit sound files
- Use Adobe Media Encoder CS6
- Understand video and audio encoding options
- Play external video from your Flash project
- Customize options on the video playback component
- Create and use cue points
- Work with video that contains alpha channels
- Embed video in your Flash project

This lesson will take approximately three hours to complete. If needed, remove the previous lesson folder from your hard drive and copy the Lesson08 folder onto it.

Sound and video add new dimensions to your projects. Import sound files and edit them directly in Flash, and use Adobe Media Encoder to compress and convert video files to use in Flash.

Getting Started

Start the lesson by viewing the finished animated zoo kiosk. You'll create the kiosk by adding sound and video files to a project in Flash.

1 Double-click the **08End.html** file in the Lesson08/08End folder to play the animation.

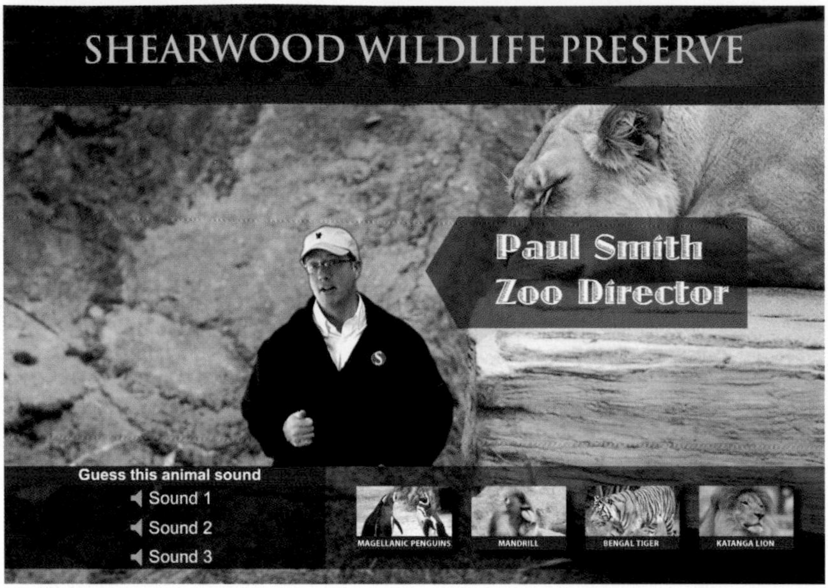

View the movie of the polar bear with a short soundtrack of an African beat. A zoo director introduces himself, and as he speaks, Flash elements appear on the stage that are synchronized with his talk.

2 Click a sound button to hear an animal sound.

3 Click a thumbnail button to view a short movie about the animal. Use the interface controls below the movie to pause, continue, or lower the volume.

In this lesson, you'll import audio files and put them on the Timeline to provide the short introductory audio flourish. You'll also learn how to embed sounds in each button. You'll use Adobe Media Encoder CS6 to compress and convert the video files to the appropriate format for Flash. You'll learn how to work with transparent backgrounds in video to create the silhouetted zoo director video. You'll also add cue points in the video of the zoo director to trigger other Flash animated elements.

1 Double-click the **08Start.fla** file in the Lesson08/08Start folder to open the initial project file in Flash.

2 Choose File > Save As. Name the file **08_workingcopy.fla**, and save it in the 08Start folder. Saving a working copy ensures that the original start file will be available if you want to start over.

Understanding the Project File

The initial setup of the project has been completed except for the audio and video portions and some of the ActionScript code. The Stage is 1000 x 700 pixels. A row of buttons of colorful animals is on the bottom row, another set of buttons on the left, a title at the top, and a background image of a resting lion.

The Timeline contains several layers that separate the different content.

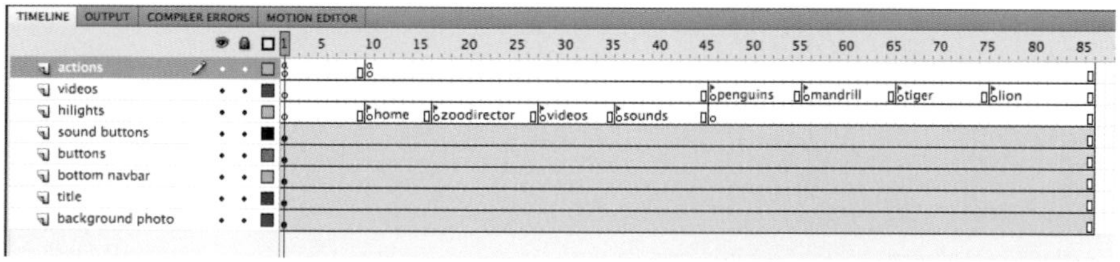

The bottom three layers, called background photo, title, and bottom navbar, contain design elements, text, and images. The next two layers above, called buttons and sound buttons, contain instances of button symbols. The videos layer and the hilights layer contain several labeled keyframes, and the actions layer contains ActionScript that provides the event handlers for the bottom row of buttons.

If you've completed Lesson 6, you should be familiar with the structure of this Timeline. The individual buttons on the bottom row are already coded so that when the user clicks a button, the playhead moves to a corresponding labeled keyframe in the videos layer. You'll be inserting content into each of those keyframes. But first you'll learn to work with sound.

Using Sounds

You can import several types of sound files into Flash. Flash supports MP3, WAV, and AIFF files, which are three common sound formats. When you import sound files into Flash, they are stored in your Library panel. You can then drag the sound files from the Library panel onto the Stage at different points along the Timeline to synchronize those sounds to whatever may be happening on the Stage.

Importing sound files

You'll import several sound files to the Library panel, which you'll use throughout this lesson.

1 Choose File > Import > Import To Library.

2 Select the Monkey.wav file in the Lesson08/08Start/Sounds folder, and click Open.

The Monkey.wav file appears in your Library panel. The sound file is indicated by a unique icon, and the preview window shows a waveform—a series of peaks and valleys that represent the sound.

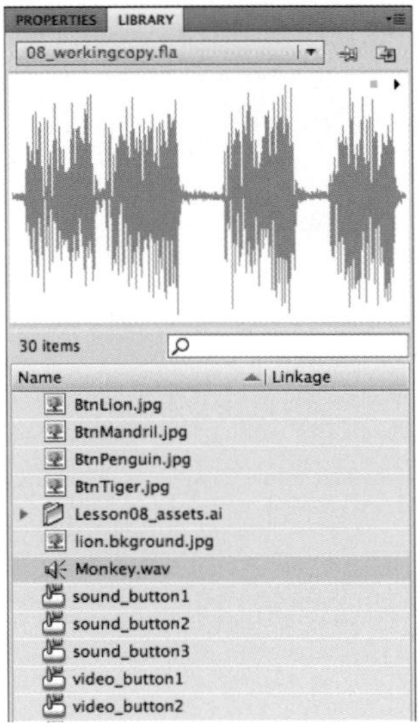

3 Click the Play button on the far upper-right corner of the Library preview window.

The sound plays.

4 Double-click the sound icon in front of your Monkey.wav file.

The Sound Properties dialog box appears, providing information on your sound file, including its original location, size, and other technical properties.

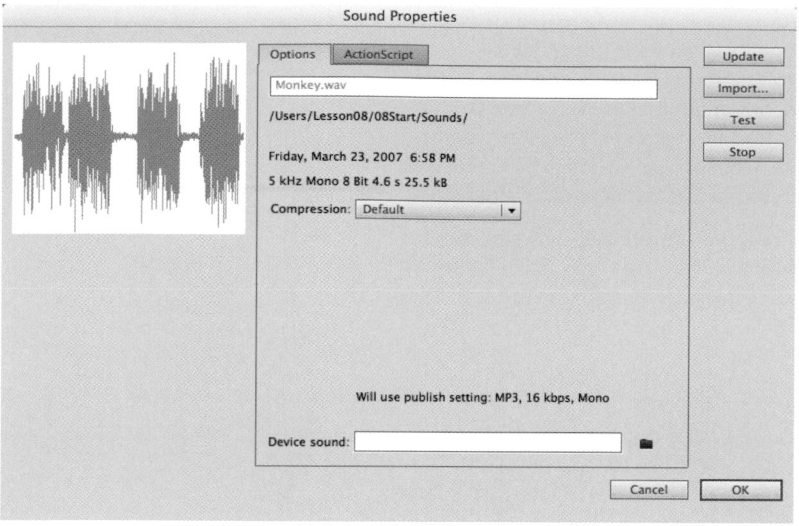

5 Choose File > Import > Import To Library and select the other sound files to import into your Flash project. Import Elephant.wav, Lion.wav, Africanbeat.mp3, and Afrolatinbeat.mp3.

Your Library panel should contain all the sound files.

6 Create a folder in your Library panel and place all the sound files in it to organize your Library panel. Name the folder **sounds**.

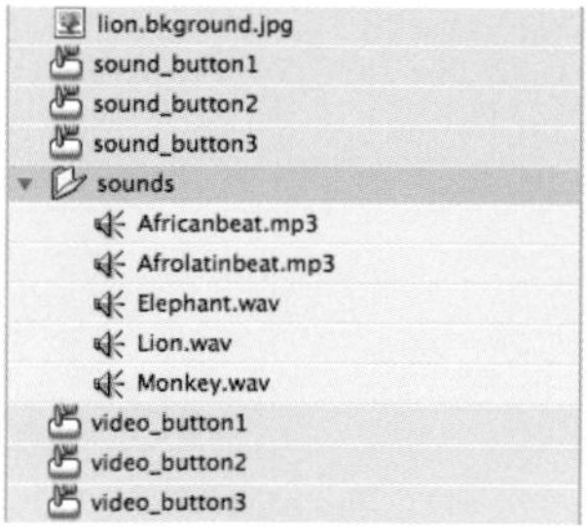

Where to Find Sound Clips

If you're looking for interesting sounds to use in your Flash movie, you can use the free sound files available from Adobe. Flash CS6 Professional comes preloaded with dozens of useful sounds that you can access by choosing Window > Common Libraries > Sounds. An external library (a library that is not connected to the current project) appears.

Simply drag one of the sound files from the external library onto your Stage. The sound will appear in your own Library panel.

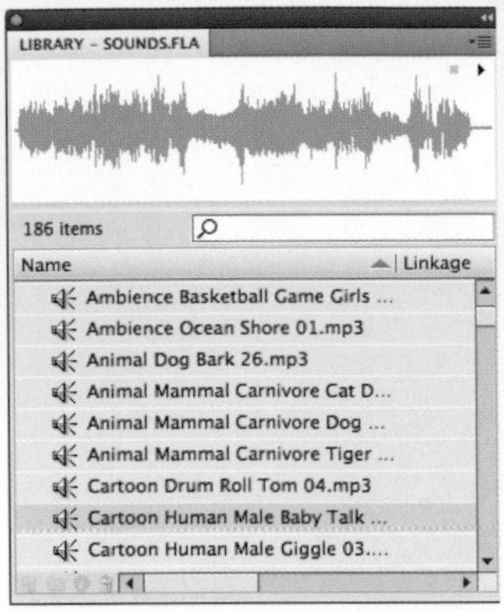

Placing sounds on the Timeline

You can place a sound at any keyframe along the Timeline, and Flash will play that sound when the playhead reaches the keyframe. You'll place a sound on the very first keyframe to play as the movie starts to provide a pleasant audio introduction and set the mood.

1 Select the videos layer on the Timeline.

2 Insert a new layer and rename it **sounds**.

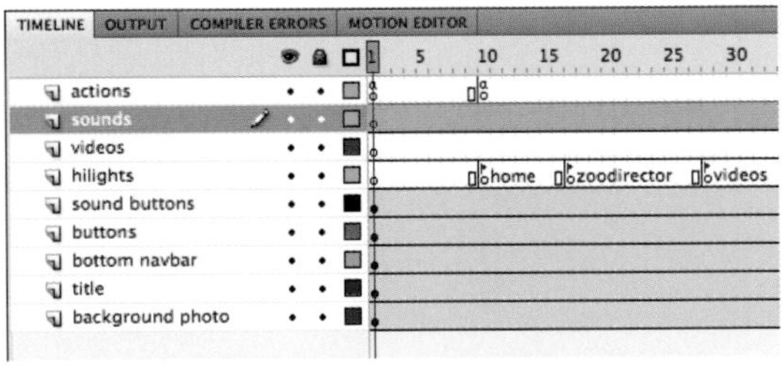

3 Select the first keyframe of the sounds layer.

4 Drag the Afrolatinbeat.mp3 file from the sounds folder in your Library panel onto the Stage.

The waveform of your sound appears on the Timeline.

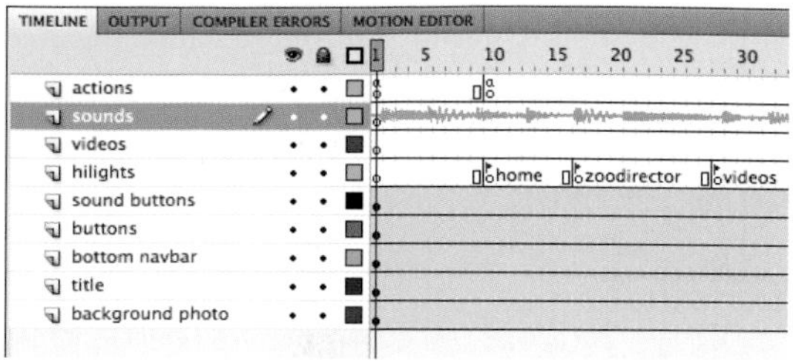

5 Select the first keyframe of the sounds layer.

In the Properties inspector, note that your sound file is now listed on the pull-down menu under the Sound section.

6 Select Stream for the Sync option.

The Sync options determine how the sound plays on the Timeline. Use Stream sync for long passages of music or narration when you want to time the sound with the Timeline.

7 Move the playhead back and forth on the Timeline.

The sound plays as you scrub the Timeline.

8 Choose Control > Test Movie > in Flash Professional.

The sound plays only for a short while before getting cut off. Because the sound is set to Stream, it plays only when the playhead moves along the Timeline, and if there are sufficient frames to play. There is a stop action at frame 9 that stops the playhead, and hence, stops the sound.

Adding frames to the Timeline

The next step is to extend the Timeline so that the entire sound (or at least the portions that you desire) plays before the stop action halts the playhead.

1 Click on the Stage to deselect the Timeline, and then place the playhead between frames 1 and 9 by clicking on the top frame numbers.

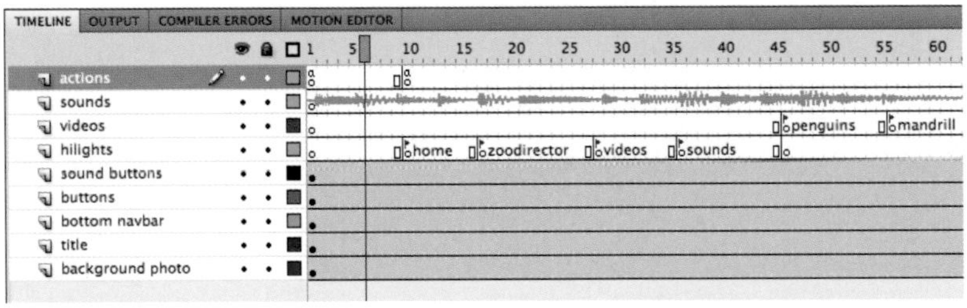

2 Choose Insert > Timeline > Frame, or press F5, to insert frames in all the layers between frames 1 and 9.

3 Insert enough frames so that there are about 50 frames to play the sound before the stop action in the second keyframe of the actions layer.

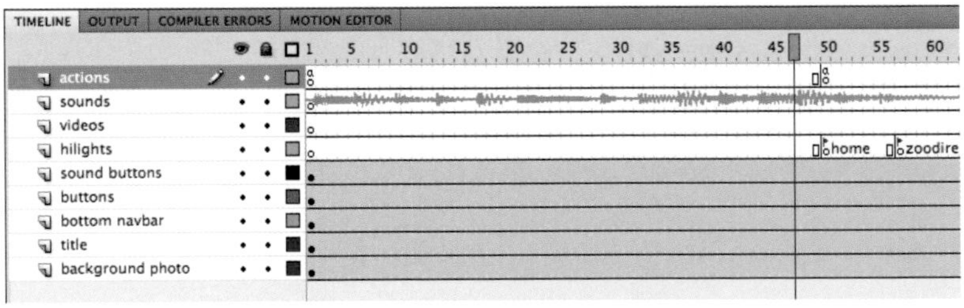

4 Choose Control > Test Movie > in Flash Professional.

The sound lasts longer because it has more frames to play before the playhead stops.

Clipping the end of a sound

The sound clip you imported is a bit longer than you need. You'll shorten the sound file by using the Edit Envelope dialog box. Then you'll apply a fade so the sound gradually decreases as it ends.

1 Select the first keyframe of the sounds layer.

2 In the Properties inspector, click the Pencil button.

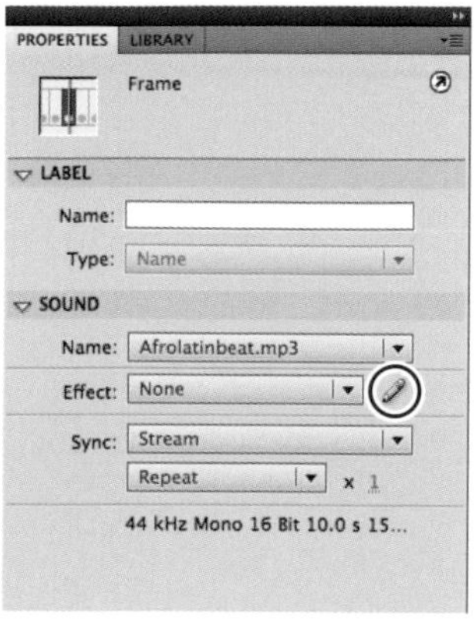

The Edit Envelope dialog box appears, showing you the sound's waveform. The top and the bottom waveform are the left and right channels of the sound (stereo). A timeline is between the waveforms, a pull-down menu of preset effects at the left corner, and view options at the bottom.

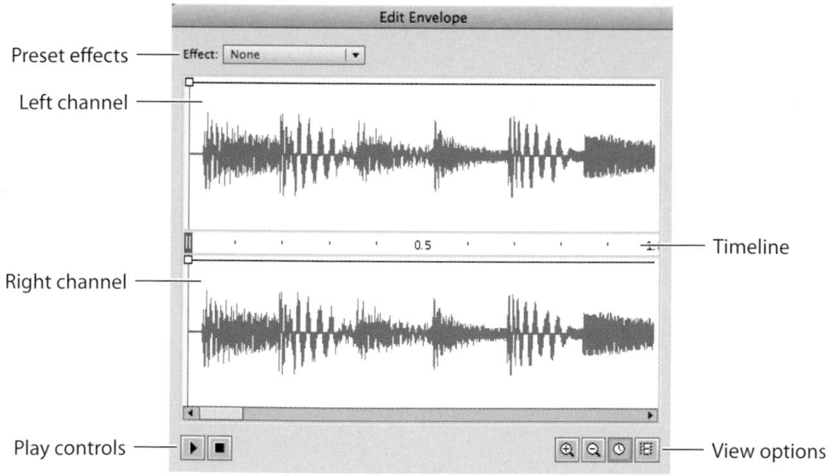

3 In the Edit Envelope dialog box, click the Seconds icon, if it isn't already selected.

The timeline changes units to show seconds instead of frames. Click the Frames icon to switch back. You can switch back and forth, depending on how you want to view your sound.

4 Click the Zoom Out icon until you can see the entire waveform.

The waveform appears to end at around 240 frames, or about 10 seconds.

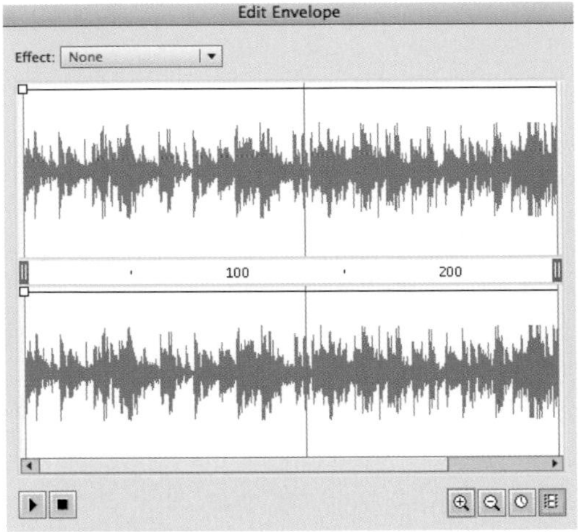

5 Drag the right end of the time slider inward to about frame 45.

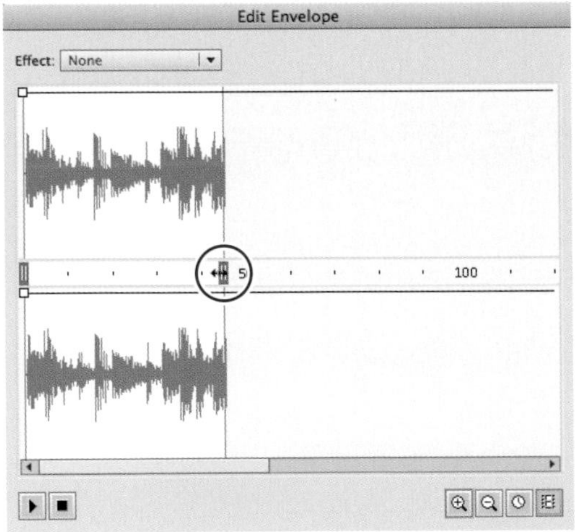

The sound shortens by being clipped from the end. The sound now plays for about 45 frames.

6 Click OK to accept the changes you've made.

The waveform on the main Timeline indicates the shortened sound.

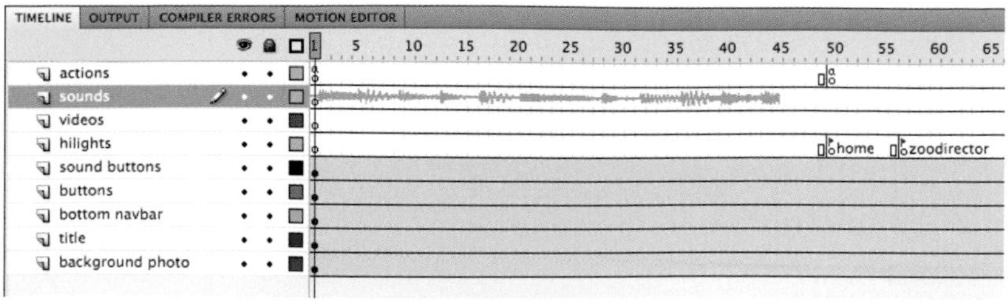

Changing the volume of a sound

The sound will be more elegant if it slowly fades out instead of being abruptly cut off. You can change the volume levels through time in the Edit Envelope dialog box. Use it to fade in, fade out, or modulate the volume of the left and right channels separately.

1 Select the first keyframe of the sounds layer.

2 In the Properties inspector, click the Pencil button.

The Edit Envelope dialog box appears.

3 Select the Frames viewing option, and zoom in on the waveform to see its end near frame 45.

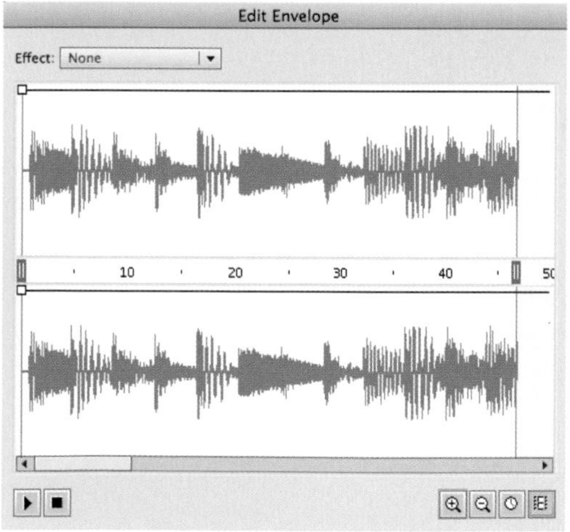

4 Click on the top horizontal line of the top waveform above frame 20.

A box appears on the line, indicating a keyframe for the sound volume.

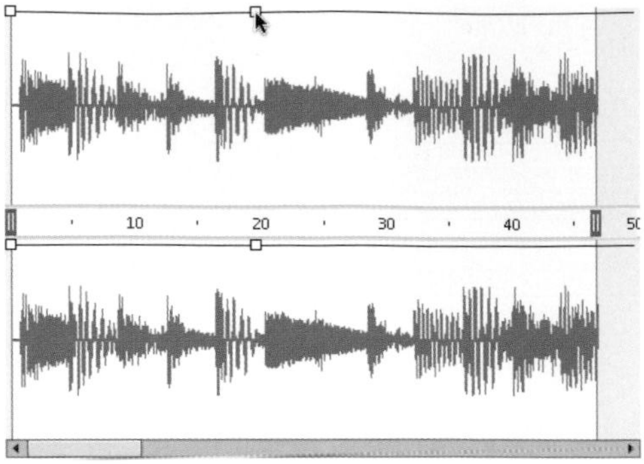

5 Click on the top horizontal line of the upper waveform above frame 45 and drag it down to the bottom of the window.

The downward diagonal line indicates the drop in volume from 100% to 0%.

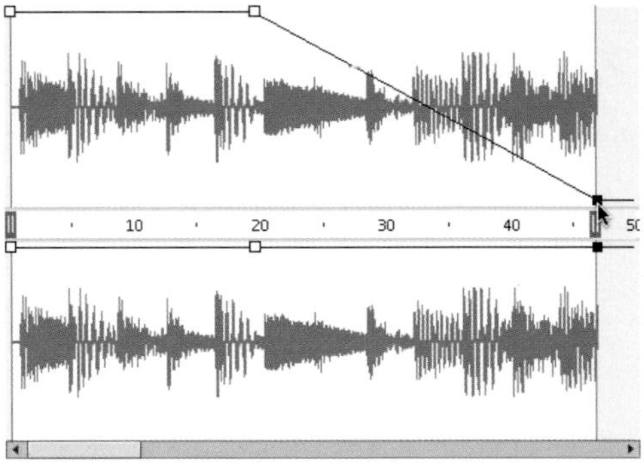

6 Click on the corresponding keyframe on the lower waveform and drag it down to the bottom of the window.

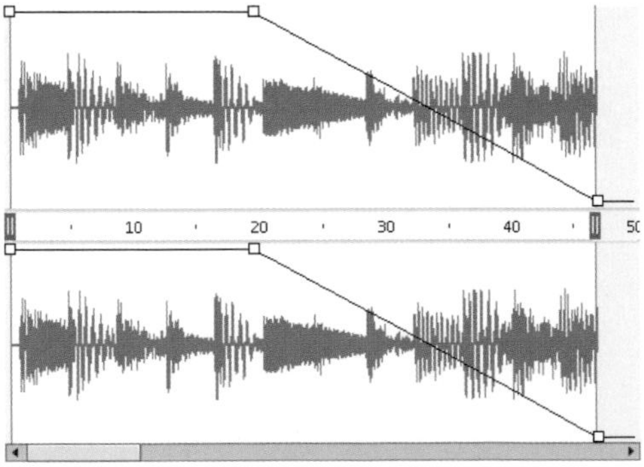

The volume levels for both the left and right channels slowly decrease starting at frame 20. By frame 45, the volume level is at 0%.

7 Test the effects of your sound edits by clicking the Play button on the lower-left side of the dialog box. Click OK to accept the changes.

Note: You can choose and apply some of the preset effects from the pull-down menu in the Edit Envelope dialog box. Common effects like a fade-in or a fade-out are provided for your convenience.

Deleting or changing the sound file

If you don't want the sound on your Timeline, or you want to change to a different sound, you can make those changes in the Properties inspector.

1 Select the first keyframe of the sounds layer.

2 In the Properties inspector, select None in the Name pull-down menu.

The sound is removed from the Timeline.

3 Now let's add a different sound. Select Africanbeat.mp3 for Name.

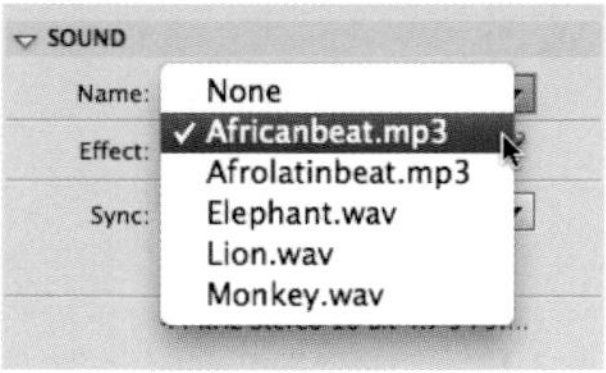

The Africanbeat.mp3 sound is added to the Timeline. The settings in the Edit Envelope dialog box that clip the sound and fade it out are reset. Return to the Edit Envelope dialog box to customize the Africanbeat.mp3 sound in the same way as the previous sound.

Setting the quality of the sounds

You can control how much or how little your sounds are compressed in the final SWF file. With less compression, your sounds will be better quality. However, your final SWF size will be much larger. With more compression, you'll have poor-quality sounds but a smaller file size. You must determine the balance of quality and file size based on the minimum acceptable level of quality. Set the sound quality and compression in the Publish Settings options.

1 Choose File > Publish Settings.

The Publish Settings dialog box appears.

2 Click the Flash check box on the left to see the Audio stream and Audio event settings.

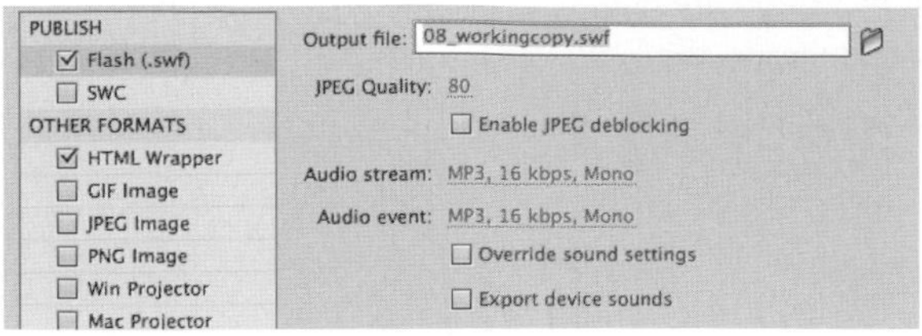

3 Click the Audio Stream settings to open the Sound Settings dialog box. Change the Bit rate to 64 kbps and deselect the Convert stereo to mono check box. Click OK to accept the settings.

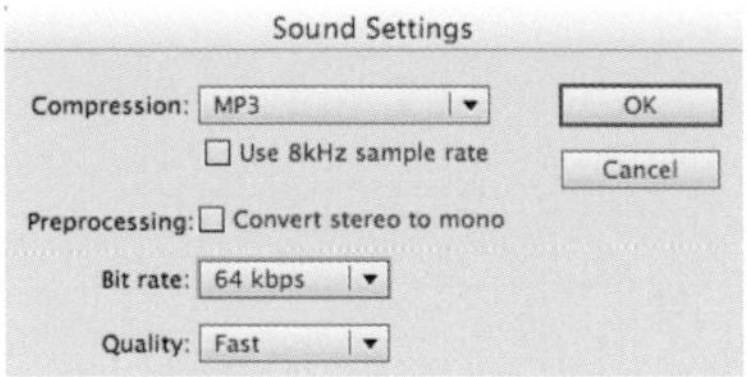

4 Click the Audio Event settings.

The Sound Settings dialog box appears.

5 Change the Bit rate to 64 kbps and deselect the Convert stereo to mono check box. Click OK to accept the settings.

Now both the Audio Stream and Audio Event settings should be at 64 kbps with stereo sounds preserved.

The Africanbeat.mp3 file in particular relies on stereo effects, so keeping both the left and right channels is important.

The Bit rate is measured in kilobits per second, and it determines the quality of the sound in your final, exported Flash movie. The higher the bit rate the better the quality. However, the higher the bit rate the larger your file becomes. For this lesson, change the bit rate to 64 kbps.

6 Select Override sound settings, and click OK to save the settings.

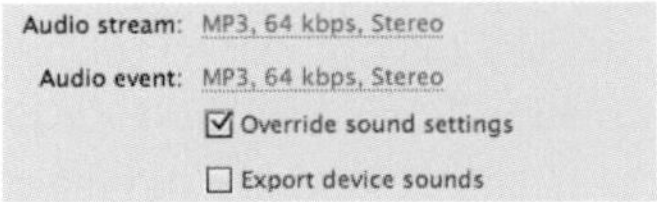

The sound settings in the Publish Settings will determine how all your sounds are exported.

7 Choose Control > Test Movie > in Flash Professional.

The stereo effect of the sound is preserved, and the quality is determined by your settings in the Publish Settings dialog box.

Adding sounds to buttons

In the kiosk, the buttons appear on your stage on the left. You'll add sounds to the buttons so that they play whenever the user clicks them.

1 In the Library panel, double-click the icon of the button symbol called sound_button1.

You enter symbol-editing mode for that button symbol.

2 The three layers in the button symbol help organize the content for the Up, Over, Down, and Hit states.

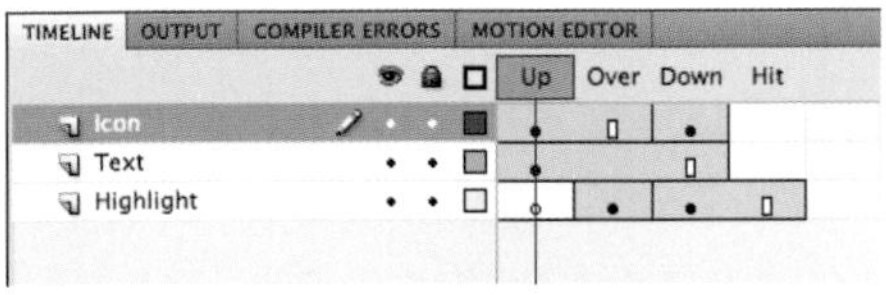

3 Insert a new layer and rename it **sounds**.

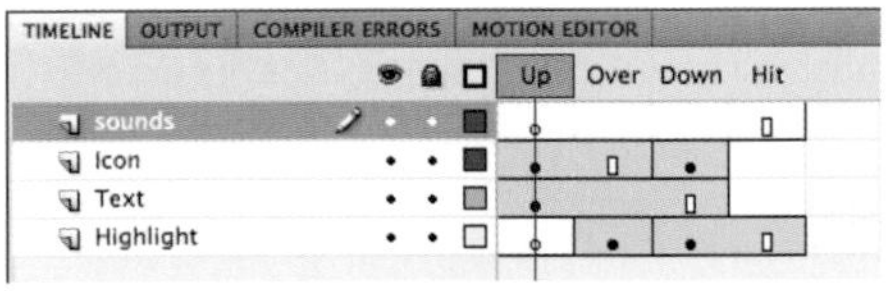

4 Select the Down frame in your sounds layer and insert a keyframe.

A new keyframe appears in the Down state of your button.

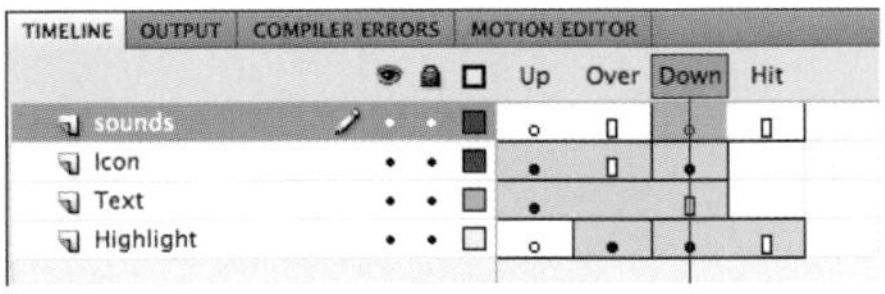

5 Drag the Monkey.wav file from the sounds folder in your Library panel to the Stage.

A waveform for the Monkey.wav file appears in the Down keyframe of the sounds layer.

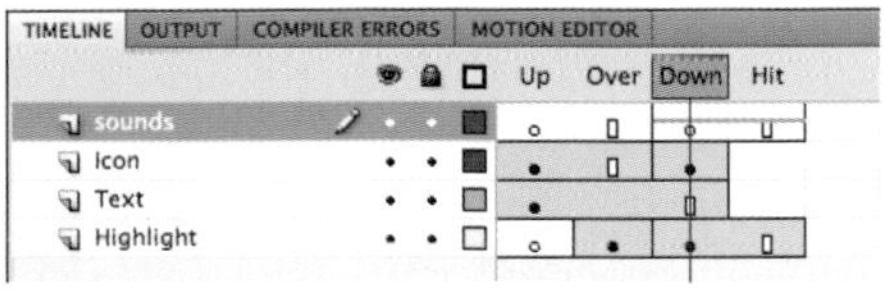

Note: You can also add sound to the Over state of a button symbol, and the sound will play whenever the mouse cursor just hovers over the button.

6 Select the Down keyframe in the sounds layer.

7 In the Properties inspector, choose Start for the Sync option.

A Start sync option triggers the sound whenever the playhead enters that particular keyframe.

8 Choose Control > Test Movie > in Flash Professional. Test the first button to hear the monkey, and then close the preview window.

9 Edit the sound_button2 and the sound_button3 to add the Lion.wav and the Elephant.wav sounds to their Down states.

Understanding Sound Sync Options

Sound sync refers to the way the sound is triggered and played. There are several options: Event, Start, Stop, and Stream. Stream ties the sound to the Timeline so you can easily synchronize animated elements to the sound. Event and Start are used to trigger a sound (usually a short sound) to a specific event, like a button click. Event and Start are similar except that the Start sync does not trigger the sound if it is already playing (so there are no overlapping sounds possible with Start sync). The Stop option is used to stop a sound, although you'll use it rarely, if ever. If you want to stop a sound with a Stream sync, simply insert a blank keyframe.

Understanding Flash Video

Note: Flash can actually play back any video encoded in H.264, so your video file doesn't have to have the .f4v extension. For example, a video with a .mov extension encoded by QuickTime Pro with H.264 is compatible with Flash.

Flash makes it very easy to deliver video over the Web. Combining video, interactivity, and animation can create a very rich and immersive multimedia experience for your viewers.

There are two options to display video in Flash. The first option is to keep the video separate from your Flash file and use a playback component from Flash to play the video. The second option is to embed the video in your Flash file.

Both methods require that the video be formatted correctly first. The appropriate video format for Flash is Flash Video, which uses the extension .flv or the extension .f4v. F4V supports the H.264 standard, a state-of-the-art video codec that delivers high quality with remarkably efficient compression. A codec (*co*mpression-*dec*ompression) is a method computers use to compress a video file to save space, and then decompress it to play it back. FLV is the standard format for previous versions of Flash and uses the older codecs Sorenson Spark or On2 VP6.

Using Adobe Media Encoder

You can convert your video files to the proper FLV or F4V format using Adobe Media Encoder CS6, a stand-alone application that comes with Flash Professional CS6. Adobe Media Encoder can convert single files or multiple files (known as batch processing) to make your workflow easier.

Adding a video file to Adobe Media Encoder

The first step to convert your video file to a compatible Flash format is to add the video to Adobe Media Encoder for encoding.

1 Launch Adobe Media Encoder CS6, which comes installed with Adobe Flash Professional CS6.

The opening screen displays the Queue in the upper left, which shows any current video files that have been added for processing. The Queue panel should be empty. The other panels are the Encoding panel, which shows any video currently being processed; the Watch Folders, which shows folders that have been identified for batch processing; and the Preset Browser, which provides common predefined settings.

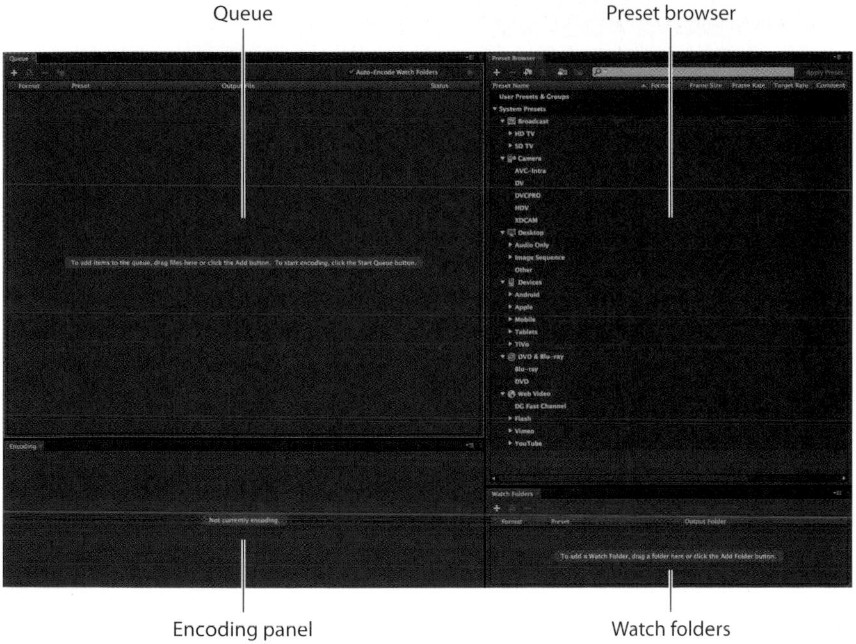

Note: You can also drag the file directly to the Queue from your desktop.

Note: In Adobe Media Encoder CS6, the default setting is not to start the Queue automatically when the program is idle. In CS5, the default setting was to start the Queue automatically. You can still change the setting by choosing Adobe Media Encoder CS6 > Preferences.

2 Choose File > Add Source or click the Plus button in the Queue panel.

A dialog box opens for you to select a video file.

3 Navigate to the Lesson08/08Start folder, select the Penguins.mov file, and click Open.

The Penguins.mov file is added to the Queue and is ready for conversion to FLV or F4V format.

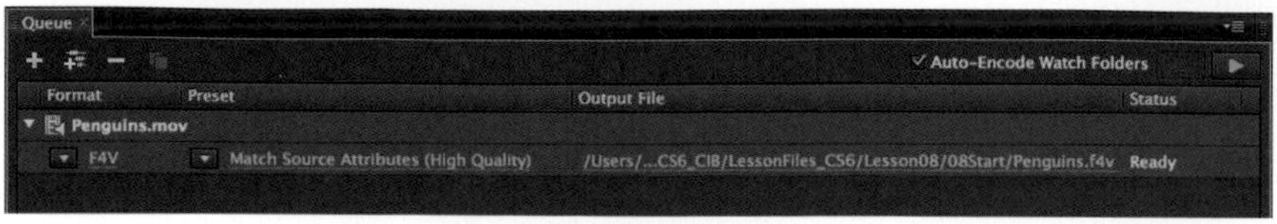

Converting video files to Flash Video

Converting your video files is easy, and the length of time it takes depends on how large your original video file is.

1 In the first column under Format, select the F4V format.

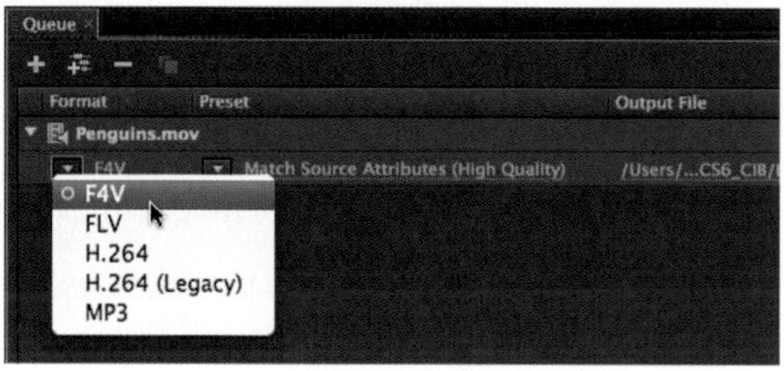

F4V is the latest video format for Flash. FLV is an older, but still valid format.

2 Under the Preset options, choose **Web – 320x240, 4x3, Project Framerate, 500kbps**.

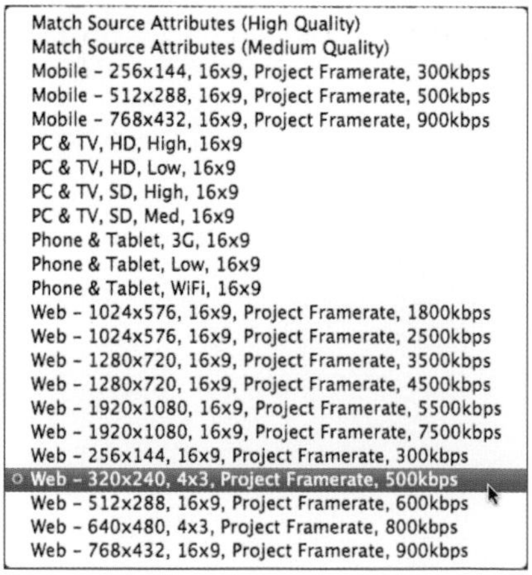

You can choose one of many standard preset options from the menu. The options determine the dimensions of the video and the quality of the video. The **Web – 320 x 240** option converts your original video to an average size to display video in a Web browser.

3 Click the Output File.

The Save As dialog box appears. You can choose to save the converted file in a different location on your computer and choose a different filename. Your original video will not be deleted or altered in any way.

4 Click the Start queue button (triangular icon) in the upper-right corner.

Flash begins the encoding process. Flash displays the settings for the encoded video and shows the progress and a preview of the video in the Encoding panel.

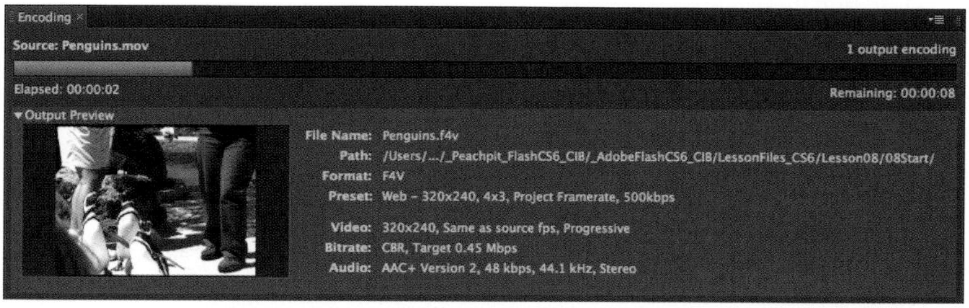

When the encoding process finishes, a "Done" label and a green check appear in the Status column of the Queue panel. A sound indicates that the file has been converted successfully.

You now have the file, Penguins.f4v in your Lesson08/08Start folder along with the original Penguins.mov file.

Note: You can change the status of individual files in the Queue by selecting the file in the display list and choosing Edit > Reset Status or Edit > Skip Selection. Reset Status removes the green check from a completed file so it can be encoded again, whereas Skip Selection makes Flash skip that particular file.

Using Watch Folders and the Preset Browser Settings

The Watch Folders panel can be helpful in processing multiple videos, while the Preset Browser stores predefined settings for specific target devices.

Adding a folder to the Watch Folders panel adds all of its contents to the queue, where they are automatically encoded. You can also add a different Output setting to the same folder, which will result in multiple formats for the same set of videos. To add a new Output setting, click the Add Output button at the top of the Watch Folders panel.

A duplicate selection appears in the list. Choose a new format and/or new preset options. If you want to apply a particular setting from the Preset Browser, choose the setting and simply drag and drop it on top of your selection in the Watch Folders panel.

This is useful when you need different video formats for high-bandwidth and low-bandwidth viewers, or for different devices such as tablets and mobile phones.

Understanding Encoding Options

You can customize many settings when converting your original video. You can crop and resize your video to specific dimensions, just convert a snippet of the video, adjust the type of compression and the compression levels, and even apply filters to the video. To display the encoding options, choose Edit > Reset Status to reset the Penguins.mov file, and then click the Format or the Preset selection in the display list or choose Edit > Export Settings. The Export Settings dialog box appears.

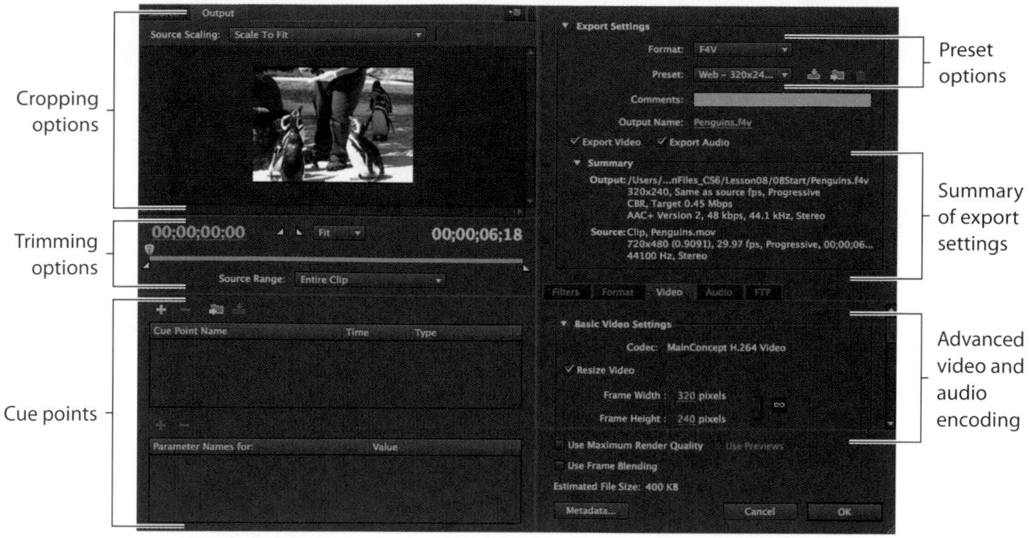

Cropping your video

If you only want to show a portion of your video, you can crop it. If you haven't done so already, choose Edit > Reset Status to reset the Penguins.mov file, and then choose Edit > Export Settings so you can experiment with the cropping settings.

1 Select the Source tab in the upper-left corner of the Export Settings dialog box, and then click the Crop button.

The cropping box appears over the video preview window.

2 Drag the sides inward to crop from the top, bottom, left, or right.

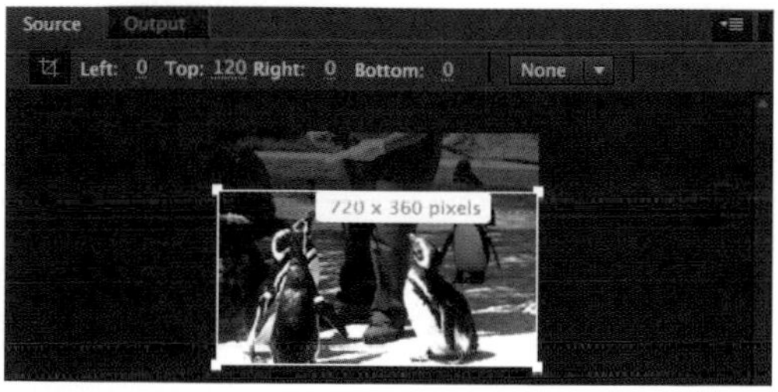

The grayed-out portions outside the box will be discarded. Flash displays the new dimensions next to your cursor. You can also use the Left, Top, Right, and Bottom settings above the preview window to enter exact pixel values.

3 If you want to keep the crop in a standard proportion, click the Crop Proportions menu and choose a desired ratio.

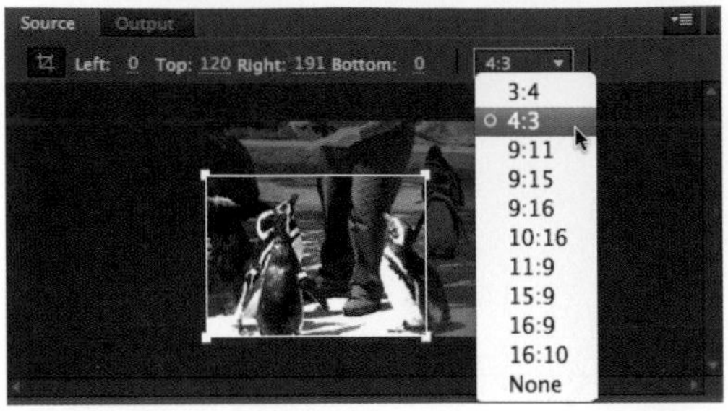

The cropping box will be constrained to the selected proportions.

4 To see the effects of the crop, click the Output tab in the upper-left corner of the preview window.

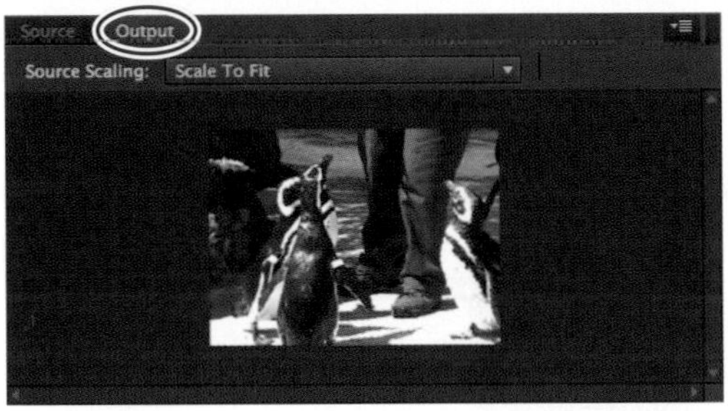

The preview window shows how your final video will appear.

5 The Source Scaling pull-down menu contains options for setting how the crop will appear in the final output file:

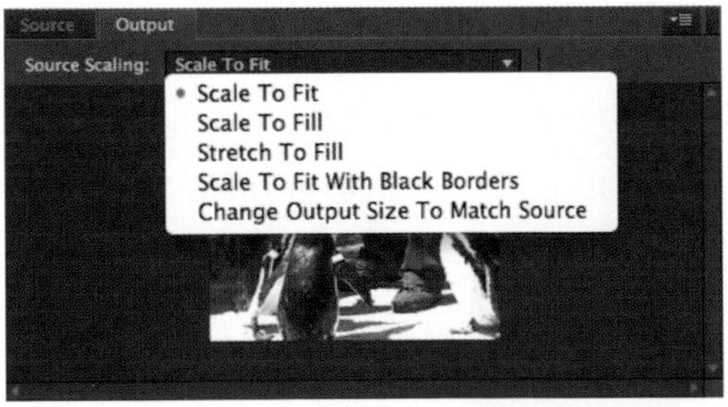

If the video has the selected crop shown here, then the Crop Setting options will affect outputted file as follows:

- **Scale To Fit** adjusts the dimensions of the crop and adds black borders to fit the output file.

- **Scale To Fill** adjusts the dimensions of the crop to fill the size of the output file.

- **Stretch To Fill** adjusts the dimensions of the crop by distorting the image, if necessary, to fill the size of the output file.

- **Scale To Fit With Black Borders** adds black bands on any of the sides to fit the crop in the dimensions of the output file.

- **Change Output Size to Match Source** changes the dimensions of the output file to match the crop dimensions.

6 Exit the cropping mode without making the crop by clicking the Crop button again under the Source tab to deselect it. You will not need to crop the Penguins.mov video for this lesson.

Adjusting video length

Your video may have unwanted segments at the beginning or the end. You can shave off footage from either end to adjust the overall length of your video.

1 Click and drag the playhead (top yellow marker) to scrub through your video to preview the footage. Place the playhead at the desired beginning point of your video.

Time markers indicate the number of seconds that have elapsed.

2 Click the Set In Point icon.

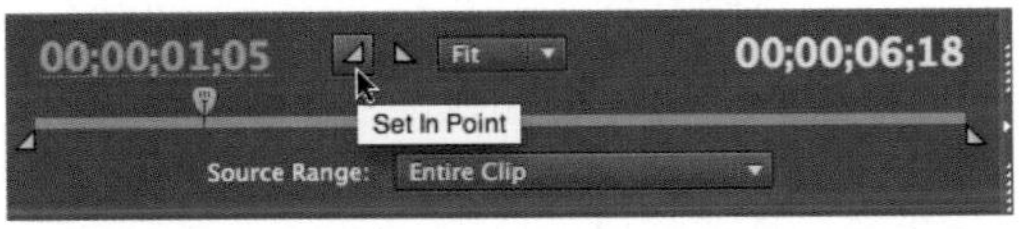

The In point moves to the current position of the playhead.

3 Drag the playhead to the desired ending point of your video.

4 Click the Set Out Point icon.

The Out point moves to the current position of the playhead.

5 You can also simply drag the In and Out point markers to bracket the desired video segment.

The highlighted portion of your video between the In and Out point markers will be the only segment of your original video that will be encoded.

Note: You can use the left or the right arrow keys on your keyboard to move back or ahead frame by frame for finer control.

6 Drag the In and Out points back to their original positions, or choose Entire Clip from the Source Range pull-down menu, because you do not need to adjust the video length for this lesson.

Cue Points

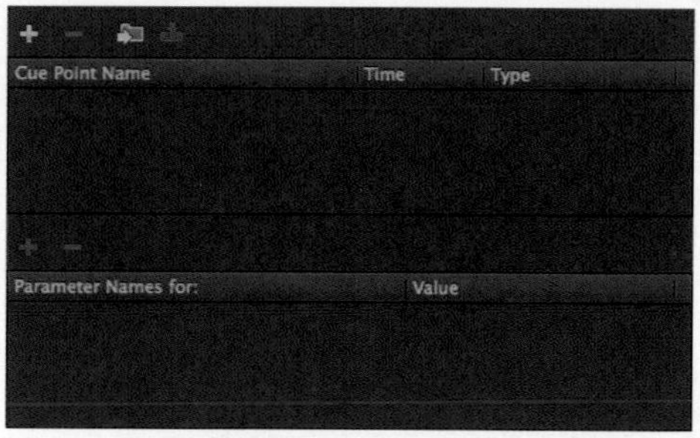

At the bottom left of the Export Settings dialog box is an area where you can set cue points for your video.

Cue points are special markers at various points along the video. With ActionScript, you can program Flash to recognize when those cue points are encountered, or you can navigate to specific cue points. Cue points can transform an ordinary, linear video into a true interactive, immersive video experience. Later in this lesson, you'll add cue points to your video within Flash when your video is directly on the Stage.

Setting advanced video and audio options

The right side of the Export Settings dialog box contains information about the original video and summarizes the export settings.

You can choose one of the preset options from the top Preset menu. At the bottom, you can navigate to advanced video and audio encoding options using the tabs. At the very bottom, Flash displays the estimated final output size.

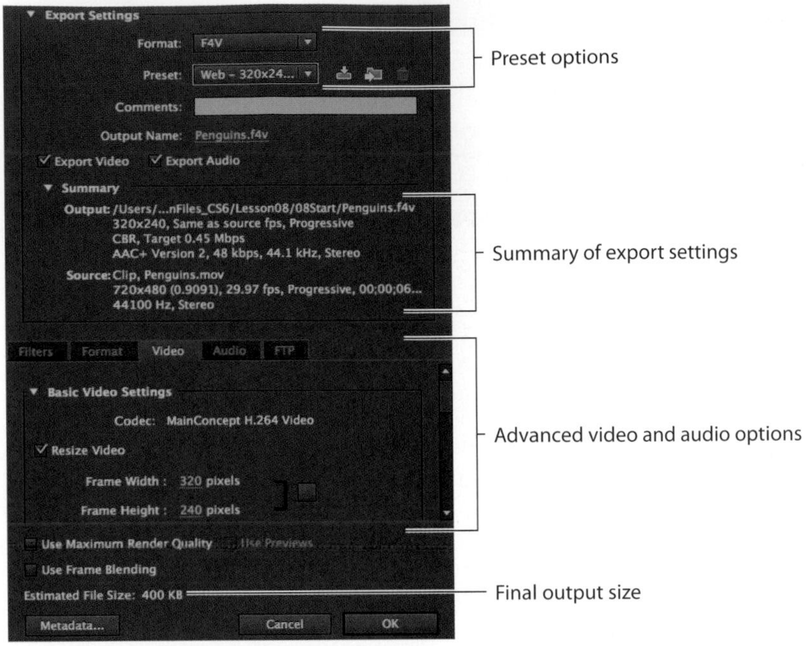

You will export the Penguins.mov file again but at a larger size.

1 Make sure the Export Video and Export Audio boxes are selected.

2 Click the Format tab and note that you're exporting the file to the F4V format.

3 Click the Video tab if it's not already selected.

4 Make sure that Resize Video and the Constrain option (chain link icon) are selected. Enter **480** for the Width and click outside the field to accept the change.

The Height automatically changes to keep the proportions of the video.

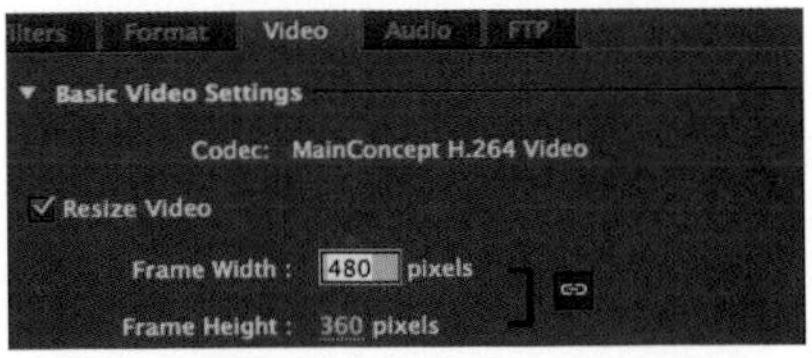

5 Click OK.

Flash closes the Export Settings dialog box and saves your advanced video and audio settings.

6 Click Start Queue to begin the encoding process with your custom resize settings.

Flash creates another F4V file of Penguins.mov. Delete the first one you created and rename the second one **Penguins.f4v**.

Saving advanced video and audio options

If you want to process many videos similarly, it makes sense to save your advanced video and audio options. You can do that in Adobe Media Encoder. Once saved, you can easily apply your settings to other videos in the queue.

1 Choose Edit > Reset Status to reset the status of your penguin video in the queue, then choose Edit > Export Settings.

2 In the Export Settings dialog box, click the Save Preset button.

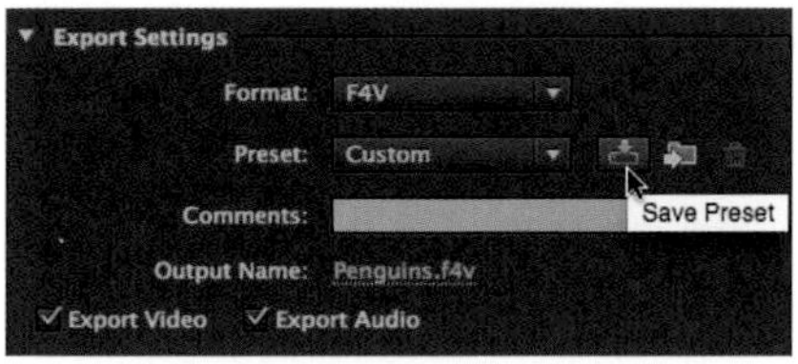

3 In the dialog box that opens, provide a descriptive name for the video and audio options. Click OK.

4 Return to the queue of videos. You can apply your custom settings to additional videos by simply choosing the preset from the Preset pull-down menu.

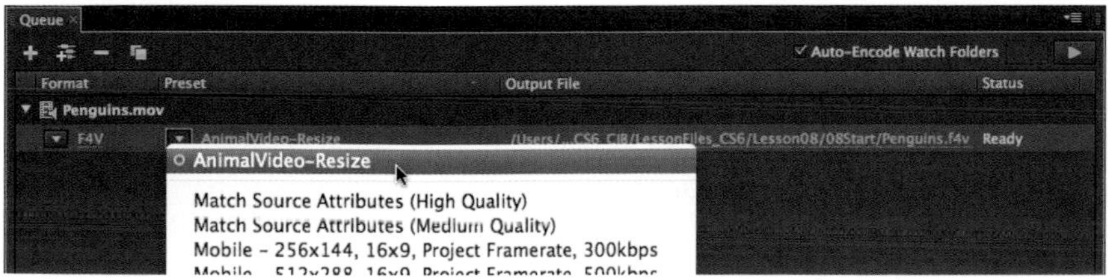

Playback of External Video

Now that you have successfully converted your video to the correct Flash-compatible format, you can use it in your Flash zoo kiosk project. You will have Flash play each of the animal videos at the different labeled keyframes on the Timeline.

You will keep your videos external to the Flash project. By keeping videos external, your Flash project remains small, the videos can be edited separately, and the videos can maintain different frame rates from your Flash project.

1 Open your 08_workingcopy.fla project in Flash Professional CS6.

2 Select the keyframe labeled penguins in the videos layer.

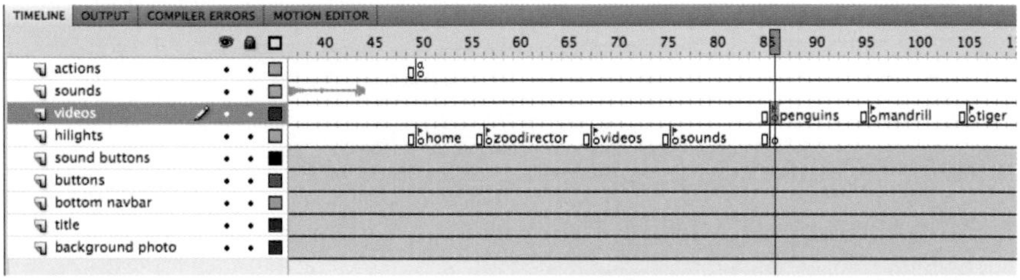

3 Choose File > Import > Import Video.

The Import Video wizard appears. The Import Video wizard guides you step by step through the process of adding video to Flash.

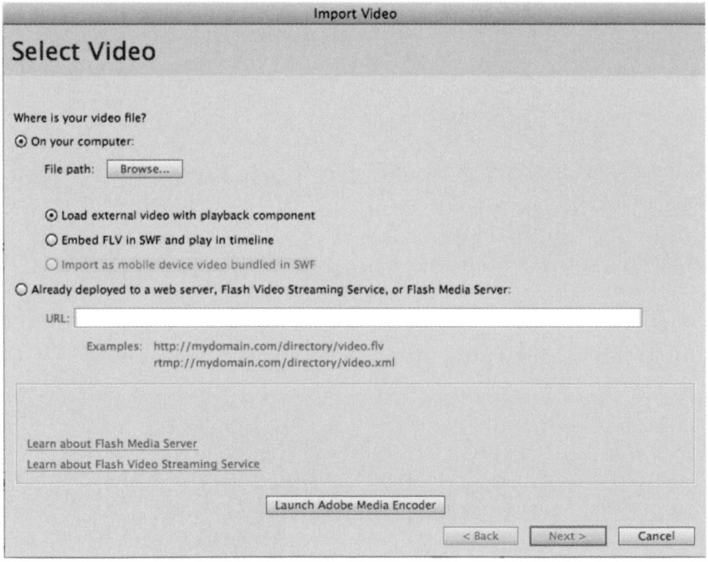

4 In the Import Video wizard, select On Your Computer and click Browse.

5 In the dialog box, select Penguins.f4v from the Lesson08/08Start folder and click Open.

The path to the video file appears.

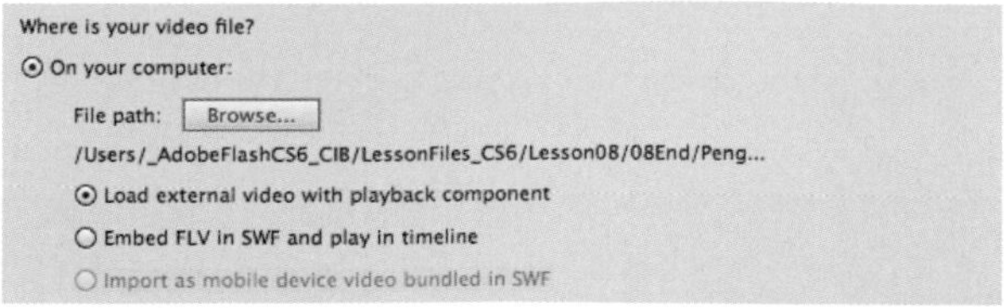

6 Select the Load external video with playback component option. Click Next or Continue.

7 In the next screen of the Import Video wizard, you select the skin, or the interface controls for the video. From the Skin menu, select the third option from the top, MinimaFlatCustomColorPlayBackSeekCounterVolMute.swf, if it's not already selected.

Note: The skin is a small SWF file that determines the functionality and appearance of the video's controls. You can use one of the skins provided with Flash, or you can choose None from the top of the menu.

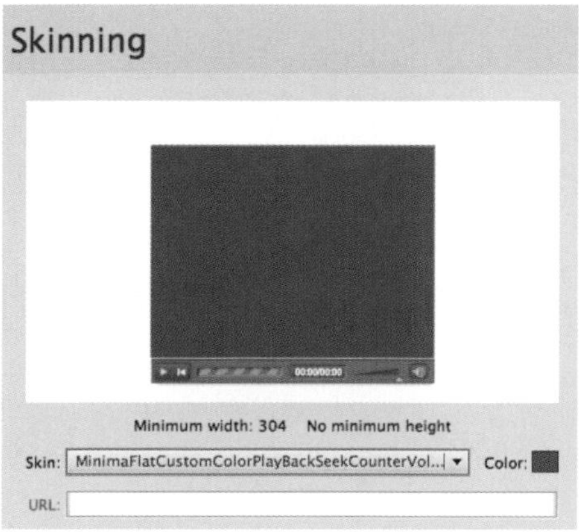

The skins fall in three broad categories. The skins that begin with "Minima" are the latest designs and include options with a numeric counter. The skins that begin with "SkinUnder" are controls that appear below the video. The skins that begin with "SkinOver" are controls that overlap the bottom edge of the video. A preview of the skin and its controls appear in the preview window.

8 Select color #333333 with a 75% Alpha. Click Next or Continue.

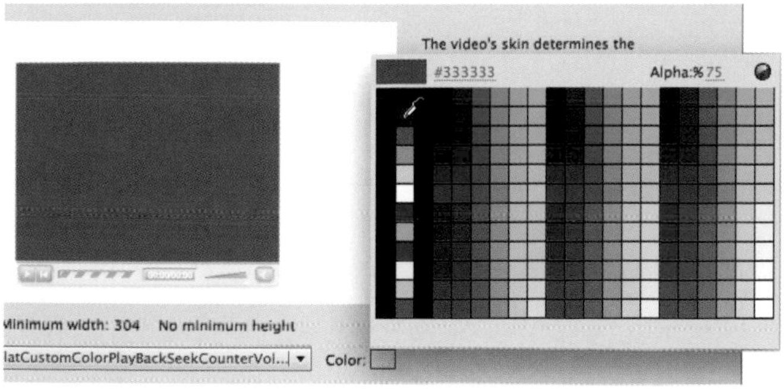

9 On the next screen of the Import Video wizard, review the information for the video file, and then click Finish to place the video.

10 Your video with the selected skin appears on the Stage. Place the video on the left side of the Stage.

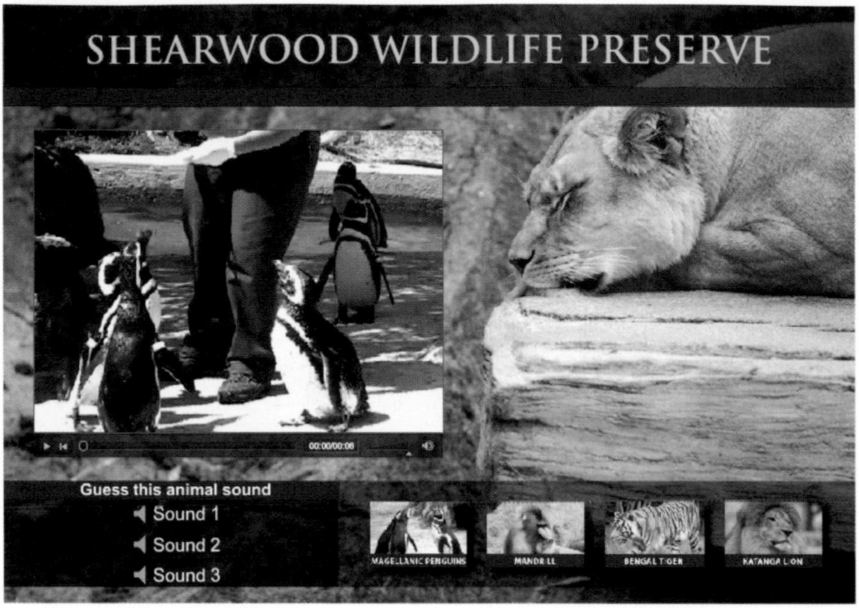

An FLVPlayback component also appears in your Library panel. The component is a special widget that is used on the Stage to play your external video.

Note: When a video on the Stage is selected, you can press the spacebar to begin or pause playback.

11 Click the play button on the skin of your video to preview the video.

The video plays on your Stage. Use the controls to play, stop, scrub, and change the volume of the movie.

Note: If you don't have a skin on your video, you can still control playback of the video on the Stage by right-clicking/Ctrl-clicking on the video and choosing Play, Pause, or Rewind.

12 Choose Control > Test Movie > in Flash Professional. After the musical introduction, click the Magellanic Penguins button.

The FLVPlayback component plays the external penguin video with the skin you chose in the Import Video wizard. Close the preview window.

13 The other animal videos have already been encoded (in FLV format) and provided in the 08Start folder. Import the Mandrill.flv, Tiger.flv, and Lion.flv videos in each of their corresponding keyframes. Choose the same skin as the Penguin.f4v video.

Note: The FLV or F4V files, the 08_workingcopy.swf file, and the skin file are all required for your zoo kiosk project to work. The skin file is published in the same folder as your FLA file.

Controlling the video playback

The FLVPlayback component lets you control which video plays, whether the video plays automatically, and other aspects of playback. The options for playback can be accessed in the Properties inspector. Individual properties are listed in the left column, and their corresponding values are listed in the right column. Select one of the videos on the Stage, and then choose among the following options:

- To change the autoPlay option, deselect the check box. When the check box is selected, the video plays automatically. When the check box is deselected, the video is paused on the first frame.

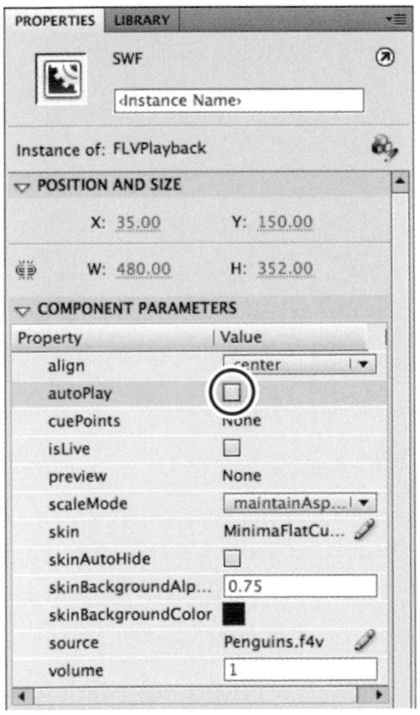

- To hide the controller and only display it when users roll their mouse cursor over the video, select the check box for the skinAutoHide option.

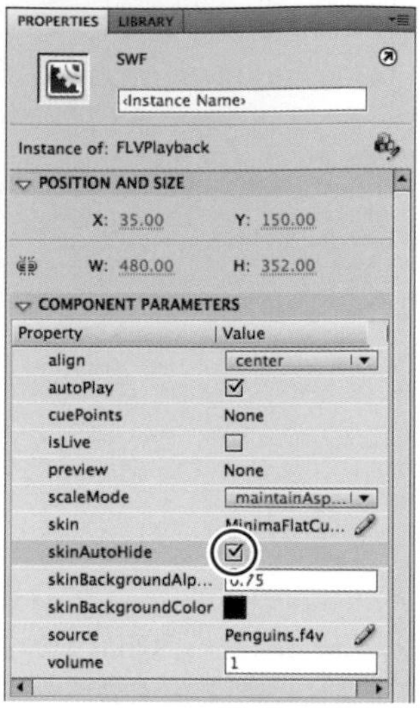

- To choose a new controller (the skin), click the name of your skin file and select a new skin in the dialog box that appears.
- To change the transparency of the skin, enter a decimal value from 0 (totally transparent) to 1 (totally opaque) for the skinBackgroundAlpha.
- To change the color of the skin, click on the color chip and choose a new color for the skinBackgroundColor.
- To change the video file or the location of the video file that Flash seeks to play, click the source option.

  In the Content Path dialog box that appears, enter a new filename or click the Folder icon to choose a new file to play. The path is relative to the location of your Flash file.

Working with Video and Transparency

For the various animal videos, you want to show the entire frame with the animals in the foreground and the lush environment in the background. But sometimes you want to use a video file that doesn't include a background. For this project, the zoo director was filmed in front of a green screen, which was removed using Adobe After Effects. When you use the video in Flash, the zoo director appears to be in front of the Flash background. A similar effect is used for news weatherpersons, where the background of the video is totally transparent and can show weather graphics behind the person.

Transparencies in video (called alpha channels) are supported only in the FLV format using the On2 VP6 codec. When encoding a video with an alpha channel from Adobe Media Encoder, be sure to choose Edit > Export Settings, click the Video tab, and then select the Encode Alpha Channel option.

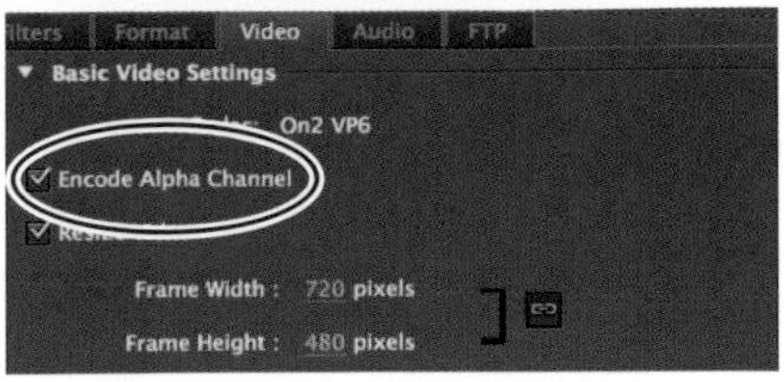

You'll import the video file, which is already in FLV format, into Flash for display with the playback component.

Importing the video clip

Now you'll use the Import Video wizard to import the Popup.flv file, which has already been encoded with an alpha channel.

1 Insert a new layer called **popupvideo**.

2 Insert a keyframe at frame 50 and insert another keyframe at frame 86.

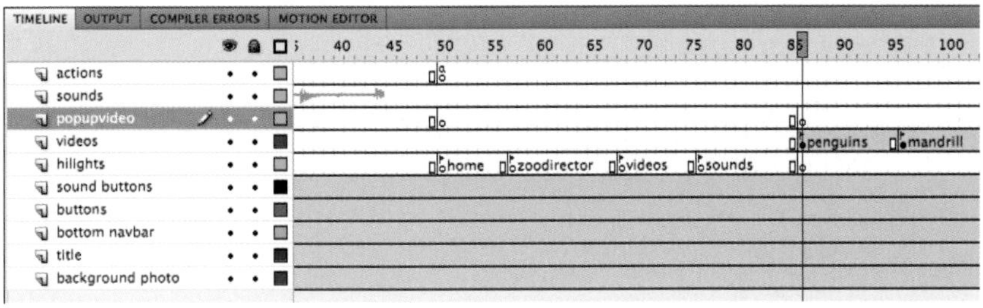

You'll place the video of the zoo director at the end of the musical introduction at the same time the stop action appears (frame 50). The keyframe at frame 86 ensures that the video of the zoo director disappears from the Stage when the animal videos appear.

3 Select the keyframe at frame 50.

4 Choose File > Import > Import Video.

5 In the Import Video wizard, select On Your Computer and click Browse. Select the Popup.flv file in the Lesson08/08Start folder and click Open.

6 Select Load external video with playback component. Click Next or Continue.

7 Select the same skin that you've been using from the Skin menu and click Next or Continue.

8 Click Finish to place the video.

The video of the zoo director with a transparent background appears on the Stage.

9 Preview the video on the Stage by clicking the play button on the skin.

10 Choose Control > Test Movie > in Flash Professional.

After the musical introduction, the zoo director appears. If you click on one of the animal video buttons, the popup video is removed from the Timeline.

● **Note:** If you don't stop one video before navigating to another keyframe containing a second video, the audio can overlap. To prevent overlapping sounds, use the command `SoundMixer.stopAll()` to stop all sounds before starting a new video. The ActionScript in the first keyframe of the actions layer in your 08_workingcopy.fla file contains the correct code to stop all sounds before navigating to a new animal video.

ACTIONS - FRAME

```
video_button1.addEventListener(MouseEvent.CLICK,clickListener1);
function clickListener1(event:MouseEvent):void {
    SoundMixer.stopAll()
    gotoAndStop("penguins");
}

video_button2.addEventListener(MouseEvent.CLICK,clickListener2);
function clickListener2(event:MouseEvent):void {
    SoundMixer.stopAll()
    gotoAndStop("mandrill");
}

video_button3.addEventListener(MouseEvent.CLICK,clickListener3);
function clickListener3(event:MouseEvent):void {
    SoundMixer.stopAll()
    gotoAndStop("tiger");
}

video_button4.addEventListener(MouseEvent.CLICK,clickListener4);
function clickListener4(event:MouseEvent):void {
    SoundMixer.stopAll()
    gotoAndStop("lion");
}
```

Using a Green Screen

Professionals often film people in front of solid green or blue backgrounds so they can easily remove, or key, the background in a video editing application such as Adobe After Effects. Then the person is merged with a different background. The image of the zoo director was filmed in front of a green screen, which was removed in After Effects. Follow these steps to use a green screen:

1 Shoot footage in front of a green screen:

- Use a green background that is flat, smooth, and free of shadows so the color is as pure as possible.
- Minimize the light that reflects off the green screen onto the subject.
- Keep movement to a minimum for Flash Video; use a tripod if possible.

2 Remove the background in After Effects or other video editing application:

- In After Effects, import the file as footage, create a new composition, and drag it onto the Composition Timeline.
- Create a garbage mask to roughly outline the shape and remove most of the background. But be sure the subject never moves outside the mask!
- Use the Color Range keying effect to delete the rest of the background. You may need to do some fine-tuning with the Matte Choker and Spill Suppressor effects. A spill suppressor removes the light that splashes onto the edges of the subject.

3 Export the file to FLV format:

Export the video file to Flash Video (FLV) format directly from the video editing application. Be sure to select Encode Alpha Channel. The alpha channel is the selection around the subject. Encoding the alpha channel ensures that the video exports without a background.

Using Cue Points

Cue points are special markers that you place in your video that Flash can detect with ActionScript. There are two ways to use cue points. Cue points can trigger an ActionScript command, letting you synchronize the video with other Flash elements. Or, you can jump to particular cue points in the video with ActionScript. Both types of cue points add more functionality to video.

In this section, you'll add cue points to the zoo director video so relevant information can be displayed on the Stage as he speaks.

Inserting cue points

Note: Recall that you can add cue points to video with Adobe Media Encoder. You can also add cue points to video with ActionScript in the Actions panel, which is not discussed in this book.

There are four points in the zoo director video at which you'll want to synchronize the display of additional information. First, when he introduces himself, you'll show his name. Second, when he instructs the audience to click on a video, you'll highlight the videos. Third, when he refers to the sounds, you'll highlight the sounds. Fourth, you'll add a cue point to mark the end of the video.

1 Select frame 50 (the first keyframe in which the zoo director video appears) of the popupvideo layer.

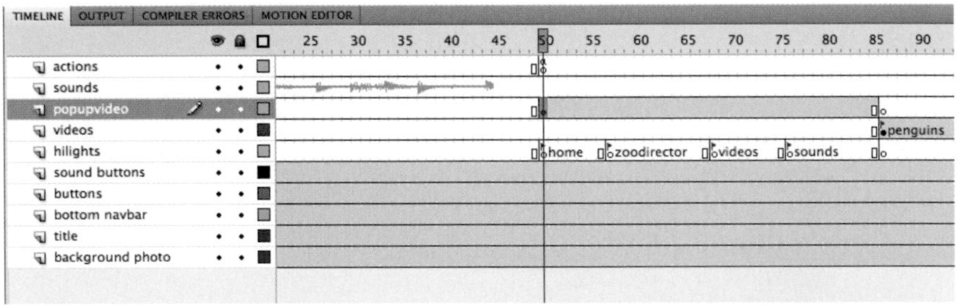

Note: If the FLVPlayback component on the Stage doesn't show a preview of the video, right-click/Ctrl-click on the video and make sure that the Preview option is selected.

2 Select the video of the zoo director on the Stage.

3 Click the play button on the skin and pause the video when the zoo director says, "…my name is Paul Smith."

The numeric counter that displays the elapsed time should read about two seconds.

4 In the Properties inspector, click the Plus button in the Cue Points section to add a cue point at the two-second mark.

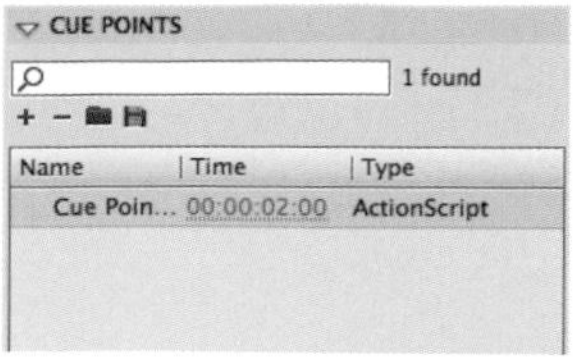

A cue point appears in the Cue Points section of the Properties inspector.

5 Click the name of the cue point in the Properties inspector and rename it **namecue**.

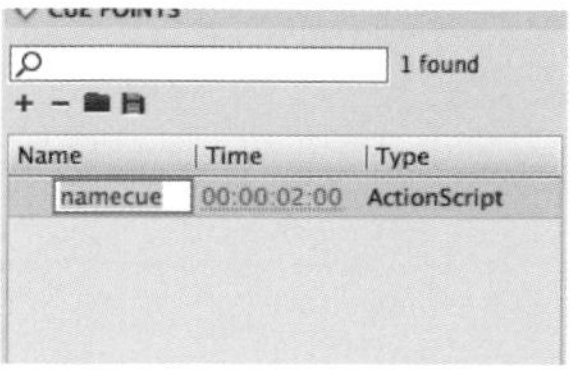

6 Continue playing the video and pause it when the zoo director says, "...so click on a video."

The numeric counter that displays the elapsed time should read about 12 seconds.

7 In the Properties inspector, click the Plus button in the Cue Points section to add a cue point at the 12-second mark, and rename the cue point **videocue**.

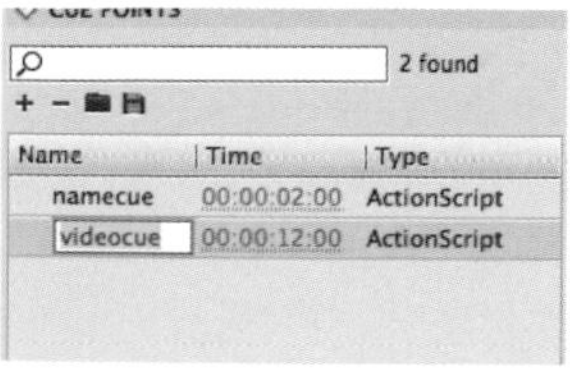

Note: If you need to adjust the time of any of the cue points, you can click and drag over the time or click to enter a time with millisecond precision.

Note: In the Properties inspector, double-click any cue point in the Type column and your video on the Stage will immediately jump to that particular cue point.

Note: To delete a cue point, select it in the Properties inspector and click the Minus sign.

8 Continue playing the video and pause it when the zoo director says, "... click on a sound."

9 In the Properties inspector, add a third cue point and rename it **soundcue**. The third cue point should be at the 14-second mark.

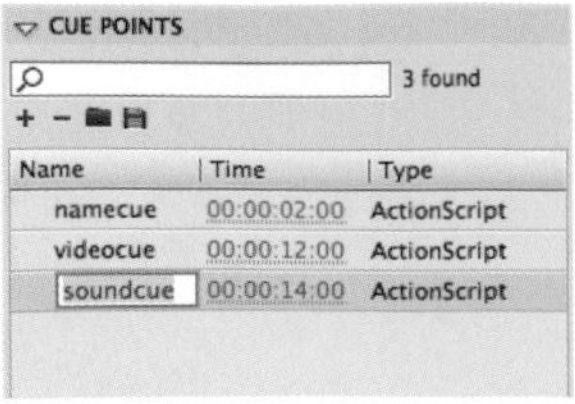

10 Continue playing the video until it reaches the end. In the Properties inspector, add a fourth cue point and rename it **endcue**.

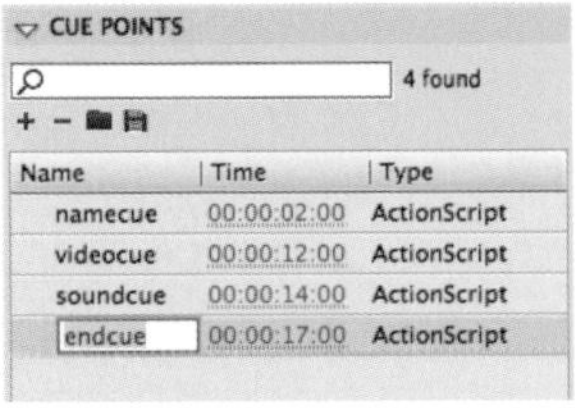

Detecting and responding to cue points

Now you'll add the ActionScript to detect the cue points and respond to them. The Code Snippets panel can help do much of the ActionScript coding.

1 Open the Code Snippets panel (Window > Code Snippets).

2 Expand the Audio and Video folder in the Code Snippets panel and select the On Cue Point Event option.

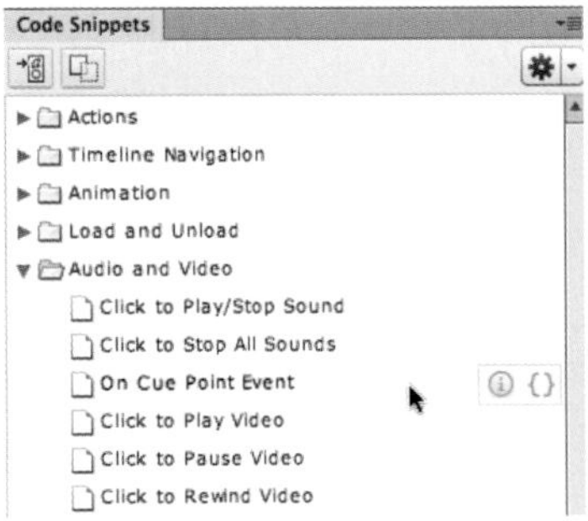

The On Cue Point Event code snippet triggers a function whenever a cue point is detected.

3 Select the Show Code button.

4 Click on the **instance_name_here** code and drag your pick whip over the video of the zoo director on the Stage.

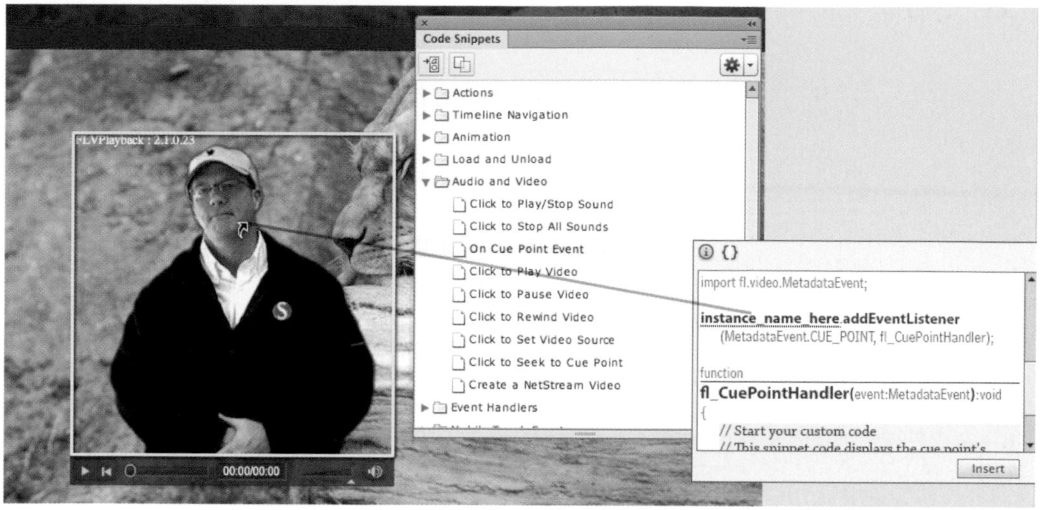

5 Since you have not yet named the instance of your video component on the Stage, Flash asks you to provide a name. Enter **paulsmithvideo** as the instance name and click OK. Remember, objects must be named in order for ActionScript to control them.

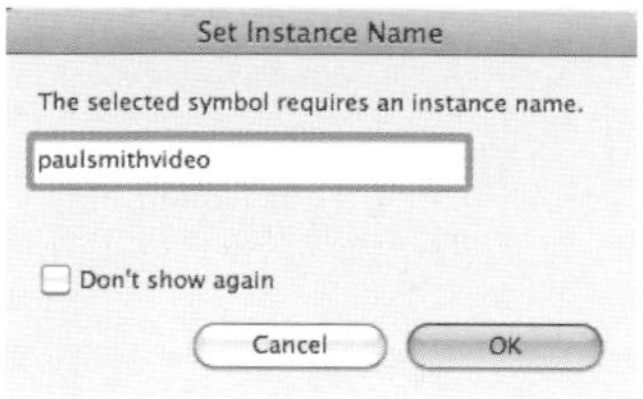

6 Click Insert.

Flash automatically adds the necessary code to detect cue points on your selected video. A temporary flag on the Timeline indicates where the new ActionScript code is inserted.

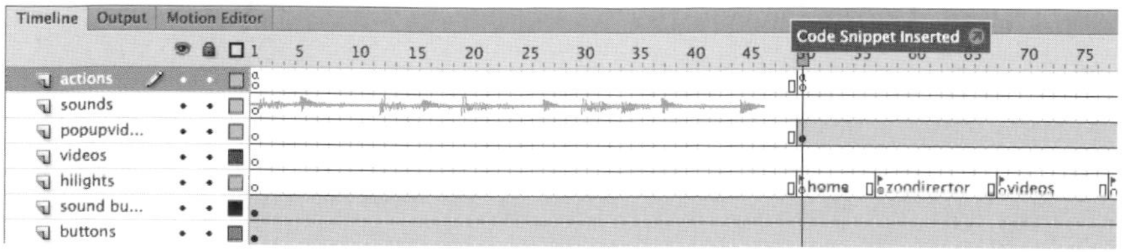

7 Select the keyframe in the actions layer at frame 50 and open the Actions panel to examine the newly inserted code.

The `stop()` command on the first line was already present in the file before you added the code snippet.

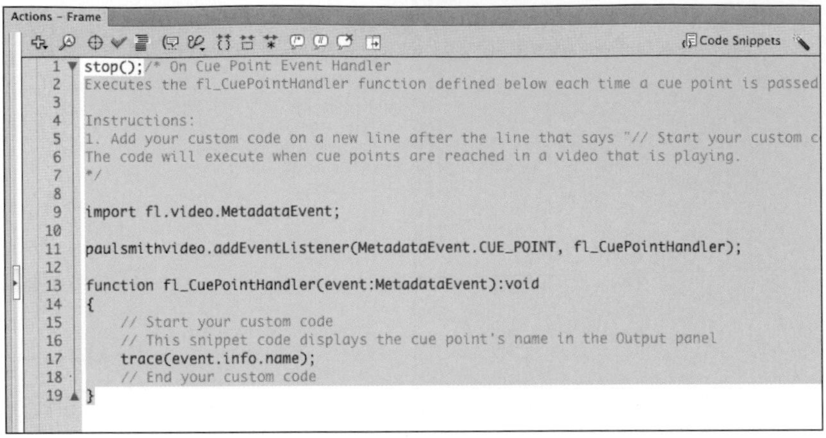
Actions - Frame
Code Snippets
stop();/* On Cue Point Event Handler
Executes the fl_CuePointHandler function defined below each time a cue point is passed
Instructions:
1. Add your custom code on a new line after the line that says "// Start your custom c
The code will execute when cue points are reached in a video that is playing.
*/
import fl.video.MetadataEvent;
paulsmithvideo.addEventListener(MetadataEvent.CUE_POINT, fl_CuePointHandler);
function fl_CuePointHandler(event:MetadataEvent):void
{
// Start your custom code
// This snippet code displays the cue point's name in the Output panel
trace(event.info.name);
// End your custom code
}

8 Now you must add conditional statements to check which of the cue points has been encountered and respond appropriately. Replace all the lines inside the function with the following code:

```
if (event.info.name=="namecue") {
  gotoAndStop("zoodirector");
 }
 if (event.info.name=="videocue") {
  gotoAndStop("videos");
 }
 if (event.info.name=="soundcue") {
  gotoAndStop("sounds");
 }
 if (event.info.name=="endcue") {
  gotoAndStop("home");
 }
```

```
stop();/* On Cue Point Event Handler
Executes the fl_CuePointHandler function defined below each time a cue point is passed

Instructions:
1. Add your custom code on a new line after the line that says "// Start your custom c
The code will execute when cue points are reached in a video that is playing.
*/

import fl.video.MetadataEvent;

paulsmithvideo.addEventListener(MetadataEvent.CUE_POINT, fl_CuePointHandler);

function fl_CuePointHandler(event:MetadataEvent):void
{
    if (event.info.name=="namecue") {
        gotoAndStop("zoodirector");
    }
    if (event.info.name=="videocue") {
        gotoAndStop("videos");
    }
    if (event.info.name=="soundcue") {
        gotoAndStop("sounds");
    }
    if (event.info.name=="endcue") {
        gotoAndStop("home");
    }
}
```

The final code checks the name of each cue point as it's detected, and if there is a match, the playhead goes to a specific named keyframe on the Timeline.

Adding the synchronized Flash elements

The Timeline already contains several named keyframes. In these keyframes, you'll place additional Flash elements that appear as the cue points in the video are detected.

1 Select the keyframe named zoodirector in the hilights layer.

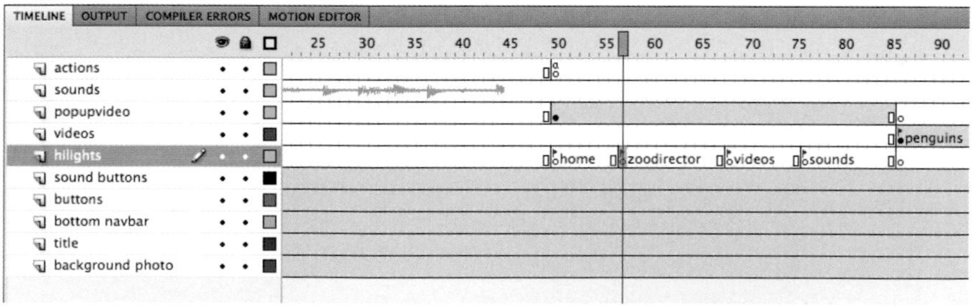

2 Drag the symbol called zoo directorname from the Library panel to the Stage and place it close to the video.

The graphic of the name appears when the playhead moves to the zoodirector keyframe.

3 Select the keyframe named videos in the hilights layer.

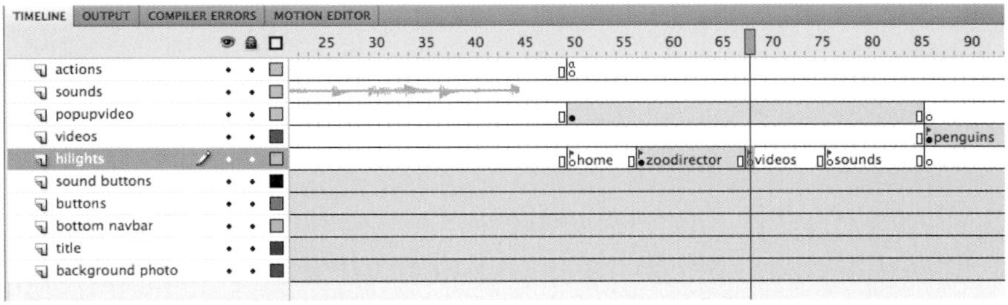

4 Select the Rectangle tool with a red 3.0 stroke and no fill. Draw a rectangle around the video buttons to highlight them.

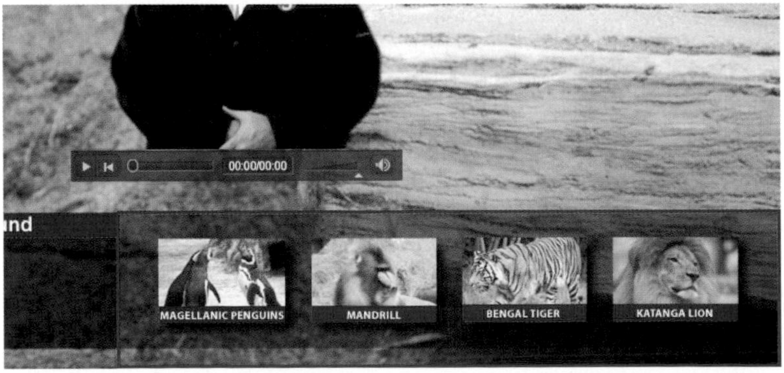

The rectangular red outline appears when the playhead moves to the videos keyframe.

5 Select the keyframe named sounds in the hilights layer.

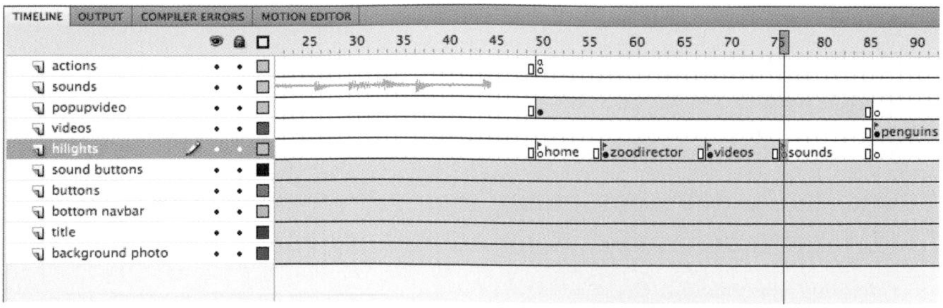

6 Draw another rectangle with the same stroke and fill settings around the sound buttons to highlight them.

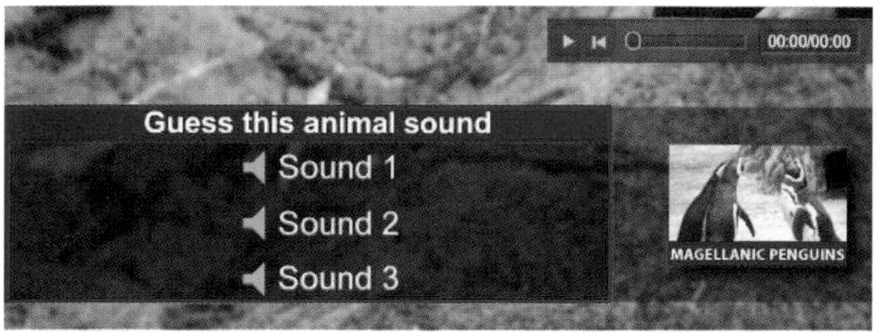

The rectangular red outline appears when the playhead moves to the sounds keyframe.

7 Choose Control > Test Movie > in Flash Professional.

As the zoo director speaks, various Flash graphic elements pop up in synchrony.

Finishing touches

At the end of the zoo director's introduction, he disappears, but the FLVPlayback component skin remains. You'll remove the skin and position the video to be better integrated with the background.

1 Select the zoo director video in the popupvideo layer.

2 In the Component Parameters section of the Properties inspector, click the Pencil button next to the skin property.

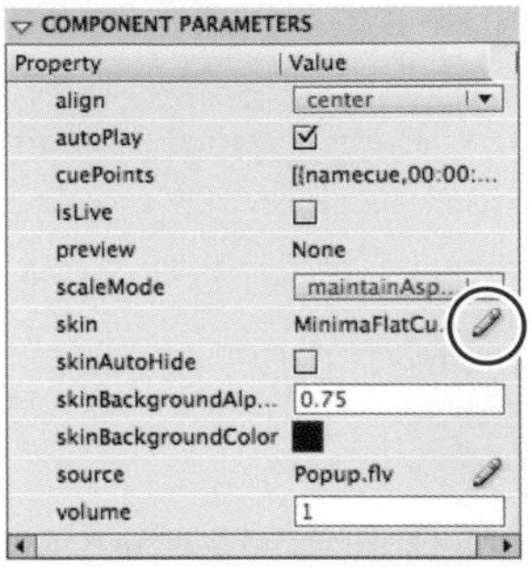

3 In the dialog box that appears, choose None from the Skin pull-down menu. Click OK.

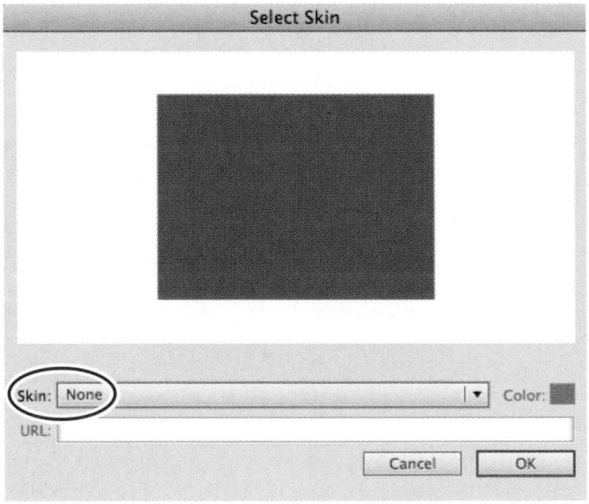

The zoo director video no longer has a skin.

4 With the Selection tool, move the video so that its bottom edge aligns with the top edge of the navigation bar. You'll also want to move the zoo director name that appears in the zoodirector keyframe of the hilights layer so it remains close to the video.

Without the skin, the illusion of the virtual zoo director greeting us is more convincing.

Embedding Flash Video

In the previous section, you added cue points to synchronize external video with Flash elements on the Stage. Another way to integrate video with Flash elements is to use embedded video. Embedded video requires the FLV format and is best only for very short clips. The FLV file is saved in the Library panel of your Flash file, where you can place it on the Timeline. The video plays as long as there are sufficient frames on your Timeline.

Embedding video in Flash is supported by Flash Player versions 6 and later. Keep in mind the following limitations of embedded video: Flash cannot maintain audio synchronization in embedded video that runs over 120 seconds. The maximum length of embedded movies is 16,000 frames. Another drawback of embedding your video is the increase in the size of your Flash project, which makes testing the movie (Control > Test Movie > in Flash Professional) a longer process and the authoring sessions more tedious.

Because the embedded FLV plays within your Flash project, it is critically important that your FLV have the same frame rate as your Flash file. If not, your embedded video will not play at its intended speed. To make sure your FLV has the same frame rate as your FLA, be sure to set the correct frame rate in the Video tab of Adobe Media Encoder.

Encoding the FLV for embedding

You'll embed a short video of a polar bear in the beginning of your zoo kiosk project.

1 Open the Adobe Media Encoder.

2 Choose File > Add Source or click the Plus button in the Queue panel and choose the polarbear.mov file in the Lesson08/08Start folder.

   The polarbear.mov file is added to the Queue.

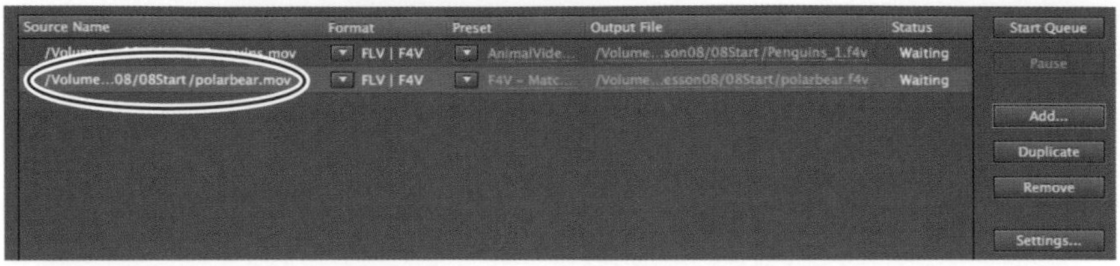

3 In the options under Format, select the FLV format.

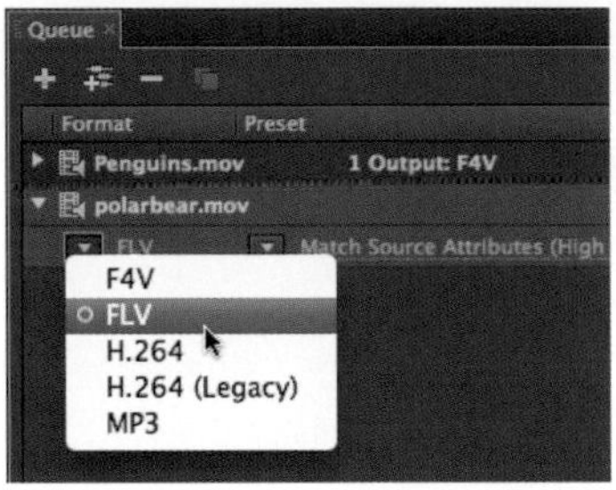

4 Click the Preset settings or choose Edit > Export Settings to open the Edit Export options.

5 Click the Video tab and set Frame Rate to **24**. Make sure that the Resize Video check box is deselected.

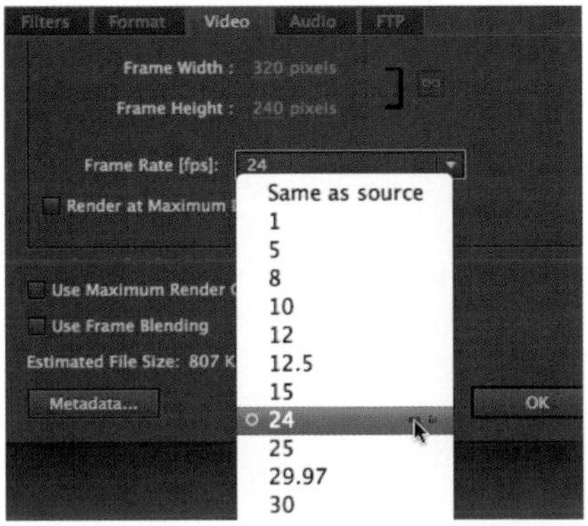

The Flash file 08_workingcopy.fla is set at 24 frames per second, so you want your FLV to also be at 24 frames per second.

6 Deselect Export Audio at the top of the dialog box. Click OK.

7 Click the Start Queue button (triangular icon) in the upper-right corner to encode your video.

The polarbear.flv file is created.

Embedding an FLV on the Timeline

Now that you have an FLV, you can import it into Flash and embed it on the Timeline.

1 Open the file 08_workingcopy.fla.

2 Select the first frame of the popupvideo layer.

3 Choose File > Import > Import Video. In the Import Video wizard, select On Your Computer and click Browse. Select the polarbear.flv file in the Lesson08/08Start folder and click Open.

4 In the Import Video wizard, select Embed FLV in SWF and play in timeline. Click Next or Continue.

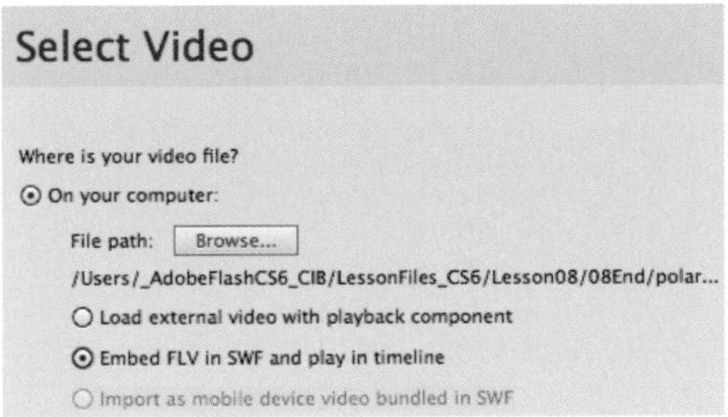

5 Deselect Expand timeline if needed and deselect Include audio. Click Next or Continue.

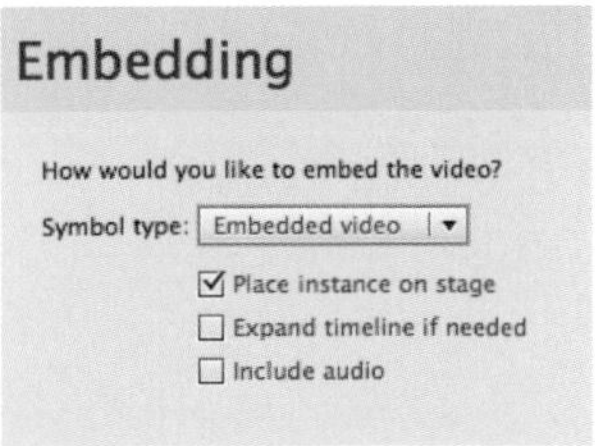

Note: You will not be able to hear audio in the authoring environment for embedded videos containing sound. To hear the audio, you must choose Control > Test Movie > in Flash Professional.

6 Click Finish to import the video.

The video of the polar bear appears on the Stage. Use the Selection tool to move it to the left side of the Stage.

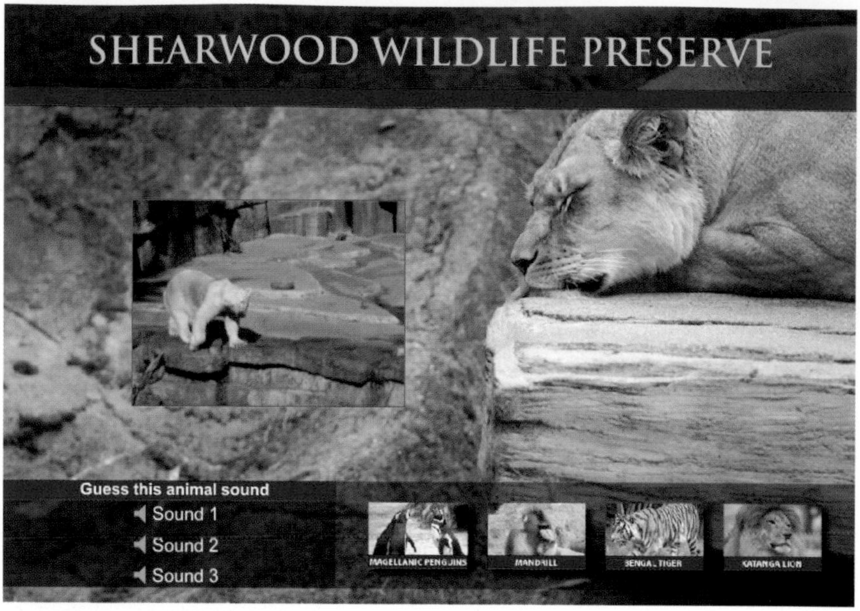

The FLV also appears in your Library panel.

7 Choose Control > Test Movie > in Flash Professional to see the embedded video file play from frame 1 to frame 49.

Using embedded video

It's useful to think of embedded video as a multiframe symbol, very much like a symbol with a nested animation. You can convert an embedded video to a movie clip symbol, and then motion tween it to create interesting effects.

Next, you'll apply a motion tween to the embedded video so it elegantly fades out just before the zoo director pops up and speaks.

1 Select the embedded video of the polar bear on the Stage, right-click/Ctrl-click it, and select Create Motion Tween.

2 Flash asks to convert the embedded video to a symbol so it can apply a motion tween. Click OK.

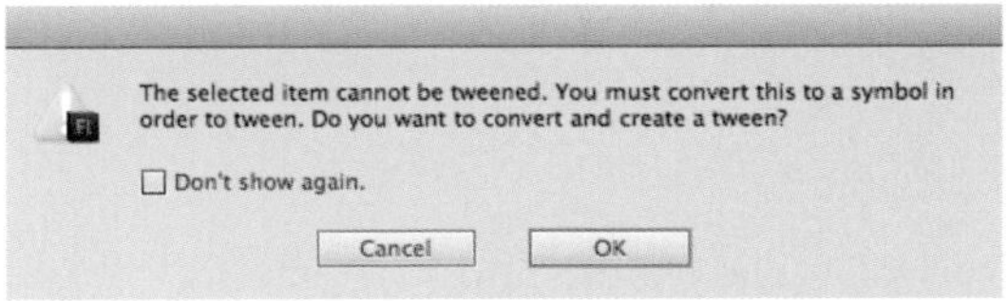

3 Flash asks to add enough frames inside the movie clip symbol so that the entire video can play. Click OK.

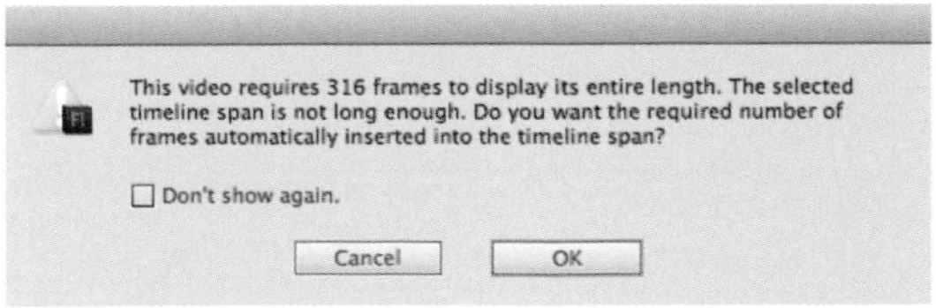

A motion tween is created on the layer.

4 Select the motion tween and click the Motion Editor tab.

5 Collapse all the property categories. Click the Plus button next to Color Effect and choose Alpha.

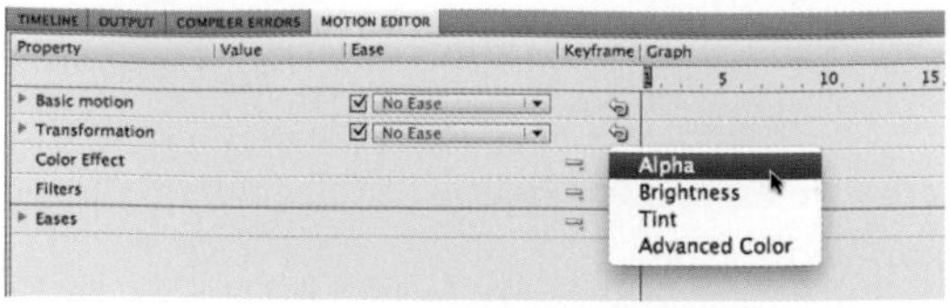

The Alpha property is added to the motion tween.

6 Select frame 1, and set the Alpha amount to 100%.

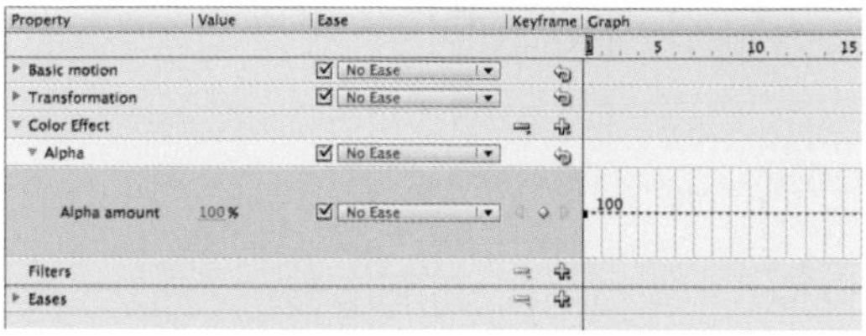

7 Select frame 30, right-click/Ctrl-click, and choose Add Keyframe.

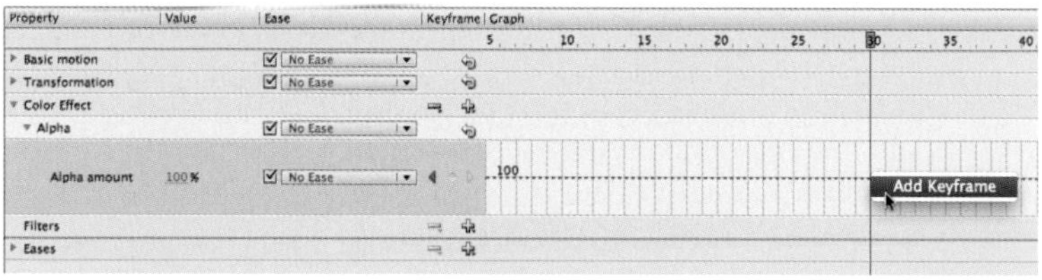

An Alpha keyframe appears at frame 30.

8 Select frame 49, right-click/Ctrl-click, and choose Add Keyframe.

An Alpha keyframe appears at frame 49.

9 Select the last keyframe at frame 49 and drag it down to 0%.

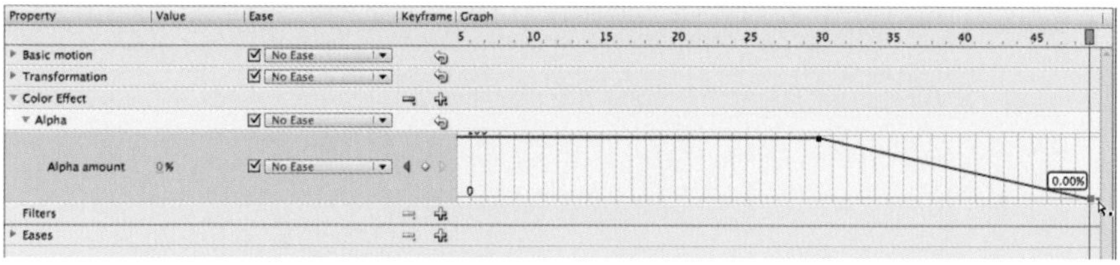

The Alpha is set to 0% at the last keyframe so the embedded video fades out from frame 30 to frame 49.

10 Choose Control > Test Movie > in Flash Professional to see the embedded video play and fade out.

Review Questions

1 How can you edit the length of a sound clip?

2 What is a skin for a video?

3 What are cue points and how are they used?

4 What are the limitations for embedded video clips?

Review Answers

1 To edit the length of a sound clip, select the keyframe that contains it and click the Pencil button in the Properties inspector. Then move the time slider in the Edit Envelope dialog box to clip the sound from the front or from the end.

2 The skin is the combination of functionality and appearance of video controls, such as Play, Fast Forward, and Pause buttons. You can choose from a wide array of combinations with the buttons in different positions, and you can customize the skin with a different color or level of transparency. If you don't want viewers to be able to control the video, apply None from the Skin menu.

3 Cue points are special markers that you can add to an external video with Adobe Media Encoder or in the Cue Points section of the Properties inspector. You can create event listeners in ActionScript that detect when a cue point is encountered and respond accordingly, for example, by displaying graphics that are synchronized with the video.

4 When you embed a video clip, it becomes part of the Flash document and is included in the Timeline. Because embedded video clips significantly increase the size of the document and produce audio synchronization issues, it's best to embed video only if it is very brief and contains no audio track.

9 LOADING AND CONTROLLING FLASH CONTENT

Lesson Overview

In this lesson, you'll learn how to do the following:

- Load and display an external SWF file
- Remove a loaded SWF file
- Control a movie clip's Timeline
- Use masks to selectively display content

This lesson will take about an hour to complete. If needed, remove the previous lesson folder from your hard drive and copy the Lesson09 folder onto it.

Use ActionScript to load external Flash content. By keeping Flash content modular, your projects remain more manageable and easier to edit.

Getting Started

You'll start the lesson by viewing the finished movie.

1 Double-click the 09End.html file in the Lesson09/09End folder to view the final movie.

The project is a fictional online lifestyle magazine called *Check*. A jazzy animation appears on the front page showing four main sections of the magazine. Each section on the front page is a movie clip with a nested animation.

The first section is an article on the star of the upcoming movie *Double Identity* (whose Web site you created in Lesson 4, "Adding Animation"), the second section describes a new car, the third section presents some facts and figures, and the fourth section is a self-improvement article.

You can click on each section on the front page to access the content. The inside content is not complete, but you can imagine that each section could contain more information. Click again to return to the front page.

2 Double-click the page1.swf, page2.swf, page3.swf, and page4.swf files in the Lesson09/09End folder.

Each of the four sections is a separate Flash file. Note that the front page, 09End.swf, loads each SWF file as needed.

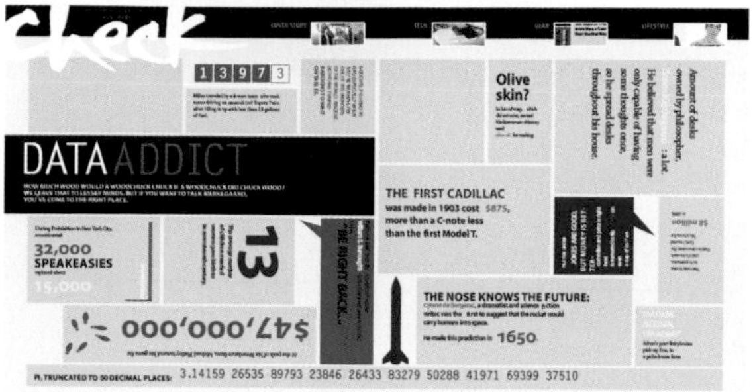

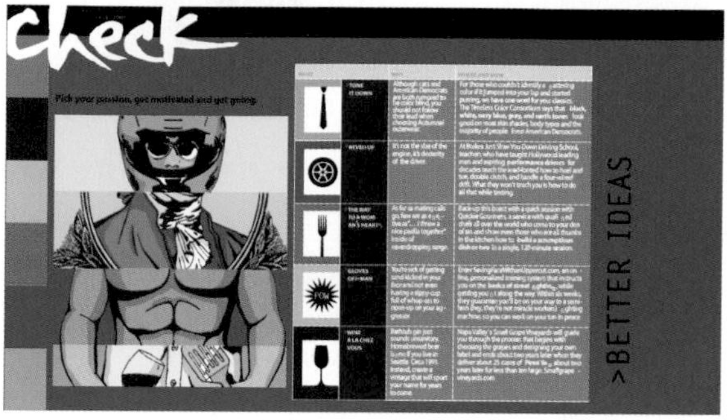

3 Close all the SWF files and open the **09Start.fla** file in the Lesson09/09Start folder.

Many of the images, graphic elements, and animations have already been completed in this file. You will add the necessary ActionScript to make the Flash file load the external Flash content.

Note: Flash warns you if your computer doesn't have the same fonts contained in a FLA file. Choose substitute fonts, or simply click Use Default to have Flash automatically make the substitutions.

4 Choose File > Save As. Name the file **09_workingcopy.fla** and save it in the 09Start folder. Saving a working copy ensures that the original start file will be available if you want to start over.

Loading External Content

You'll use ActionScript to load each of the external SWFs into your main Flash movie. Loading external content keeps your overall project in separate modules and prevents the project from becoming too bloated and difficult to download. It also makes it easier for you to edit, because you can edit individual sections instead of one, large, unwieldy file.

For example, if you wanted to change the article on the new car in the second section, you would simply open and edit the Flash file page2.fla, which contains that content.

To load the external files, you'll use two ActionScript objects: one called a ProLoader and another called a URLRequest.

1 Insert a new layer at the top and rename it **actionscript**.

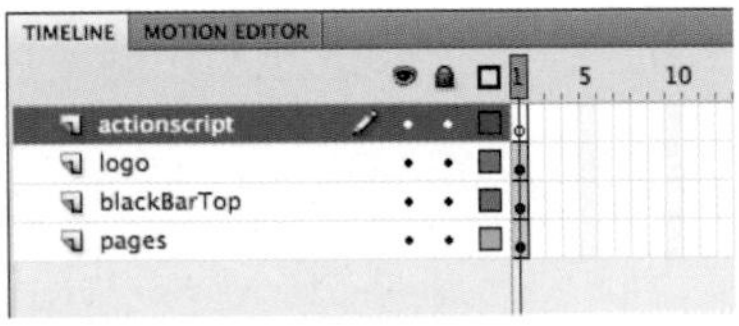

2 Press F9 (Windows) or Option+F9 (Mac) to open the Actions panel.

3 Type the following two lines exactly as they appear here:

```
import fl.display.ProLoader;
var myProLoader:ProLoader=new ProLoader();
```

This code first imports the necessary code for the ProLoader class, and then creates a ProLoader object and names it myProLoader.

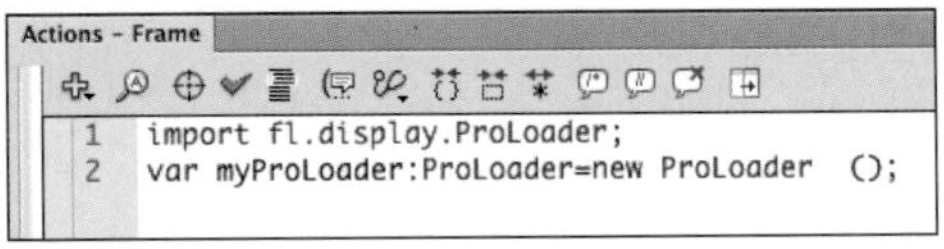

Note: The ProLoader object is an ActionScript object introduced in Flash Professional CS5.5. Older versions of Flash relied on a similar object called the Loader object. The ProLoader and the Loader objects are identical except that the ProLoader handles the loading of TLF text better for more reliable and consistent performance.

4 On the next line, type the following lines exactly as they appear here:

```
page1_mc.addEventListener(MouseEvent.CLICK, page1content);
function page1content(e:MouseEvent):void {
 var myURL:URLRequest=new URLRequest("page1.swf");
 myProLoader.load(myURL);
 addChild(myProLoader);
}
```

Note: To compare punctuation, spacing, spelling, or any other aspects of the ActionScript, view the Actions panel in the 09End.fla file.

```
1  import fl.display.ProLoader;
2  var myProLoader:ProLoader=new ProLoader  ();
3  page1_mc.addEventListener(MouseEvent.CLICK, page1content);
4  function page1content(e:MouseEvent):void {
5      var myURL:URLRequest=new URLRequest("page1.swf");
6      myProLoader.load(myURL);
7      addChild(myProLoader);
8  }
```

You've seen this syntax before in Lesson 6. On line 3, you create a listener that detects a mouse click on the object called page1_mc. This is a movie clip on the Stage. In response, Flash executes the function called page1content.

The function called page1content does several things: First, it creates a URLRequest object referencing the name of the file you want to load. Second, it loads the URLRequest object into the ProLoader object. Third, it adds the ProLoader object to the Stage so you can see it.

5 Select the movie clip on the left side of the Stage with the movie star.

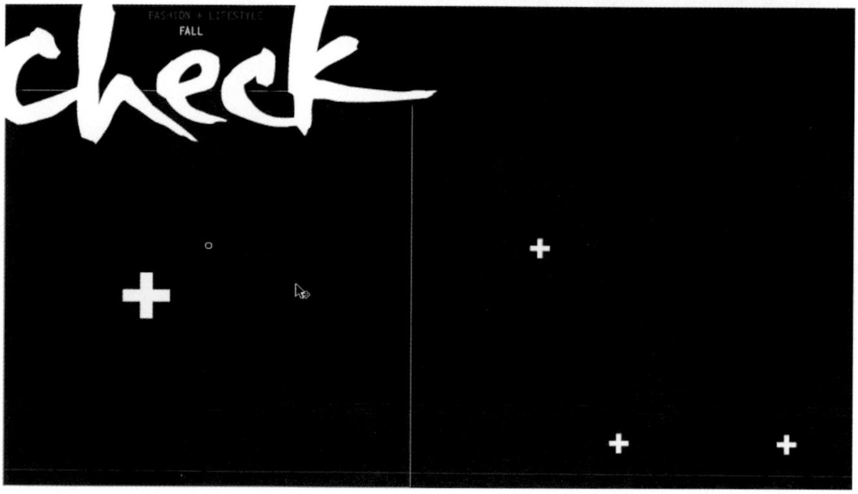

6 In the Properties inspector, name it **page1_mc**.

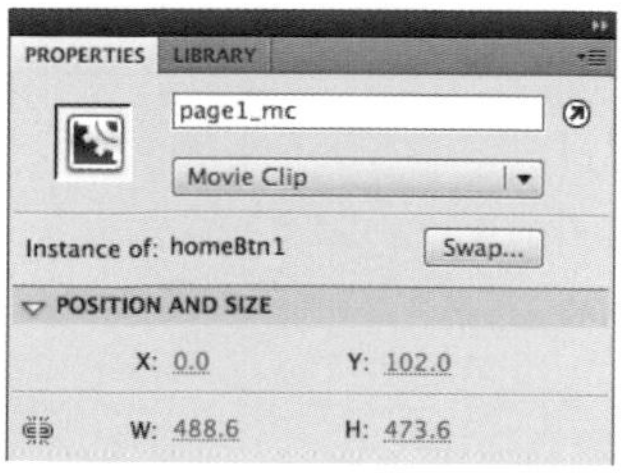

The ActionScript you entered refers to the object called page1_mc, so you need to apply the name to one of the movie clips on the Stage.

Note: You can also use the ProLoader and URLRequest objects to dynamically load image files. The syntax is identical. Simply replace the SWF filename with a JPEG filename, and Flash loads the specified image.

7 Choose Control > Test Movie > in Flash Professional to see your movie so far.

The front page plays its animation and stops. When you click on the movie star, the file called page1.swf loads and is displayed.

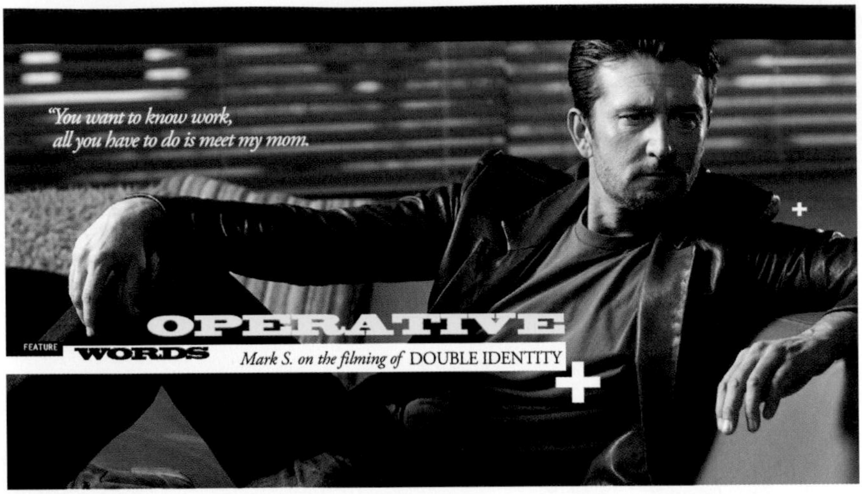

8 Close the SWF called 09_workingcopy.swf.

9 Select the first frame of the actionscript layer and open the Actions panel.

10 Copy and paste the event listener and the function so you have four distinct listeners for each of the four movie clips on the Stage. The four listeners should appear as follows:

```
page1_mc.addEventListener(MouseEvent.CLICK, page1content);
function page1content(e:MouseEvent):void {
 var myURL:URLRequest=new URLRequest("page1.swf");
 myProLoader.load(myURL);
 addChild(myProLoader);
}
page2_mc.addEventListener(MouseEvent.CLICK, page2content);
function page2content(e:MouseEvent):void {
 var myURL:URLRequest=new URLRequest("page2.swf");
 myProLoader.load(myURL);
 addChild(myProLoader);
}
```

```
page3_mc.addEventListener(MouseEvent.CLICK, page3content);
function page3content(e:MouseEvent):void {
 var myURL:URLRequest=new URLRequest("page3.swf");
 myProLoader.load(myURL);
 addChild(myProLoader);
}
page4_mc.addEventListener(MouseEvent.CLICK, page4content);
function page4content(e:MouseEvent):void {
 var myURL:URLRequest=new URLRequest("page4.swf");
 myProLoader.load(myURL);
 addChild(myProLoader);
}
```

Note: Adding event listeners to movie clips can make them respond to mouse clicks, but your cursor doesn't automatically change to a hand icon to indicate that it is clickable. In the Actions panel, set the property `buttonMode` to `true` for each movie clip instance to enable the hand cursor. For example, `page1_mc.buttonMode=true` makes the hand cursor appear when you move your mouse over that movie clip on the Stage.

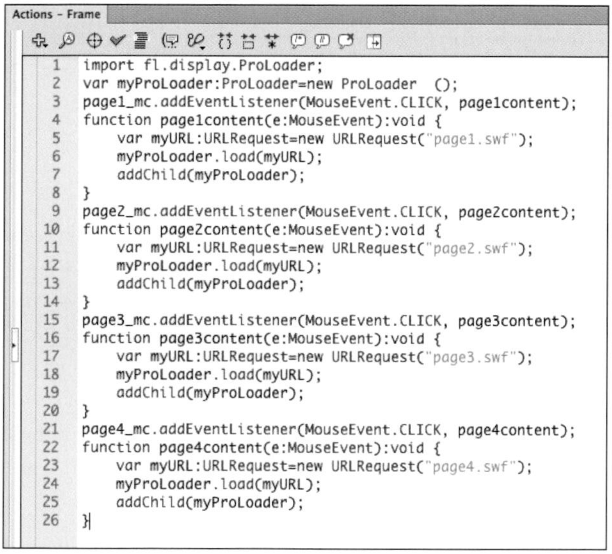

Actions - Frame
import fl.display.ProLoader;
var myProLoader:ProLoader=new ProLoader ();
page1_mc.addEventListener(MouseEvent.CLICK, page1content);
function page1content(e:MouseEvent):void {
var myURL:URLRequest=new URLRequest("page1.swf");
myProLoader.load(myURL);
addChild(myProLoader);
}
page2_mc.addEventListener(MouseEvent.CLICK, page2content);
function page2content(e:MouseEvent):void {
var myURL:URLRequest=new URLRequest("page2.swf");
myProLoader.load(myURL);
addChild(myProLoader);
}
page3_mc.addEventListener(MouseEvent.CLICK, page3content);
function page3content(e:MouseEvent):void {
var myURL:URLRequest=new URLRequest("page3.swf");
myProLoader.load(myURL);
addChild(myProLoader);
}
page4_mc.addEventListener(MouseEvent.CLICK, page4content);
function page4content(e:MouseEvent):void {
var myURL:URLRequest=new URLRequest("page4.swf");
myProLoader.load(myURL);
addChild(myProLoader);
}

11 Click on each of the remaining three movie clips on the Stage and name them in the Properties inspector. Name the yellow car **page2_mc**, name the data section **page3_mc**, and name the self-improvement section on the lower left **page4_mc**.

Using the Code Snippets Panel

You can also use the Code Snippets panel to visually point and add code to load external SWF or image files. Using the Code Snippets panel can save you time and effort, but writing your own code by hand is the only way to understand how the code works and will help you begin building your own more sophisticated, customized projects.

Follow these alternate steps if you wish to rely on the Code Snippets panel. However, the remainder of this lesson will refer to the code presented in the previous section.

1 Choose Window > Code Snippets, or if your Actions panel is already open, click the Code Snippets button at the top right of the Actions panel.

   The Code Snippets panel appears. The code snippets are organized in folders that describe their function.

2 In the Code Snippets panel, expand the folder called Load and Unload and select Click to Load/Unload SWF or Image.

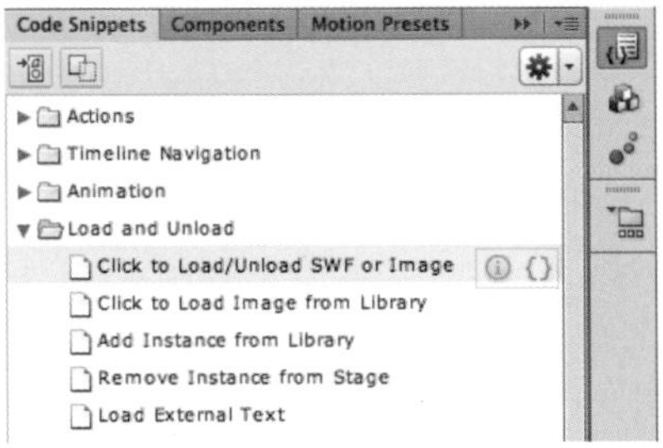

3 Click the Show code button.

   The actual code appears. There is a commented portion of the code that describes the function of the code and the different parameters. The colored parts of the code are the parts that you need to change.

4 Move your mouse over the blue words **instance_name_here**.

   Your mouse cursor turns into the pick whip icon that appears as a small curl.

5 Click and drag your cursor from the blue code words to the first movie clip on the Stage.

   The movie clip instance becomes highlighted with a yellow border, indicating that the selected code snippet will be applied to it.

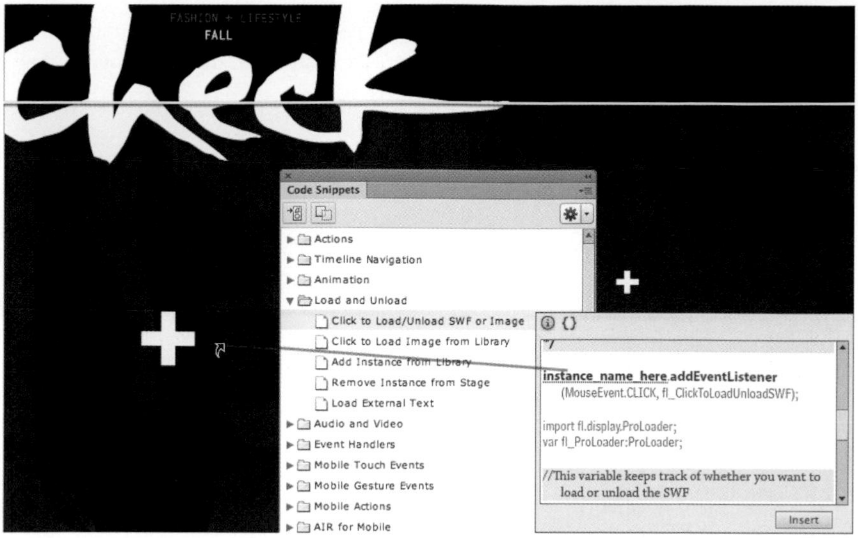

6 Release your mouse cursor.

A dialog box appears to allow you to give a name to the instance. Name the instance **page1_mc**.

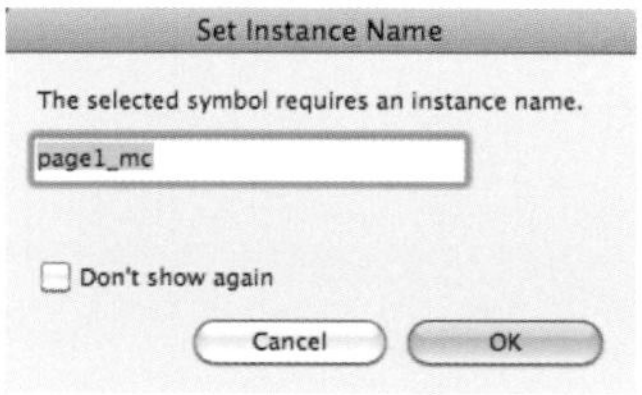

7 Replace the blue URL with the filename **page1.swf**.

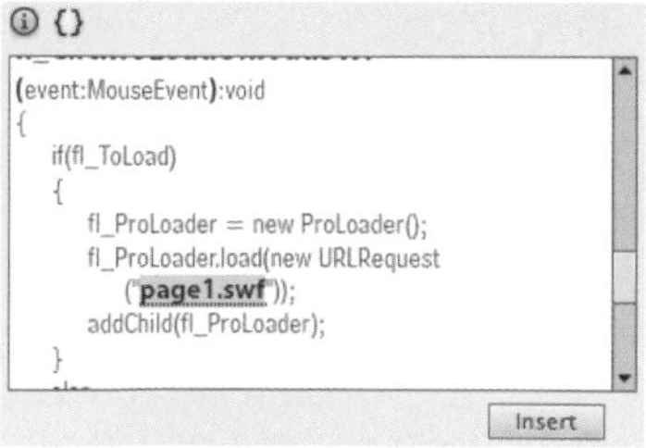

The filename page1.swf refers to the external SWF file that will be loaded.

8 Click Insert.

Flash adds the code snippet to the current keyframe on the Timeline. A flag appears on the Timeline to let you know that the code has been added, and to indicate where on the Timeline it's been placed.

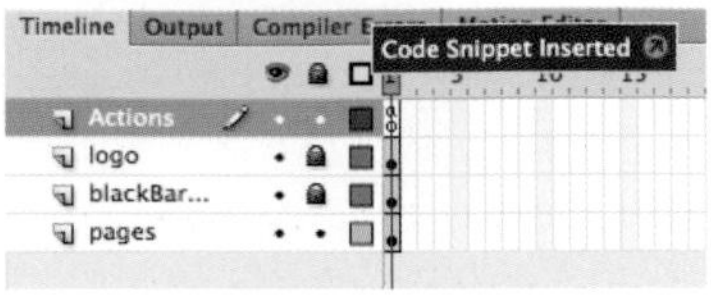

9 Click on the flag to open the Actions panel to view the code.

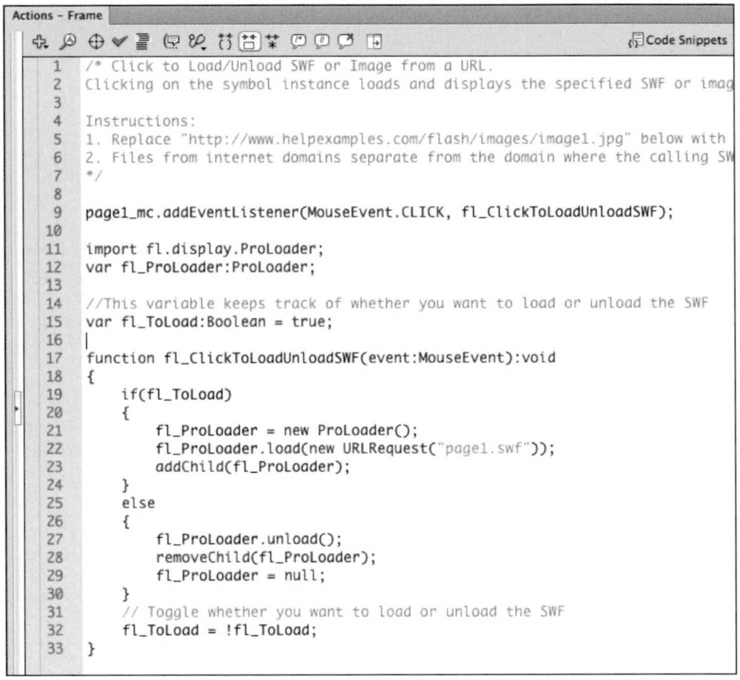
Actions - Frame
Code Snippets
/* Click to Load/Unload SWF or Image from a URL.
Clicking on the symbol instance loads and displays the specified SWF or imag
Instructions:
1. Replace "http://www.helpexamples.com/flash/images/image1.jpg" below with
2. Files from internet domains separate from the domain where the calling SW
*/
page1_mc.addEventListener(MouseEvent.CLICK, fl_ClickToLoadUnloadSWF);
import fl.display.ProLoader;
var fl_ProLoader:ProLoader;
//This variable keeps track of whether you want to load or unload the SWF
var fl_ToLoad:Boolean = true;
function fl_ClickToLoadUnloadSWF(event:MouseEvent):void
{
if(fl_ToLoad)
{
fl_ProLoader = new ProLoader();
fl_ProLoader.load(new URLRequest("page1.swf"));
addChild(fl_ProLoader);
}
else
{
fl_ProLoader.unload();
removeChild(fl_ProLoader);
fl_ProLoader = null;
}
// Toggle whether you want to load or unload the SWF
fl_ToLoad = !fl_ToLoad;
}

Examine the code. The code is a little more complex than the code presented in the previous section. The code includes a toggling functionality, so the user can click once to load the SWF and then click again to unload the SWF. However, because the external SWF that loads covers the entire Stage, the original movie clip is hidden and inaccessible to click on. Use this code snippet if your layout allows the button or movie clip that triggers the loading function to remain visible on the Stage.

Positioning of the Loaded Content

Loaded content is aligned with the Stage (or whatever it is loaded into). The registration point of the ProLoader object is at its top-left corner, so the top-left corner of the external SWFs align with the top-left corner of the Stage (where x=0 and y=0). Since the four external Flash files (page1.swf, page2.swf, page3.swf, and page4.swf) all have the same Stage size as the Flash file that loads them, the Stage is completely covered.

However, you can position the ProLoader object wherever you want. If you want to place the ProLoader object in a different horizontal position, you can set a new X value for the ProLoader object with ActionScript. If you want to place the ProLoader in a different vertical position, you can set a new Y value for the ProLoader. Here's how: In the Actions panel, enter the name of the ProLoader object, followed by a period, the property x or y, and then the equals symbol and a new value.

In the following example, the ProLoader object called myProLoader is repositioned 200 pixels from the left edge and 100 pixels from the top edge.

```

myProLoader.x = 200;
myProLoader.y = 100;
```

When the external SWF content loads, it shows up exactly 200 pixels to the right and 100 pixels down.

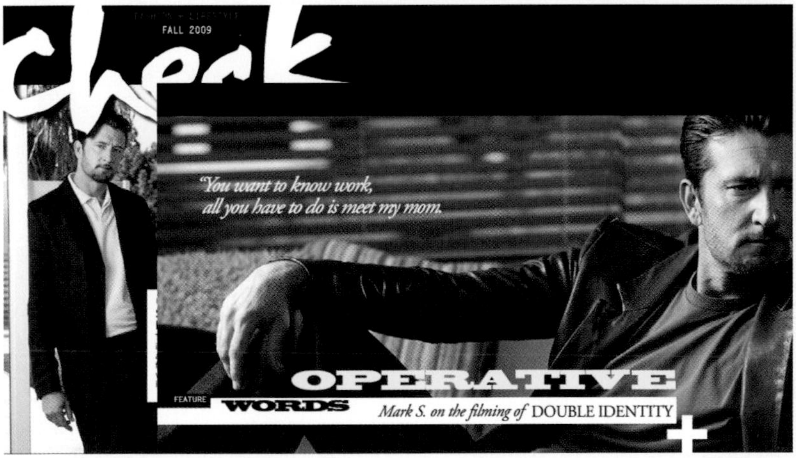

Removing External Content

Note: If you want to remove the ProLoader object from the Stage entirely, you can use the removeChild(). command. The code `removeChild (myProLoader)` removes the ProLoader object called myProLoader so that it is no longer displayed on the Stage.

Once an external SWF file is loaded, how do you unload it to return to the main Flash movie? One way is to unload the SWF content from the ProLoader object, so the audience can no longer see it. You will use the command `unload()` to do this.

1 Select the first frame of the actionscript layer and open the Actions panel.

2 Add the following lines to your code in the Script pane:

```
myProLoader.addEventListener(MouseEvent.CLICK, unloadcontent);
function unloadcontent(e:MouseEvent):void {
 myProloader.unload();
}
```

Note: If your loaded content contains open streams (such as video or sounds), those sounds may continue even after you've unloaded the SWF from the ProLoader object. Use the unloadAndStop() command to extinguish the sounds as well as unload the SWF content.

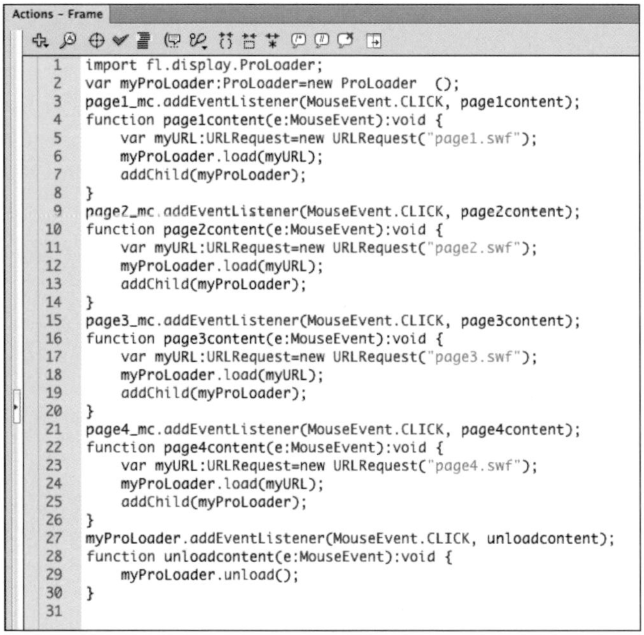
Actions - Frame

```
import fl.display.ProLoader;
var myProLoader:ProLoader=new ProLoader  ();
page1_mc.addEventListener(MouseEvent.CLICK, page1content);
function page1content(e:MouseEvent):void {
    var myURL:URLRequest=new URLRequest("page1.swf");
    myProLoader.load(myURL);
    addChild(myProLoader);
}
page2_mc.addEventListener(MouseEvent.CLICK, page2content);
function page2content(e:MouseEvent):void {
    var myURL:URLRequest=new URLRequest("page2.swf");
    myProLoader.load(myURL);
    addChild(myProLoader);
}
page3_mc.addEventListener(MouseEvent.CLICK, page3content);
function page3content(e:MouseEvent):void {
    var myURL:URLRequest=new URLRequest("page3.swf");
    myProLoader.load(myURL);
    addChild(myProLoader);
}
page4_mc.addEventListener(MouseEvent.CLICK, page4content);
function page4content(e:MouseEvent):void {
    var myURL:URLRequest=new URLRequest("page4.swf");
    myProLoader.load(myURL);
    addChild(myProLoader);
}
myProLoader.addEventListener(MouseEvent.CLICK, unloadcontent);
function unloadcontent(e:MouseEvent):void {
    myProLoader.unload();
}
```

This code adds an event listener to the ProLoader object called myProLoader. When you click on the ProLoader object, the function called unloadcontent is executed.

The function performs just one action: It removes any loaded content from the ProLoader object.

3 Choose Control > Test Movie > in Flash Professional to preview the movie. Click on any of the four sections, and then click on the loaded content to return to the main movie.

Controlling Movie Clips

When you return to the front page, you'll see the four sections, so you can click another movie clip to load a different section. But wouldn't it be nice to replay the initial animation? The initial animations are nested inside each movie clip, and you can control the four movie clips that are on the Stage. You can use the basic navigation commands that you already learned in Lesson 6 (`gotoAndStop`, `gotoAndPlay`, `stop`, `play`) to navigate the Timelines of these movie clips. Simply precede the command with the name of the movie clip and separate them with a dot. Flash targets that particular movie clip and moves its Timeline accordingly.

1 Select the first frame of the actionscript layer and open the Actions panel.

2 Add to the commands in the function called unloadcontent so the entire function appears as follows:

```
function unloadcontent(e:MouseEvent):void {
 myProloader.unload();
 page1_mc.gotoAndPlay(1);
 page2_mc.gotoAndPlay(1);
 page3_mc.gotoAndPlay(1);
 page4_mc.gotoAndPlay(1);
}
```

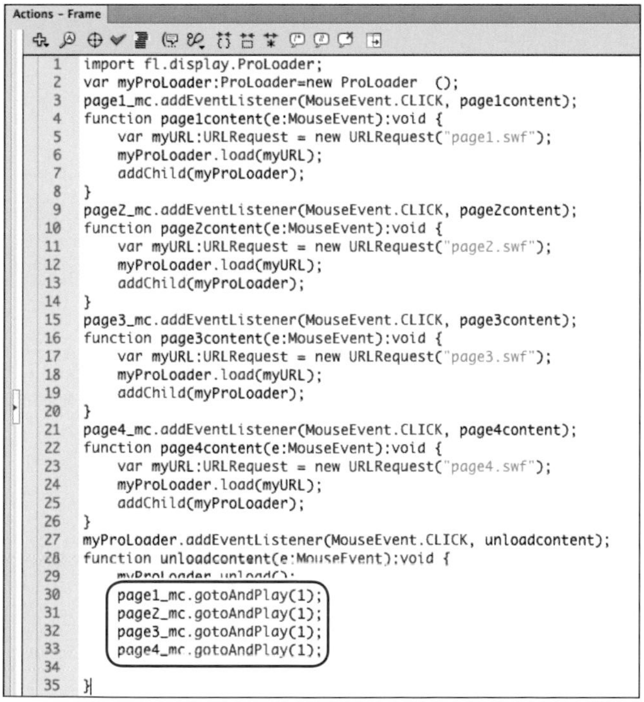
Actions - Frame
import fl.display.ProLoader;
var myProLoader:ProLoader=new ProLoader ();
page1_mc.addEventListener(MouseEvent.CLICK, page1content);
function page1content(e:MouseEvent):void {
var myURL:URLRequest = new URLRequest("page1.swf");
myProLoader.load(myURL);
addChild(myProLoader);
}
page2_mc.addEventListener(MouseEvent.CLICK, page2content);
function page2content(e:MouseEvent):void {
var myURL:URLRequest = new URLRequest("page2.swf");
myProLoader.load(myURL);
addChild(myProLoader);
}
page3_mc.addEventListener(MouseEvent.CLICK, page3content);
function page3content(e:MouseEvent):void {
var myURL:URLRequest = new URLRequest("page3.swf");
myProLoader.load(myURL);
addChild(myProLoader);
}
page4_mc.addEventListener(MouseEvent.CLICK, page4content);
function page4content(e:MouseEvent):void {
var myURL:URLRequest = new URLRequest("page4.swf");
myProLoader.load(myURL);
addChild(myProLoader);
}
myProLoader.addEventListener(MouseEvent.CLICK, unloadcontent);
function unloadcontent(e:MouseEvent):void {
page1_mc.gotoAndPlay(1);
page2_mc.gotoAndPlay(1);
page3_mc.gotoAndPlay(1);
page4_mc.gotoAndPlay(1);
}

In this function, which is executed when the user clicks the ProLoader object, the ProLoader object is removed from the Stage, and then the playhead of each movie clip on the Stage moves to the first frame and begins playing.

3 Choose Control > Test Movie > in Flash Professional to preview the movie. Click on any of the four sections, and then click on the loaded content to return to the main movie.

When you return to the main movie, all four movie clips play their nested animations.

Creating Masks

Masking is a way of selectively hiding and displaying content on a layer. Masking is a way for you to control the content that your audience sees. For example, you can make a circular mask and allow your audience to see only through the circular area, so that you get a keyhole or spotlight effect. In Flash, you put a mask on one layer and the content that is masked in a layer below it.

Masks can be animated, and the content that is masked can also be animated. The circular mask can grow bigger to show more content, or the content can scroll under a mask like scenery whizzing by a train window.

Define the Mask and Masked layers

You'll create a rectangular mask that starts small and grows larger to cover the Stage. The resulting effect reveals the contents of the Masked layer slowly, similar to a sliding door opening.

1 Open the file page2.fla.

A single layer called content contains a movie clip of the second section about a new car.

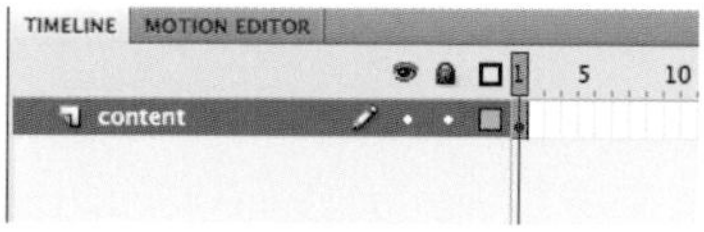

2 Insert a new layer above the content layer and rename it **mask**.

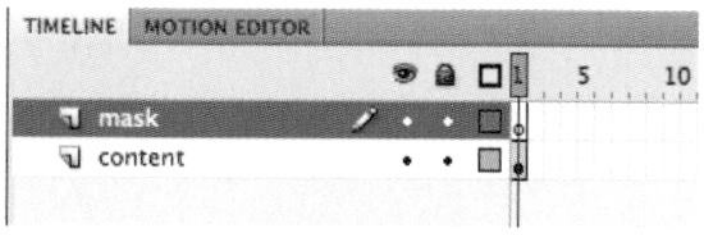

3 Double-click the icon in front of the layer name, or choose Modify > Timeline > Layer Properties.

The Layer Properties dialog box appears.

4 Select Mask and click OK.

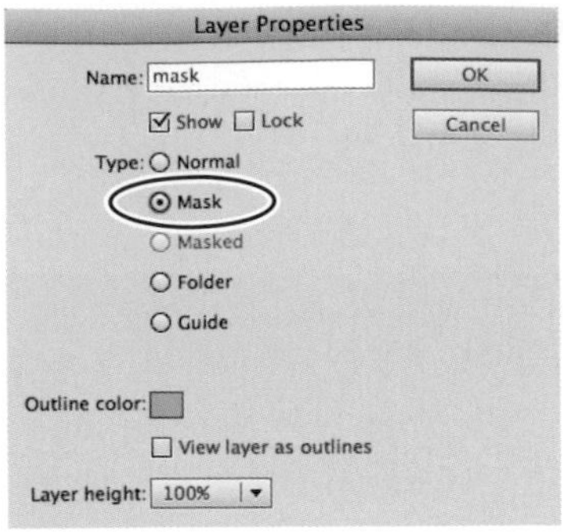

The top layer becomes a Mask layer. Anything that is drawn in this layer will act as a mask for a Masked layer below it.

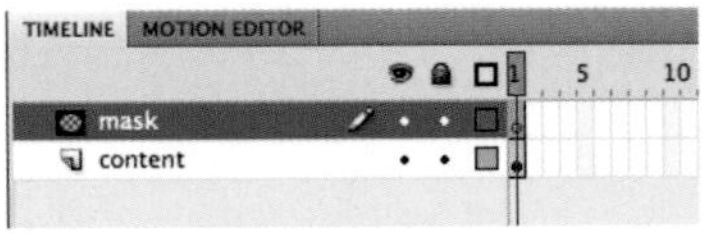

5 Double-click the icon in front of the bottom layer named content, or choose Modify > Timeline > Layer Properties.

The Layer Properties dialog box appears.

6 Select Masked and click OK.

Note: You can also simply drag a normal layer under a Mask layer, and Flash will convert it to a Masked layer.

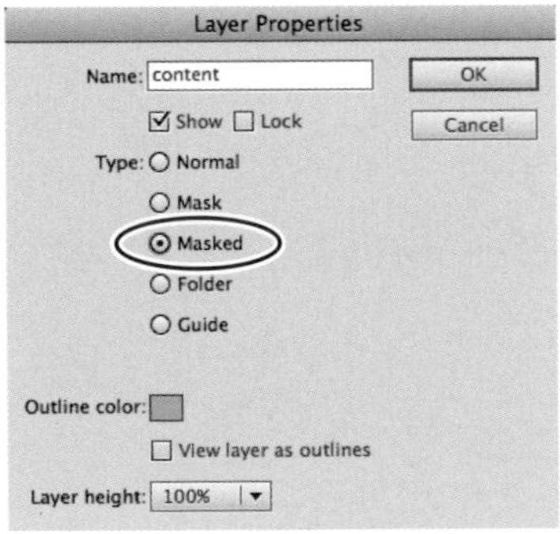

The bottom layer becomes a Masked layer and is indented, indicating that it is affected by the mask above it.

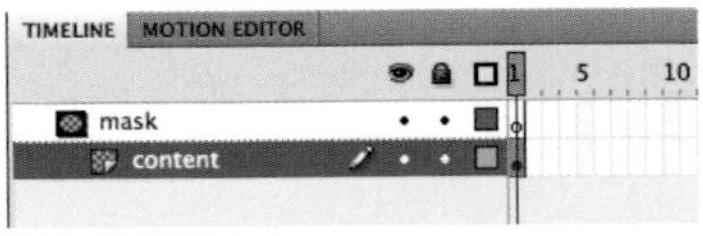

Create the mask

The mask can be any filled shape. The color of the fill doesn't matter. What's important to Flash is the size, location, and contours of the shape. The shape will be the "peephole" through which you'll see the content on the layer below. You can use any of the drawing tools to create the fill for your mask.

1 Select the Rectangle tool.

2 Choose any color for the Fill and no stroke for the Stroke.

3 Select the top Mask layer and draw a thin rectangle just off to the left of the Stage. Make the height of the rectangle slightly larger than the Stage.

4 Right-click/Ctrl-click the rectangle and select Create Motion Tween.

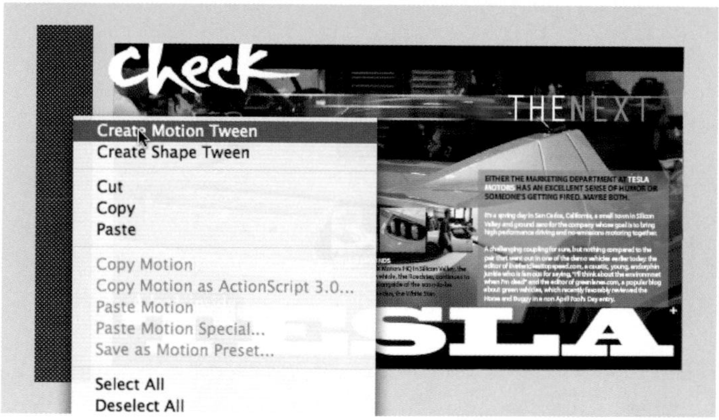

5 Flash asks to convert the rectangular shape to a symbol so you can apply a motion tween. Click OK.

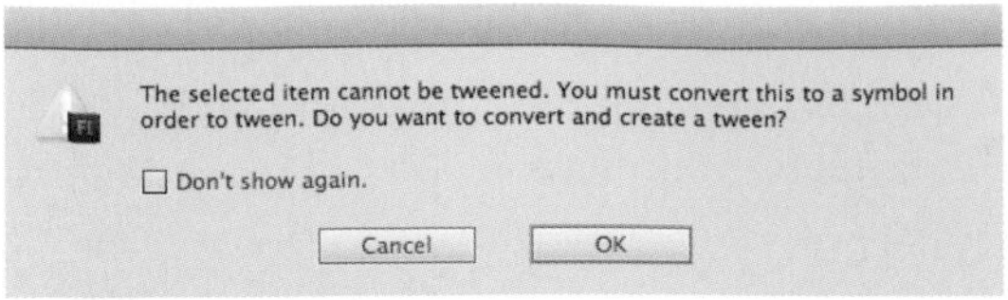

The top layer becomes a Tween layer, and one second's worth of frames is added to the Timeline.

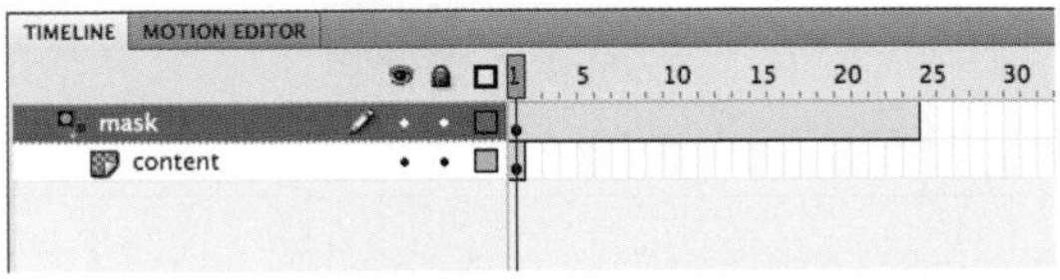

6 Insert the same number of frames in the bottom layer.

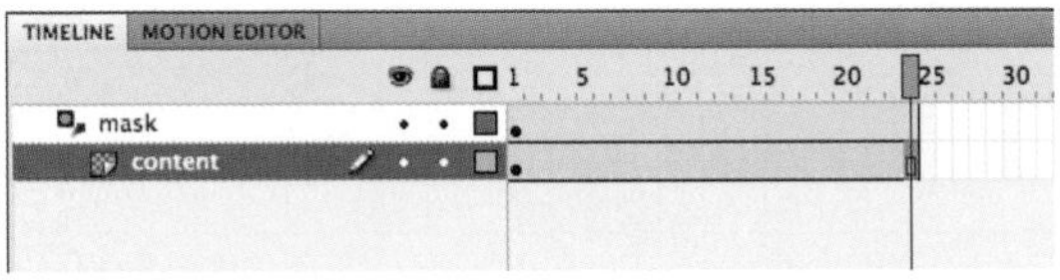

7 Move the playhead to the last frame, frame 24.

8 Select the Free Transform tool.

9 Click on the rectangular symbol.

The free transform handles appear around the rectangular symbol.

10 Hold down the Alt/Option key and drag the right edge of the free transform handle to expand the rectangle to cover the entire Stage.

Flash creates a new keyframe in the last frame, where the rectangle becomes wider. The motion tween creates a smooth animation of the rectangle growing wider and covering the Stage.

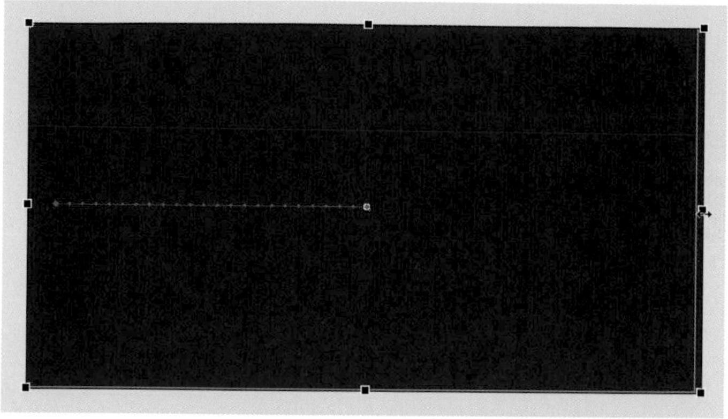

11 To see the effects of the Mask layer on its Masked layer, lock both layers. Scrub the red playhead back and forth along the Timeline to see how the motion tween uncovers the content in the bottom layer.

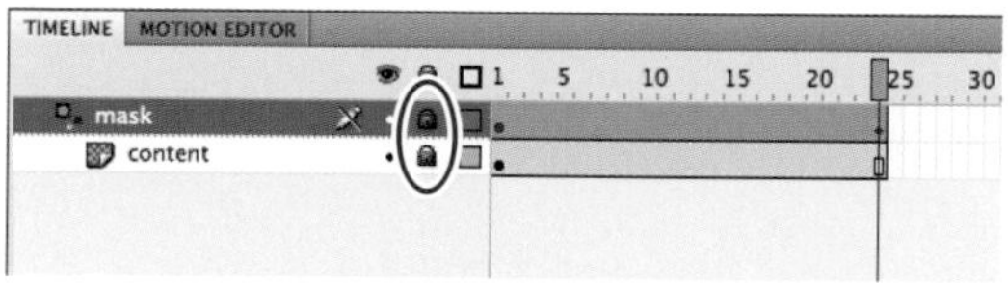

12 Insert a new layer and rename it **actionscript**.

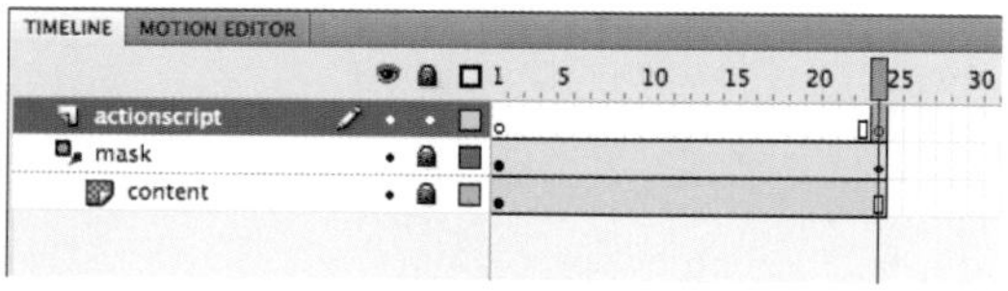

13 Insert a keyframe at the last frame of the actionscript layer and open the Actions panel.

14 Enter `stop();` in the first line of the Script pane of the Actions panel.

> **Note:** Flash does not recognize different Alpha levels of a mask. For example, a mask drawn with a fill at an Alpha value of 50% will not reveal the underlying content at 50%. However, with ActionScript you can dynamically create masks that will allow transparencies. Masks also do not recognize strokes.

15 Choose Control > Test Movie > in Flash Professional.

As the motion tween proceeds in the Mask layer, more of the Masked layer is revealed, creating a cinematic transition known as a wipe. If you open 09_workingcopy.fla and choose Control > Test Movie > in Flash Professional, and then click on the car movie clip, you'll see that the masking effect is preserved even as it is loaded into another Flash movie.

Review Questions

1 How do you load external Flash content?

2 What are the advantages of loading external Flash content?

3 How do you control the Timeline of a movie clip instance?

4 What is a mask and how do you create one?

Review Answers

1 You use ActionScript to load external Flash content. You create two objects: a ProLoader and a URLRequest object. The URLRequest object specifies the filename and file location of the SWF file that you want to load. To load the file, use the `load()` command to load the URLRequest object into the ProLoader object. Then display the ProLoader object on the Stage with the `addChild()` command.

2 Loading external content keeps your overall project in separate modules and prevents the project from becoming too bloated and difficult to download. It also makes it easier for you to edit, because you can edit individual sections instead of one, large, unwieldy file.

3 You can control the Timeline of movie clips with ActionScript by first targeting them by their instance name. After the name, type a dot (period), and then the command that you desire. You can use the same commands for navigation that you learned in Lesson 6 (`gotoAndStop`, `gotoAndPlay`, `stop`, `play`). Flash targets that particular movie clip and moves its Timeline accordingly.

4 Masking is a way of selectively hiding and displaying content on a layer. In Flash, you put a mask on the top Mask layer and the content in the layer below it, which is called the Masked layer. Both the Mask and the Masked layers can be animated. To see the effects of the Mask layer on the Masked layer, you must lock both layers.

10 PUBLISHING FLASH DOCUMENTS

Lesson Overview

In this lesson, you'll learn how to do the following:

- Test a Flash document
- Change publish settings for a document
- Understand the various Flash runtime environments
- Publish a project for the Web
- Add metadata
- Detect the version of Flash Player a viewer has installed
- Publish a project as a desktop application
- Publish a self-contained projector file
- Test a project by simulating mobile interactions

This lesson will two hours to complete. If needed, remove the previous lesson folder from your hard drive and copy the Lesson10 folder onto it.

When you've finished your Flash project, publish it in a variety of formats for playback on different devices and environments. Author once and publish (nearly) everywhere with Flash Professional CS6.

Getting Started

In this lesson, you'll publish several projects that have already been completed to learn about various output options. The first project is an animated banner for the familiar fictional city of Meridien. You'll publish the movie for playback in a desktop browser. The second project is the interactive restaurant guide for Meridien that you completed in Lesson 6. For that project, you'll target Adobe AIR, which creates a stand-alone application that runs on the desktop outside the browser. Finally, you'll test the interactivity for a third project for a mobile device.

1 Double-click the 10Start_banner.fla, 10Start_restaurantguide.fla, and 10Start_mobileapp.fla files in the Lesson10/10Start folder to open the three projects.

   The three projects are relatively simple, each having unique Stage dimensions that are suited for their final published playback environments.

2 In the Properties Inspector for each project, notice that the Target is set for different options.

The banner ad targets the Flash Player, the restaurant guide targets AIR for Desktop, and the mobile app targets AIR for Android.

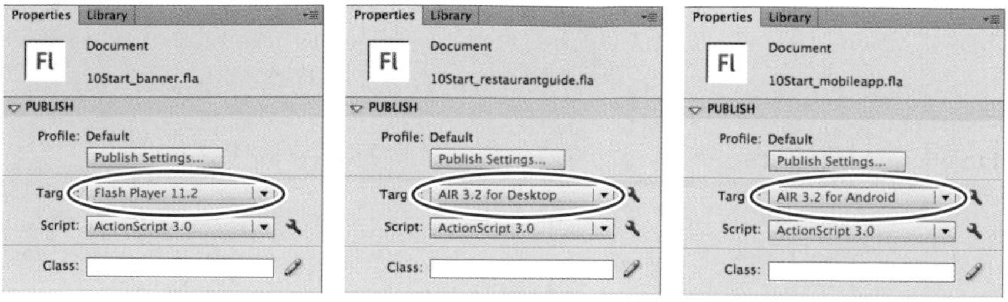

Testing a Flash Document

Before we get to the completed Flash files, consider the troubleshooting process that happens before you publish. Troubleshooting is a skill you develop over time, but it's easier to identify the cause of problems if you test your movie frequently as you create content. If you test after each step, you know which changes you made and therefore what might have gone wrong. A good motto to remember is "Test early. Test often."

One fast way to preview a movie is to choose Control > Test Movie > in Flash Professional (Ctrl+Enter/Command+Return), as you've done in earlier lessons. This command creates a SWF file in the same location as your FLA file so you can play and preview the movie directly within the Flash application; it does not create the HTML file necessary to play the movie in a Web browser.

When you believe you've completed your movie or a portion of the movie, take the time to make sure all the pieces are in place and that they perform the way you expect them to.

1 Review the storyboard for the project, if you have one, or other documents that describe the purpose and requirements of the project. If such documents do not exist, write a description of what you expect to see when you view the movie. Include information about the length of the animation, any buttons or links included in the movie, and what should be visible as the movie progresses.

2 Using the storyboard, project requirements, or your written description, create a checklist that you can use to verify that the movie meets your expectations.

Note: The default behavior for your movie in Test Movie mode is to loop. You can make your SWF play differently in a browser by selecting different publish settings, as described later in this lesson, or by adding ActionScript to stop the Timeline.

3 Choose Control > Test Movie > in Flash Professional. As the movie plays, compare it with your checklist. Click buttons and links to ensure they behave as expected. You should click on every possibility that a user may encounter. This process is called QA, or quality assurance. In larger projects, it may be referred to as beta testing.

4 For movies that play with the Flash Player, choose File > Publish Preview > Default-(HTML) to export a SWF file and an HTML file required to play in a browser and to preview the movie.

   A browser opens, if one is not already open, and plays the final movie.

5 Upload the two files (the SWF and HTML) to your own Web server and give your colleagues or friends the Web site address so they can help you test the movie. Ask them to run the movie on different computers with different browsers to ensure that all the files are included and that the movie meets the criteria on your checklist. Encourage testers to view the movie as though they were its target audience.

   If your project requires additional media, such as FLV or F4V video files, skin files for your video, or imported external SWF files, you must upload them along with your SWF and HTML file in the same relative location as they were on your computer hard drive.

6 Make changes and corrections as necessary to finalize the movie, upload the revised files, and then test it again to ensure it meets your criteria. The iterative process of testing and making revisions may not sound like fun, but it is a critical part of launching a successful Flash project.

Clearing the Publish Cache

When you test your movie by choosing Control > Test Movie > in Flash Professional to generate a SWF, Flash puts compressed copies of any fonts and sounds from your project into the Publish Cache. When you test your movie again, Flash uses the versions in the cache if the fonts and sounds are unchanged to speed up the export of the SWF file. However, you can manually purge the cache by choosing Control > Clear Publish Cache. If you want to clear the cache and test the movie, choose Control > Clear Publish Cache and Test Movie.

Understanding Publishing

Publishing is the process that creates the required file or files to play your final Flash project for your viewers. Keep in mind that Flash Professional CS6 is the authoring application, which is a different environment from where your viewers experience your movie. In Flash Professional CS6, you author content. In the target environment, such as a desktop browser or a mobile device, your viewers watch the content when it plays back, or runs. So developers make a distinction between "author-time" and "run-time."

Adobe provides various runtime environments for playing back your Flash content. The most common for a browser running on the desktop is the Flash Player. Flash Player 11.2 is the latest version and supports all the new features in Flash Professional CS6. The Flash Player is available as a free plug-in from the Adobe Web site for all the major browsers and platforms. In Google Chrome, the Flash Player comes pre-installed and updates automatically.

Adobe AIR is another runtime environment to play Flash content. AIR runs Flash content directly from your desktop, without the need for a browser. When you publish your content for AIR, you make it available as an installer that creates a stand-alone application. You can also publish applications that can be installed and run on Android devices and even iOS mobile devices such as the iPhone or iPad, whose browsers do not support the Flash Player.

Knowing your audience and understanding the target playback environment is essential for your success.

Publishing for the Web

When you want to publish a movie for the Web, you target a Web browser's Flash Player. Flash content for the Web requires a SWF file for the Flash Player and an HTML document that tells the Web browser how to display the Flash content. You need to upload both files to your Web server along with any other files your SWF file references (such as FLV or F4V video files and skins). By default, the Publish command saves all the required files to the same folder.

Note: When you change the settings in the Publish Settings dialog box, they are saved with the document.

You can specify different options for publishing a movie, including whether to detect the version of Flash Player installed on the viewer's computer.

Specifying Flash file settings

You can determine how Flash publishes the SWF file, including which version of Flash Player it requires, which version of ActionScript it uses, and how the movie is displayed and plays.

1 Open the **10Start_banner.fla** file.

2 Choose File > Publish Settings, or click the Publish Settings button in the Profile section of the Properties inspector.

The Publish Settings dialog box appears with the general settings at the top, the formats on the left, and additional options for selected formats on the right.

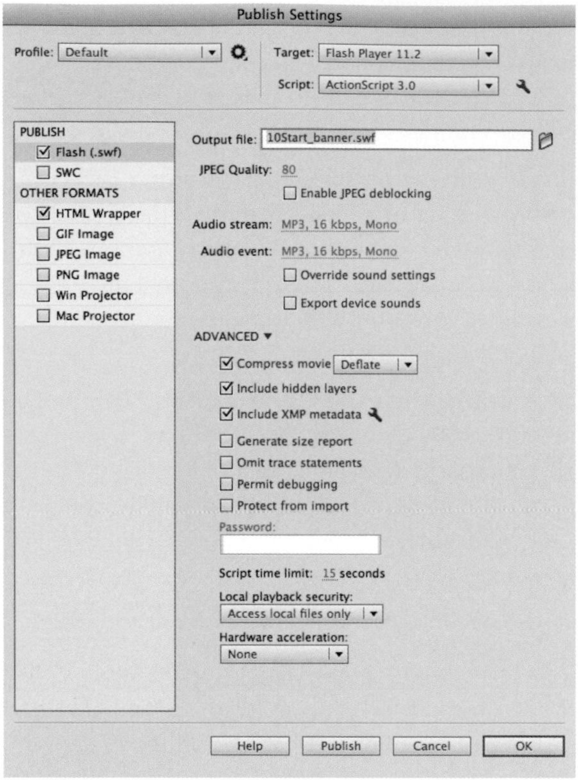

The Flash and the HTML Wrapper formats should already be checked.

3 At the top of the Publish Settings dialog box, select a version of Flash Player. The latest version is Flash Player 11.2.

Some Flash Professional CS6 features will not play as expected in versions of the player earlier than Flash Player 11.2. If you're using the latest features of Flash CS6, you should choose Flash Player 11.2. Only choose an earlier version of the Flash Player if you are targeting a specific audience that does not have the latest version.

4 Select the appropriate ActionScript version. You've used ActionScript 3.0 in lessons in this book, so choose ActionScript 3.0.

5 Select the Flash (.swf) format on the left side of the dialog box.

The options for the SWF file appear on the right. Expand the ADVANCED section to see more options.

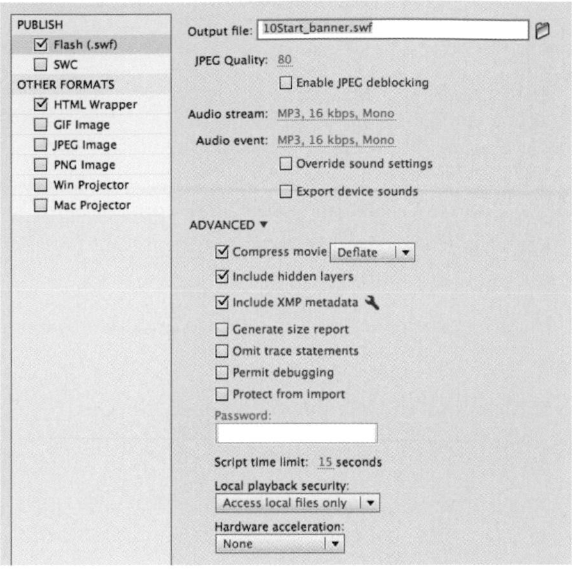

6 If you wish, you can modify the output filename and location by entering a new filename. For this lesson, leave the Output file as **10Start_banner.swf**.

7 If you've included bitmaps in your movie, you can set a global quality setting for JPEG compression levels. Enter a value from 0 (lowest quality) to 100 (highest quality). The value of 80 is the default, which you can leave as is for this lesson.

Note: In the Bitmap properties dialog box for each imported bitmap, you can choose to use the JPEG Quality set in the Publish Settings, or choose a setting unique for that bitmap. This allows you to publish higher-quality images where you need it—for example, in photos of people, and lower-quality images where you can get away with it—for example, in background textures.

8 If you've included sound, click on the Audio stream or Audio event values to modify the quality of the audio compression.

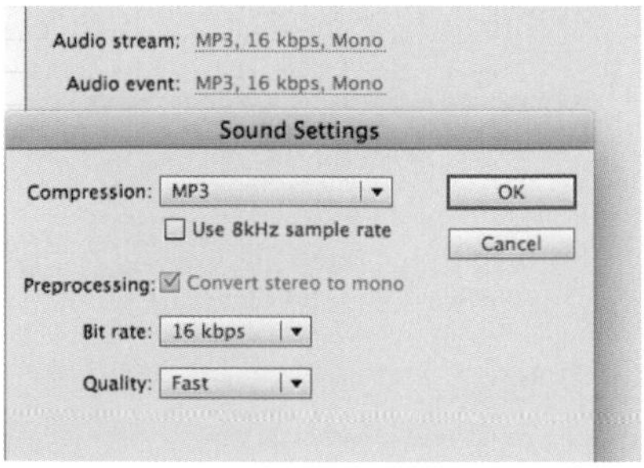

The higher the bitrate, the better the sound quality will be. In this interactive banner, there is no sound, so there's no need to change the settings.

9 Make sure Compress movie is checked to reduce file size and download times.

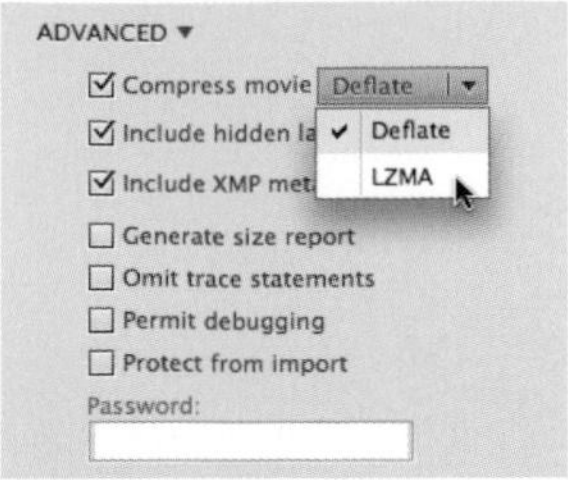

Deflate is the default option. Choose LZMA for better SWF compression. You'll see the biggest improvements in file size compression if your project consists of more ActionScript code and vector graphics.

10 Make sure Include XMP metadata is checked if you want to include information that describes your movie.

11 Select the HTML Wrapper format on the left side of the dialog box.

Note: To learn about other template options, select one and then click Info.

12 Select the Flash Only option from the Template menu.

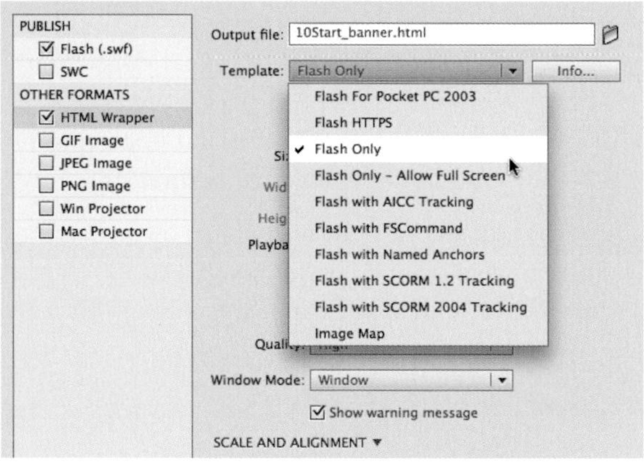

Detecting the version of Flash Player

You can automatically detect the version of Flash Player on a viewer's computer; if the Flash Player version is not the one required, a message will prompt the viewer to download the updated player.

1 If necessary, choose File > Publish Settings, or click the Publish Settings button in the Profile section of the Properties inspector.

2 Select the HTML Wrapper format on the left side of the dialog box.

3 Select Detect Flash Version.

4 In the Version fields, enter the earliest version of the Flash Player to detect.

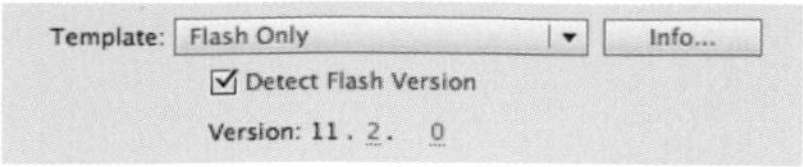

5 Click Publish, and then click OK to close the dialog box.

Flash publishes three files. Flash creates a SWF file, an HTML file, and an additional file named **swfobject.js** that contains extra JavaScript code that will detect the specified Flash Player version. If the browser does not have the earliest Flash Player version you entered in the Version fields, a message is displayed instead of the Flash movie. All three files need to be uploaded to your Web server and are necessary for your movie.

Changing display settings

You have many options for changing the way your Flash movie is displayed in a browser. The Size and Scale settings for the HTML Wrapper work together to determine the movie's size and amount of distortion and cropping.

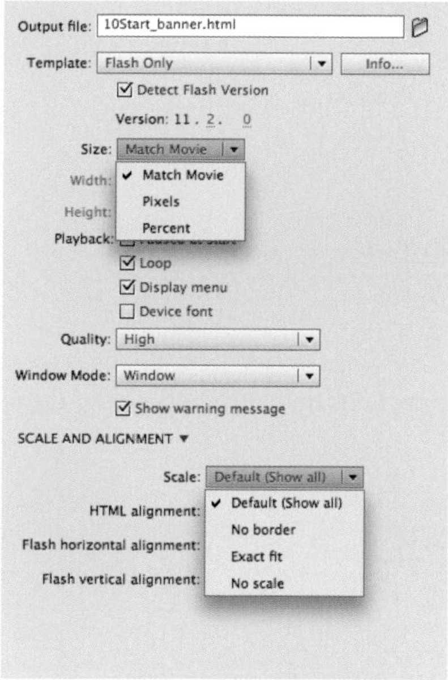

1 Choose File > Publish Settings, or click the Publish Settings button in the Profile section of the Properties inspector.

2 Select the HTML Wrapper format on the left side of the dialog box.

- Select Match Movie for the Size to play the Flash movie at the exact Stage size set in Flash. This is the usual setting for almost all your Flash projects.

- Select Pixels for the Size to enter a different size in pixels for your Flash movie.
- Select Percent for the Size to enter a different size for your Flash movie as a percentage of the browser window.

3 Click on the Scale and Alignment option to expand the advanced settings below it.

- Select Default (Show all) for the Scale option to fit the movie in the browser window without any distortions or cropping to show all the content. This is the usual setting for almost all your Flash projects. If a user reduces the size of the browser window, the content remains constant but is clipped by the window.

- Select Percent for Size and No border for the Scale option to scale the movie to fit the browser window without any distortions but with cropping of the content to fill the window.

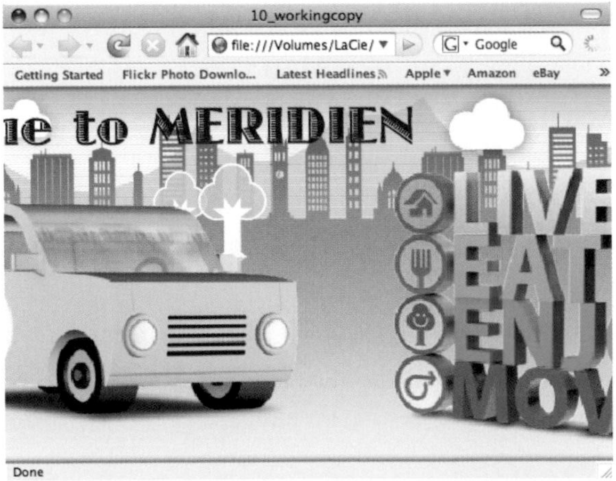

- Select Percent for Size and Exact fit for the Scale option to scale the movie to fill the browser window on both the horizontal and vertical dimensions. With these options, none of the background color shows, but the content can be distorted.

- Select Percent for Size and No scale for the Scale option to keep the movie size constant no matter how big or small the browser window is.

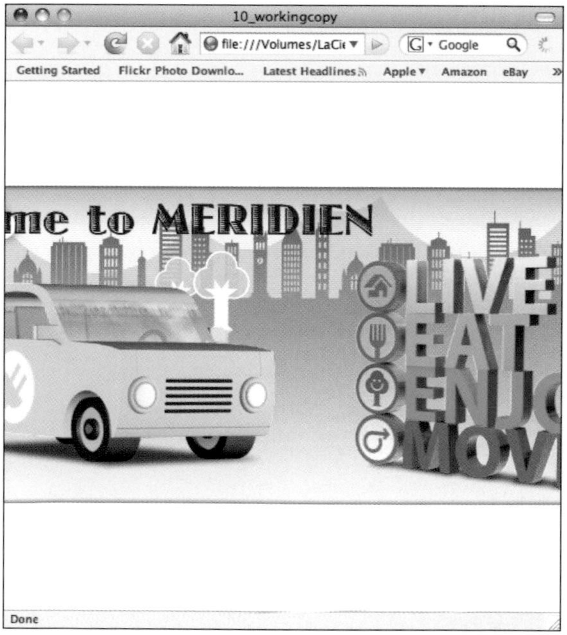

Changing Playback settings

You can change several options that affect the way your Flash movie plays within a browser.

1 Choose File > Publish Settings, or click the Publish Settings button in the Profile section of the Properties inspector.

2 Select the HTML Wrapper format on the left side of the dialog box.

- Select Paused at start for the Playback option to have the movie pause at the very first frame.
- Deselect Loop for the Playback option to have the movie play only once.
- Deselect Display menu for the Playback option to limit the options in the context menu that appears when you right-click/Ctrl-click on a Flash movie in a browser.

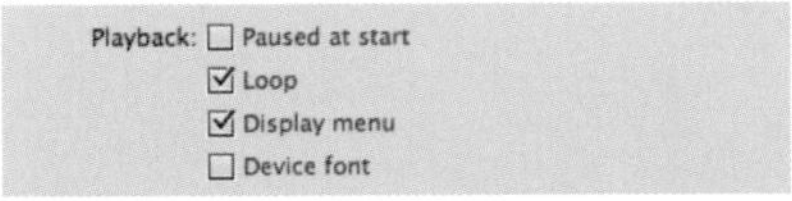

Note: In general, it is best to control a Flash movie with ActionScript than to rely on the Playback settings in the Publish Settings dialog box. For example, add a stop() command in the very first frame of your Timeline if you want to pause the movie at the start. When you test your movie (Control > Test Movie > in Flash Professional), all the functionality will be in place.

Understanding the Bandwidth Profiler

You can preview how your final project might behave in different download environments by using the Bandwidth Profiler, a useful panel that is available when you are in Test Movie mode.

View the Bandwidth Profiler

The Bandwidth Profiler provides information such as the overall file size, the total number of frames, the dimensions of the Stage, and how your data is distributed throughout your frames. You can use the Bandwidth Profiler to pinpoint where there are large amounts of data so you can see where there may be pauses in the movie playback.

1 Choose Control > Test Movie > in Flash Professional.

Flash exports a SWF and displays your movie in a new window.

2 Choose View > Bandwidth Profiler.

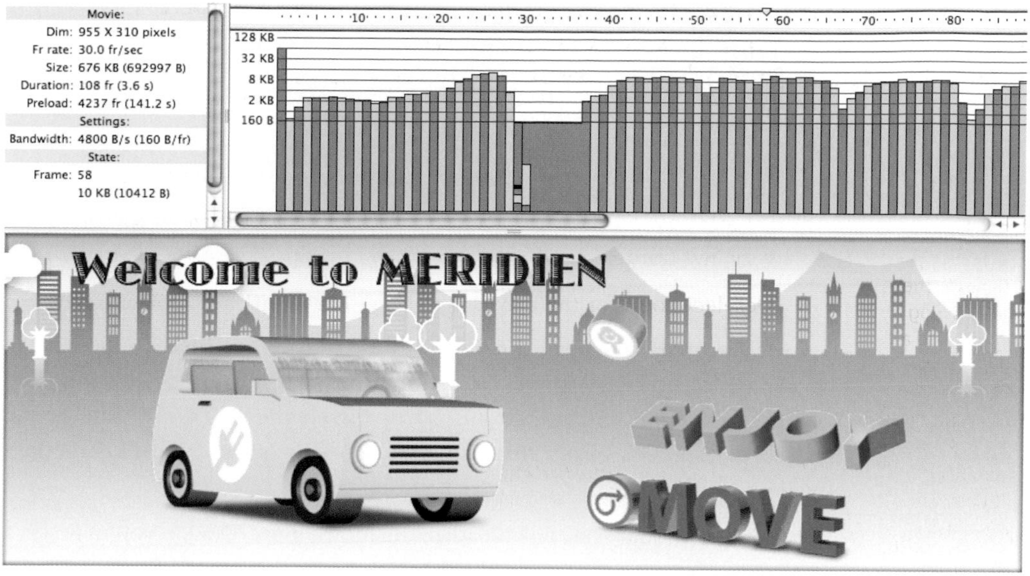

A new window appears above your movie. Basic information about your movie is listed on the left side of the profiler. A timeline appears on the right side of the profiler with gray bars representing the amount of data in each frame. The higher the bars, the more data is included.

You can view the graph on the right in two ways: as a Streaming Graph (View > Streaming Graph) or as a Frame By Frame Graph (View > Frame By Frame Graph). The Streaming Graph indicates how the movie downloads over the Web by showing you how data streams from each frame, whereas the Frame By Frame Graph simply indicates the amount of data in each frame. In Streaming Graph mode, you can tell which frames will cause hang-ups during playback by noting which bar exceeds the given Bandwidth setting.

Test download performance

You can set different download speeds and test the playback performance of your movie under those different conditions.

1 While in Test Movie mode, choose View > Download Settings > DSL.

The DSL setting is a type of Internet connection and a measure of the download speed that you want to test. It corresponds to 32.6 kilobytes per second. Choose higher or lower speeds depending on your target audience.

Note: The download speeds listed for DSL, T1, and the other preset options represent Adobe's estimate of those standard Internet connections. You should determine the actual speed of your Internet provider. You can customize the options and their speeds by choosing View > Download Settings > Customize.

2 Choose View > Simulate Download.

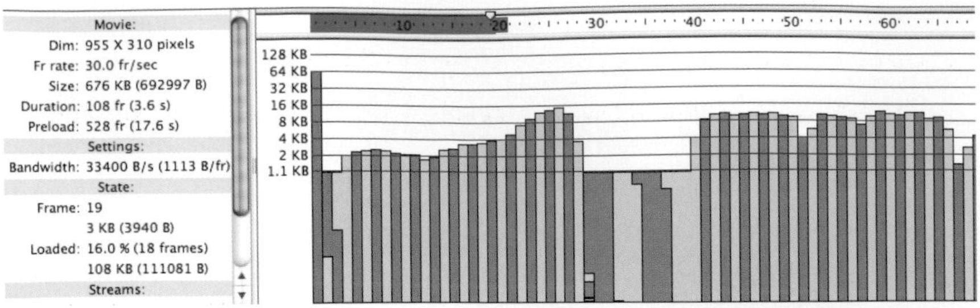

Flash simulates playback over the Web at the given Bandwidth setting (DSL). A green horizontal bar at the top of the window indicates which frames have been downloaded, and the triangular playhead marks the current frame that plays. Notice that there is a slight delay at frame 1 while the data downloads. Anytime a gray data bar exceeds the red horizontal line (the one marked 1.1 KB), there will be a slight delay in the playback of your movie.

Once sufficient data has downloaded, the movie plays, though you may still see some pauses when the playhead catches up to the downloaded portions.

3 Choose View > Download Settings > T1.

T1 is a much faster broadband connection than DSL, which simulates download speeds of 131.2 kilobytes per second.

4 Choose View > Simulate Download.

Flash simulates playback over the Web at the faster speed. Notice that the delay at the beginning is very brief, and the movie plays almost seamlessly as the movie downloads quick enough so the playhead never catches up.

5 Close the preview window.

Adding Metadata

Metadata is information about data. Metadata describes your Flash file so other developers with whom you share your FLA can see details that you want them to know, or a search engine on the Web can find and share your movie. Metadata includes a document's title, a description, keywords, the date the file was created, and any other information about the document. You can add metadata to a Flash document, and that metadata is embedded in the file. Metadata makes it easier for other applications and Web search engines to catalog your movie.

1 Choose File > Publish Settings, or click the Publish Settings button in the Profile section of the Properties inspector.

2 Select the Flash (.swf) format on the left side of the dialog box.

3 In the Advanced section, make sure Include XMP metadata is checked and click the wrench icon.

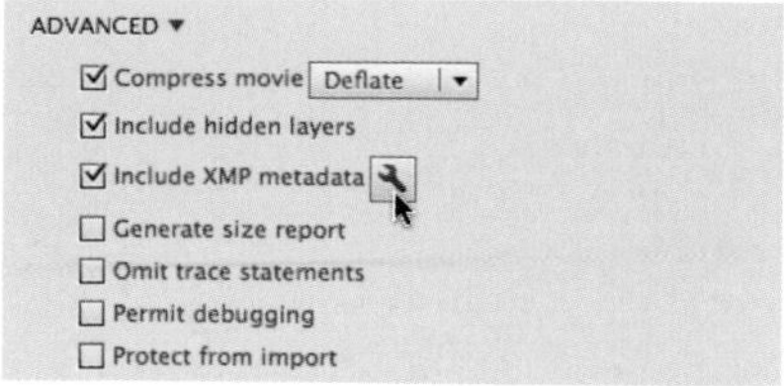

The XMP Metadata dialog box appears.

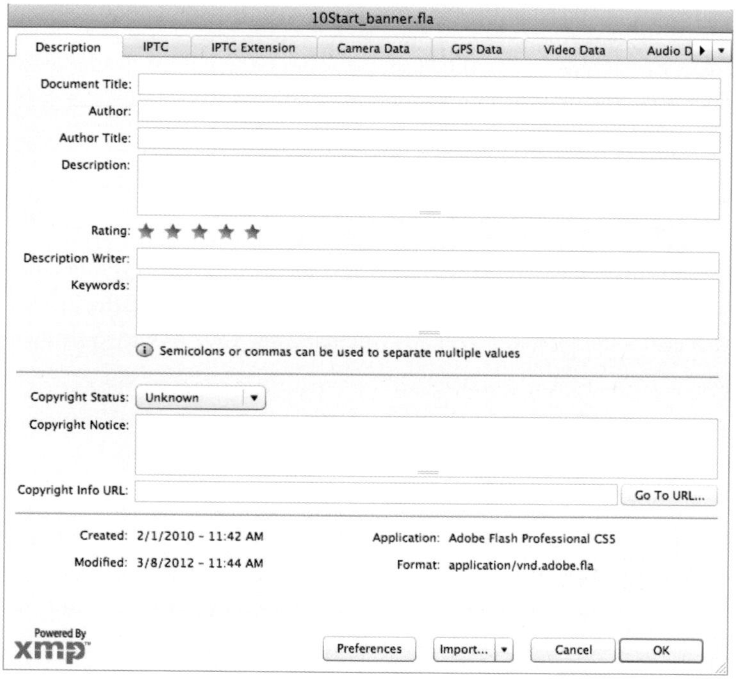

4 Click the Description tab.

5 In the Document Title field, type **Welcome to Meridien**.

6 In the Keywords field, type **Meridien, Meridien City, relocation, tourism, travel, urban, visitor guide, vacation, city entertainment, destinations**.

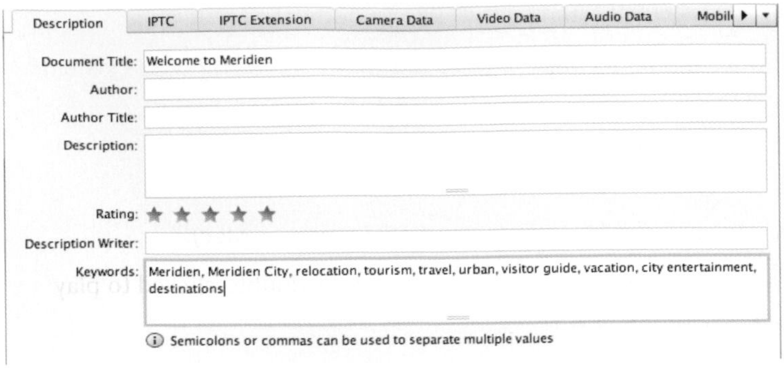

7 Enter any other descriptive information in the other fields. Click OK to close the dialog box. Click OK to close the Publish Settings dialog box.

The metadata will be saved with the Flash document and will be available for other applications and Web search engines.

Publishing a Desktop Application

Most desktop computers have the Flash Player installed with their browsers, but you may want to distribute your movie to someone who doesn't have the Flash Player or who has an older version. Perhaps you just want your movie to run without a browser.

You can output your movie as a projector, which is a stand-alone file that includes the Flash Player with your movie. Because a projector contains the Flash Player, projector files are larger than SWF files.

You can also output your movie as an AIR file, which installs an application on the user's desktop. Adobe AIR is a more robust runtime environment that supports a broader range of technologies. Viewers download the free Adobe AIR runtime from Adobe's Web site at http://get.adobe.com/air/.

Creating a projector

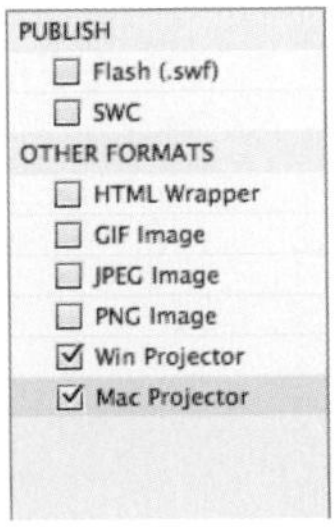

You must create a projector that is specific for Windows or for the Macintosh. However, you can create both kinds of projectors from either platform.

1 Choose File > Publish Settings, or click the Publish Settings button in the Profile section of the Properties inspector.

2 Deselect the Flash and HTML Wrapper formats. Select Win Projector and Mac Projector.

3 Click Publish.

4 When the files have been published, click OK to close the dialog box.

5 Open the Lesson10/10Start folder.

The Windows Projector file has an .exe extension and the Mac Projector file has an .app extension, though your operating system may hide the extension in the filename.

6 Open the projector file for your platform (Windows or Mac).

Both the Windows and the Mac projectors can be double-clicked to play without a browser.

Projectors and TLF Text

The interactive banner in this lesson doesn't contain any TLF Text. However, if your movie includes TLF Text and you want to create a projector, you must merge the Text Layout SWF into the projector. The Text Layout SWF contains the necessary code that supports the new TLF Text engine. Click the Edit button for ActionScript Settings in the Properties inspector or the ActionScript Settings button in the Publish Settings dialog box.

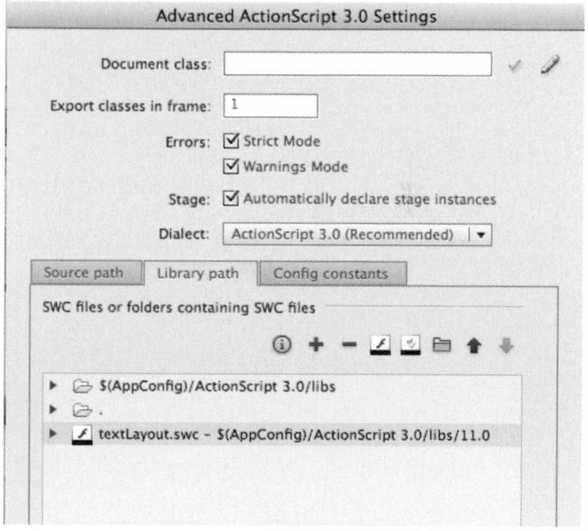

In the Advanced ActionScript 3.0 Settings dialog box that appears, click the Library path tab and then the textLayout.swc file in the window below the tab.

Select Merged into code for the Default linkage in the Runtime Shared Library Settings near the bottom.

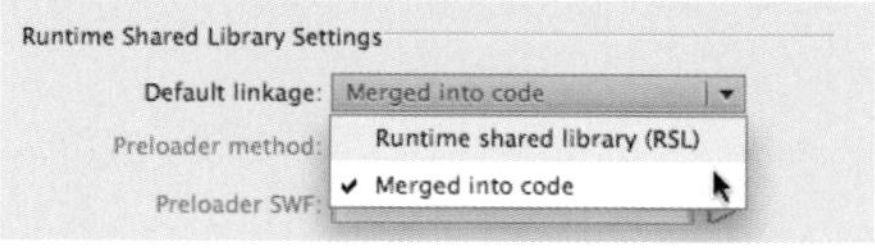

The TLF Text engine that is listed in the display window now shows that its Link Type is to be merged into code rather than linked to a shared external library. This means that the code for the TLF Text engine will be included in the single projector file.

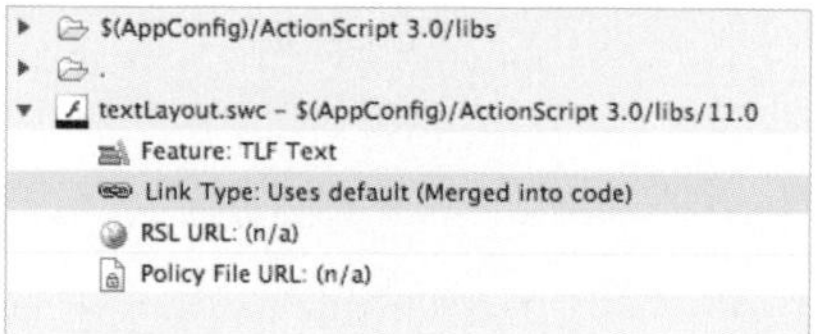

Refer to Lesson 7 for more information about TLF Text and the additional Text Layout SWF.

Creating an AIR Application

Adobe AIR allows your viewers to see your Flash content on their desktop as an application.

1 Open **10Start_restaurantguide.fla**.

  This is the same interactive restaurant guide that you created in Lesson 6, with a few modifications to the background image.

2 In the Properties inspector, note that the Target is set to AIR 3.2 for Desktop.

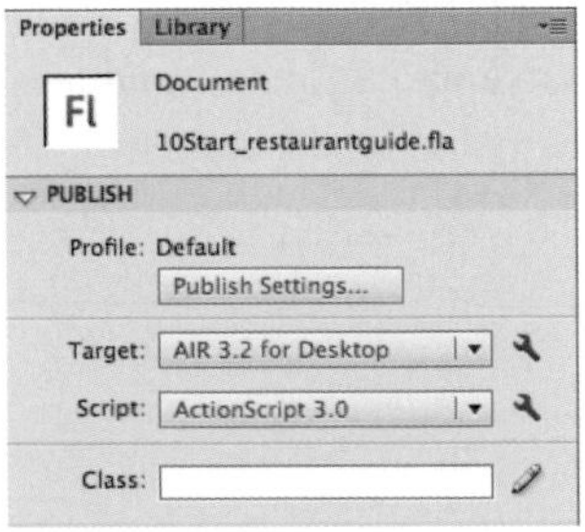

  AIR 3.2 is the latest version of the Adobe AIR runtime.

3 Click the Edit application settings button (wrench icon) next to the Target.

  The AIR Settings dialog box appears.

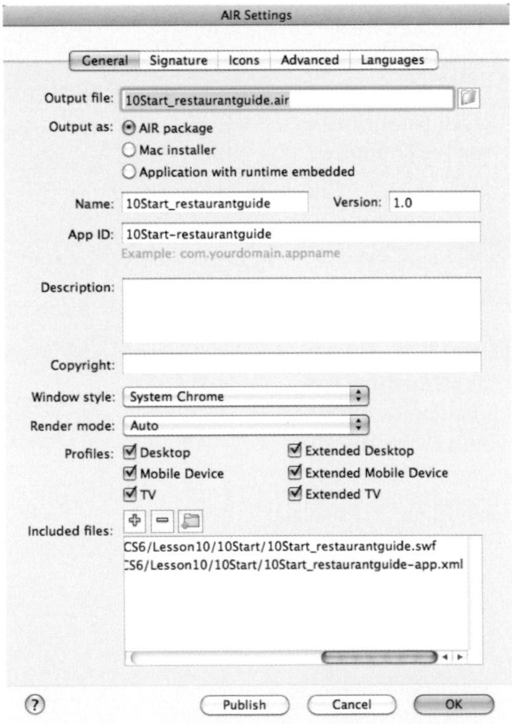

You can also open the AIR Settings dialog box from the Publish Settings dialog box. Click the Player Settings button (wrench icon) next to the Target.

4 Examine the settings under the General tab.

The Output file shows the filename of the published AIR installer as 10Start_restaurantguide.air. The Output as options provide three ways to create an AIR application. The first choice should be selected:

- AIR package creates a platform-independent AIR installer.
- Mac or Windows installer creates a platform-specific AIR installer.
- Application with runtime embedded creates an application without an installer or the need for the AIR runtime already on the desktop.

5 In the Name/App Name field, enter **Meridien Restaurant Guide**.

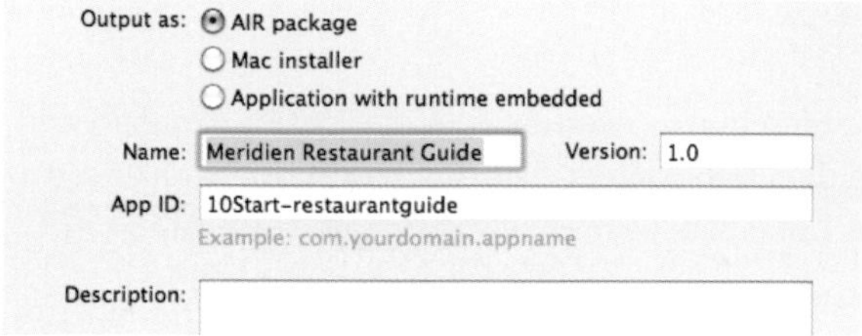

This is the name of your application.

6 In the Window style, choose Custom Chrome (transparent).

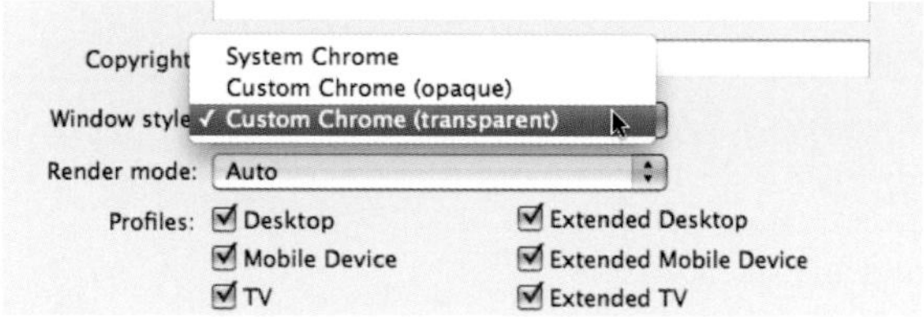

Custom Chrome (transparent) creates an application without any interface or frame elements (known as chrome), and with a transparent background.

7 Click the Signature tab at the top of the AIR Settings dialog box.

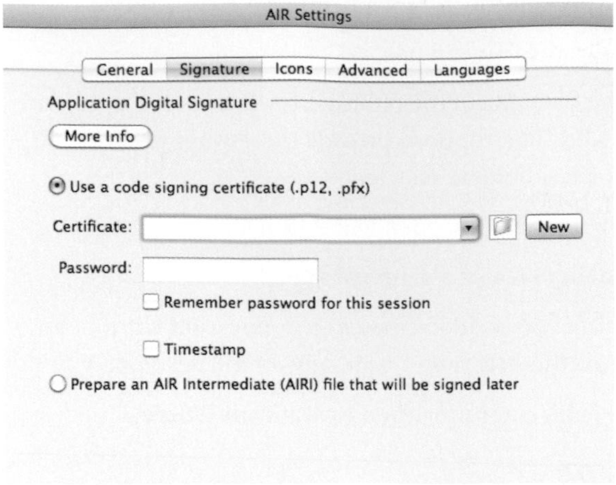

Creating an AIR application requires a certificate so that users can trust and identify the developer of the Flash content. For this lesson, you won't need an official certificate, so you can create your own self-signed certificate.

8 Click the New/Create button next to Certificate.

9 Enter your information in the empty fields. You can use **Meridien Press** for Publisher name, **Digital** for the Organization unit, and **Interactive** for the Organization name. Enter your own password in both password fields, and then save the file as **meridienpress**. Click on the Folder/Browse button to save it in a folder of your choice. Click OK.

A self-signed certificate (.p12) file is created on your computer. Make sure that the Password field is filled, and that Remember password for this session and Timestamp is checked.

10 Now click on the Icons tab at the top of the AIR Settings dialog box.

11 Select icon 128x128 and click the folder icon.

12 Navigate to the AppIconsForPublish folder inside the 10Start folder and choose the restaurantguide.png file provided for you.

The image in the restaurantguide.png file will appear as the application icon on the desktop.

13 Finally, click on the Advanced tab at the top of the AIR Settings dialog box.

14 Under Initial window settings, enter **0** for the X field and **50** for the Y field.

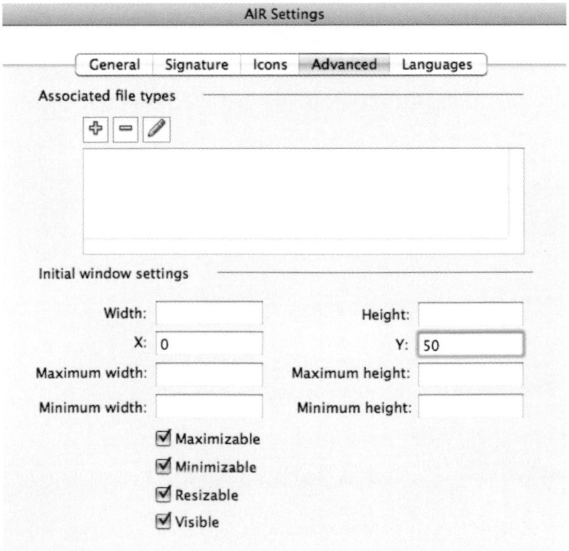

When the application launches, it will appear flushed to the left side of the screen and 50 pixels from the top.

15 Click Publish.

Flash creates an AIR installer (.air).

10Start_restaurantguide.air

Installing an AIR Application

The AIR installer is platform-independent, but requires that the AIR runtime is installed on the user's system.

1 Double-click the AIR installer that you just created, **10Start_restaurantguide.air**.

The Adobe AIR Application Installer opens and asks to install the application. Since you used a self-signed certificate to create the AIR installer, Adobe warns of a potential security risk.

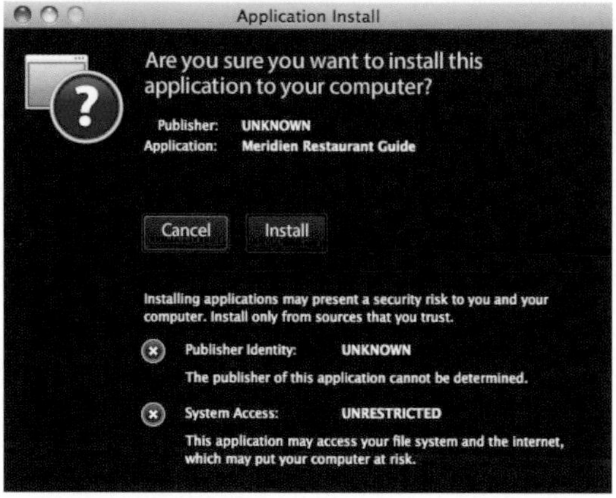

2 Click Install, and then click Continue to proceed with the installation at the default settings.

The application called Meridien Restaurant Guide is installed on your computer and automatically opens.

Notice that the application is positioned at x=0, y=50, and that the Stage is transparent so your graphic elements float over the desktop, much like the appearance of other applications.

3 Quit the application by pressing Alt+F4/Cmd+Q.

Publishing for a Mobile Device

You can also publish Flash content for mobile devices running on Android or on Apple's iOS, such as the iPhone or iPad. To publish Flash content for a mobile device, you target AIR for Android or AIR for iOS to create an application that viewers download and install on their devices.

Creating an app for mobile devices is a little more complicated than creating an application for the desktop because you have to obtain specific developer certificates for distribution. Moreover, you have to factor in the additional time and effort required for testing and debugging on a separate device. However, Flash Professional CS6 features a mobile device simulator that can help make that testing and debugging easier. The simulator can emulate specific mobile device interactions such as tilting the device (using the accelerometer), touch gestures such as swiping and pinching, or even using the geolocation functions.

Simulating a mobile app

You'll use the Adobe SimController to simulate mobile device interactions within Flash Professional CS6.

1 Open **10Start_mobileapp.fla**.

The project is a simple application with four keyframes that announces an imaginary sports challenge set in our familiar city of Meridien. The project already contains ActionScript that enables the viewer to swipe the Stage left or right to go to the next or previous frames.

Examine the code in the Actions panel. The code was added using the Code Snippets panel, which includes dozens of code snippets for interactivity on mobile devices.

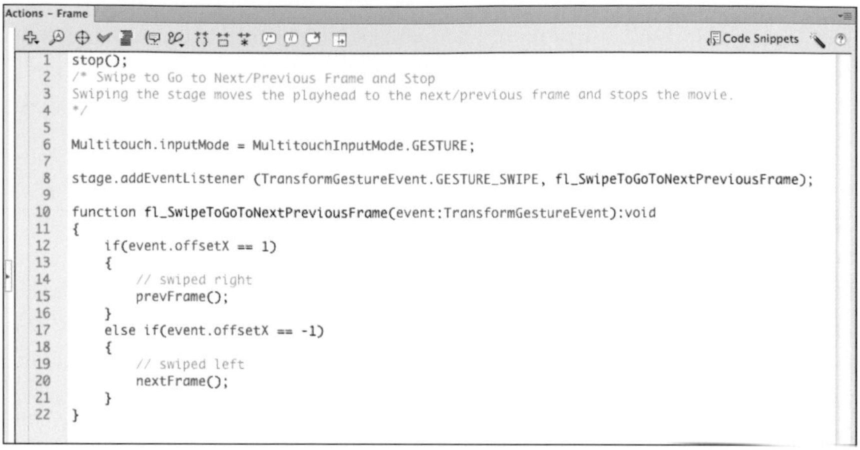


```
stop();
/* Swipe to Go to Next/Previous Frame and Stop
Swiping the stage moves the playhead to the next/previous frame and stops the movie.
*/

Multitouch.inputMode = MultitouchInputMode.GESTURE;

stage.addEventListener (TransformGestureEvent.GESTURE_SWIPE, fl_SwipeToGoToNextPreviousFrame);

function fl_SwipeToGoToNextPreviousFrame(event:TransformGestureEvent):void
{
    if(event.offsetX == 1)
    {
        // swiped right
        prevFrame();
    }
    else if(event.offsetX == -1)
    {
        // swiped left
        nextFrame();
    }
}
```

Note: On Windows, a security warning may appear when you use the AIR Debug Launcher. Click Allow access to continue.

2 In the Properties inspector, notice that the Target is set for AIR 3.2 for Android.

3 Choose Control > Test Movie > in AIR Debug Launcher (Mobile), which should already be checked.

The project publishes to a new window. In addition, the SimController launches, which provides options to interact with the Flash content.

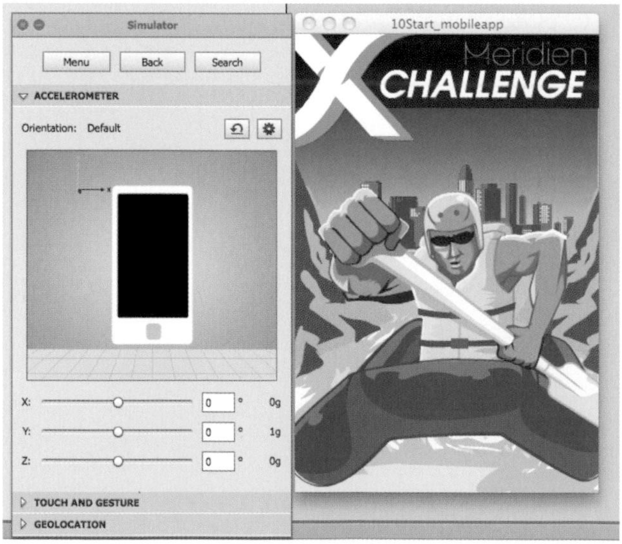

4 In the Simulator panel, click Touch and Gesture to expand that section.

5 Check the Touch layer box to enable it.

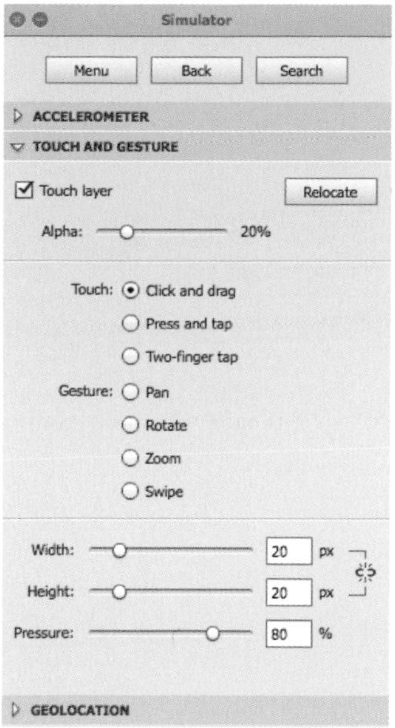

The simulator overlays a transparent gray box over the Flash content to simulate the touch surface of the mobile device.

You can change the opacity of the touch layer by changing the Alpha value, if you wish.

6 Choose Gesture > Swipe.

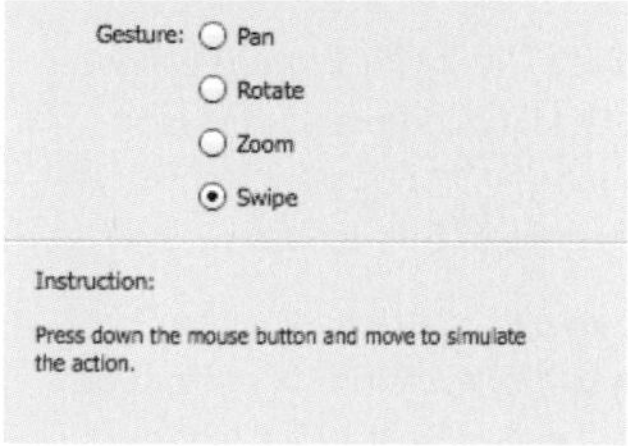

The simulator is now enabled to emulate a swipe interaction. The instructions at the bottom of the panel detail how you can create the interaction with just your mouse cursor.

7 Press down on the touch layer over your Flash content, drag to the left, and then let go of your mouse button.

The yellow dot represents the contact point on the touch layer of the mobile device.

The project recognizes the swipe interaction, and the second keyframe appears.

8 Swipe left and right.

Flash advances ahead one frame, or moves back one frame.

Publishing a Movie for HTML5

A free extension available for Flash Professional CS6 called Toolkit for CreateJS allows you to publish your Flash content as HTML5. HTML5 is the latest Web standard for browsers. One of the key features of HTML5 is the new <canvas> tag, which supports more sophisticated rendering and animation without the need for the Flash Player.

Once installed, the Toolkit for CreateJS extension appears as a new panel within Flash Professional CS6. From the panel, you can export Flash content, including animation, sounds, and images, to HTML5. The Toolkit uses several JavaScript libraries (collectively known as CreateJS) to output a faithful representation of your Flash content.

At the time of this publication, the Toolkit supports only Classic Tween animations and a small subset of Flash Professional's capabilities. The Toolkit for CreateJS is in only its first iteration, and in time, Adobe will be adding additional support and features. Keep your eye on Adobe's Web site for any updates and news about this exciting new tool. It will undoubtedly become a valuable bridge between the Flash Professional platform and the emerging standard of HTML5.

Keeping Organized with Projects

If you intend to target multiple target environments with the same Flash content—for example, you want to create a game that runs as both a Web site and as a mobile app—then it's useful to begin your project through the Project panel rather than as individual documents. The Project panel (Window > Project, or Shift+F8) organizes more complex projects by streamlining the sharing of common assets.

Starting a new project

You'll create a new project through the Project panel.

1 In Flash, choose Window > Project, or press Shift+F8. You can also click on the Projects icon ( ).

The Project panel appears.

2 From the top of the Project panel, choose Projects > New Project.

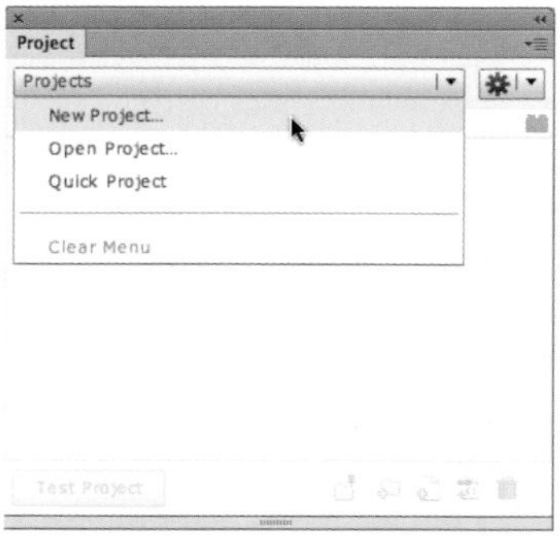

The Create New Project dialog box appears.

3 For Project name, enter **animation_web**.

4 For Root folder, click on the folder icon to browse your computer directory. Create a new folder in the 10Start folder called **myproject**.

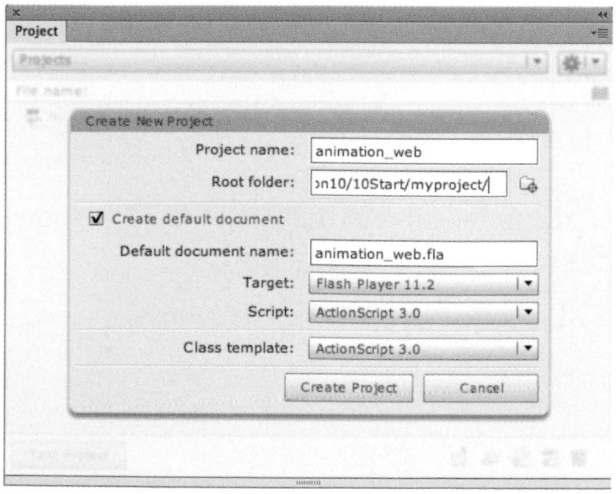

5 Click Create Project.

Flash creates your new folder and creates a new project document called animation_web.fla. Associated with the file is another file called AuthortimeSharedAssets.fla. Additional project documents can share common Library assets through this file.

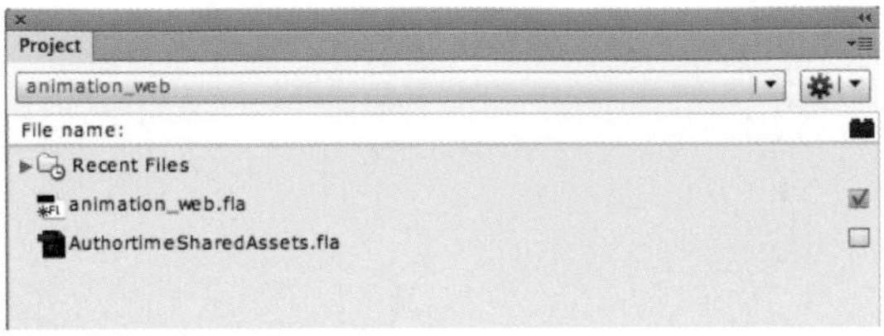

Sharing Library symbols

You'll create a second document for your project, and both files will share a common Library symbol. This makes editing simple and efficient. You can make changes to the symbol in one document, and those changes will be automatically reflected in the other document.

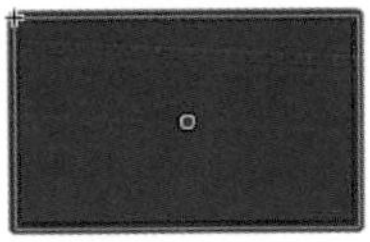

1 In the new animation_web.fla file that's open in Flash, create a simple shape and convert it to a movie clip symbol. Leave an instance of your symbol on the Stage.

In this example, you see a simple square created with the Rectangle tool.

2 In the Library panel, check the box under the Linkage column next to your new symbol.

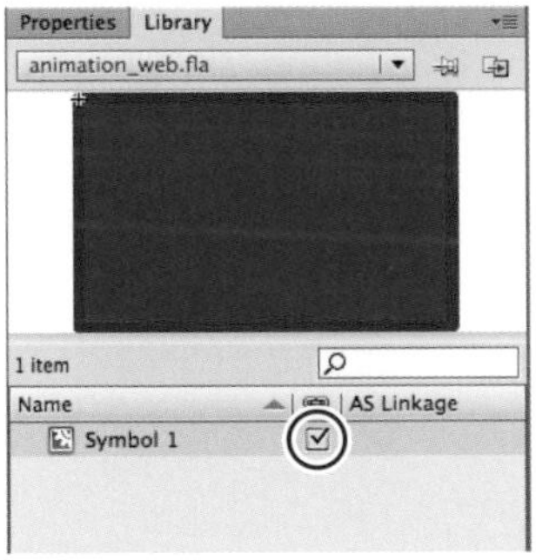

Flash stores your new symbol in the AuthortimeSharedAssets.fla file so other files in the same project can access it.

3 Open the Project panel and click the New File button at the bottom.

The Create File dialog box appears.

4 For Name, enter **animation_mobile**, and for Target, choose AIR 3.2 for Android. Check the Open file after creation box.

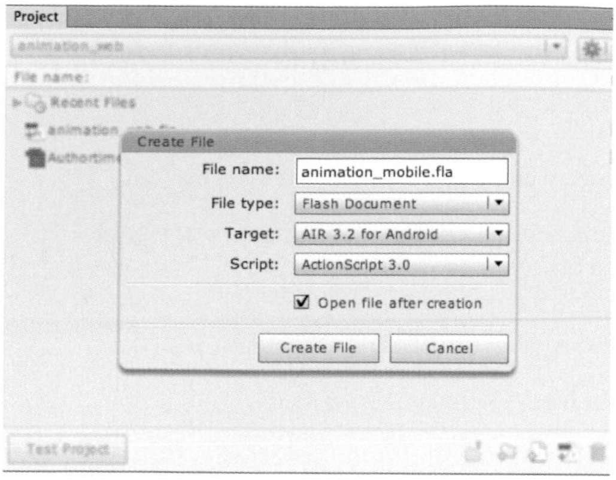

5 Click Create File.

Flash creates and opens a new document in your project. You now have two documents open, the animation_web.fla file and the animation_mobile.fla file.

6 Now you'll add the shared movie clip symbol to animation_mobile.fla. In the Project panel, double-click the AuthortimeSharedAssets.fla file.

The AuthortimeSharedAssets.fla file opens. Notice that the shared symbol is in the Library.

7 Go back to the animation_mobile.fla file, and from the top of its Library, choose AuthortimeSharedAssets.fla.

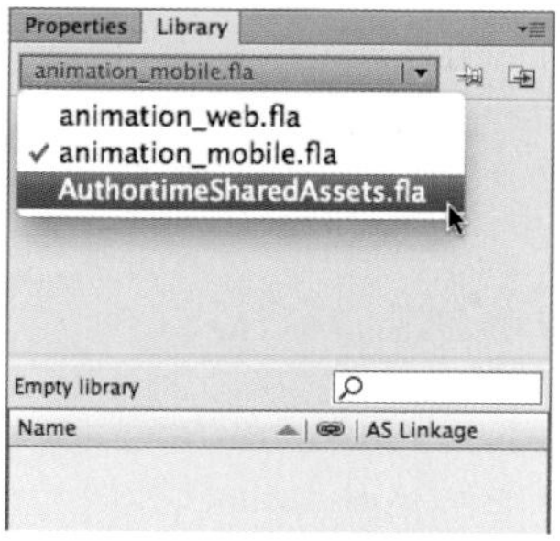

Flash opens the Library for AuthortimeSharedAssets.fla for your current document.

8 Drag the shared symbol from the Library to the Stage of the animation_mobile.fla file.

The symbol appears on the Stage.

9 From the top of the Library panel, choose animation_mobile.fla to see the document's own Library. Check the box under the Linkage column next to the symbol.

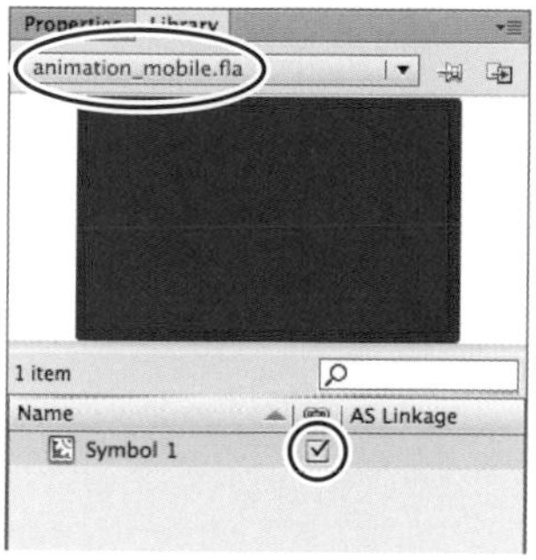

Flash links the symbol to the AuthortimeSharedAssets.fla file. Now both files share the same symbol. Making and saving changes in any of the three documents will make changes in all of them.

Editing Shared Library symbols

You'll make a simple edit to the symbol in one file and see the changes reflected in the other file.

1 In the animation_web.fla file, double-click the symbol instance on the Stage to enter symbol-editing mode.

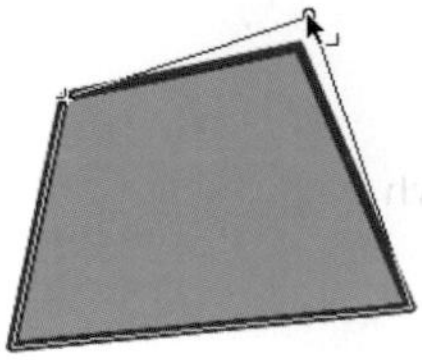

2 Modify the shape of the symbol by changing its color or contours.

   The red square in this example has been changed to a green trapezoid.

3 Save your file.

   Flash updates the symbol in the AuthortimeSharedAssets.fla file.

4 Open the animation_mobile.fla file.

   The shared symbol automatically reflects all the modifications from the animation_web.fla file.

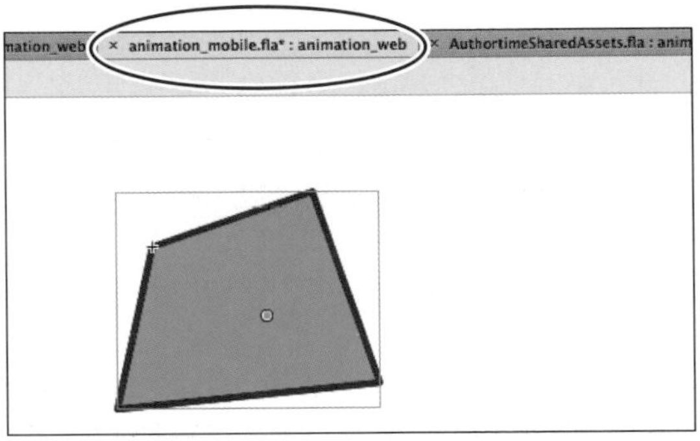

Next Steps

Congratulations! You've made it through the last lesson. By now you've seen how Flash Professional CS6, in the right creative hands (your hands!), has all the features to produce media-rich, interactive projects that run on multiple platforms. You've completed these lessons—many of them from scratch—so you understand how the various tools, panels, and ActionScript work together for real-world applications.

But there's always more to learn. Continue practicing your Flash skills by creating your own animation or interactive site. Get inspired by seeking out Flash projects on the Web. Expand your ActionScript knowledge by exploring the Adobe Flash Help resources and other fine Adobe *Classroom in a Book* manuals.

Review Questions

1 What is the Bandwidth Profiler, and why is it useful?

2 What files do you need to upload to a server to ensure your final Flash movie plays in Web browsers?

3 How can you tell which version of Flash Player a viewer has installed, and why is it important?

4 Define metadata. How do you add it to a Flash document?

5 What is a projector file?

Review Answers

1 The Bandwidth Profiler provides information such as the overall file size, the total number of frames, the dimensions of the Stage, and how your data is distributed throughout your frames. You can use the Bandwidth Profiler to preview how your final project might behave under different download environments.

2 To ensure that your movie plays as expected in Web browsers, upload the Flash SWF file and the HTML document that tells the browser how to display the SWF file. You also need to upload the swfobject.js file, if one was published, and any files your SWF file references, such as video or other SWF files; be sure that they are in the same relative location (usually the same folder as the final SWF file) as they were on your hard drive.

3 Select Detect Flash Version in the HTML tab in the Publish Settings dialog box to automatically detect the version of Flash Player on a viewer's computer. Some Flash features require specific versions of Flash Player to play as expected.

4 Metadata is information about data. Metadata includes a document's title, a description, keywords, the date the file was created, and any other information about the document. Metadata in a Flash document is published with the Flash file, making it easy for others to identify the project.

5 A projector is a stand-alone application that includes all the information necessary to play the movie without a browser, so people who don't have the Flash Player or who don't have the current version can view your movie.

INDEX

C

D

E

F

G

M

N

O

T

U

V

W

X

Y

Z

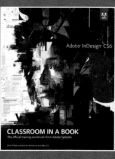

WATCH
READ
CREATE